BATH BETWEEN THE WARS

To Luca, Marco, Saul and Jonah

Bath between the Wars

1919-1939

DAVID G WILLIAMSON

THE HOBNOB PRESS

First published in the United Kingdom in 2024

by The Hobnob Press,
8 Lock Warehouse, Severn Road, Gloucester GL1 2GA
www.hobnobpress.co.uk

© David G Williamson 2024

The Author hereby asserts his moral rights to be identified as the Author of the Work.

All rights reserved. No part of this publication may be reproduced, stored in a retrieval system, or transmitted in any form or by any means, electronic, mechanical, photocopying, recording or otherwise, without the prior permission of the publisher and copyright holder.

British Library Cataloguing in Publication Data
A catalogue record for this book is available from the British Library

ISBN
978-1-914407-67-3 paperback
978-1-914407-68-0 casebound

Typeset in Adobe Garamond Pro, 11/14 pt
Typesetting and origination by John Chandler

Front cover illustration:
Therese Lessore, Walcot Street from Hedgemead, Bath, 1942, oil on canvas (Victoria Art Gallery, Bath & North East Somerset Council). The author and publishers are grateful to Jim Riseley, Collections Manager, Victoria Art Gallery, for granting permission to reproduce this picture.

CONTENTS

Acknowledgements	ix
List of Abbreviations	x
Notes on Imperial weights and measures	xii
Bath Street Maps, 1939	xiii–xv

Introduction — 1

1 From War to Peace of a Sort, 1918-19 — 3
- The Armistice — 7
- Post war problems — 16
  - *Demobilisation* — 17
  - *Bolshevism* — 22
  - *Afghanistan and India* — 25
- Germany and the Germans: the view from Bath — 26
- Peace Celebrations — 29
- Bath in 1919: Unemployment, poverty and labour unrest — 31
- Reconstruction and plans for the future — 37
- Christmas 1919 — 44

2 Bath and the Turbulent Aftermath of War, 1920-24 — 46
- Noises off: The impact of the European crisis on Bath — 47
- Bath and Empire — 53
- Ireland — 57
- Unemployment and industrial strife — 60
- Political turmoil: November 1922-October 1924 — 70
  - *A whiff of revolution* — 74
  - *Foxcroft triumphant* — 78

3 Bath: Health Resort, City of Culture and Sport, 1920-24 — 81
- Bath as a tourist centre — 84
- Culture, ideas and philanthropy — 88

Music and Drama	89
Cinema	91
Societies and Clubs	93
The Churches	97
Controversies and debates	99
Sport	101

4 Ambitious Plans for Bath: The 1925 Corporation Act — 106

    Gaining the approval of Parliament — 111
    The toll bridges — 113
    The City Improvement Scheme — 118
    The backlash: revival of the Bath Preservation Society — 119

5 The impact of the General Strike and the Coal Strikes on Bath 1925-26 — 122

    The approaching crisis — 123
    The General Strike — 130
        The aftermath — 139
    The miners remain on strike — 142
        The impact on Bath — 144
    Christmas, 1926 — 149

6 Education and Health — 151

    Schooling in Bath — 151
        Schools and popular memory — 155
    Medical services — 158
        Hospitals — 158
        Doctors, nurses and midwives — 160
    The Health of Bathonians — 164
        The Bathwick typhoid outbreak — 167
        Mental Health and eugenics — 172

7 Bathonians at the turn of the decade — 175

    Work — 178
    Home Life and Leisure — 188

8 Into the Thirties — 191

    The end of an era — 191

The Wall Street Crash and the formation of the National Government	193
High Drama in Bath's Conservative Party	195
Devaluation	197
The Great Depression	199

9 The Empire, the Dictators and the Abdication Crisis — 212

Bath and the Empire	212
The moral dilemmas of Empire	216
The Triumph of the Nazis in Germany	219
The Blackshirts in Bath	222
Support for the League of Nations and the Peace ballot	223
Bath and the Abyssinian crisis	225
Emperor Hailie Selassie in Bath	227
Sitting on a 'powder barrel'	229
The city's air raid precautions: the preliminary stage, 1935-36	232
The Silver Jubilee	236
The General Election, November 1935	237
The Death of George V and the Abdication Crisis	238

10 Bath in the late Thirties — 241

The Bath Corporation Act of 1937	242
The renaissance of the Assembly Rooms	246
Still a City of Culture?	248
The battle to save the Orchestra	249
The challenge of modern art	251
Planning The Bath Festival of the Arts, 1939	254
Migration from the Distressed Regions, 1936-39	257
Bath and Modernity	265
The impact of the car and aeroplane	268
The expansion of the city and the impact of modern architecture	268
Wireless, cinema and television in 1930s Bath	269
The decline of religion	269
Female emancipation	271
Sex	275

11 War draws ever closer — 277

    The Spanish Civil War — 277
    The Sino-Japanese War — 280
    Austria and Czechoslovakia, 1938-39 — 282
    Jewish Refugees in Bath — 286
    Christmas, 1938 — 289
    The European crisis intensifies, March-April 1939 — 290
    'Be Prepared' — 290
    Planning to receive evacuees — 304
    'There's going to be a war .... my son' — 305
    The Link — 309
    War again — 311

Conclusion — 317

Notes — 321
Select Bibliography — 337
Index — 342

ACKNOWLEDGEMENTS

I WOULD LIKE to thank *all* the staff of the Bath Record Office (that is Richard Meunier, Anne Buchanan, Hannah Whittingham, Veronica Howe, Holly Trant, Stephanie Adams, Drew Westerman and Lucy Powell) for their patience and assistance. Usually, on Wednesday mornings, they guided me to relevant source material, answered my queries and when through my own carelessness I lost or muddled a reference, they went to great lengths to find it. Stuart Burroughs at the Bath Museum of Work was equally helpful and patient in directing me to relevant material and was always cheerful and welcoming during those strange periods between the repeated lockdowns of 2020 and 2021. I would also like to thank Patricia Connett, Doreen Williams, Alan Gait, Philip Morris and Mary Dale for finding time to talk to me about their childhood in pre-war Bath. Mary Dale also sent me an invaluable copy of her memoirs entitled *Florence Mary Keyes*, the maiden name of her mother. Andrew Swift and Kirsten Elliott of the Akeman Press have been unfailingly helpful in answering obscure questions, lending me material and reading and checking several chapters of the manuscript of *Bath between the Wars*. Special thanks are also due to John Chandler and Louise Ryland-Epton of the Hobnob Press for their encouragement and decision to publish *Bath between the Wars*. Last but not least I would like to thank Sue for all her patience and encouragement during the writing and researching of this book.

ABBREVIATIONS

AFS	Auxiliary Fire Service
ARP	Air Raid Precautions
B&WC&H	*Bath and Wilts Chronicle and Herald*
BC	*Bath Chronicle*
BCS	Bath Cooperative Society
BPM	Bathford Paper Mills
Bn	Battalion
BPT	Bath Preservation Trust
BTLC	Bath Trades and Labour Council
BTCS	Bath and Twerton Cooperative Society
BUF	British Union of Fascists
BVRA	Bath Vigilance and Rescue Association
CAD	Central Ammunition Depot
CBU	Committee of the Bath Unemployed
CO	Company
Cttee	Committee
CWT	Hundredweight
Exec.(Cttee)	Executive committee
FEU	Fuller's Earth Union
Ft	Foot or feet (pre metric measurement)
GP	General Practitioner
GPI	General Paralysis of the Insane
GPO	General Post Office responsible both for the postal and telecommunications system
GWR	Great Western Railway
HE	High Explosive
LCC	London County Council
LMS	London, Midland and Scottish Railway
LNU	League of Nations Union
Lt	Lieutenant
MCU	Middle Class Union
MFGB	Miners' Federation of Great Britain
Mins	Minutes
MOBAW	Museum of Bath at Work
MOH	Medical Officer of Health
NCU	National Citizens' Union

NUR	National Union of Railwaymen
NUT	National Union of Teachers
NUWM	National Unemployed Workers' Movement
OBPS	Old Bath Preservation Society
OHP	Oral History Project
OMS	Organisation for the Maintenance of Supplies
OTC	Officers Training Corps
PAC	Public Assistance Committee
PDSA	People's Dispensary for Sick Animals
POW	Prisoner of War
RAOC	Royal Army Ordinance Corps
RASC	Royal Army Service Corps
RDC	Rural District Council
RIBA	Royal Institution of British Architects
RNHRD	Royal National Hospital for Rheumatric Diseases
RUH	Royal United Hospital
SLI	Somerset Light Infantry
TCS	Twerton Cooperative Society
Sh	Shilling
SMO	Schools Medical Officer
Tel	Telegramme
TGWU	Transport and General Workers' Union
TUC	Trades Union Congress
VAD	Voluntary Aid Detachment (member)
WEA	Workers' Education Association
WI	Women's Institute
YMCA	Young Men's Christian Association

NOTES ON IMPERIAL WEIGHTS AND MEASURES

Length
Inch   2.54 cms
Foot   0.3 of a metre or 30.4 cms
Yard   0.9 metre

Weight
Ounce   28.3 grams
Pound   0.4 Kg
Stone   6.3 Kg
Hundredweight 50.8 Kg
Ton   1.016 metric tons

Note on pre-decimalisation currency
12 pence to the shilling
20 shillings to the pound.
21 shillings to a guinea

Value of money
Certainly as far as money values go, the past is indeed 'a foreign country'.
In purchasing power £100 in 2022 was worth about £6,580 in 1930. To put this into context the average wage of a working man in 1935 was between £3 and £4 a week, and a modest semi-detached suburban house cost £500.

BATH STREET MAPS, 1939

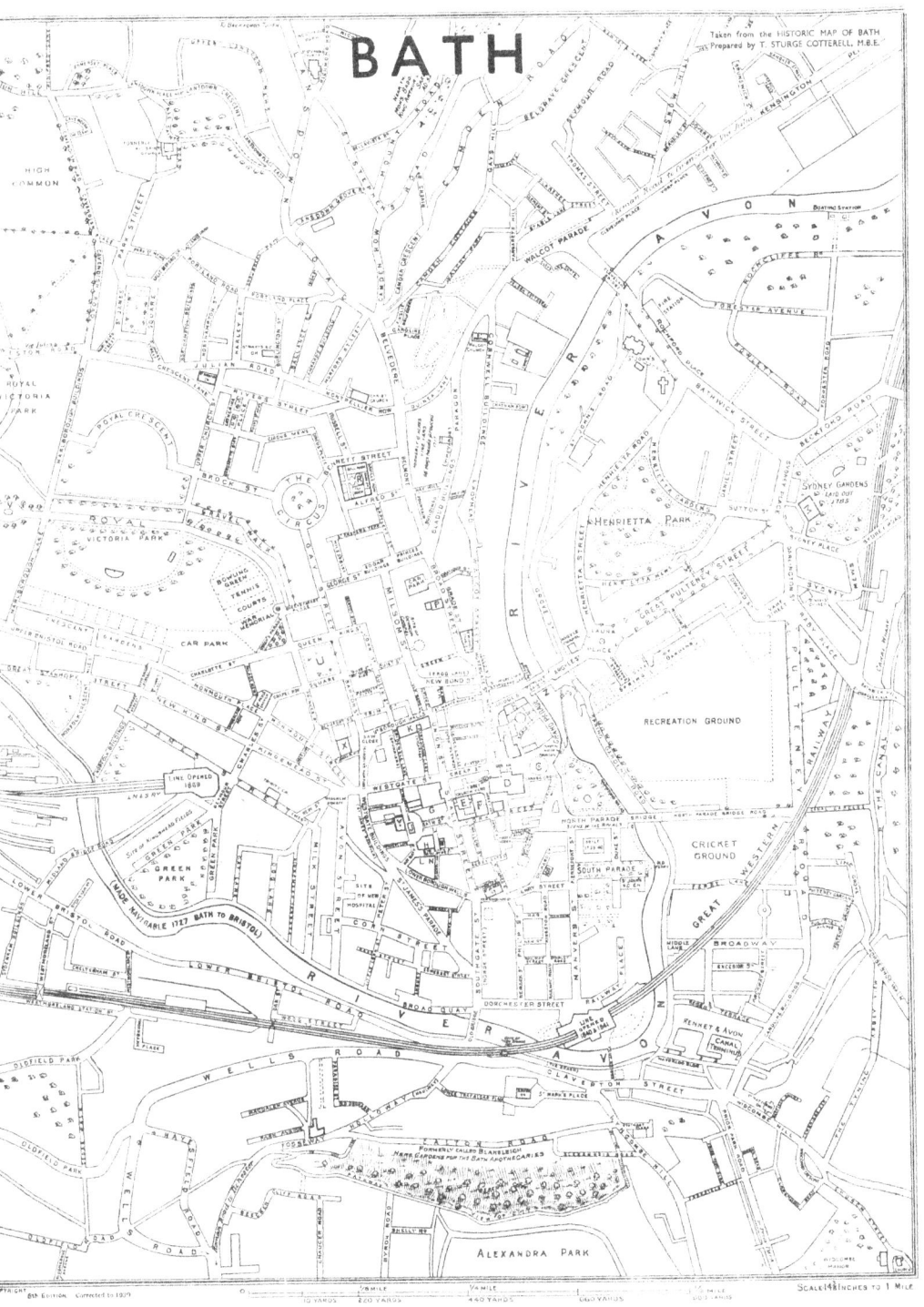

xiv

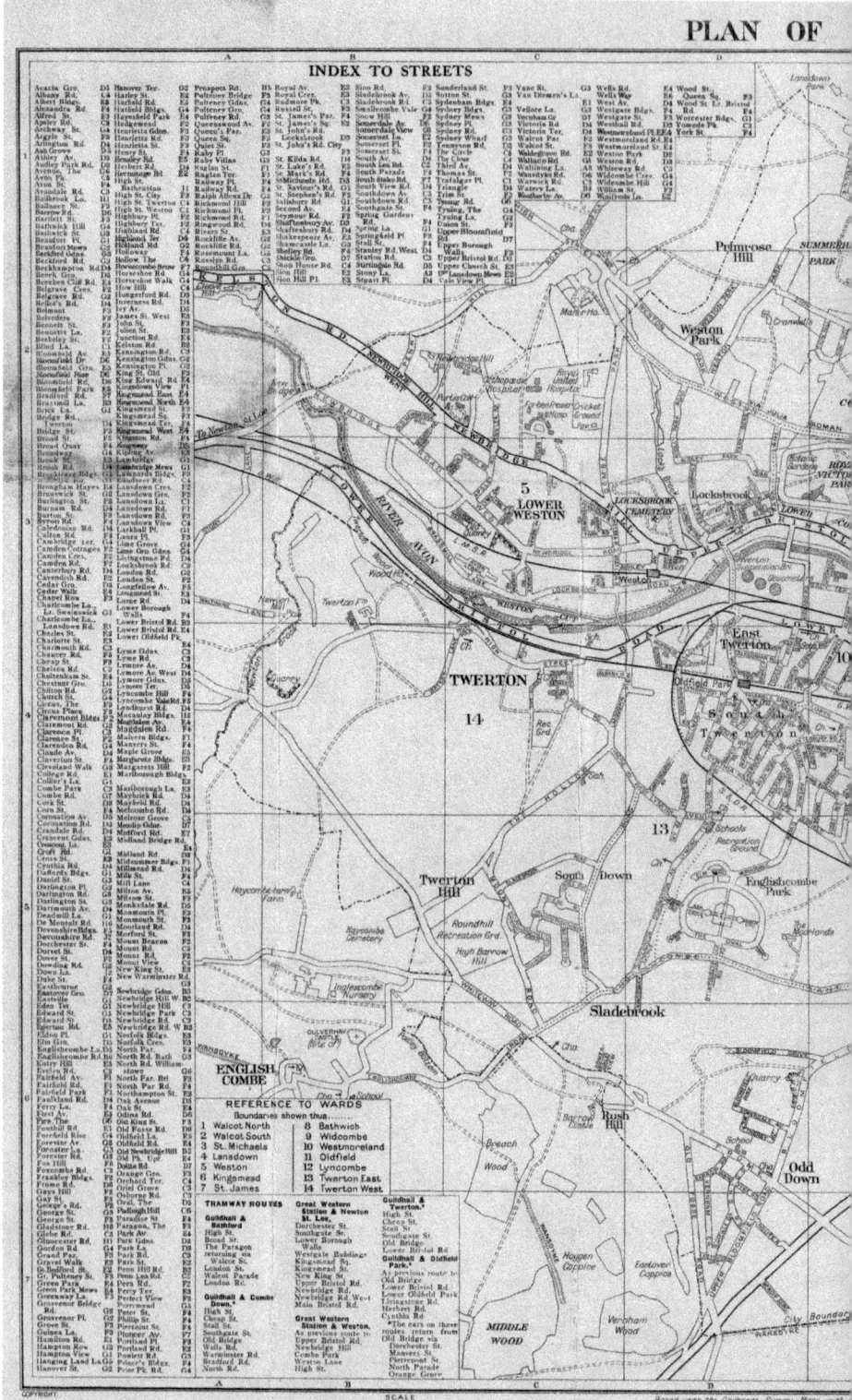

CITY OF BATH

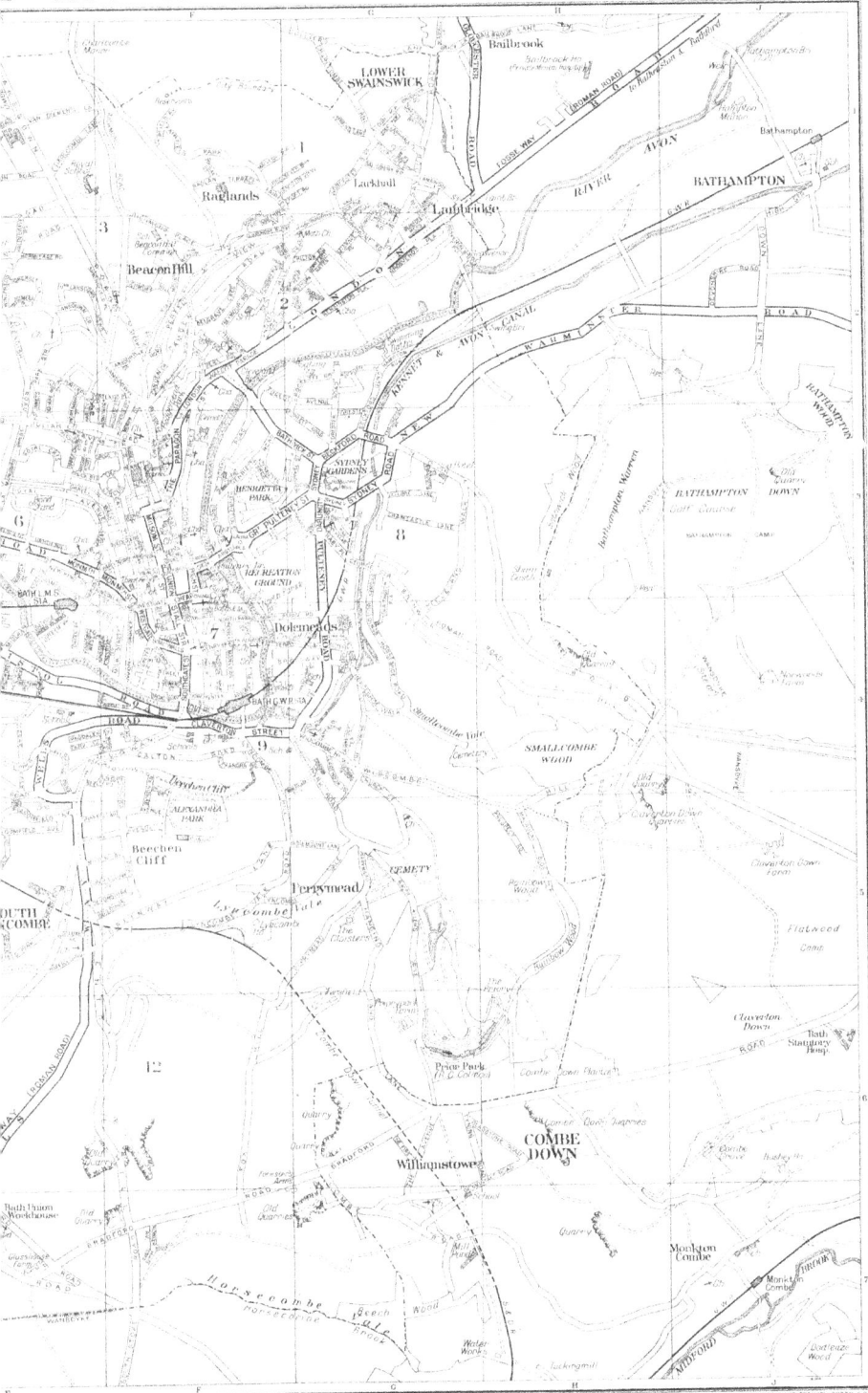

INTRODUCTION

THE YEARS 1919-39 form a coherent period of history, which began in the aftermath of one conflict and ended with the start of another, that was to be even more devastating in its consequences. A major theme of this book is how global events, be they economic, political or cultural, impinged on the everyday life of Bath and its citizens. Inevitably when studying 'local history', newspapers are a major source of information, but I have been fortunate to have been able to supplement this source with diaries, private correspondence, council minutes, school logbooks and the records of a wide range of societies and organisations, most of which are kept in the Bath Record Office. Another invaluable source of information has been the Oral History Project undertaken by the Bath Industrial Heritage Centre, which provides a host of insights into the reality of life during this period. I have also been privileged to interview several Bathonians, who can remember this era as children. Of particular value have been the archives of local firms such as the Fuller's Earth Union, the Bathford Paper Mills Co. and Horstman Cars Ltd, as they indicate how global economic and political events affected local businesses and their workers. One omission is the absence of substantial records from Stothert and Pitt covering the years 1919-39. Sadly for historians they were most likely disposed of during the Second World War as they were a potential fire hazard in the event of incendiary attacks by the *Luftwaffe* on the firm's workshops and offices.

While studying the inter-war history of Bath I have constantly recalled LP Hartley's oft quoted observation that ' the past is a foreign country. They do things differently there'. Inevitably attitudes in inter-war Bath were very different from today, particularly as far as the Empire went, but at times in the cut and thrust of debate in the hustings, society meetings and on council committees, ideas and attitudes emerged which are both recognisable and current today, and which indicate the sophisticated nature of political and intellectual life in inter-war Bath. It is sobering to realise that one day our own antics and shibboleths will also be seen by future historians 'as a foreign country'.

1
FROM WAR TO PEACE OF A SORT, 1918-19

By the autumn of 1918 the optimistic days of August 1914 were but a distant memory. Instead of a quick victory over Germany and its allies, the struggle had developed into a desperate war of attrition making ever greater demands on what became called the home front. By 1916 the great flood of enthusiastic volunteers, to which Bath had contributed its share, was drying up, and the government had no option but to introduce conscription in January – first for single men between 18 and 41, and then a few months later for married men as well. Exemption on the grounds of conscience or the prior claims of war industries at home could only be obtained by permission of local tribunals. In 1917 war socialism dominated Britain. The opening hours of pubs were rigorously controlled and the press was censored. Above all, food and fuel rationing was introduced.

The war vitally affected Bath's industries. Although 'Bath's economy had always been founded to a certain degree on the three-legged pursuits of health, wealth, and happiness', it did possess modern industries.[1] These lay for the most part along a narrow strip of land running from Green Park to Twerton, parallel to the River Avon and the Great Western and Midland railway lines. Bath's industries, like those in the rest of the country, had been turned over to the production of war materials. Stothert and Pitt, with a workforce of 1,185 men and about 300 women, made 18-pounder high explosive shells, submarine parts and the vital paravanes –torpedo shaped floats with steel cutters which were towed on both sides of a ship and were able to deflect mines – as well as an experimental but ultimately unsuccessful tank. Aircraft parts ranging from struts and propellers to whole planes were made by W & T Lock, Bath Cabinet Makers and Bath Aircraft Ltd, with a combined workforce of 510 men and 640 women. Horstmann Gear Company manufactured the vital gauges for the Ministry of Munitions, which tested the measurements of the various shells and guns manufactured across the country to ensure that they were all of the standard size. When campaigning in Twerton as a Coalition candidate in the Coupon Election of December 1918, Captain Charles Foxcroft went out of his way to stress the services of the local munition workers, who 'had "stuck it" from six in the morning until half past seven at night'.

In the spring of 1918 there seemed to be no end to the war in prospect. Russia was paralysed by revolution, and in March the Germans launched a massive offensive on the western front, which smashed through the Entente's lines at the hinge between the British and French armies. By early June they were just 56 miles from Paris, but they had over-reached themselves, and by July the tide had begun to turn. On 8 August, the so called 'black day of the German Army', the British Fourth and French First Armies attacked across the Somme and forced the Germans to retreat. By September Germany and its allies were facing defeat. On 17 October British troops entered the key city of Lille. A description of its liberation by Signaller Leonard Sims, a former Bath Post Office worker from 6 Railway Street, was published in the *Chronicle*:

> We have entered a whopping big French town, one of the largest in France; you should have seen the reception we got. The people nearly went mad at the sight of the English soldiers. They were giving us flowers, sticking flags, rosettes and ribbons in our button-holes and rifles, shaking hands with us and kicking up an awful row in their joy. When we halted, they ran out with big jugs of steaming hot coffee for us.[2]

Yet there still seemed little prospect of an immediate end to the war. The Germans remained a formidable enemy, as the list of casualties continued to testify. On 26 October, when Lord Bath opened the headquarters and club rooms of the Somerset division of the Comrades of the Great War in Beau Nash House, he cautioned against immediate expectations of peace, and stressed that the 'German Army was nor yet beaten' and was still 'fighting well'. In September his younger brother, Colonel Lord Alexander Thynne, who was one of Bath's two MPs, had been killed by a German shell, while in the process of moving his headquarters nearer the front. Right up to the time the Armistice took effect at 11 o'clock on 11 November, the armies were locked in combat and men were still being killed on the western front. Sapper W Long of 10 Highbury Place, Snow Hill, who had witnessed Thynne's death back in September, was himself killed three days before the Armistice when a shell smashed into a cellar where he was working with several other Royal Engineers signallers. His death was made all the more poignant by the fact that he had served unwounded at the front for three and a half years. As the *Chronicle* reported on 16 November, he had recently been home on leave and 'returned to France about ten days ago, telling his mother before he left that he would not for the world miss being out there with the boys when peace was proclaimed'.

Another Bathonian, Sergeant Stanley Silvester, who was serving as a pilot in the RAF, participated in a string of raids on German positions from 8 to 11 November. The final one on Charleroi was at 2am on the 11th, just nine hours before the Armistice was signed. He survived this experience, but early in December he had a potentially fatal accident: while he was flying near Zeebrugge his plane burst into flames and he was forced to make a crash landing. He had no option but to borrow a bicycle and head towards a German occupied aerodrome where he was able to send a wireless message back to his own base and arrange for a car to pick him up.[3]

The front page of Sergeant Stanley Silvester's diary (Bath Record Office)

'Spanish flu', the earliest documented case of which had been in Kansas in March 1918, threatened to kill both servicemen and civilians just at the point when the guns fell silent. At the beginning of July a few cases occurred in

Oldfield Boys' School. The Schools' Medical Officer (SMO) issued instructions for the

> flushing of the classrooms several times morning and evening with fresh air and extra playtime for the children, also simple hints on the prevention of the disease by gargling and attention to the nose, etc; teachers were advised to send the children home if ill.[4]

These measures were insufficient and by 8 July there were a hundred cases in the school. All elementary schools were then closed for ten days, and the SMO reported that 'the outbreak seemed staved off'.[5]

In early autumn, however, the second and most deadly wave of the flu struck Europe. In Bath this was reflected in the ever increasing number of children catching the virus. Initially the Walcot group of schools appeared to be worst hit. On 19 September East Walcot Girls' School reported that 'there were many cases of colds and sickness among the older children since Monday'.[6] These were in fact influenza symptoms. Ten days later the school was closed for 24 hours. Meanwhile, cases in the city's other schools were rising exponentially and on 18 October all elementary schools were closed. It was estimated that 39 teachers and over 2,692 children had been affected, and, while 'many others no doubt were ill afterwards', there were no accurate figures.[7] The Walcot group of schools reopened on 11 November and the other schools a week later. The recorded number of children who died during the period up to 30 November in this second wave was nine.

School closures helped control the spread of the virus amongst children, but outside the schools relatively little could be done to check its progress – the possibility of a 'lockdown' during war and its immediate aftermath was inconceivable. In Bath, Dr Collins, the Acting Medical Officer of Health, thanks to the Public Health (Influenza) Regulations of 1918, managed to ensure that cinemas and other places of entertainment were limited to three consecutive hours of entertainment 'unless there was an interval of not less than 30 minutes to allow for the effectual and thorough ventilation of the premises'. To enforce this, the medical authorities carried out 65 visits. School children were also excluded from the local cinemas until 6 May 1919.[8]

The general public was showered with advice through notices in the local press and at factories and workshops, which in the conditions of wartime was not easy to follow. Margaret Osborne, a regular contributor to the *Chronicle*, observed that to keep warm, to eat good food and to avoid overcrowding would be easy enough for a good many of us in peace-time, but with rationed food, with rationed fuel and with trains and omnibuses full to bursting point, we might as well ask for the moon.[9]

By 21 November 1918 the epidemic had caused 121 deaths, 88 of them in October. The number of cases in the city could only be guessed at. Dr Collins observed that 'there must have been some thousands in the city [which] were not reported', and that his department only knew of the deaths and the number affected in the schools. He also conceded, when questioned by the Bath Sanitary Committee on 25 October, that sometimes a case could be wrongly recorded as influenza as none of the doctors were 'infallible'!

Reports in the *Chronicle* ensured that the reality behind these statistics was made clear to its readers. In its weekly roll of honour, there were several recorded cases of death from influenza in France, Salonika and on board HMS Ajax. Sergeant W Carthew, who was the driver of General Robertson, the Chief of the Imperial General Staff, died of flu at the Connaught Hospital, Aldershot. His body was returned to his home at 27 Park Avenue and then borne on a gun carriage to St James Cemetery on 30 November. General Robertson himself attended the funeral. The *Chronicle* also reported deaths of civilians from flu in the city. For instance, on 22 October, Charles Cleverly of 96 Entry Hill, a legal clerk and 'a zealous and active church worker' at St Lukes, caught flu, which developed into double pneumonia, and led to his death eleven days later.

By the end of January the virus was in retreat and only seven deaths from influenza were recorded. At the Sanitary Committee meeting on 27 January, the following exchange took place:

Councillor Dawe: Is the influenza epidemic gone?
The (Acting) Medical Officer (Dr Collins); Oh, yes; there are very few cases now.[10]

The epidemic was waning but there were still fatalities. Amongst those who died in March were Albert Neathey, who before the war had been a much-loved postman in Bath, and JW Wrayford, a farmer from Bathampton.

THE ARMISTICE

By the first week of November the German fleet was paralysed by mutinies and the whole country teetered on the brink of revolution. On 5 November, the Kaiser fled to Holland and a de facto government calling itself the Council of People's Representatives and composed of the German Democratic and Socialist parties was set up under the moderate Socialist Friedrich Ebert. The next day it sent a delegation to the allied headquarters in Spa to negotiate the terms of the Armistice. One Bathonian, Bugler Arthur Bell of Monmouth Street, who had been a POW in a camp near Berlin. witnessed some of the mayhem in Germany at first hand. As he told the *Chronicle*, he saw 'the revolutionaries swarm into the Kaiser's palace and bring out stores of food that the "All Highest" hoarded, while his people starved'.

By Sunday 10 November, the imminence of an armistice was common knowledge and its announcement was expected at any time. In the early hours of that Sunday at the Bath War Hospital, Kathleen Ainsworth, a VAD nurse, who was on night duty, was able to snatch a few minutes to write to her parents. She told them about the new night orderly, a variety artist in peace time, and of one her patients who talked incessantly in his sleep. She also speculated on what the coming days would bring:

I wonder if we shall have peace by Monday. Things are looking like that aren't they?

Good going, it's Sunday morning. I have just heard the first cock crow and the clock says five to four. Perhaps it will be one of the most momentous Sundays in history. I shall be rather pleased if peace comes in my birthday month.[11]

Katherine had to wait until Monday for the announcement of the Armistice. WS Read, who wrote a whimsical weekly column in the *Chronicle* entitled 'Armchair Musings' under the nom de plume of the Bellman, summed up the atmosphere in the city on that momentous day:

In Bath, as in every other city in the Empire and in Allied lands, in every town and hamlet, was released the pent up suspense of over four years duration … City streets, which were of normal aspect, with little to suggest the imminence of a mighty happening save the frequent enquiry as to whether there was 'any news yet' became within a few minutes the theatre of vast surging crowds demonstrating their joy with pardonable disregard of the usual very decorous behaviour of staid and unemotional citizenship.[12]

There was an immediate race to raise Union Jacks on all the public buildings and churches in the city – St Mary's Bathwick being the first.

Henry Whitmore, who was harvesting potatoes on his family's farm some five miles away in Swainswick, recalled as an 85-year-old that he was first aware of the Armistice 'when he heard shouting and commotion in the city below' and then the pealing of the bells'. It was, he said, 'not a moment to forget', and he used to return to that field 'almost every year on November 11th'.[13] Later, the mayor attended a service of thanksgiving in the Abbey, which was so packed that that crowds had to stand in the Abbey Church Yard.

By a happy coincidence, the Walcot group of schools reopened on that fateful Monday after their enforced closure. According to the East Walcot Girls' School log book,

> at 10.46 the signal was given throughout the city that the Armistice had been signed, so the flag was hoisted in the playground, the children stood in lines and sang the Doxology, God save the King and Flag of Britain, in the chorus of which the children saluted, then cheered and clapped. During the next lesson [the vicar] came and proclaimed a holiday for the afternoon, so after the singing of the Grace, the children were dismissed.[14]

In the evening an effigy of the Kaiser was hung up outside a carpentry workshop on Holloway, and on Saturday afternoon it was driven around the city on a lorry accompanied by a band, a bellringer and a small crowd. The intention was to burn it as a surrogate Guy Fawkes in Sawclose, but the police intervened, and the procession was halted at the Old Bridge. To some, their action seemed rather too zealous, and made no concessions to the popular desire to celebrate the end of the war. On Tuesday 19 November, the council, at the conclusion of business, decorously approved a motion conveying to the King 'on behalf of all the citizens of Bath' congratulations on the 'happy issue of the war ... and the splendid achievements' of the armed forces.

On the home front the most pressing matter was the election of a new parliament. The sitting parliament had been elected under very different circumstances in 1910. As a result of the 1918 Reform Act, the old double-member constituencies had been abolished and replaced with single-member constituencies. Sir Charles Hunter, who had been elected in tandem with Lord Alexander Thynne to represent Bath in 1910 resigned in favour of Charles Foxcroft as the sole candidate. The Bath constituency had also expanded to include Twerton and part of Weston, which had been absorbed by the borough in 1911. The new franchise act of 1918 added more voters to the register than all its predecessors put together, as it extended the vote to all males over 21 and to women over 30. In Bath, the number of electors expanded from 8,000 to just over 30,000, and the number of polling stations had to be increased from 15 to 60. As there were insufficient ballot boxes, converted shell cases had to be used in several polling stations. Soldiers on active service could send postal votes or vote by proxy, and the counting of the votes right across the country was delayed until 28 December to enable their votes to arrive safely.

Shortly after the Armistice, parliament was dissolved and Lloyd George went to the country as leader of the wartime coalition, opposed only by the Labour Party and those Liberals still loyal to their pre-war leader, Herbert Asquith. Captain Charles Foxcroft, the Conservative candidate in Bath, was an old Etonian, a poet and a staunch Unionist and imperialist. He had been the unsuccessful conservative candidate for the Frome constituency in 1910. He had joined the 4th Somerset battalion in 1914 and been posted initially to India, only to return in February 1915 on sick leave. In 1916 he was posted to Italy and, on account of his good Italian, seconded to the Italian authorities to write articles about Italy's role in the war for the British public.

Captain Charles Talbot Foxcroft: campaign poster, November 1918 (Bath Record Office)

Foxcroft's only opponent was the labour candidate, Alfred Bethell. In some ways he was a controversial choice as he had stood as Conservative candidate in Central Bradford in 1894, and in 1916 had unsuccessfully applied to represent Reigate in Surrey as a Conservative. The issues in Bath as elsewhere were primarily concerned with reconstruction. As a consequence of war socialisation, there was a certain amount of common ground between the Coalition and Labour. Indeed, Bethell accused the Coalition of stealing 'snippets of Labour policy, but as there was never any hint of how they were to be paid for', he drew the conclusion that 'the gentlemen who put forward those snippets would drop them as soon as convenient'. Both sides stressed the need to eliminate unemployment, build houses and pay attention to child welfare.

In contrast to many previous contests, the election campaign was conducted in an atmosphere of calm and restraint. In Twerton in 1910, which then belonged to the Frome constituency, Foxcroft, for his own safety, had to be escorted from the village hall by three mounted policemen. When he returned in December 1918, he was well received. There was, however, an unsuccessful attempt to smear Bethell as a renegade Tory and opportunist in the *Chronicle*, and an equally unsuccessful effort to blow up into a scandal a poem in Foxcroft's recently published collection of verse entitled *The Night Sister*. This included a short poem entitled 'A Veteran's View', which in the hyper-patriotic climate of December 1918, could well have been seen as unpatriotic, especially the following couplet:

> You want to fight if you've the chance!
> You must be mad! You must be drunk.

Apparently, Bethell had suggested that he should withdraw the volume, but Foxcroft deftly averted any criticism by explaining to a meeting of Conservatives in Twerton that that the poem represented 'only the opinion of an old and much decorated campaigner' whom he had met in Italy.[15]

The subdued atmosphere on polling day, December 14, was described by a local journalist:

> So far as outward indications were concerned a stranger in Bath might have been in the city the whole of the morning and early afternoon without being aware that one of the most important elections in the history of the country was in progress. There was no excitement, party colours were not being worn, and there was a complete absence of many of the outstanding factors of the general election in the past. Polling booths opened at 8 o'clock, but owing to heavy rain in the early morning, the number voting in the first few hours was small.[16]

The results were announced at three o'clock on 28 December, to a large crowd that had been waiting patiently in the High Street. It was generally assumed that the Coalition candidate, Charles Foxcroft. would win, but the size of his majority came as a considerable surprise. The state of the parties in Bath was as follows:

> CT Foxcroft (Coalition Unionist) 15,605
> AJ Bethell (Labour) 5,244

Once the election campaign was over, Christmas beckoned. In the centre of Bath, street lights were permitted, but only at half their potential power, and in the suburbs, where gaslights were still in use, only every other lamp was lit. To cope with the seasonal increase in letters, cards and parcels, a temporary post office was opened in New Bond Street. Traditionally, one of the delights of Christmas was the abundance of rich and delicious food. However, the Christmas of 1918 was bound to be a more modest affair than those great pre-war feasts. The International Stores placed a series of advertisements in the *Chronicle* informing its customers that, even though 'peace, longed for and fought for, has at last arrived ... the plenty of pre-war days will not return yet awhile'. Indeed, on 23 November, Bathonians were informed by an anonymous correspondent in the *Chronicle* called 'Smallholder' that, unlike armament factories, which could fairly rapidly switch over to peace time production, the Ministry of Food faced a daunting task which was going to become 'even more complicated than ever'. There would still be a shortage of shipping to bring in food and raw materials and, 'consequent upon the complete subjugation of the Hun', it might be necessary 'in the interests of humanity ... to provide food for our late ignoble enemies'. These observations would have come as no surprise to members of the Bath Cooperative Society whose minutes recorded complaints of 'shortages of good's on 10 December.[17]

A week after the Armistice, the Bath Food Control Committee had expressed alarm that some food committees elsewhere in the country were threatening to seize more than their fair share of turkeys simply by offering to pay more for them. A letter of complaint was sent off to the Ministry on November 22, but it was only answered after a delay of two weeks. In the meantime, the Bath Committee acted unilaterally and fixed prices for turkey, goose and rabbits in an attempt to ensure an adequate supply. This drew a rebuke from the Divisional Food Commissioner, who pointed out that, as no increase in the price of poultry and game had been sanctioned, Bath had not been unfairly treated. In reply, the mayor, Alfred Wills, heroically stood up for his city's right to a Christmas feast and criticised the Ministry's inefficiency:

> I must point out that headquarters ... failed to reply for days to my original letter. When they did reply, it was the customary official method of evading an awkward point – viz. to pass on the correspondence to another quarter ... We have loyally endeavoured to carry out the instructions of the Ministry hitherto, but in view of the fact that we find other towns break regulations which we insist upon, and that this adversely affects us, we are getting little tired. The effect of the regulation as to rabbits has been that we have had practically no

supplies, and we are not prepared to find this applying to turkeys. The whole value of Food Control is that we all shall share equally, and we are not prepared to see specially 'favoured towns'.[18]

Despite the continuation of wartime restrictions, something of the magic and excitement of Christmas remained. Harbutt's plasticine factory in Bathampton offered home modelling outfits, and the *Chronicle*, in its pre-Christmas edition, ran articles on various Christmas games. One instructed readers in the art of making puzzles with matches, string and paper; another explained a party trick which involved picking up a handkerchief from the floor with your teeth while balancing a bottle on your head. The pantomime at the Theatre Royal was *Humpty Dumpty*, which, according to the *Chronicle*, was 'a most ambitious production ... far and away exceeding anything yet attempted on this historic stage'. At the Pump Room there was a series of concerts, including Old English Songs on the 23rd and *Messiah* on the 27th.

Christmas Eve witnessed some frenetic scenes in the city. There were huge crowds at the tram stop outside the Guildhall. One woman attempting to board a tram for Combe Down was elbowed aside and punched in the right eye in a decidedly unseasonal bout of bad temper. Right up until Christmas Eve the weather was mild and wet, but on Christmas Day and Boxing Day it turned cold with a sparkling frost, before reverting to the mild, damp norm.

Inescapably, war still dominated the Christmas of 1918. Even though American and Dominion troops began to sail home, demobilisation for the overwhelming mass of British servicemen had hardly started, and large numbers of Bathonians were still serving with the armed forces. It was also business as usual at the Bath War Hospital, where the nurses continued to tend the wounded. Kathleen Ainsworth was on duty in the tents, where the soldiers who were well on the way to recovery slept. She told her mother how she slithered up and down duck boards shivering and thinking longingly of her cosy ward inside the hospital, explaining that 'you get horribly dirty and plastered in mud from head to foot – if it's wet.'[19]

Some families were blessed by the return of a son, father or brother who had been a POW. Mr and Mrs Gay of 1 Bailbrook Buildings, Batheaston, had not heard of their son, Private Wallace Gay of the 6th Somerset Light Infantry (SLI), since he had been captured in March 1918. Just before the Armistice he had been working in a cavalry barracks in West Germany. On 9 November, riots broke out and several German officers were attacked by workers and their own soldiers. He obeyed the advice of a German corporal 'to keep quiet and interfere with nobody'. Shortly afterwards Wallace and the other POWs were taken to within a few miles of the front line and told to find their 'own way to their friends'. His parents first heard that he was still alive when a postcard from France reached them. Then, on the night of Wednesday 27 November, to the joy and relief of his parents, he walked into his old home.

Their joy was matched by that of the parents of Lt J Hill who had been shot down over German lines on 12 August and only released from captivity in Karlsruhe on 18 December. With the most fortuitous timing he arrived back home on Christmas Day. Henry Harwood, a porter living at 23 Stall Street, and his wife experienced what some might have perceived as a miracle when their son, who had served four years in the Royal Artillery and had been wounded, gassed and subsequently rendered completely mute, regained his speech at home while on hospital leave, at midnight on Sunday, December 22. He suddenly called for his mother and from then on was able to sing as well as speak.

For some, like the parents of two young Sappers, CH Morgan of 8 Nelson Place and MV Case of 3 Coronation Road, who both died in Salonika just after the Armistice, these accounts must have made poignant reading since Morgan had died of malaria, and Case of pneumonia. Some other families still did not even know the fate of their sons, brothers or husbands who had been reported missing. On 4 January 1919, for example, Mrs Evry of Avon Lodge, London Road appealed through a letter in the *Chronicle* to returning POWs for any information as to the fate or whereabouts of Private HJ Every, a market gardener, who had been missing since 22 March 1918. She stressed that she would 'gladly pay any expense incurred'.

The shooting had stopped along the western front, but the occupation of the Rhineland by allied and American troops, which was one of the conditions of the Armistice, was in itself a major military operation. By 26 November, the German army had completed its withdrawal, and allied forces, amongst which was the British Second Army, began their march to the Rhine. On 6 December, a force of British cavalry and armoured cars entered Cologne, and by mid-December the Cologne Zone was occupied by British and Dominion troops. Although it was not until January that the 2/4 Bn of the SLI was moved from Belgium to Bonn and Troisdorf, there were some soldiers from Bath who spent Christmas in Germany. In January, a picture was published in the *Chronicle* of a group of Bathonians at the Headquarters of the 18th Motor Transport Corps at Düren, a small town west of Cologne. The eminent Bath surgeon, Captain Forbes Fraser, was also appointed consulting surgeon for the British Rhineland Army in December.

In December, Private WG Wolfe of the Royal Marines provided his family with a detailed first-hand account of defeated Germany. Wolfe, who had joined the Marines before the outbreak of war, was on board HMS Hercules as she led a flotilla of British ships through the Kiel canal to supervise the surrender of German naval units at Wilhelmshaven and Kiel. Based on his son's letters, Mr Wolfe was able to give the *Bath Chronicle* a succinct account of his experiences in Germany just after the Armistice:

> The trip to Kiel took eleven hours and Private Wolfe was impressed by the magnificent engineering feat in its construction. The bridges guarded by soldiers with [revolutionary] red flags gave sufficient access to allow the Hercules to pass with feet to spare though the height of her masts is 160 feet. The surrounding country proved monotonous and practically devoid of agriculture.

The Hercules passed four British prisoners of war working on the land. One of the party, a Scot, saluted the group of admirals on the bridge with grave precision and then as the stern of the ship passed shouted delightedly, 'How's "Blighty"? I'm going back home next week.'

Before sailing to Kiel the *Hercules* docked at Wilhelmshaven, where Wolfe formed the impression there were adequate food supplies. But the situation in Kiel was very different:

> At Kiel several inhabitants came out in boats and surrounded the ship asking for food and clutching their throats to signify their desperate plight. One old couple even offered their fishing tackle – presumably their only means of livelihood to obtain food. The clothing of the population of Kiel appeared to consist largely of papers and their boots resembled sandals with wooden sides without heels.[20]

The old year in Bath was seen out on a note of optimism. On New Year's Eve, well over 400 people attended the Fancy Dress Victory Ball at the Pump Room. Such a gathering had not been seen since 1909, the year of the great Bath Pageant. A sumptuous supper was laid on by Bath's leading restaurant, Fortt & Son in Milsom Street. According to newspaper reports, there was a glittering array of costumes: service uniforms 'mingled with Spaniards, Italians and Moors; Red Cross nurses, jesters and rajahs, gallants, beaux and clowns, fictional characters, Beau Nash costumes and original devices in endless confusion'. Earlier in the day, a children's party was also held in the concert hall of the Pump Room. Again the allied victory over Germany was celebrated when Father Christmas entered with a Christmas tree laden with allied flags. The atmosphere of innocence led the *Chronicle* to observe that 'we elder folk

'... will be failing in our duty towards these merry little people if we leave aught undone to ensure that they might indeed dwell safely and without fear all the days of their life'. Sadly, that was not to be.

POST WAR PROBLEMS

THE VICTORY BALL in the Pump Room saw the New Year in on a confident and optimistic note, but for Bath, as for the rest of the country, 1919 was to prove a complex and paradoxical year. For the most part there was agreement that the war had created an entirely new situation. This view was particularly strong on the left. For instance, TW Allan, the Director of the Cooperative Wholesale Society, warned his audience at the annual festival organized by Twerton Cooperative Society in January that 'those who were going to build up a new world on the conditions of the old were to get a rude awakening'. It was obvious, too, that many women were not going to return to the *status quo* of 1914. Kathleen Ainsworth summed up this mood very clearly when contemplating her imminent demobilisation as a nurse in the Bath War Hospital. She told her mother in January that, 'I want a job. I'm not going to settle down into the old groove again'. She hoped to obtain temporary employment with a friend or relative, and then find a permanent job in Swindon. She stressed that 'the idea of an aimless life makes me positively shudder – I'd soon become the old useless, lethargic Kathleen I was four years ago'.[21]

Even the staid *Chronicle* reinforced this message when it reminded its readers on 1 March that, now that peace 'is in sight [women] are not willing to return to the old monotonous routine of doing nothing in particular from dawn till night', and advised girls seeking ways of helping the community to look at the possibilities of free training and salaried posts offered by the Church Army. This sense of profound change was best summed up by the 87-year-old 'national treasure', Frederic Harrison, a well known radical writer, when he addressed the girls at the High School on their prize giving day:

> It was the common opinion of almost everyone who spoke in public that we were now finding ourselves in a new world socially and economically, and also a new world in the matter of education and also of women's work ... The youngest of them must realise that they were coming into an age totally different from that which their grandmothers, or even their mothers, had expected.[22]

All wanted a lasting and effective peace, speedy demobilisation of their sons and husbands, an end to the housing crisis and lasting economic prosperity.

Striving to achieve these goals, however, led to bitter debates, strikes and the clash of political principles. At a confirmation service at St Stephens's in late March, the Bishop of Bath and Wells complained of 'a feeling of restlessness, a want of purpose ... Instead of finding people prepared to support each other in the great efforts which were needed, we find a house divided'.

Demobilisation

It was against this domestic background that Bathonians read about, and in some cases participated actively in, the tumultuous events sweeping across much of Europe, Asia and the Middle East. At the Paris Peace Conference, which opened on 18 January, the allied leaders eventually agreed on what appeared at the time to be draconian peace treaties with Germany and its allies, Turkey, Austria, Hungary and Bulgaria. Besides occupying the Rhineland, allied troops were also required to occupy the former territories of the Ottoman Empire in the Middle East. Many British and Indian troops were also still deployed in Mesopotamia during its transition from Turkish rule to British control. These commitments inevitably entailed the unwilling retention of men who had either volunteered or were conscripted for active service during the war. In early February, the *Chronicle* quoted from a letter from a Bathonian in the Royal Engineers, who had joined the army as a volunteer in 1914 and was now stationed in Salonika:

> I am longing to get my discharge, and the quicker I am out of it, the happier I shall be for I don't know what we are doing here. It is not right after spending some of the best part of our lives in the war ... Any man with common sense would say, 'well, they are the men to come home for they went out first'. But we stand just as much hope of coming home as the conscripts – in fact they stand a better chance than a man like me. [23]

The *Chronicle* rightly observed that the writer had 'grounds for his grumble'.

Initially, the government had worked out a complex scheme which gave priority to the release of men required for skilled work, but this proved slow and cumbersome. As the sub-agent of Lord Temple's estate at Newton St Loe observed, after filling in applications for the release of one of the estate workers, 'if all that performance applies to every man in the army, most of them will die of old age before they get home'. [24] During the election, Lloyd George bowed to public pressure and promised to accelerate demobilisation, and regulations were rapidly changed, but even so, they seemed to lack any justice or logic, and men who had only served for a year or so, who could prove they had a job to return to, were often released before married veterans from 1914.

Not surprisingly the mood of those left behind became increasingly ugly and strikes and demobilisation riots took place on both sides of the Channel. At two army camps in England, soldiers alarmed the authorities by forming soldiers and workers councils similar to those set up by the Bolsheviks in Russia. In early January, delay in the transmission of demobilisation forms triggered a demonstration among SLI troops stationed in Belfast. It started with the band boys but rapidly spread to the rest of the unit. The situation was defused by the tactful intervention of the battalion's officers, who explained the measures were being taken to speed up demobilisation. Yet even while the officer was explaining the delays, a telegram arrived cancelling outright the discharge of 27 men who had already packed up their kits and were waiting to leave for England. The *Chronicle* remarked dryly on 1 February that 'it says a lot for the patience of the men and for the discretion of their officers that the battalion returned to duty and the demonstration was conducted as good-humouredly'.

A potentially far more serious incident occurred at Calais on 30 January when around 5,000 troops mutinied. Fortunately, order was restored without bloodshed, and only the three ringleaders were arrested. Not surprisingly, a week later a party of soldiers from Bath who were en route to the GWR station for embarkation to Calais, hastily had their orders cancelled and were sent back to their homes. Ironically, on the very day of the Calais mutiny the government announced that all men who had enlisted as volunteers between 1914 and 31 December 1915 would be demobilised as soon as there was transport to bring them home. Those who had joined the army after that date would still have to serve but would be given extra leave and pay, and the Cologne Zone was to be garrisoned primarily by young soldiers, called up in 1918, many of whom had seen no action at all.

Although these measures ultimately defused the demobilisation crisis, delays still occurred causing predictably angry and frustrated reactions from those affected. For instance, soldiers of the 1/4 SLI were actually on their way home in late February from Mesopotamia when they were abruptly ordered back to Baghdad, and informed that they might have to join the army of occupation. In protest Private Harry Mathews, a former organ builder at Sweetland's factory in Walcot, who had joined up in 1914, wrote to his parents telling them that there was every possibility that he might have to 'spend another summer in this hell of a country', and that demobilisation had 'been a mess up all through'. It was, he wrote, 'time the people at home took up the case on our behalf'. In response, his parents sent the letter to the *Chronicle* which was published on 12 April. Some of his fellow soldiers, meanwhile, wrote to their MPs. Their protests were evidently effective and resulted in the return of most of the 1/4 Somersets in early May, although a few unlucky ones remained in Mesopotamia until the end of the year.

For employers, demobilisation was a complex bureaucratic process. The personnel records of the Fuller's Earth Union at Combe Hay illustrate just how byzantine the whole process was.[25] To secure the demobilization of its former employees, the manager, Owen Keevil, first had to inform the Employment Exchange and send the men letters formally offering them their jobs back. These needed to be stamped by the local Employment Exchange, but since the majority of the men were in France, this was difficult to arrange. For most of the younger employees, demobilisation was wishful thinking. Only one man, Corporal Bull, stationed at a Base Depot in France, had the right credentials for early release: he was 41 and had enlisted voluntarily in 1915. Two younger men, G Staddon and Bert Miles both faced delays in demobilisation. The former, an army driver, wrote to Keevil on 26 January complaining that he had 'his fill of Army life', but Keevil could not offer much hope of an early release:

> As you did not join up until May 1916, I am now afraid that there is very little chance of you being released for some time ahead. I am very sorry about this as I could do with you back here at once ... I am afraid I cannot do more than I have done. We can but stand by now to see what the future brings forth.[26]

Another former employee, Driver FR Withers of the Army Service Corps, was also desperate to be demobilised. He was in a company engaged in baling forage for army horses in an isolated stretch of country on Salisbury Plain about three miles from the nearest village, which he complained was turning him into a 'hermit'. He had attempted unsuccessfully to see Keevil shortly before the New Year to discuss his demobilisation. On his return to duty he heard that his company was to be disbanded at the end of January and that its members were to hand in all their equipment by 21 January. Worried that some of his comrades had already received demobilisation forms, he wrote to Keevil on 7 January seeking reassurance that all the right paperwork had been completed correctly. He tactfully told him that, 'I know you are doing your best for me', optimistically adding that perhaps his papers were 'on the road'. Keevil replied by return of post and reassured him that, just 'because some fellows in your unit have got forms to fill in and you have not ... I have not been forgetting to do anything possible in connection with your release'. He also sent Withers another letter informing the authorities that he had a definite job to return to, which Withers duly forwarded to his commanding officer. Eleven days later an officer brought him Form Z16 and helped him complete it. The officer, who was 'a decent fellow', apparently told him that the army were 'going to hang on to you fellows for some considerable time, so get your employer to get you off if he can'.

Once again, Withers complained bitterly to Keevil about his work and most of the officers in the company:

> As long as the present officers remain in the company, it will never be no good, I have always thought that it was run chiefly by civilians, we have had officers out to us today asking for complaints and we didn't half tell him [sic] something, now the War Office is taking it over, they are trying to cover up there [sic] blunders. I told him that our work was nothing else but conscript labour, he answered, 'I'll admit the Forage Dept. is different to other coys [companies]', of course, it's the same old tale (I'll see what I can do for you) and that is as far as it goes.[27]

There was also a muddle about the exact nature of Withers' peacetime job at the Fuller's Earth Union. His employment had been listed in error as 'mixer' rather than 'miner', but in fact he was a steam-wagon driver. This error could have worked to his advantage, because as a miner he would have been assured early release, whereas drivers were a long way back in the queue for demobilisation. Withers was tempted not to correct this error and asked his employer's advice. Keevil agreed to 'do the best I can for you in this matter', but added

> personally I do not think it is any use for you to describe yourself to the authorities as a miner or mixer. The last-named description is only a subterfuge, and I do not think it would in any way deceive the authorities, besides which, I am very averse to doing anything (in connection with the release of men) which can at all be regarded as 'shady'. The best thing you can do in my opinion is to describe yourself at every opportunity as a steam-wagon driver, which you really were when you left our employ to join the army.[28]

Keevil also observed that the continued uncertainty surrounding the demobilisation of the younger servicemen was a very worrying one for employers as they have promised to take a number of men back when they are released, but they can get no kind of idea from the authorities when this release will take place. While most employers are anxious to get their men back, they cannot of course agree to keep jobs open indefinitely. I am perfectly ready to employ you if you are released within a reasonable time, but Heaven only knows what will happen within the next six months.

Withers was not demobilised until September, when he was offered a job of a driver, which he declined on the grounds that he would be paid only 'a labourers wage'. He was not the only man in Bath to decline working for what he considered a pittance (see page 32), and Keevil duly wrote to the Employment Exchange in early December, advising it not to pay him any unemployment benefit as 'he had turned down a good constant job at a fair rate of remuneration and it is entirely his own fault today that he is out of employment'. Withers' decision can possibly be explained by the relatively low wages paid by the Fuller's Earth Union and the impact of inflation on earnings. According to the firm's historians, Neil Macmillen and Mike Chapman, it paid twopence less an hour than any other Bath firm in April 1920.[29]

The men returning to the Fuller's Earth Union were all manual workers, with one exception – 19-year-old Lt Nicholds of the Royal Air Force, who had worked in the office at Combe Hay. Keevil offered him his old post, which had been filled while he was on active service by a highly efficient 16-year-old girl. When Nicholds took over a month to reply to a letter requesting certain details which were needed to secure his demobilisation, Keevil made it very clear in a second letter that he was more than satisfied with his temporary replacement and would keep the post open for only another week. This time Nicholds responded quickly and received six forms from the Ministry of Labour, which led Keevil to complain about 'all this red tape'. He was demobilised in April and his temporary replacement applied for a post as book keeper and short hand typist at the offices of the *Daily Press* in Bristol. Keevil in a glowing reference expressed his 'extreme regret' that he was duty bound to replace her with an employee returning from war service. On 25 January, Keevil instructed Nicholds to take a month's leave before starting at Combe Hay 'so as to give my lady assistant as long a period as possible for finding another position before leaving me'. In fact Nicholds more than proved his worth and replaced Keevil as manager in 1927.

By June, the tempo of demobilisation had increased. Parties were organised by employers, clubs and associations to welcome the men back home. The Postal Telegraph and Telephone Christian Association entertained some 80 demobilised postal employees at the Post Office Chambers early in the month. On the 21st the Earl and Countess Temple welcomed back over 60 of their demobilised employees and their families. Together with her sub-agent, Tarrant- Bailey, the Countess planned an elaborate occasion, which was reported fully in the *Chronicle*. Each man was presented with a souvenir in a glazed frame illustrated with pictures of Newton Park and the three villages which belonged to the estate. They marched down to a supper at the estate club room laid on by Fortt's and then danced to the music of Tarrant - Bailey's Seven-Piece Jazz Band. It was, to quote Graham Davis, an eminent historian of Bath, 'an unmistakable blend of patriotism and patronage'

Bolshevism

While the allies discussed the peace terms to be imposed on their defeated enemies, fighting continued in Russia and flared up in Afghanistan. In both these theatres conscript Bathonians participated, often unwillingly. Allied troops had initially been sent to Russia after the outbreak of the Revolution to ensure that military equipment did not fall into the hands of the Germans. With Germany's defeat in November 1918, allied intervention was stepped up in order to support the anti-Bolshevik forces in the Russian civil war. What this meant for the allied troops involved was explained to the *Chronicle* by Sapper Broad, a house decorator of 7 Chatham Row, when he returned home for two weeks leave in June after serving a year in Murmansk with the Royal Engineers:

*A group of soldiers in Bath serving reluctantly in Russia in the winter of 1918/19 (*Bath Chronicle, *12 April 1919)*

The cold was intense, the thermometer registering 35 degrees below zero ... During the whole time spent out there Sapper Broad never saw so much as a green vegetable, and they had to live on tinned foods, including tinned potatoes, which he says was 'more like pigs' food than anything else'. Among the things he pleasurably remembers is the Aurora Borealis, which was a sight of peculiar grandeur and one he was glad to have seen. From the middle of December to the end of February there was practically no sunlight and it seemed to be night all the time.[30]

Not surprisingly Broad had no desire to return to Russia. His was a familiar litany: there was great dissatisfaction at the unfairness of the government's demobilisation policy; younger men without family responsibilities were demobilsed, while in Russia there were men still serving, who were over age and with three or four wound stripes. Somerset MPs were bombarded with letters from other men from the SLI who were serving in Russia. Seventeen of them wrote to the MP for Frome, Percy Hurd, claiming that they had not been back to England since they left in November 1914. Hurd approached the Secretary of State for War, and was told unambiguously that all troops in Russia except those who volunteered to join the military missions would be brought home before the winter.

Military intervention in Russia was bitterly condemned by the Labour Party and many independent Liberals, who perceived Bolshevism to be essentially a democratic force, whereas most Conservatives, in Sir Samuel Hoare's words, 'were convinced that the whole future of Europe and indeed of the world depends ... upon the destruction of Bolshevism'. Echoes of these opposing points of view could be heard in Bath. In an open-air meeting in Sawclose to mark Labour Day, Lt Malcolm Hardyman bitterly attacked the War Minister, Winston Churchill, for sending troops to 'the frigid death trap, the White Sea territory'. Hardyman was an interesting man who was to become a vocal critic of the Coalition. His father was a distinguished surgeon and his brother, the late Lt Col John Hardyman, DSO, MC, was a poet and member of the Union of Democratic Control, which had supported ending the war through negotiations with the Germans. He had been killed on the western front in August 1918.

In June, the Somerset Miners' Association sent Percy Hurd a resolution condemning the British government for 'using British money and British blood for the purpose of establishing Czarist rule at the expense of the present Russian government'. Hurd's reply was somewhat ambiguous. He argued, admittedly at a time when the White Russians seemed to be winning the civil war in Russia, that the government, like the miners, wanted to see the expeditionary force withdrawn as soon as possible, leaving an independent non-Bolshevik northern Russia. Bath's MP, Captain Foxcroft, in his speech to the Conservative Association at the end of June was more forthright. He was adamant that, before peace could truly be restored, 'the poisonous growth of Bolshevism' needed to be eliminated. To prove his point, he gave his audience a spine chilling example of 'Bolshevik atrocities':

> A traveller, lately returned from Russia just before leaving that country entered a peasant's cottage, to find father, mother, and three children sitting around the table dead! They had been nailed to it – by the Bolsheviks. [31]

The emotive issue of Bolshevik atrocities was a key to the debate on Bolshevism. If true, it was a powerful way to discredit its ideology, justify allied intervention and fill the British bourgeoisie with the fear of a Bolshevik take over in Britain. To those on the left this was mere propaganda and, in Lt Hardyman's words, 'a monstrous perversion of the truth'. In October, F Redwood of the National Union of Railwaymen, while addressing a meeting in Sawclose, claimed that the Bolsheviks in Russia, like the working men in Britain, were 'only fighting for their rights'.

These arguments failed to convince the staunchly Conservative *Chronicle*, which continued to publish accounts of Bolshevik brutality. On 22 November it published a poem entitled 'A Warning To Labour Party Extremists' by BM Sullivan, an extract from which will give an idea of its tone:

> Someone gets up and makes a speech to you;
> Says 'hands off Russia' and you all applaud
> How nice to sit and smoke, as you all do,
> Nor hear death cries, nor feel the knotted cord.
> Someone else says, 'I am a Bolshevist'!
> You take your pipes out and remark,'Hear hear'! ...
> Remember, if the Bolshies get firm hold
> They'll rule, not you, with a murderous hand. [32]

In retrospect, the history of Soviet Union shows that Sullivan was right, but he, like Foxcroft and many others on the right, ignored the atrocities committed by the White Russians. As the historian Orlando Figes observes in *The People's Tragedy*, 'White Terror was a mirror image of the class resentment that drove the Red Terror. Terror lay at the heart of both regimes.' [33]

Afghanistan and India

In April, the British government was also faced with war on the North-West frontier when Emir Amanullah of Afghanistan attempted to exploit the nationalist unrest in the Punjab by invading British India. This led to the Third Afghan War, which ended with an armistice in August and delayed the return home of the 2/5 SLI until November. Before fighting the Afghans, the battalion had been involved in containing the unrest in the Punjab, which had been inflamed by the Amritsar massacre.

The experiences of Sergeant Silcox. a Bathonian who had been a junior reporter before the war, were not untypical. He had been transferred from Mesopotamia to Karachi where his demobilisation orders were cancelled because of the Punjab riots. When the Afghan War broke out, his period of service was abruptly extended, and he took part in the fighting with units of the SLI and the Devon Regiment at Dakka, at the far end of the Khyber Pass. It was not until early September that he arrived home. Another Bathonian, Private Hulance, who in civilian life had been a barman in Westgate Street, had a similar story to tell. He had joined up in 1914 and had a four-year-old child whom he had never seen. He was transferred from Mesopotamia to India and sent up to the North West Frontier. In early summer 1919, he wrote to his wife from Rawalpindi that 'I will be lucky if I get home by Christmas next'. Nevertheless, his fate was preferable to that of Private Wherrett, a former employee of Lipton's. Like Hulance, his demobilisation was cancelled, and he was sent to the North West Frontier where he contracted bronchial pneumonia and died in early July. It was not until November that the Guildford Castle, after a stormy voyage lasting a month rather than the usual 18 or 19 days, reached Liverpool with a draft of a thousand troops from India, about 400 of which were from the SLI. Amongst them were 19 Bathonians and the Battalion mascot, 'a fine buck' which had to be loaded into a car on arrival in Bath and taken to the headquarters of the 1/4 SLI on the Lower Bristol Road.

Despite nationalist unrest in the Punjab and General Dyer's notorious order in April to fire on an unarmed Indian crowd in the Jallianwala Bagh at Amritsar, causing over 300 deaths and 2,000 casualties, on Empire Day in May 1919 the message given to schools was still one of Indian loyalty to the British Crown. Sir Harry Hatt, a former mayor, for instance, told Oldfield Boys' School that Germany had expected India 'to throw off the yoke of British rule ... but the inspiring spectacle had been witnessed of loyal Indian princes pouring out their treasure and begging to be allowed to lead armies ... and all had seen how India like the rest of Britain's possessions, recognized in the British flag the flag of liberty'.

Curiously a not dissimilar message was given by Annie Besant when she gave a lecture on 'India Past and Present' on Saturday 20 September at the Assembly Rooms. Besant was an ardent socialist and supporter of Indian Home Rule, who had been elected president of the Indian National Congress in 1917. She made a robust defence of Indian civilisation and its 'splendid past', but her main point was that the Montague-Chelmsford proposals for introducing limited Indian self-government should 'with some alterations be passed into law'. The Indians wanted 'the gate of liberty' to be opened, she explained, so that they could begin 'to work out step by step their own emancipation and system of government', but she was emphatic that India did not want to break its ties with Britain – 'she knew our history and had seen our struggles for freedom … India believed our cry that the late war was a war for liberty and making democracy safe for the world'.

Indians were not frequent visitors to Bath, but after Besant's lecture 'an elegant speech' was given by a 'Hindoo [sic] gentleman' on the trade union movement in India. A week earlier, the Bath Bathing Establishment had been visited by two distinguished Indians: the journalist Nihal Singh and Dr Chowry-Muthu, a friend of Mahatma Gandhi, who had set up Hill Grove Sanatorium on the Mendips for patients suffering from pulmonary tuberculosis. Singh provided striking evidence of the achievement of Indian civilisation, about which Annie Besant had waxed so lyrical, by pointing out that the pattern of flat bricks used by the Romans was in fact a traditional feature of Indian architecture.

GERMANY AND THE GERMANS: THE VIEW FROM BATH

MESOPOTAMIA, INDIA AND RUSSIA were not popular postings for conscript soldiers anxious to return home, but in the occupied Rhineland life was comfortable, the population friendly and the rate of exchange thoroughly favourable to the occupiers. Civilians visiting the Cologne Zone in 1919 were astonished at the apparently amicable relations between the Germans and the British troops. Most SLI soldiers were withdrawn from Germany in June, but a small number remained behind and were amalgamated with the Hampshire Regiment. For many British servicemen a posting to the Rhineland gave them an opportunity to explore western Europe. Take for example the experience of Air Mechanic FP Edwards of 51st Wing HQ, RAF, a former post office official, as relayed by letter to his father at 16 Milton Avenue. He described his visit to Cologne, where he found the trams far superior to those back home:

Why is it that our tram system in England is so poor? Here the cars are palatial, being fitted up regardless of cost and are run on the trailer system – three or four together ... Allied troops ride free anywhere – any time – any distance ... I had a good supper at the British Empire Leave Club – late dinner in fact – soup, a cut from the joint and vegetables, bread and cheese and beer, served in a fine dining hall complete with a German orchestra and waiters, price 3 marks 50 (about 1sh. 1d).

He then went on to enthuse about Brussels – 'the whirl of enjoyment, the blaze of light from cafes and shops, the endless string of cinemas and shows.'[34]

Back home in England the mood was, with significant exceptions. still one of fierce hatred for the Germans. A good example of this was Countess Temple's appeal to her tenants on the Newton Park estate at the party in June to mark the homecoming of those who had fought in the war, when, as the vice-president of the British Empire Union, she asked them 'to promise never again do business with or be on friendly terms with a German'. Just before Christmas some 259 German and Austrian aliens had been released from internment and exempted from repatriation on the grounds of their long residence in the United Kingdom and marriage to British women. Two of them were now working in Bath: Jacob M Murschel, who was employed as a cabinet maker at the Albion Cabinet Works on the Upper Bristol Road, and AP Blass, who was working at a local bakery. On Saturday 11 January, a large crowd assembled in Sawclose to protest against the employment of foreign labour. The meeting had been organised by the Comrades of the Great War, which had been founded in 1917 to represent the rights of ex-servicemen. The prime target of their anger was the alleged employment of enemy aliens at the expense of demobilised servicemen who needed a job. One speaker, Captain Gerald Coningham, appeared to advocate direct action against 'enemy aliens': 'If they were employed, then they could not blame the "boys" if they took the law into their own hands.' He then went on to sing his own 'hymn of hate' and urge the citizens of Bath to drive every alien out of the city, adding for good measure that, without exception, the Germans were 'a lot of dirty swine'.

Two weeks later, on 29 January, there was a lively debate about the employment of baker Blass at the annual meeting of the Bath Trades and Labour Council (BTLC). The injustice of employing a German, albeit a man who had probably spent decades in Britain, instead of an unemployed ex-soldier was keenly felt. In the discussion it was stressed that 'several bakers were out of employment at the present time – men who were demobilised and walking about the streets'. A fortnight later, when the matter was again discussed, one of the members observed that they should not just pick on 'working men Germans [sic] but on Germans who were in high places – rich and poor alike, without any distinction of class'. It is possible he may have been referring to the Horstmanns, long-standing Bath residents of German extraction, who owned several large businesses in the city. In April, the Bath Board of Guardians considered the case of 'a German lunatic' in Wells. One of the guardians, William Harbutt, the Plasticine manufacturer, urged repatriation to Germany, but the chairman did not think it practical to have him moved. During 1919 many German immigrants, who had been interned during the war, returned to Germany, a large number gravitating to the British Zone in the Rhineland.

Some voices in Bath, as elsewhere in the country, were beginning to be raised on Germany's behalf. The official policy pursued by the Coalition government was to make Germany pay for the war, but already there was a growing awareness that Germans needed to be fed. In January, the allies agreed to supply Germany with grain, cereals and pork, but otherwise the blockade remained in force. Initially the case for feeding Germany met with a tepid response in Bath, as elsewhere in the country, but in early February the Bath branch of the Women's International League passed a resolution urging the government to raise the blockade so that 'the civilian population of the enemy countries should not suffer the continued horrors of starvation'. At the Labour Day rally in Sawclose Malcolm Hardyman advocated the immediate raising of the blockade and sounded a warning that harsh peace terms would bring back 'the Prussian mob'. He welcomed the fact that 'our humane soldiers (in the Rhineland) remain in close touch with the German population'.

Despite the frequent showing of propaganda films and talks on various aspects of German 'frightfulness', in 1919 it was Germany's commercial ambitions that worried many Bathonians, who feared that its exports would undercut British firms and put them out of business. The BTLC criticised the government for closing down the factories opened during the war, instead of using them to make goods which would otherwise have to be bought from Germany. An unambiguous and implacable message was given by Major Meade, who presided over the dinner held in Combe Down on Saturday 14 June to celebrate the return of its servicemen. They were told that 'they must realise that they had to fight the *Boche* in commerce …only they would be doing it at home and much more comfortably than they did it "out there"'.

However, this phobia of all things German did not lead to a boycott of German music despite the demands of some super-patriots. In the *Chronicle* at the end of March, the Bellman reminded readers that, 'had musical circles in this country banned those great composers, who were writing their masterpieces when Britain and Germany were friendly states, and in some instances our allies, they would have eliminated ... much that is best and most admirable in music'. In October, Frederic Lamond, a Scottish composer and one of the last surviving pupils of Franz Liszt, who been interned in Germany during the war, played in the Pump Room a programme of predominantly German classical music. A revealing comment on the mixed feelings that German culture awoke in this country in the immediate aftermath of the war was expressed in a lecture on *Hamlet* to the members of the Bath branch of the British Empire Shakespeare Society in early February 1919. After analysing the character of Hamlet, who was dismissed as a dithering passivist, Edith Thompson, a leading light in the society, turned her attention to Horatio. He was a Dane, but his spiritual home was in the ancient university city of Wittenberg, 'a town that sounds so ill in our ears' today. Here she was probably referring to the typhus outbreak, which killed so many British POWs in Wittenberg in the winter of 1914-15, and the lack of German medical assistance for them.

In August, amidst the still prevalent hatred of Germany, a brief notice appeared in the *Bath Chronicle*:

> A Plucky German
> In the presence of a large number of German prisoners a German soldier was, at Dorchester, presented with a silver watch and a gift of money in recognition of his plucky conduct in extricating two British officers from a burning plane on Salisbury Plain. The authorities sent the man home to Germany.[35]

PEACE CELEBRATIONS

THE TREATY OF VERSAILLES was signed in the Hall of Mirrors at Versailles on 28 June. It was an uneasy Anglo-French compromise, which was to destabilise Europe until the Locarno Agreements of 1925. Britain's local authorities had little time to organise peace celebrations. With just a fortnight's notice, they were told by the government that Saturday 17 July would be Peace Day. A week earlier, services of thanksgiving were held in Bath. At the Abbey, Prebendary Boyd sounded an interesting note more reminiscent of 1945 than 1919, when he said that 'the victory of the allies did not mean the *extinction* of the liberties of the conquered. Indeed, for Germany, it was better to be beaten than to be victorious and still dominated by the Prussian spirit.'

Several trade unionists and members of the Labour Party boycotted the peace celebrations The Somerset miners were quick to condemn the treaty as both unjust and an incentive to further strife. This was an attitude shared by many of the trade unions and some members of the BTLC. AE Bragg, for instance, at a meeting on 9 July, decided to boycott the celebrations on the grounds 'that this peace was no peace at all', and that they had been 'fighting for a settlement that had not been granted'. The BTLC, however, decided to leave the decision on whether to participate or not to individual members. The celebrations started on Friday the 18th with a party for all Bath children at Sydney Gardens in glorious weather. Around 7,000 children attended and Fortt's provided two tons of cake, 50,000 buns, a large quantity of biscuits and 100 gallons of milk. After singing the national anthem the mayor addressed the children. He emphasised that the war was fought for honour and truth, but went on to say that 'some people might tell them that war was glorious, but peace was even more glorious'.

The following day the weather was very different as rain swept in overnight. The celebrations started with the singing of the Te Deum on the Abbey Tower during a torrential downpour. The rain eased somewhat as a procession of around 2,000 soldiers, ex-service men, nurses, members of friendly societies, clergy, along with the mayor preceded by the sword and mace bearers, wended its way towards the Royal Crescent where a service was conducted by Prebendary Boyd. At its conclusion a flight of pigeons, which were supposed to be 'the doves of peace', were released to the cheers of the crowd. In the afternoon some 5,000 guests attended a garden party, again in pouring rain, in Sydney Gardens. The city's celebrations ended with a bonfire at Sham Castle. More modest celebrations took place at the workhouse on Frome Road, where patients and inmates sat down to a special Peace Day dinner of roast pork, new potatoes and cabbage, followed by stewed rhubarb and custard.

The only unruly incident reported was a verbal fracas on the evening of the 18th between a retired Sergeant-Major, Ernest Alfred Lee of Westgate Buildings, and a group of four Australian soldiers, who allegedly claimed that Australia had won the war for Britain, as a result of which the magistrates fined Lee £1. Over the next few weeks there were celebrations in the surrounding suburbs and villages. At Fairfield Park and Bathampton, effigies of the Kaiser were paraded around and then burnt. Arguably, the Bathonian who experienced the most adventurous peace celebrations was Private FW Tanner from the British Rhine Army, who was selected to be in the British contingent at the great victory procession in Paris on 14 July –Bastille Day. Tanner was so struck with Paris that he described it as 'the best place he has ever seen'.

The question of how best to remember the fallen caused considerable debate. Should there be a memorial or should they be commemorated by a club, hostel or even a public library? On 19 February 1919 Sir Harry Hatt, convened a public meeting in the Guildhall to discuss the matter. He made out a compelling case for a memorial. He pointed out that 'a club for comrades of the Great War' would not last for ever, and that there was a considerable risk that 'something which might appeal to us at the moment as supplying the needs of those who have returned', would in a couple of generations have completely lost its significance. This argument was to go on for nearly eight years, and it was not until 1927 that a memorial was unveiled in Royal Victoria park, although in December 1922 two chapels in Wells Cathedral were dedicated to the fallen of Somerset. Amongst the 11,275 names in the Book of Remembrance there were 1,808 Bathonians. In the suburbs, decisions to build war memorials were taken far more quickly. As early as March, for instance, Walcot decided to erect a 'war memorial pure and simple'.

BATH IN 1919
UNEMPLOYMENT, POVERTY AND LABOUR UNREST

WHILE MUCH OF the world was in turmoil, Bathonians adapted, often fearfully and angrily, to the new post-war world. The most dramatic impact on their life during this period was the return of those who had fought in the war. The Liberal politician and writer Charles Masterman, writing in 1922, called the whole process of the formation and demobilisation of the mass armies a 'gigantic migration', with most of the men returning home having endured 'unspeakable suffering, and looked into the face of Death'. He also pointed out that, before serving 'in France and Italy, in Gallipoli and Salonika, in Egypt and Palestine and India and Mesopotamia, in the frosty Caucasus and the White Sea', few of them had ventured abroad.[36]

The concern of the great majority of men was to return to civilian life, adequate living quarters and secure employment. Some, like the former postmen at Bath Post Office, were able to slip back easily into their old jobs as early as March 1919. Others, like G Raward of the examination staff at Isaac Pitman and Sons, took over their former positions from the women who had temporarily assumed their posts. Raward's replacement, Mrs Warran, on her departure in May was presented with a silver and ivory manicure set and was assured by the general manager that women like her 'had rendered great service to the country during a national crisis'. Both 2nd Lt Pilot Ernest Carter and the gifted young organist and choirmaster of St Mary's Bathwick, Benjamin

Maslin, who had been called up as late as February 1918, were successful in securing posts: the former in the Bath Constabulary, in which he went on to serve for 30 years, eventually becoming superintendent, and the latter as assistant librarian in the city's reference library. Neither, however, on account of their youth, were able to leave the army until the autumn. [37]

Many other demobilised men, particularly unskilled workers, were not so successful. On 30 April the mayor, Alfred Wills, was informed by the Re-employment Advisory Committee that there were 894 ex-servicemen, compared to 239 civilian males, drawing the dole. Councillor AE Withy, the committee chairman, pointed out that these figures were 'in striking contrast to the rest of the country' and 'were really enormous with regard to the discharged soldiers'. Over the next two months the situation deteriorated still further. Figures given on 7 July to the Surveying Committee by Withy showed that, while the number of civilians without a job had fallen to 92, the number of unemployed ex-servicemen had risen to 1,013. Initially, it was assumed that Bath employers were not reinstating men in their former jobs, but statistics showed that there were barely more than half a dozen such cases. Sir Harry Hatt suggested that one possible reason for the high unemployment figures was that many young men who had joined the colours at 18 were now in their mid-20s, and, whereas before they had been prepared to worked for ten or twelve shillings a week, they now demanded £3 or £4. Councillor Chamberlain quoted examples of young men from Bath, who, before being called up, had found work away from the city, but were now returning to their home town. As the mayor went on to observe, this 'put Bath in an unenviable position in comparison with other towns', as it unfairly cast a negative light on local employers. To correct this impression, Councillor Withy appealed to employers to inform the Labour Exchange when a job offer was turned down. In subsequent meetings, various proposals for work creation projects were discussed, including building a swimming pool in Oldfield Park, widening Englishcombe Lane in preparation for the construction of houses, and painting bridges and railings. Trade union opposition and the council's dilatory progress in purchasing the land needed for future building projects, however, ensured that these schemes were slow to be implemented.

Unemployment was the reason why there was such hostility towards the employment of women in jobs that had, before the war, been filled by men, and towards the very small number of 'enemy aliens' who were re-instated by their former employers. It was also the main reason why, at the council meeting on 10 November, Labour councillors opposed the council's decision to grant Lloyd George the freedom of Bath. Councillor Chamberlain explained 'that when they saw fewer men walking about the streets in want of employment, then by all means ... give the Freedom of the City to Mr Lloyd George'.

Bath was still a beautiful city. It had not been physically ravaged by the war, but it had its slums and pockets of extreme poverty in Widcombe, Walcot, Southgate Street, Kingsmead Square and, above all, in the notorious Avon Street. John New, later the managing clerk of Stone, King and Wardle, when interviewed in 1989, remembered Carlton Road, which as late as the thirties was composed of 'horrible houses'. They were built 'right up against Beechen Cliff – never had any sun – three houses with one lavatory and one tap between them'.[38] Children from more prosperous families, right up to the 1930s, were kept well away from these areas. For instance, Patricia Connett, whose father had a butcher's shop on Camden Road was forbidden to go a fair on the quayside as it was too near to Avon Street.[39]

Proceedings in the police courts often afford a glimpse of the poverty and misery that still existed in Bath. On 13 December 1919, the *Chronicle* reported that Albert Freemantle, an unemployed 43-year-old widower, was accused by the National Society for the Prevention of Cruelty to Children (NSPCC) of neglecting his two children. Initially, he had lived with his family in one room at 18 Grove Street, where there was only one bed 'to accommodate all the parties'. Albert then disappeared, and, before applying to the Salvation Army for assistance, stayed briefly in Avon Street. He was advised to go to the workhouse, but 'declined to stay as he objected to having to turn out his pockets on admission'. The NSPCC conceded that 'he had done his best for his family according to his lights'. The court had no option but to send the children to the Cottage Homes attached to the Frome Road Workhouse, and Albert was remanded in custody for a week – the main object of which was to give the NSPCC time to arrange for a permanent home for the children. Figures released by the Bath Schools' Medical Officer and published in the *Chronicle* in December 1919 provide further evidence of poverty in Bath: a routine examination of 8,605 children showed that 18.8% were classed as being 'under normal nutrition' and 1.5% were very badly nourished. The figures were by no means uniform across the city. In the inner-city slums, malnourishment ran at 32.3%, while in Twerton and Oldfield Park, where, for the most part, tradesmen, skilled workers and small shopkeepers lived, it was only 5.9%.

Unemployment, malnourishment and ultimately the workhouse awaited those who could not support themselves and their families. It was the fear of falling into this abyss that haunted the impoverished middle classes and inflamed their fear of Bolshevism and organised labour. Increased taxation and rising prices had hit their incomes very hard. Clergymen and school teachers were particularly badly paid. For instance, at the Diocesan Conference in Wells on 30 October, the Rev J Boyle, an 'outspoken Irish clergyman', complained bitterly about the poverty of many parish priests in Somerset, and the church's decision to appeal for funds to maintain the cathedral. He called the Church of England 'the biggest sweating institution in the country', and went on to say

> I am not a proud man ... and I don't mind telling you what I have had to do this summer. I have had to turn my house into a lodging-house and my wife and I have been sleeping in the harness room; my children in the hay-loft, in order to provide an upkeep for the mansion which you, my lord, recommended should be purchased for a vicarage, and the purchase price for which I am helping to pay, and which you have made it as difficult as possible to get rid of.[40]

Teachers were also under acute financial pressure. As the minutes of a special meeting of the National Union of Teachers (NUT) on 29 August put it, 'owing to devaluation of money your authority's teachers almost without exception are in receipt of smaller remuneration than in pre-war days'.[41] Reluctantly the Education Committee agreed on 11 October that established teachers should be given an outright bonus of £30, and that when national pay scales were introduced in December, Bath would have to match them. One councillor went as far to concede that 'many Bath teachers were paid less than the historic dustman'.

Increases in the salaries of teachers were paid for out of the education rate. This often met with opposition from the beleaguered middle classes, whose standard of living was threatened by the steady increase in the city's rates. In September, a local branch of the Middle Class Union (MCU) was set up. The aim of the MCU was, in Councillor Sturge Cotterell's words, to defend the interests of the middle classes, who, 'it appeared, were at present unorganised wanderers in No Man's Land between the ramparts of capital and the trenches of labour'. Particularly vulnerable to rising prices were those on fixed pensions. Single women of modest means, as well as elderly couples eking out an existence, often in furnished rooms, felt particularly under pressure. A few fortunate elderly ladies, provided they were communicants of the Church of England, found refuge in Partis College, where they were given modest apartments, looked after until their death and granted a small pension. One member, Miss Patricia Risk, for example, became so frail that she requested permission to leave the college in April 1918 'for a time' to be looked after in a nursing home. She returned to Partis College in January 1919 to find 'her bed clothes, etc dripping', and the maid, 'a viper in a fury'! Eventually she moved out to a nursing home in Torquay, before moving to another in Clifton. Generously the Trustees allowed awarded her a small pension of £30, which, combined with the modest income from her investments, just about enabled her to stay there.⁴² She was, of course, lucky compared to many elderly people in the city, who, through the inability to support themselves, ended up in the Frome Road Workhouse. To help some avoid this humiliation, in March the Monmouth Street Society appealed to the citizens of Bath to raise £291 to enable the Society to increase its contributions to the income of 112 elderly people from one to two shilling a week, as 'the day of miracles is ... past when an old man or old woman can support life under the present conditions of high prices upon so tiny an amount'.

Rising prices and the demand for an eight-hour day caused a wave of strikes, which were countered by lockouts throughout the country. In 1919-21 there were more strikes in Britain than in revolutionary Germany or Italy, and Bath had its fair share. Even such a benevolent employer as the Bath Cooperative Society was put under pressure by its employees to pay more. In December, the secretary of the Society's committee advised his colleagues that 'we should have to seriously tackle' the question of pay, as it was well below what the National Union of Distributive and Allied Workers was demanding. Initially, as the committee minutes show, this did not 'find favour and the matter was allowed to remain in abeyance' until March, when the union's demands were at last accepted. The chairman, however, reminded his employees that 'the salary increases would be a serious matter unless the whole of the employees pulled together and tried to make the business go'.⁴³

There were bitter disputes in two of Bath's major industries: the furniture trade and the engineering firm of Stothert and Pitt. A dispute originating in Barnstaple in July over the application of mass-production techniques to the furniture trade rapidly escalated into a major industrial conflict. The National Federation of Furniture Employers decided to coerce their employees into accepting the new work conditions through a lock out. In Bath, between 250 and 300 employees were affected at the Bath Cabinet Makers on Bellott's Road and W&T Lock's factory at Charlton Buildings in Twerton. The strikers were financially supported by local trade unions and the Labour party as well as the BTLC. The strike was bad news for the local economy, as companies in other parts of the country, which were independent of the National Federation, were able to exploit the situation to secure orders that would normally have gone to the Bath workshops. In October, the employers ended the lockout, and, after a brief strike, which won further concessions, the men went back to work. In September, pipe fitters at Stothert and Pitt also went on strike to gain recognition as skilled workers, and so move up to a higher wage scale, but their efforts were sabotaged by members of another union carrying out their work. Next the moulders struck. Their case was eloquently put by one of the members of their strike committee, who pointed out in November that the price of castings had risen by 300 per cent during the war, but their wages had only gone up by 20 per cent. [44]

It was, however, a lightning railway strike, triggered by government attempts to reduce railwaymen's pay, that most affected Bath. It lasted from the night of 26/27 September to 5 October, when the government climbed down. The Bath Labour Party was fully behind the strike, letting the local railway strike committee use its rooms at Post Office Chambers, and organising meetings in its support. The strike caused considerable disruption: county court hearings had to be delayed and exhibitions and tours cancelled. Tourists were trapped in Bath and Bathonians away from home could not get back. Councillor Withy, a lawyer by profession, was holidaying in Cornwall and was unable to return to defend a client in court, a local fishmonger accused of profiteering. Some of the more fortunate were able to reach their destinations by finding seats on a charabanc. One enterprising charabanc driver, who had brought a load of passengers to Bath from Bournemouth, ensured that he did not travel back empty by contacting the local hotels, and managed to secure 14 passengers. The strike inevitably accelerated the growth in road traffic. A regular charabanc service was introduced between Bath and London, and so busy was motor traffic along the main roads that the Home Office reintroduced the Vehicles Lights Order, which had been rescinded after the war. From half an hour after sunset all vehicles now had to have a red tail light and two white front lights.

The strike also led to the temporary reimposition of strict food rationing. Thomas Wills, the Executive Officer of the Food Control Committee, which had been set up in 1918, was, in the dramatic language of the Bellman,

> summoned from his bed when the crisis arose, by startling rappings of his door knocker, and persistent peals upon his door bell. Mr Wills 'went forth in the darkness of the dark night' to the Food Office and remained in constant attendance. [45]

Strict rationing of coal and essential foods such as meat, butter and lard ensured that food and fuel supplies were adequate for the duration of the strike. The chief constable appealed for volunteers as special constables, but the strike passed off peacefully in Bath where there were no violent clashes between strikers and strike breakers. The only recorded strike breakers were the lady workers of the Citizens' House Art Centre, who took a small hand cart to the Great Western goods depot to pick up a consignment of a hundredweight of sugar. Apparently, according to the *Chronicle*, 'the passage of the lady strike breakers through the city occasioned a great deal of appreciative comment from passers-by'.

Given the degree of class conflict throughout the country, it was clear that Labour would gain some council seats in the local elections in November. At a meeting of the Bath Educational Committee in late April, Councillor Baker gloomily pronounced that 'after November next very few of us will be here'. In fact it was not quite the bloodbath predicted. Elections took place in eight wards. Labour candidates won outright in four – Westmoreland, Widcombe, Walcot South and Twerton East – and in three others their share of the vote increased.

RECONSTRUCTION AND PLANS FOR THE FUTURE

THROUGH SUCCESSIVE ACTS in the late nineteenth and early twentieth centuries, local authorities had gained responsibility for public health and education. The 1919 Housing and Town Planning Act now required them to establish their local housing needs and within three months draw up plans for meeting them. Government subsidies were to be made available to pay for the construction of new housing. A second measure, the Housing (Additional Powers) Act, was designed to encourage local builders by granting them a subsidy of between £120 and £130 for building houses not exceeding a certain size for sale or rent.

There was general agreement that Bath needed more housing to replace the slums. The new mayor, Alfred Wills, was the senior partner of the local building company, A Wills & Sons, and had a reputation for 'getting things done'. The Chief Medical Officer saw slum clearance as the key to a healthier city, while Alderman Bush, the chairman of the Education Committee, pointed out 'that the best will never be got out of the expenditure upon education so long as the conditions, which exist in some parts of the city, continue to exist'. Lloyd George's wife joined the demand for new housing by rather mischievously observing that 'one reason why our houses were inconvenient was that men planned them and men built them'. This inspired Margaret Osborne to write an article in her usual light-hearted tone in the *Chronicle*:

> There are few women architects ... and hardly any women who order and pay for houses. And yet women commonly spend most of the 24 hours under their own roof, while their sons and husbands only sleep and have their morning and evening meals and perhaps a Sunday pipe or an attack of influenza at home, year in year out. It does not matter to them if the stairs are so steep that mothers of young children might think them planned by Herod for the destruction of infants.[46]

By January 1919, the Housing Committee, which was chaired by the councillor for Twerton East, George Long, had produced a plan which received a good reception in the national press, and many other councils requested a copy of it. It proposed that 1,000 new houses should eventually be built on various sites on the eastern and western borders of the city, starting with a more modest total of 250, the gradual clearing of slum areas and the provision of affordable accommodation for the elderly by purchasing some of Bath's large and dilapidated old houses. The plan was approved by the council on 14 January, but, as the Bellman observed, 'between the adoption of the report and the beginning of the actual work a good deal of negotiating, of estimating, and a hundred other preparatory necessities interpose'. In March, the council acquired 35 acres in Englishcombe where they planned to build 'over 400 model houses'. The inspector of the Local Government Board judged the site to be 'better than any in England that [had] come under his notice'. The council also decided to replace slum property in the Dolemeads with double-fronted semi-detached cottages. When Dr Addison, who was about to take over the newly created Ministry of Health, which was also responsible for housing, visited the city in June to open an extension to the Royal Baths, he was so impressed by the Dolemeads scheme that he gave 'his consent at once'. Progress was, however, slow and by November only two houses were in the course of construction. It took another two years to build a further twelve.

Bath's main industry was tourists, especially those wealthy invalids and hypochondriacs who were attracted by the healing qualities of the spa waters. During the war, when travel to foreign spas in France and Germany had been impossible, Bath prospered, and the hotels paid handsome dividends to their backers. The Grand Pump Room Hotel was reopened and the accommodation in both the Pulteney and Spa Hotels was extended. In late January 1919, a conference of local hoteliers and boarding-house proprietors was convened by the chairman of the Baths' Committee. Optimistically it concluded that 'even when travelling facilities are restored and foreign countries are again easy of access, Bath has a future of great prosperity before her'. To secure this, however, both the council and local businesses would have to invest money in improving facilities and above all in advertising.

By June 1919, a new wing had been added to the Royal Baths in Bath Street. It provided state-of-the-art spa facilities, which included whirlpool and aeration baths. New improved electric hot-air baths were also fitted, and in each room in the new block there was 'a handsome spinal douche for the application of mineral water'. The Spa Committee staged a considerable publicity coup by inviting Dr Addison to open the extension on 5 June. In his welcoming address the mayor lost no chance to extol Bath's national importance as a spa and 'the healing virtues of its streams'. In reply Dr Addison was effusive. He observed that, 'notwithstanding its long history', Bath 'seemed to be as virile and full of imagination today as it had been in the past', and was sure that, in the future, the new Health Ministry 'would not look in vain to the Bath Corporation for assistance and support'.

One consequence of Dr Addison's visit was that three weeks later the Chamber of Commerce agreed to contribute to a fund to finance the advertising of the city's attractions. DA Evans, its vice-chairman, in a speech at the Guildhall, compared the sleepy old Bath of twenty years earlier, when one of its main attractions 'was a threepenny concert in the Guildhall on Saturday nights', to the modern city which was now 'absolutely bubbling with life'. The fund was an investment in its future. The renaissance of Bath was endorsed by the literary critic, SR Littlewood, the son of the former vicar of St James, who had recently visited the city. Writing in the Sunday edition of *The Referee*, he contrasted the Bath of his youth with the Bath of today:

> What a change in Bath itself from the Bath of my childhood ... with its dingy old Pump Room, its shabby old chairmen, its permanently closed hotels, its houses like empty tombs, its air of stagnant somnolent respectability, beneath the weight of which retired majors went up Milsom Street and down Milsom Street and the grasshopper was a burden. In the nearly half century between Bath has renewed its youth almost beyond recognition

He then added an interesting interpretation of why this had happened:

> I think it was from the hills that its help really came –the spreading out into white villas round the rim of that great green cup and over the downs beyond; motors, trams, golf, everything that took folk out of the swelter into the breezes, and heartened them to continue this process every day instead of

making it their custom always of an afternoon to draw the sun blinds and settle themselves to a little more slumber, a little more sleep.[47]

The importance for British spas of advertising was further emphasized in an article in the *National Review* in October. Its author, Captain E Brown, warned that foreign competition would return and that 'the valetudinarian of the gouty, dyspeptic, rheumatic order' will go to the spa where he thinks he will get the best treatment. His solution was threefold. First, the British spa industry needed to 'gain the ear of the medical profession if they are to continue to enjoy the wave of prosperity that war has unexpectedly thrust upon them'. It was crucial that there should be no return to the pre-war habit of Harley Street consultants, who were often bribed with free holidays, recommending Continental spas to their patients. Second, they should try and reach out to the public through 'kinema publicity' – 'Bath and its Healing Properties' would, for instance 'make an interesting … one reel film on the movies'. Third, British Spas should think of marketing their spa waters, as Vichy, Karlsbad and Ems did.

Both the council and the Chamber of Commerce was receptive to this advice. A few months earlier, in June, Sturge Cotterell, the deputy chairman of the Library and Arts Committee, had suggested that an aeroplane should be

John Hatton, the Baths' Director, exploits the unavailability of German and Austrian spas to British visitors to attract patients (Museum of Bath at Work)

chartered to tour the empire with a supply of films advertising Bath. The new mayor, Percy Jackman, who, to quote his predecessor, Alderman Wills, was full of 'breezy, cheerful optimism', had, as the owner of the Pulteney Hotel, a vested interest in the success of the spa. Before the war he had visited rival spas on the continent and could therefore speak with some authority on the potential competition confronting Bath.

Reassuringly, the spa continued to draw crowds of guests throughout 1919. At the end of November, the Francis Hotel, then in Bennett Street, which had been taken over by the RAF in July 1918, reopened after a complete refurbishment. Reflecting the booming health and tourist trade, the dining room was doubled in size, the bedrooms and sitting rooms were 'furnished with every consideration for comfort, convenience and sanitation' and electric lighting was installed throughout. As soon as the work was finished, almost all the rooms were occupied or booked. It was, as the *Chronicle* pointed out, 'another proof of the popularity of Bath and its establishments of repute'.

The essential ingredient of the Bath tourist trade was still the spa, but the cultural life of the city was also important. The concerts in the Pump Room and the Assembly Rooms were almost always of high quality, often featuring well-known musicians and vocalists. The Pump Room Festival of 10-15 February, for example, included Moisewitch, Albert Sammons, Myra Hess, and the Philharmonic String Quartet. Edward Elgar was also due to conduct some of his works, but at the last moment was unable to attend through illness. In May, the leader of the Philharmonic Quartet, a young musician called Frederick Holding, was appointed leader of the Pump Room Orchestra.

The 1919 summer season was, according to the Director of Music, GB Robinson, 'quite phenomenal'. His ambition was to make Bath a major centre of music, but he risked being thwarted by the council's determination to keep a tight grip on the city's finances. In August, when the programme for the forthcoming winter events had been drawn up, relations between the council and the orchestra reached crisis point. The members of the Municipal and Pump Room Orchestras, as well as the director, demanded increases in salary. The Musicians' Union, negotiating on behalf of the orchestra, demanded not only pay rises of about 25-30 per cent for individual members of the orchestra, but also an end to the contractor system whereby they were recruited by the Director of Music, and a return to the former system under which they were paid directly by the corporation. To sugar the pill, the orchestra was ready to work 24 rather than 16 hours a week.

On 27 August, John Brand, oboist with the orchestra, wrote to the *Chronicle* explaining why the pay rises were necessary. He had been a member of the orchestra before the war on a salary of £3 a week, but was able to supplement this by accepting private work. After serving in the army, he resumed his former position, but with a salary increase of just 7/6 a week, which did not cover the steep rise in the cost of living since 1914. He declared that

> this policy of 'accept a starvation wage or clear out' will not do, sir! And it is not the right treatment to extend towards a body of serious men, engaged in a serious art, who have long been faithful servants, and many of whom have taken an active part in saving England, and those left behind from the hands of a savage foe. All we are asking is a little justice and a glimpse of the 'land fit for heroes to live in' about which we hear so much, and of which we see so little.[48]

The council faced with the prospect of a musicians strike when the winter programme had been nearly finalised had little option but on 16 September to accept the union's demands in full.

It was not just classical music that was popular in Bath. Jazz was regularly played at *thés dansents* in the Pump Room and the Spa Hotel. The music scene in Bath was also enriched by the Ragtime Banjo Band run by the Tarrant-Baileys, a husband and wife team. Richard Tarrant-Bailey, besides being a banjo player and teacher, was also the highly efficient if somewhat obsequious sub-agent on the Earl and Countess Temple's estate at Newton St Loe. He was credited as the man who introduced the banjo not only to Bath but also to the South West.[49] Over Christmas 1918, at their home at 2 Park Street the Tarrant-Baileys assembled a group of friends and expert banjo players, and formed a 'Syncopated Quintette', which, as Richard was later to tell a friend, 'is quite the goods and the dancing set here seem to love it'. His band played at dinners, private parties and fetes, and, when they played a song called *Peaches* at the Spa Hotel, it was so popular that no less than four encores were called for, and even after that 'the crowd of mad human beings [were] howling for more'.[50]

The theatre, too, was important for the cultural reputation of Bath. The city had a large number of leisured and well-educated citizens who were potential theatre goers. Under the management of Mrs Valentine Munro, the Theatre Royal had, according to SR Littlewood, been transformed 'from something very much like the old Tottenham Court Road dust hole into the cleanest, brightest, little gem of an old fashioned playhouse'. It was now a considerable commercial success, but, its repertoire was unadventurous, with very few classics or new productions. Again, this was not surprising as Munro had gained a reputation as a producer of light and comic operas. Her successor as manager was Shelford Walsh from the King's Theatre, Gainsborough, who launched his first season in August with the popular drama *Romance* by the American playwright Edward Sheldon, which played to a full house.

Not everybody felt that Bath's claims to be the 'Athens of the South West' should rely solely on its high culture. At a meeting in the Guildhall to discuss the revival of the Bath Horse Show at the end of February, Lt Powell, a member of the Horse Show Committee, argued that 'we certainly need more diversions than music in the Pump Room and Park', and suggested polo, hunting and steeplechase meetings. In May, there were suggestions that a Temple of Agriculture should be erected in the city, where the Bath and West Society could display its 'good work over the past 140 years' and educate the public in the problems, achievement and needs of British farming.

Bath was also an industrial city, which needed to face the future and attract new industries. What was arguably Bath's principal industrial undertaking, Stothert and Pitt, was booming and exporting all round the world. In August, a commercial delegation from Brazil paid it a visit and were given a guided tour of both the Newark and Victoria Works where they saw cranes being made not only for the home and imperial markets but also for Portugal, France, Chile and China. Other factories were also taking advantage of the post-war boom. At Locksbrook Rubber Mill, Messrs Fussell & Co installed a modern plant for producing vulcanised rubber. The Corsham Bath Stone Company had also made significant progress in standardising the production of Bath stone, so that it could more easily be used in the construction of mass housing. There was talk, too, of turning Bath into a centre for the film industry. In response to tentative approaches from the Ministry of Labour in May, the Chamber of Commerce enthusiastically stressed Bath's advantages, 'there being good light, lack of impediment in the air and the city being full of architectural and historical features, while the scenery is unequalled'. It is an interesting thought that Bath might have become the British Hollywood.

There was too a growing awareness of the coming importance of air travel. Just after Christmas 1918, an RAF officer flew from Andover to Bath – 140 miles in just 40 minutes – to visit friends, but had to return as he could find nowhere to land. When the *Chronicle* heard of the story, it stressed how important it was 'to open the eyes of progressive folk to the fact that before long Bath and other places among the eternal hills will need to face the problem of providing landing and starting stages for the purpose of aerial travel'. Yet, for much of Bath, this perspective was more science fiction than reality, as horse-drawn vehicles were still very much the order of the day. In January, for instance the Bath Cooperative Society was concerned with the fate of the 'horse Bob', who had fallen lame and with the breaking in of a new colt from Marshfield. [51]

CHRISTMAS 1919

BY DECEMBER, TRACES of the war still lingered. Although the Red Cross Hospitals at Bathampton, Rock House and Marlborough Buildings had closed, the Bath War Hospital, which was now under the control of the Pensions Ministry, remained open to care for the long-term wounded. Some food and price controls were still in place: in August controls over the distribution of dried fruits had been reintroduced and new ration books were issued as late as September. Some young soldiers were still serving with the colours, but the majority of men had been demobilised, and both the German POWs and the Belgian refugees had gone home. However, the psychological and social damage of the war remained, and cases of venereal disease, bigamy, marital breakdown and mental illness were reported daily in the newspapers. In just one week in the summer of 1919, three Bath bigamists were brought before the courts. As the historian Andrew Swift has pointed out, during the war, 'with large numbers of men continually on the move, and the prospect of sudden, violent death an everyday reality, it is hardly surprising that the consequences of bigamy often paled into insignificance beside the prospect of immediate sexual gratification'. [52] In late November, a sharp reminder of the human cost of the war was the discovery of an unemployed ex-soldier, William Parry, sleeping rough under Newton Bridge. Parry, who had been there since 18 October, was suffering from pneumonia and mental depression and later died in the Royal United Hospital (RUH).

The damp, rainy Christmas of 1919 was inevitably a more relaxed occasion than the previous Christmas, but, as the Bellman observed, 'full many a grief [was] still fresh'. Despite food restrictions, Magnolia Grace, the *Chronicle's* cookery expert, confidently assured her readers that 'there is enough to go round and no one need go without Christmas fare, who has any money at all'. Given the poverty and unemployment in Bath, this was a considerable qualification.

In the weeks before Christmas, however, Bath assumed a festive appearance. The Pump Room laid on ten days of music and parties, *Jack and Jill* was the pantomime at the Theatre Royal, while the Palace Theatre had a special holiday programme of clowns, jugglers and acrobats. Evans and Owen and Colmer in Union Street opened toy bazaars, while Carter, Stoffell & Fortt offered Christmas hampers 'with carriage free to your station'. Despite its social problems and the aftermath of war, Bath for many was a pleasing 'bubble' to live in. The contrast with the situation in Russia and central Europe could not have been more striking. Mindful of this, the collection at St John's Roman Catholic Church on Holy Innocents' day was 'for the poor of Central Europe'.

2
BATH AND THE TURBULENT AFTERMATH OF WAR, 1920-24

In Bath, as elsewhere, memories of war were still fresh. Dedications of war memorials in the outlying villages and suburbs, and the annual Remembrance Day inevitably stirred painful memories and emotions. At Twerton on Armistice Sunday 1924, the *Chronicle* reported that the Cross of Remembrance 'gleamed like a tall spectre in the waning light' and the green slopes of the churchyard reminded some who attended 'of the Hill of Calvary'.

Out of sight but not out completely out of mind, the Bath Pension Hospital, which in August 1920 had 427 patients, had become the centre for the specialist treatment of wounded servicemen who could not be nursed in ordinary hospitals. In 1920 a second operating theatre was opened as well as a new physiotherapy department and plans were drawn up for the production of artificial limbs. From time to time, brief reports appeared in the *Chronicle* announcing the death of patients. In August 1922, for instance, Captain Henry James Allin, a long term victim of poison gas, died in the hospital, leaving a widow and five children. Concerts and other treats were frequently organised for the patients and once a year the Bath and West of England Motor Club would arrange an outing. On a fine but rather chilly Thursday in late September 1923, the club took over 300 patients in a convoy of 70 cars, ranging from a Daimler to a humble sidecar-combination, for a tour of the countryside ending up at Corsham Court where 'well provisioned tea tables' were laid out in one of the buildings on Lord Methuen's estate. The convoy aroused considerable interest as it drove through Trowbridge and the surrounding villages not only because of the eclectic collection of cars, but also because spectators glimpsed the once familiar blue uniform which wounded servicemen used to wear in public.

At least the fate of these 'broken men', as they were often called, was known to their nearest and dearest. As late as the autumn of 1920, a War Office Mission was still active in France and Belgium attempting to ascertain the fate of British soldiers reported missing. The hope that many of their relatives still held on to was that their loved one had lost his memory and possibly become a tramp in France or Germany. It was not until October 1920 that Mrs Stafford of 5 Park View, Lower Bristol Road, was finally informed by the War Office that no trace could be found of her husband, a former employee of Stothert and Pitt's, who had been posted as missing in April 1918 in the Merville area of Northern France. She was told:

> You can be quite certain that your husband is not suffering from loss of memory. A thorough search for any man who did not know who they were has been conducted throughout Germany and the occupied districts of France and Belgium, but none such have been discovered. [1]

NOISES OFF

THE IMPACT OF THE EUROPEAN CRISIS ON BATH

THE TURBULENCE IN Germany and Russia remained for the most part ominous noises off stage. Local concerns, such as the cost of living, the housing shortage, the weather, the Pump Room Orchestra and even such a trivial matter as the exact date of the first cuckoo were usually uppermost in people's thoughts. Nevertheless, from time to time international events intruded on residents' consciousness and made a significant impact on opinion and politics in Bath. The Bolshevik Revolution in Russia continued to act as both an inspiration and a blueprint for a better society to many of those on the left, while being seen by many of the middle and upper classes as an existential threat. When Albert Purcell, the prospective Bath Labour Candidate, spoke to a large meeting at the Guildhall in August 1920 of his impressions of Bolshevik Russia after an 18-day visit, he painted an engaging if wildly optimistic picture of a new classless society emerging where doctors, nurses and cleaners were all in the same union, and where workers had a month's holiday in the former mansions of grand dukes. A very different message was presented in the same month by the sitting member for Bath, the diehard Tory, Charles Foxcroft, who described Bolshevism as 'an international conspiracy' which was 'designed to destroy the world's existing industrial, political and religious systems'.

While the Russian revolution inspired either enthusiasm or revulsion, feelings towards Germany were more nuanced. Germany was from time to time referred to in an aside as 'the disgraced country', as in a lecture on satire to the Bath Poetry Society in May 1920, and MPs were criticised in the *Chronicle* for drinking German wines. Yet people with this attitude towards Germany were increasingly seen as 'never enders' by those who had served in the British

Rhineland Army or lived and worked in post- war Germany. The voice of moderation was heard clearly when Lord Methuen opened the headquarters of the Bath Comrades of the Great War in George Street in early January 1920. He told his audience that Germany deserved 'anything she got for the manner in which she treated civilians and everybody else during the war, but they had to recollect that, if their own exports and imports were to work out, they must put Germany in the position in which she could also put her hand to the wheel and see that every country worked together for the common good'.

In March 1920, the arguments of the 'Never Enders' were momentarily strengthened by news of a putsch in Germany. The east Prussian politician, Wolfgang Kapp, backed by elements of the German army, occupied Berlin, and the legitimate government fled to Stuttgart. Briefly a restoration of militarism and the monarchy seemed a real possibility. Max Aberstone, the managing director of Stones, the opticians in the Corridor, who had relatives in Poland, skillfully blended political comment with promoting his shop's optical skills when he placed an advertisement in the *Chronicle* on 20 March. He voiced the worry shared by many that 'treaty obligations would be scattered to the winds' at a time when 'troubles everywhere' were distracting the allied governments, and concluded that there is nothing 'so valuable or so indispensable as a clear vision'. The putsch was, however, rapidly defeated by a general strike, and warrants were issued for the arrest of the generals involved.

Both the German and Russian problems converged dramatically in July 1920. The Russian Red Army had driven the Poles out of Ukraine and was poised to take Warsaw and advance to the German frontier. If this occurred, it was feared that the Germans might well make common cause with the Soviets, and the whole post-war structure created by the Treaty of Versailles would collapse. France was already aiding the Poles, and it now seemed as if Lloyd George was also about to commit Britain to what was essentially a war against Russia, which the Labour Party and trade unions were determined to stop at all costs. Labour's policy was fully supported by both the local Labour Party and the BTLC. Councils of Action sprang up throughout the country, including Bath, and on 10 August the government was threatened with a general strike if it supplied the Poles with weapons. This was unanimously endorsed by the BTLC, which also accepted an invitation from the Labour Party to send representatives to a special conference to be held at Central Hall, Westminster. One member, Sam Day, observed that for 'too long had governments considered that they had the right to call the working man to war whenever they liked'. In its annual report for 1920, the BTLC described the formation of the Councils of Action as 'one of the most momentous happenings in the history of the Labour Movement', as they forced Lloyd George, in an abrupt U-turn, to advise the Poles to negotiate a peace settlement with the Russians.² This became practical politics once the Polish army had defeated the Russians in the Battle of Warsaw on 16 August. However, to some in Bath these councils seemed uncomfortably reminiscent of the Russian soviets. The constitutional argument against them was put trenchantly by the Dominican Prior of Hawkesyard Priory in a sermon at St John's Roman Catholic Church in October:

> It was necessary to look facts in the face. A couple of months ago, when it was thought that Poland was about to be swamped by Russia a body of men went to the constitutionally appointed government and said: 'unless you promise not to lift a finger in aid of Poland we shall strike. They were all horror struck, but how many people realised what it meant? It meant that a body of men not trained to govern and knowing nothing of the difficulties appeared to say, 'We prefer our own will to those of the British constitution, and if you don't go as we want you to go, then all is over with government and constitution.³

The Prior had made a telling point, but this line of argument was rejected at a meeting at the Guildhall at the end of August by RH (Bob) Hope, a prominent member of the Bath Labour Party, who reminded his listeners that parliament itself was brought into being 'during the time of King John and that there had been many unconstitutional acts in this country's history with good effect'.

To some in Bath the League of Nations offered an opportunity to create a new and peaceful world. The local branch of the League of Nations Union (LNU) was established in February 1920 and opened by Crawford Vaughan, the former President of New South Wales, who ominously warned that, if another war came, 'the last one would be child's play'. The LNU was supported by both the Co-operative Movement and the BTLC as well as by a broad cross section of local Bath worthies embracing all three political parties and the churches. Yet it soon became clear that the League, as it stood, was no magical panacea for world peace. From the early Spring of 1921 through to the summer of 1924 Europe was in a state of paralysis. On 7 March 1921, when British and French troops occupied the Ruhr ports of Düsseldorf, Duisburg and Ruhrort to bring pressure to bear on Germany to pay reparations, military reservists in Bath were instructed 'to hold themselves ready' in case they were called up for a march into Germany', although this did not become necessary. With this incident in mind, the Rev FW Norwood from the Temple Church in London, in a talk in the Guildhall on 9 March observed:

> For one thing, the political situation was exceedingly grave; in his judgement it was graver now than before the war began. With what happened on Tuesday in the marching of forces of the Allies into Germany, there was driven a nail into the coffin of their best hopes. That after two years we should come to this was, however one looked at it, a very disappointing thing. And whatever its results, it was going to mean disorder and tension and chaos for years to come
>
> ... We must recognise that the ideal of the League of Nations had been smitten in the face. [4]

The crisis in Europe intensified when French and Belgian troops occupied the Ruhr itself in January 1923 to compel Germany to pay reparations. The German government retaliated with a campaign of passive resistance, the financing of which led to hyperinflation and the impoverishment of the middle classes. Britain adopted a line of 'benevolent neutrality' and refused to contribute any troops to the occupation. The reaction to the crisis in Bath was muted. The Labour and Liberal Parties opposed the occupation, and Conservative voters were puzzled by their government's lack of support for France.

The reports reaching Bath about the economic and humanitarian situation in Germany caused by inflation and defeat were mixed. In July 1922 Lady Pierse, the wife of Admiral Sir Richard Pierse of Bathwick Hill observed after a visit to Germany and Austria that, when she returned to London and Bath, she saw 'more shabbily dressed men and poverty stricken and starving little children' than she had seen anywhere on her travels. In July 1923, at the height of the Ruhr Crisis, Prebendary Horten-Starkie, the Vicar of Wellow, went to Germany to take the waters at Bad Homburg and then to visit his son, who was adjutant of 2nd Bn of the King's Royal Rifles in the Cologne Zone. He noted that Hanover appeared to be a 'ghost town' and that its children appeared 'thin and underfed'. German agriculture on the other hand was markedly prosperous with well-tilled fields and a lot of building going on in the villages. While poverty, hunger and disease were realities in inflation-racked Germany, many in Britain, particularly unemployed ex-soldiers were sceptical about helping the Germans, believing that charity began at home. Just before Christmas a provocative letter appeared in the Chronicle from P Brewer, an ex-rifleman from Lansdown Road:

> Sir, As an unemployed man I ask the public why are German travellers allowed to do business in our cities? Only on Tuesday in Milsom Street, I saw and spoke to one whom I knew well. I worked in Germany seven years previous

to the war, in Berlin, in the same firm as the above mentioned gentleman. He said I could obtain employment at once if I returned. How's that? And paid in English sterling! He tells me hundreds of British soldiers married German girls in the last five years and all are doing well. I am writing to the firm in question. Nothing turns up in our own country. I think it is about time we threw in out lot with the late enemy. In any case I shall, rather than do nothing for another twelve months. I get all travelling expenses refunded, so its worth the while, and I shall take my hat off to Germany.[5]

The bitterness expressed in this letter about the lack of employment explains the events which took place on the evening of 13 February 1924. Carl Heath, the General Secretary of the International Service of the Society of Friends (Quakers), arrived in Bath to address a meeting in the Guildhall 'in aid of the starving children of Germany'. He was, according to the *Chronicle*, given a boisterous and rowdy reception that threatened to erupt into violence. Before the meeting began, there was a demonstration by ex-soldiers addressed by the former commandant of the Bath Comrades of the Great War, the well known eye surgeon, staunch Conservative and supporter of the Bath Harlequins, Alexander Beck Cluckie, who had himself been a POW. At one stage the temper of this demonstration threatened to get out of hand, but the two police constables on duty managed to persuade the crowd to disperse, although not before several people who were trying to get into the Guildhall to attend the lecture were 'rather severely crushed against the doors'. Inside the Guildhall the combined efforts of Gordon Dudley of the Bath Branch of the British Legion, Father Kendal, the Benedictine Friar, and the writer and former mayoress Sarah Grand, to secure a hearing for Carl Heath, were all howled down. Sarah Grand opened the meeting amidst a chorus of booing and cries of 'this meeting is an insult to us' and was unable to make herself heard. Gordon Dudley appealed, as an ex-service man to other ex-servicemen in the audience, to give her a 'fair hearing'. Eventually she was able to explain why she was chairing this meeting: she had come, she said, 'because she was moved by compassion to come, compassion for little innocent children [in Germany] that she heard were starving'. A voice called out that there were plenty of those in Bath, to which she replied, 'the more shame to Bath'. She added that her own feeling was that if the parents of a child had done her the greatest injury and she knew their child was starving, she would feel bound to do all she could to rescue that child. 'That was practical Christianity.' This was greeted with applause, but also by more signs of disturbance, as someone shouted, 'What did the Germans do to the Belgians? Cut them to pieces.'

Carl Heath stood up to speak and was met with a chorus of boos and cries of 'sit down'. When he was briefly able to make himself heard above the din, he declared that, 'British troops on the Rhine and in Cologne shared their rations with the suffering children there.' This was greeted with a few cheers, quickly drowned out by boos as prolonged uproar broke out, as people stood on their seats to look at the back of the hall where what looked like a collection box had been knocked out of the hand of one of the stewards and was being trampled on by the crowd.[6]

All attempts to secure a fair hearing for Heath failed and Sarah Grand brought the meeting to an end at about 8.45. Given the hostile crowd outside, Heath and the others on the platform left the Guildhall down the stairway from the police court to the police station before proceeding home in small groups. The crowd hung round outside the Guildhall for another thirty minutes and then after singing Auld Lang Syne and the National Anthem, dispersed, and by 930pm the High Street had almost returned to normal.

The Bellman attributed the blame for the fracas to the Quakers, whom he accused of thoughtlessly provoking the audience of ex-servicemen and widows by showing 'a lamentable instance of greater concern for Germans than Englishmen'. The Bath Branch of the British Legion was sent a gift of £10 from an anonymous donor to alleviate distress amongst local ex-servicemen, while another letter from a 'London correspondent' enclosed a cheque for £2 in protest against the meeting, specifically asking the Legion to convey his 'congratulations to the ex-servicemen of Bath'. On his return to London, Carl Heath wrote a restrained and dignified letter to the *Chronicle* explaining the work of the Quakers amongst the starving in Europe and reminding its readers that it had the backing of the leaders of the three main political parties in Britain. Despite his experiences in Bath, he still felt that there was 'a generous, intelligent and Christian community' in the city.

In the summer of 1924, Germany's finances were at last stabilised with the help of an American loan, and, for the time being at least, reparation payments were regulated on a more manageable basis by the Dawes Plan. Many agreed with the prime minister, Ramsey MacDonald, that the acceptance of the plan was a sign that 'we have turned our backs on the terrible years of war and war mentality'. The following year the Locarno Treaties promised a new era of Franco-German harmony and were greeted throughout western Europe and the US with enormous enthusiasm and optimism. It seemed that real peace had at last come. To mark the day of their signature, on 11 December, 1925 the Bath Free Church Council and the League of Nations Union arranged a meeting of thanksgiving and prayer at the Argyle Church.

Bath and empire

The British Empire, which covered a quarter of the world's surface, formed the backdrop to life in Bath. There were frequent talks in the churches, the YMCA and the schools on aspects of the Empire. The war both consolidated and paradoxically weakened the Empire. It accelerated the emergence of the Dominions of Australia, Canada, New Zealand and South Africa as independent nations and allies, and also brought the intricate question of Indian independence onto the agenda. On the other hand in the inter-war period, the hold of the empire on the popular imagination intensified. In 1917, after honours for service to the empire, such as the CBE, OBE and MBE were created, many Bathonians were awarded them, as the local newspapers recorded. In 1916, 24 May was officially declared Empire Day, when children throughout the empire saluted the flag and sang patriotic songs before enjoying a half holiday.

It was Australia, Canada, and India which attracted the most attention in Bath. Sub-Saharan Africa in the perception of most Bathonians remained a 'dark' and unknown continent, with its mysterious beauty and the apparently strange customs of its inhabitants from time to time the subject of lectures by missionaries or colonial bishops. Almost every week, advertisements would appear in the *Chronicle* appealing for British immigrants to Canada or Australia. In December 1924 the Chronicle received a letter from a Bathonian who had emigrated to Australia to work on a sheep farm. He was an avid reader of the Bath papers and inevitably suffered much joshing from his Australian work mates, who asked, 'Where is this place called Bath? Nothing but damn Bath papers everywhere!'. However, as he pointed out,

> Bath ... is not a complete stranger to this outlandish place, as in the railway siding there is one of Messrs Stothert and Pitt's cranes. The assistant storekeeper [on the sheep station] was in Messrs Cater, Stoffell and Fortt's business in the High Street a good many years ago.'[7]

Recently he had been joined by several other young men from England. His advice to would-be emigrants was that only on the land could reasonably well-paid jobs be found. In Sydney, unemployment was almost as bad as in England. Unemployed young women were also encouraged to find work in Australia by the Society for Overseas Settlement of British Women, but the BTLC in June 1923 refused outright to give the scheme its support on the grounds that there had been several scandals concerning the ill treatment of women and children. One member tellingly accused the government of betraying its promises to create a land fit for heroes by trying to force unemployed men overseas and 'now with so many unemployed women on the books, they were trying to do the same with them'.

The exotic atmosphere of India was frequently evoked in lectures and bazaars. Yet in 1919 the very future of the Raj seemed to be in question. This was of great concern to the many old 'India hands' in Bath, who had served in the Indian civil service, the Indian army, or run businesses and tea plantations. The British were confronted with a growing Indian nationalism, which had been inflamed by the Amritsar massacre on 13 April 1919. General Dyer, the officer responsible, was controversially relieved of his command in 1920. In the subsequent debate in the House of Commons the government successfully defended this decision against many of its Conservative supporters, including Charles Foxcroft. When the Lords debated the motion in July, Foxcroft watched the proceedings from the visitors' gallery, and was delighted to see the government decisively defeated. He sent the *Chronicle* a triumphant and romanticised account of the proceedings, the gist of which was that 'the Lords in this instance reflected the opinions of the people'. Given the number of Bathonians who had links with India, it is not surprising that many saw Dyer as the man who had saved the Indian empire rather than the brutal practitioner of 'frightfulness' on – or even beyond – a Prussian scale. There were consequently many subscribers from Bath to the fund which the *Morning Post* opened for Dyer. Foxcroft himself contributed five guineas.

The nature of British rule in India was changing. In 1919 a new constitution was drawn up which provided for limited participation by Indians in the government of their own country. India was now on the road to self-government – too quickly for many Anglo-Indians but not quickly enough for many Indians. In Bath, not surprisingly, opinion was divided about these changes. Opposed to any change were the diehards such as Major Woolley, formerly of the Indian Army and now a pig farmer in Swainswick, who told his fellow Rotarians in May 1923 that the Indian Army would become 'a rabble' without British officers to hold it together. On the other hand, there were more enlightened voices who supported the constitution, ranging from the BTLC to the Britain and the India League, which held its first meeting in October 1920 at 99 Sydney Place. The meeting was chaired by Lady Woodroffe, whose husband Sir John, a former Chief Justice in India, was an expert in Sanskrit and Indian philosophy. His biographer, Kathleen Taylor, observed that he had 'an Indian soul in a European body'. Christian missionaries viewed the constitutional changes in India with mixed feelings.

The chairman of the Missionary Association of St Mary's, Bathwick, observed in December 1922 that while 'giving more and more self government ... might mean a great deal for many people in India, it also meant a very hard thing for a very large class known as the pariah class' who were afforded protection in the Christian missions. Charles Foxcroft was convinced that it was the 'Prayer of the Untouchable' that the British should remain in India.[8]

The acquisition of Mesopotamia – or Iraq as it became in 1921 – and Palestine as League of Nations' Mandates in 1919 overextended British power at a time when it faced challenges in India, Egypt and Ireland. In May 1920, a rebellion broke out against British rule at Tel Afar, near Mosul, which took four months to defeat. The situation was followed with particular interest by many in Bath, who had served in Mesopotamia with the SLI. A few had even decided to remain with the army of occupation there. One former soldier with the SLI, Charles Hepher, who had married 'a local Christian lady', stayed on when he was demobilised in July 1920, and worked as a civilian in the army's wireless and telegraphy department in Baghdad, sadly only to die there from dysentery in January 1921. His parents, of 10 Lark Place, Upper Bristol Rd had not seen him since 1914 when he left Prior Park for the Andaman Islands. Three times in 1919 he was about to be demobilised but each time he was sent back to Baghdad because of a shortage of men in the wireless service. Another Bathonian, Sergeant CF Butcher, who before the war had worked in Cater, Stoffell and Fortt's, was demobilised, but, after looking in vain for employment in Bath, decided to re-enlist in 1920 and was posted back to Mesopotamia where he worked as a clerk at the army's headquarters in Baghdad. In August 1921 his father, a retired policeman living at 21 Hampton View, Fairfield Park, received a cable from the Army Records Office in Woolwich informing him that his son had died of pneumonia, but on 13 September there came what any family in a similar position would have secretly longed for – a telegram from Woolwich 'cancelling the report of his death'. Another telegram a few days later explained what had happened:

> The error was caused through incorrect telegrams being received in this office from the authorities in Basra and Baghdad reporting your son's death instead of that of another soldier named Butcher serving in the same area as your son. The sorrow and inconvenience that have been caused through the wrong report are much regretted, and it will be taken up very seriously for those concerned.[9]

The Balfour Declaration of 1917 committed Britain to providing the Jews with 'a national home' in Palestine, which was incompatible with the wishes and aspirations of the Arabs. These contradictions were hinted at from time to time by speakers in Bath. At a garden party in July 1922 organised by the British Society for the Propagation of the Gospel amongst the Jews at Ivy Bank, Entry Hill, Dr A Gold- Levin, a Christian convert, observed that 'if there were no wire-pullers the Jews and Arabs would settle down very soon', but his solution to the problems created by Zionism was to convert the Jews to Christianity. The MP for Bath, Charles Foxcroft, did not share Gold-Levin's optimism. When the House of Commons was asked to approve the maintenance of the Balfour Declaration as the basis for British policy in Palestine on 4 July 1922, 35 MPs – mainly Conservatives – voted against it, including Foxcroft. Partly as a demonstration against the government and partly to reassure the Arabs that they had friends in London, he helped organise a reception on 27 July in the Hyde Park Hotel to give a send-off to the Arab delegation, which had arrived in London a year earlier with the intention of persuading the British government to modify its support for Zionism. It was, as Foxcroft observed, an attempt 'to restore the trust and friendliness of the Arabs – a most important factor for our future work in the East'. A year later Foxcroft joined a group of colleagues to sign a petition to the chairman of the Cabinet Committee on Palestine, drawing his attention to 'the definite PLEDGES given to the Palestine Arabs'. [10]

In the early 1920s, Bath, apart from the existence of a few Chinese laundries, was very far from a modern multi-racial city. The occasional Indian academic or Maharajah did pass through the city, however. On 1 July 1921, for instance, the Indian delegate to the Empire Conference, the Maharao of Kutch, together with the prime ministers of Australia and New Zealand, were given the freedom of the city. Very occasionally an African or West Indian seaman from Bristol or Cardiff might be seen in the streets. In August 1923, when the West Indies cricket team, composed of 'six men of colour and five whites' toured England and played Somerset at Weston-super- Mare, the *Chronicle* was particularly impressed by the skills and smiles of Learie Constantine, who later became the High Commissioner for Trinidad and was made a life peer.

The empire was celebrated by a monumental exhibition at Wembley in the summer of 1924, which it was hoped would boost trade and stimulate public interest in the imperial idea. The King's opening speech was broadcast on radio on St George's Day. In Bath, many firms, clubs, businesses and cafes installed wireless sets so that the opening ceremony could be heard. Amongst them were the headquarters of the British Legion in Queen Square, the YMCA in Broad Street and the City Café in Stall Street. In Bathampton, Owen Harbutt closed his plasticine works at 11 o'clock for 90 minutes, and the employees and a large number of local residents assembled in the yard to hear the opening ceremony from Wembley. Bath had its own pavilion there. where it advertised itself as 'the premier spa of the Empire'. Over the summer many Bathonians and their families visited Wembley, most of them travelling to Paddington on special excursion trains provided by the GWR. Private parties could also book a tour through Bell's Travel Office with Major T Grenfell, who would later have the distinction of being one of Bath's few communists. On Friday 11 July, more than 1,200 children from the city's elementary schools went by train to the exhibition. For many of them, their first novel experience of the day was the sight of tube trains in suburban London. When they reached Wembley station they were marshaled by their teachers and parents into a crocodile and walked to the exhibition, where they spent seven action-packed hours looking at the numerous pavilions including the Bath exhibit. The most popular, according to a *Chronicle* reporter was the Palace of Engineering with its huge locomotive and, of course, the Amusement Park where the great attraction was the Safety Racer.

The first page of the booklet advertising Bath at the Empire Exhibition at Wembley, 1924 (Akeman Press)

IRELAND

THE GREATEST CHALLENGE to the image of an invincible empire arose in what Bernard Shaw called 'John Bull's other island' – Ireland. Until the cease fire between the rebels and the British government in July 1921, events in Ireland provided a sombre backdrop to politics on the mainland. In the election of December 1918, Sinn Fein, the Irish Nationalist Party, achieved a large majority and proceeded to set up an independent parliament in Dublin. In early 1919, it initiated a campaign of assassinations against its enemies, in response to which the British government declared martial law. Over the next eighteen months the conflict escalated, and it was not until July 1921 that a ceasefire was negotiated. In December, a treaty was signed which gave Eire, or Southern Ireland, dominion status within the British Empire, while Ulster remained an integral part of the British state.

The horrors that erupted in Ireland during the Trouble of 1919-22 could not be ignored in Bath. As early as January 1919, the local branch of the Comrades of the Great War was worried about the treatment of Irish ex-servicemen in the west and south of the island 'where people are hostile to discharged men'. At the annual meeting of the Anglican Irish Church Mission in May 1921, JA Kensit, the fanatical anti-Catholic, informed a meeting in the Assembly Rooms that it was the Church of Rome which had sown 'dragons' teeth' in Ireland. The turmoil in Ireland was seen by some to be providing a dangerous precedent for unruly behaviour in Bath itself. After fights broke out at a race meeting at Lansdown in August 1921, Alderman Jackman was convinced that these miniature riots were

> a sign of the times, and to be considered in association with the present spirit of the government's negotiations with Ireland [where] the principle of concession to armed resistance has been conceded with the result of the general undermining of that power behind the throne which is the real source of law and order. [11]

A Bathonian who had volunteered to join the Auxiliary Division of the Royal Irish Constabulary found when he came home on leave in January 1921 that there was a 'complete lack of knowledge of the work and hardships of the crown forces in Ireland ... but plenty of inaccurate knowledge of the so called reprisals'. Presumably by that he meant incidents such as the setting fire to Cork's commercial centre in retaliation for an IRA ambush, which had killed one auxiliary and wounded ten others. To remedy this ignorance he sent the *Chronicle* a description of what life was like fighting the IRA:

> Life in the Auxiliary Division RIC resembles the late war in one respect, in all the others it certainly does not. The resemblance lies in the fact that you are more or less on active service conditions and have an enemy to fight; but in all other respects the difference is great. Here in the Emerald Isle your 'friends the enemy' are all round you. You never know when you go out on a trip to raid a certain place if you are going to be bombed at, shot at, 'held up' or simply allowed to go and return. [12]

Not surprisingly members of the crown forces were only too glad to come home on leave and to escape the 'Shinnies'(Sinn Feiners) for a time. In January, four young soldiers from the Royal Field Artillery, who were on the 5 o'clock Fishguard Boat Express jumped out of the train when it stopped at Bath, crossed the line to the up platform and tried to hide in the lavatory, but were spotted by the ticket inspector, who called the police. After appearing before the magistrates, they were handed over to the military police.

To the Quakers and many in the Labour Party in Bath, the British army in Ireland was 'an army of occupation'. Herbert Elvin, who had succeeded Purcell as Bath's parliamentary Labour candidate, was applauded when he remarked, in a speech at the Guildhall in June 1921, that if 'only the Irish in the North and the Irish in the South were able to get together without let or hindrance and work out their own solution, their redemption would come'. Arguably the most authoritative assessment of the Irish crisis was given by the well known London Quaker, John Barlow, at the Friends' Meeting House in April 1921. A year earlier he had led a mission to Ireland to study the problem at first hand, the results of which were published in the *Times* and presented to the American Commission assessing conditions in Ireland. He conceded that both sides had done 'terrible things' but pointed out that 'to the foreigner England appeared to be the big bully'. His solution was one of faith rather than detail; if Britain renounced violence and admitted its mistakes in Ireland, he thought that the Irish – 'a generous hearted people' – would quickly respond. When questions were invited from the floor, one member of the audience suggested organising a tax strike until the army was removed from Ireland.

Such opinions were an anathema to Charles Foxcroft and the diehard wing of the Conservative party. In the words of the Labour councillor, Walter Barrett, Foxcroft wanted 'to carry the sword further in Ireland than it had been carried by the Black and Tans'. Foxcroft was a consistent critic of the government's Irish policy, believing that the maximum of force was needed to crush the IRA, which he called the Irish Red Army, and he frequently drew comparisons between Michael Collins, its leader, and Trotsky, the Soviet leader in charge of the Red Army in the USSR. When at last a settlement of sorts was negotiated between the British government and Sinn Fein in December 1921, Foxcroft, along with a minority of fellow Conservatives and Ulster Unionists MPs, voted against it. He justified his stance in no uncertain words, pointing out that, 'we find the man in power is the man with the gun'.

Foxcroft did not abandon the Irish Loyalists who were left stranded in the South, often facing attacks on their property and persons. On the death of the Anglo-Irish peer Lord Bessborough in 1921 he became acting chairman for the Assistance of Distressed and Persecuted Loyalists in Southern Ireland and worked tirelessly to raise funds for them. In March 1922, he organized a concert and produced his own play, *Lady Diana's Bracelet* in the Aeolian Hall in London's Bond Street, in which he himself played the leading part. On 1 November, a well-attended meeting took place at 30 Royal Crescent to raise further funds. Amongst those present were many from distinguished Anglo-Irish families, the venerable Frederic Harrison and several church dignitaries. In concluding the proceedings, Foxcroft stressed that the meeting was non-political in character and 'deplored the indications of an indifference among some people in England to the sufferings of the Irish loyalists, which could not be exaggerated'. There is no doubt that Foxcroft worked hard to help the Loyalists. On his death in 1929 two Anglo-Irish sisters who had moved to 27 The Paragon, in their letter of condolence to his sisters, wrote that 'he has been such a staunch, loyal, true friend to all of us distressed Irish Loyalists and has fought our cause in parliament', and mourned that such 'a useful and unselfish life has been brought to a close'.[13]

UNEMPLOYMENT AND INDUSTRIAL STRIFE

DESPITE THE SHORT-LIVED economic boom of 1919-20, the total number of unemployed in Bath was still high by pre-war standards, and the fact that many were ex- servicemen, some with severe physical handicaps, made the issue potentially incendiary. Although the local Labour Party and the BTLC were for the most part moderate in their policies and recommendations, from time to time a more militant note was sounded by groups of unemployed men from South Wales or Bristol on protests marches to London. On the evening of Wednesday 14 July 1920, a march from Bristol to London organised by the militant and fiercely anti-capitalist National Union of Ex-Servicemen stopped in Bath. Each marcher wore a red rosette in his jacket and its leader, Mr H Gilmore, was conspicuous by wearing a red shoulder sash. The marchers dragged with them a piano organ on which was written the slogan 'Returned warriors of 1914-18 on their march from Bristol to London to demand their rights – the right to work and live in the land they fought for'. Gilmore's address to a large crowd in Sawclose was essentially a call for direct action, and he was soon interrupted by a police constable, who warned him 'in a friendly way' to moderate his language. Incensed, Gilmore replied that he was fighting for employment' and told him that, 'you have got your job at £3 10sh a week'. This was greeted with applause, and another voice added 'and rent'. Ten minutes later, after Gilmore had called on the workers to create 'merry hell' and to smash 'the whole damned show', he was asked to close the meeting and accompany the police sergeant back to the station. According to the *Chronicle*:

> Some in the crowd jumped to the conclusion that Mr Gilmore had been placed under arrest, and for a minute or two the position was critical, there being an evident inclination on the part of a few of those present to 'rush' the police.
>
> One broad shouldered Bath man was observed thrusting his way through what had grown to a large crowd, to the rescue, but on it being understood that there was no arrest, the movement for releasing Mr Gilmore subsided.[14]

The police detained Gilmore for an hour, while they confirmed his identity. When he emerged from the police station, he was greeted with muted applause, and the marchers moved on to pitch camp on the the outskirts of the city before heading to Swindon.

Scene at the ex-servicemen's meeting in Sawclose on 14 July 1920
(Bath Chronicle, *17 July 1920)*

At the end of December 1920 the Bath Labour Exchange had over 1000 people on its books, and two months later this had increased to nearly 1,400. This was reflected in the number of school children being given free school dinners. At the St Michael's Place Centre numbers had risen from 80 in the summer to 110 by November, and plans were being made for restarting dinners at Walcot Hall in Guinea Lane for children on the eastern side of the city. Free dinners were also available at Odd Down and at St Michael's Special School in Broad Street. Pressure for effective work creation projects was increasing from the ex-servicemen's organisations, the unions, and the Labour Party. Local employers were also under intense pressure from both the government and the council to find places for disabled ex-servicemen. Following appeals from the

King, Field Marshall Lord Haig and other notables in the press in September 1920, the mayor wrote to all local employers urging them to recognise their obligations to disabled ex-servicemen, whom he suggested should constitute at least 5% of their total workforce. Thirty-three employers in Bath had already provided work for 296 disabled men. At the Bathford Paper Mills, for example, four out of its labour force of 68 were in receipt of disablement pensions.[15]

By 1920, with inflation running at 15.5%, middle-class pressure groups started to emerge as an increasing number of white-collar and unskilled workers organised themselves into trade unions. Demands for wage increases came from every quarter. At a well-attended meeting at the end of March in Citizen House, organised by the National Clerks Union, the consensus was that 'the average clerk is living from hand to mouth'. The popular weekly, *John Bull*, championing the cause of the council's rate collectors in Bath, who earned just £2 17s a week, pointed out that

> these men have to maintain a respectable appearance and are entrusted with large sums of public money; and it is discreditable to a city so celebrated as Bath that they should receive less for their responsible services than does a horny handed labourer for his toil.[16]

A similar message came from the Bath Branch of the National Union of Teachers in October 1920 when it passed a motion urging its executive to 'speed up' negotiations with the newly appointed Burnham Committee, since 'the continued increase in the cost of living has made the provincial minimum scale quite inadequate to meet the needs of teachers'.[17]

Bath, like the rest of the country, experienced a series of strikes and threats of strikes in 1920. Some were local like the sudden walkout of builders engaged on the construction of houses on Englishcombe Lane on 15 November, which was caused by one building firm sub-contracting labour. At one time it even looked as if the National Agricultural Labourers' Union would strike at harvest time over its demand for a weekly wage of £6. The brief miners' strike in October 1920, like the railway strike the previous year, had the potential to affect life in Bath drastically. In anticipation of its impact the council appointed an emergency committee under the former chairman of the Food Committee, Thomas Wills. Not only would coal deliveries be disrupted; so would the numerous commodities in the production of which coal was essential.

The United Alkali Co at Bristol, for example, informed Bathford Paper Mills that if the strike went ahead it would face a temporary closure and could make no 'definite promises as to deliveries' of soda ash, a key ingredient in the manufacture of paper.[18] The mere threat of the strike also disrupted the tourist trade, since, to quote the Marquis of Bath, 'certain timid souls ... proceeded to scuttle away like so many rabbits for fear of being caught in this city'. His landed neighbours, the Earl and Countess Temple, were advised by their sub-agent to curtail their holiday on the Isle of Skye and return home four days earlier than planned, as 'the strikers seem so very keen to make trouble ..., and the long journey needs every plausible comfort to make it tolerable'.[19] The government, however, played for time, and granted the miners a temporary six-month wage increase, which persuaded them to call off the strike.

The post-war boom ended abruptly in the winter of 1920-21 when the demand for British exports collapsed spectacularly. The *Economist* called 1921 'one of the worst years of depression since the industrial revolution'. The only positive consequence was that inflation also fell dramatically. The government responded by radically slashing public spending and abandoning its ambitious plans for post-war reconstruction. Employers reacted by sacking staff and cutting the wages of those that remained. Bath's flagship industry, Stothert and Pitt's, for instance, had to suspend many employees and put the remainder on short time due to a decline in orders.

Another Bath company facing severe economic problems was Hortsman Cars Ltd (the company had dropped the Germanic second 'n' from its name in 1922). In early 1921, Sidney Horstmann had expanded his factory to increase the output of the Horstman Light Car. He also had ambitious plans for cooperating with Douglas Hawkes, the motor car designer, to produce a single-seater racer, but had run out of money, and his business was on the verge of liquidation. It was temporarily saved by an injection of cash in March 1921 from Charles Lister, the managing director of RA Lister Co Ltd of Dursley, which produced diesel engines and agricultural machinery. Lister strongly advised him to look 'at once into labour efficiency' and to dispense 'with anyone not really efficient and paying'.[20] This advice seems to have had no effect, and in July Lister pointed out:

> the fact is that the car that bears your name has a very bad reputation ... It is heartbreaking to feel that what might have been a great success is in grave danger of failure through want of proper forethought or direction.[21]

In January 1922 the company closed down, but Horstmann was determined to raise further capital and reopen his factory. He advertised for investors in the *Financial Times*, the *Western Gazette* and the *Daily Telegraph*.[22]

In his private papers there is an interesting letter to an anonymous potential investor, dated 14 January 1922, which puts the situation at Horstman's into the context of the current economic crisis:

> You have no doubt heard that a young and promising industry for Bath, viz. the manufacture of the Horstman car has had to close down, for want of adequate capital and consequently swell the number of unemployed .Knowing that you are keenly interested in this city and its welfare I venture to bring to your notice that a capital investment of £10,000 in this company would mean the reinstating of two or three hundred men and boys.[23]

One of Horstman's cars being driven by Gladys de Havilland, a 'well known woman racing motorist' (Museum of Bath at Work)

By June 1922 the future of the firm, at least in the short term, was secured when fresh capital was raised from Messrs Mortimer Rooke and GS Butler.[24] Some firms, of course, could ride out the recession more easily than others. The Bathford Paper Mills produced a product which – recession or no recession – was vital both for individual and commercial use. It had lucrative markets in Australia, and in March 1921 was still able to export ten tons of paper to Melbourne. Reduced global demand also ensured that Shell-Mex was able to offer the BPM an advantageous contract for fuel oil.[25]

In February 1921 there was a total of 1,384 unemployed in Bath – of whom 888 were men, 222 women and 84 'juveniles' – and a further 409 people on 'short time'. In the outlying towns of Midsomer Norton, Corsham, Keynsham, Clutton and Marshfield there were another 600 unemployed. By July, the total number in Bath had risen to 1,873, and in November it climbed to 1,970. In its yearly report for 1921, the BTLC observed that 'unemployment has reached dimensions hitherto unknown, and much privation and suffering has been caused to our unfortunate fellow citizens'. Those workers who remained employed faced swingeing wage reductions. The council cut the wages of its municipal workers by seven shillings a week. The salaries of the police and teachers were also cut, and even at the Co-op wages were reduced by 5% in August 1921, and in March 1922 by a further two shillings a week.[26]

In March 1921, the government decided not to nationalise the coal industry and, when the mines were returned to their owners, they immediately reduced the miners' wages. In response, the Miners' Federation (MFGB), which was backed by the transport and railway unions decided to strike. Faced by such a formidable nationwide alliance, it was no wonder that the *Chronicle* reported that an atmosphere of deep gloom had fallen over the city. At the last moment on 15 April – 'Black Friday' – the MFGB was deserted by the other two unions but persevered with the strike. The council once again formed a special emergency committee with subcommittees dealing with coal and food supplies. The managers of the municipal tramway services and the gas works attended meetings by invitation, but as the feared threat to public order did not materialise, the chairman of the Watch Committee and the chief constable made only one appearance.

When the strike started, coal supplies in Bath were already low and a system of coal rationing had to be introduced. This was followed three weeks later by a series of restrictions on the use of gas and electricity. Street lighting was reduced to just one light in four. Plans were also drawn up for communal kitchens to prepare food for those who had no gas cookers. One 'large school' which possessed steam ovens offered to cook 'the dinners of all poor dwellers', in its locality, and the master of the Frome Road Workhouse informed the Emergency Committee that its ovens could bake all the bread made by the bakers of Odd Down. The mayor appealed to the more prosperous residents to hand over their surplus coal supplies to the council. The response was generous and by the end of the strike in July 221 tons had been received, enabling 'the poorer members of the community' to be issued with coal permits that entitled them to a quarter of a hundredweight of coal each. If they had a gas cooker in their house, however, permits were withheld. The brother of Earl Temple, the Hon Chandos Gore-Langton, gave four tons of coal to Keynsham Rural

District Council, to be distributed through a coal merchant to the the poor in Newton St Loe.

The impact of the strike on the more prosperous citizens was relatively light. As a result of the coal shortage several train services were cut. On 19 April, the interval during the Pump Room concert had to be 'very drastically' curtailed so that the musicians could catch the last train back to Bristol. Fortt's immediately exploited the crisis by placing a prominent advertisement in the *Chronicle* appealing to customers to save coal by eating lunch in their restaurant. Unexpectedly, in early June the firm experienced the anger and frustration of the striking miners at first hand when a van carrying one of its famed three-tier wedding cakes to Swansea, was stopped at Ebbw Vale by about 50 miners, urged on by their wives, who suspected it 'was loaded with 'blackleg coal' Only after a thorough investigation was it allowed to proceed on its way.

Although coal rationing and limited imports of foreign coal enabled local industry to function for the duration of the strike, production was inevitably affected. Bathford Paper Mills, for example, were told by the haulage firm, Joseph Fish of Bristol, that it was unable to transport paper consignments from the Mills because of a lack of coal for its steam lorries. The acute shortage of coal predictably ensured that there was a run on fuel oil. At the end of June, the British Petroleum Company told Henry Tabb, the managing director, that it could not make any fresh deliveries, as the demand was 'absolutely phenomenal'. [27] By the end of June there was just one week's supply of coal left in Bath, and the Emergency Committee was on the verge of considering the introduction of further drastic measures, when, in the nick of time, on 2 July the miners called off the strike. A week later the *Chronicle* was able to report that 'coal was arriving by rail in a fairly steady stream and carmen and teams engaged in the work of delivery have come to the end of their enforced holiday'. Two days after the strike ended, Priston Collieries at Tunley were quick to write to Tabb, informing him that they would be able to deliver a load of small coal 'on or after Tuesday next'. [28]

The issues raised by the coal strike were discussed in mass meetings in Sawclose – Bath's equivalent of Speakers' Corner in London. In early May there was a series of meetings on the rights and wrongs of the coal strike, promoted by the Re-Construction Society, the successor to the Anti-Socialist Union. The case for the miners was put in another meeting organised by the BTLC where representatives from the Somerset, Bristol and South Wales Miners Federations were present. Oliver Lewis, vice-president of the Somerset Miners' Federation sounded a note of defiance:

The miners were going to fight, and only from the point of view of the starvation of their wives and kiddies would they accept the damnable wage offered by the government and the owners. The workers of the world had common interests. They had got to destroy capitalism.[29]

In fact, it was, as Lewis feared, the imminent starvation of their wives and children that forced the miners back to work in July. The suffering the strike caused to the miners' families was evident in the North Somerset coalfield villages around Radstock. The local Co-operative Societies and the BTLC did all they could financially to support them. On 14 June, the Twerton Co-op raised £3 in the local shop for the Somerset miners' children, which was supplemented on the same day by a further £16 and nearly two weeks later by another £15 17sh.[30] The BTLC set up a special fund on behalf of the Somerset miners and their wives and children and raised a substantial sum through door to door collections and a further £10 10s when a choir of Welsh miners sang in Kingsmead square.[31] When the North Somerset branch of the newly created federation of trade councils met in the Labour Rooms on 28 May in Northgate Street, it appealed to members to take miners' children 'as visitors until the termination of the struggle'.

Nationally in late summer 1921 there was a slight decline in the numbers of the unemployed, but the rate started to increase in October, and by Christmas it stood at 18% of the workforce. In Bath the number of unemployed on 30 December was 2,319, or 4,388 if the surrounding villages are included. In February 1922 the figure for Bath had risen to 2,656. The unemployment problem was exacerbated in the spring of 1922 by the national engineering dispute, caused by the employers' insistence that they had the right to introduce overtime without prior consultation with the employees. The Amalgamated Engineers Union (AEU) argued that at a time of high unemployment work should be shared out equally amongst the unemployed. In response, on 2 May the employers locked out members of the AEU and attempted to persuade their non-unionised workers to report back to work. In Bath local members of the AEU picketed Stothert and Pitt's Newark Works. A week later, on 9 May, the *Chronicle* reported that a 'scab' was subjected to 'the taunts and shouts of a raucous gang' who followed him home for lunch along Dorset Street and Caledonian Road to Brook Road. The man, who apparently set up 'a mile a minute speed', was easily able to outpace his tormentors. The strike dragged on for a further month until the AEU voted in favour of a return to work. A 'friendly meeting' between union and management took place at Stothert and Pitt's on 14 June and arrangements were made 'for work to be recommenced ... as and when they can be put on'.

The most constructive way to ameliorate the effects of unemployment was through a full-scale programme of public works supplemented by the efforts of local employers.. At the annual meeting of shareholders on 14 October 1921, Sir Percy Stothert remarked that he could 'readily visualise the nightmare of being out of employment, especially to men who are married with young children', and it was 'the patriotic duty of employers ... to keep their works going'. He was particularly worried by the inroads German competition was making into British industry and emphasised that 'no contract should be allowed to pass so long as the bare cost of carrying it out be covered'. Even though lack of orders forced him to suspend some of his workforce, in October 1922 he launched a programme of relief work, which involved levelling and turfing the new recreation ground at Newton St Loe and opening a new boiler shop at the Victoria Works.

At the council's finance committee meeting on 4 October 1921, the chairman, Alderman Spear, trenchantly expressed the intention of the council to help the unemployed and 'to see that all hungry men and women and children in the city were fed'. He believed that 'it was quite possible in Bath to deal with the difficulty if they all as one man co-operated in doing what had to be done', but many of the councillors feared what they saw as the corrosive affect of the dole on a person's willingness to work. At a meeting of the surveying committee on 26 September, Sir Harry Hatt had argued that instead of employing, say, 500 men continuously on a project, it would be better to employ 1,000 on alternate weeks as 'hardship should be shared'. He also suggested that payment for relief work should be the minimum a family could live on so that the unemployed 'should have every possible inducement to look for other work and to get it'.

It was the government, in combination with local authorities, which in the final analysis could provide the finance for effective work creation schemes. In December 1920, it set up the Unemployment Grants Committee to help local authorities implement approved schemes. The committee was responsible to the Treasury but was supervised by the Ministry of Health. The council sought to take advantage of this scheme, as it needed financial help if it was significantly to ameliorate local unemployment. Like every other local authority in the country, its civic debt rose during the depression of 1921-22, and rates in many wards of the city were, in the words of the city surveyor, 'very near breaking point'. The council was also well aware of mounting opposition to rate increases from the National Citizens' Union, which in February 1922 decided to run candidates in the forthcoming municipal elections. Plans were drawn up over the summer and early autumn of 1921, and applications made to the Unemployment Grants Committee for grants towards widening both Shophouse Road in Twerton and the Upper Bristol Road from Park Lane to Marlborough Buildings, as well as for giving the Parks Committee a grant to construct a bowling green and tennis courts on the field behind Queen's Parade known as Queen's Parade Paddock. Despite wearisome bureaucratic delays, Bath was eventually successful in obtaining money for a number of projects, and in the course of 1922 several road widening schemes, including Upper Bristol Road and Englishcombe Lane, had been approved, and a grant of £1,920 obtained towards the Queen's Parade Paddock scheme.

It is all too easy to quote unemployment statistics and to forget that each statistic represented a sentient being. Reports in the *Chronicle* and scattered references in the Bath Record Office do, however, reveal personal stories behind a handful of those statistics. The brief jottings in William Chun's diary record that his apprenticeship at Cedric Chiver's bookbinding business came to an end in October and that he was unemployed until he started work at the end of December at Eyres and Sons Milliners and Court Dress Makers in Milsom Street. For him, two months unemployment was no great burden. He was young, lived in a secure family and was a keen boy scout as well as a regular student at the Bible Class at Manvers Street. For others who had a family to feed, or had themselves no secure parental backing, it was a very different matter as is shown by the case of 22-year-old Leonard Hemmings, who had been unemployed for twelve months. He was found asleep under one of the benches in the grandstand on the Recreation Ground on 19 August 1921 by a policeman. He lived with his mother in Chapman Cottages, Widcombe, but, as he had no income, left home so as not to be a burden on his mother. Hemmings later told the magistrate that, 'if I could get employment, I should be all right. That is the only thing that worries me.' The bench dismissed the case, and he promised to seek assistance at Frome Road Workhouse. Forty years later, Ted Ashman, the Branch Secretary of the WEA in Bath, wrote a moving description of what it was like to be unemployed in the early twenties in the city. He had won a Cassell Trust Scholarship for a term at Bristol University, for which he gave up his job as a pattern maker. On his return he found his job had vanished and he had to join

> the growing army of unemployed workers and sign on at the Labour Exchange and live on the hated so-called dole. This was for me a soul-destroying experience. How I envied the chaps who made some sort of livelihood sweeping

the streets. They were at least doing a useful job, albeit for a miserable wage, while I was a little more than a peasant existing in conditions which inhibited any attempt at sustained or serious study.[32]

Political turmoil, November 1922-October 1924

By the summer of 1922, support for the coalition government under Lloyd George had all but disappeared. It had presided over an unprecedented rise in unemployment, tumultuous labour unrest and rising prices as well as chaos in Ireland. When welcoming Herbert Elvin at his adoption meeting as the Labour parliamentary candidate for Bath on 16 August 1921, Councillor Tom Chamberlain observed that 'the state of the country was such that not only Labour but many not in sympathy with Labour were absolutely sick of the present government'. The government seemed to have failed on every front, and increasingly the Conservatives were becoming convinced that they must quit the coalition. What was the last straw for the Party was Lloyd George's apparent willingness in September 1922 to risk war with Turkey when forces under Mustapha Kemal, the Turkish nationalist leader, swept up the Straits threatening territory under Allied control.

In preparation for the Conservative party conference in November, local constituency parties were busy preparing motions of no confidence in the coalition. On 22 September the secretary of the Somerset Branch of the Conservative and National Unionist Association wrote to Charles Foxcroft emphasising how 'very important' it was that 'the position of Lloyd George should be boldly challenged by a motion of no confidence'. Foxcroft, deeply disillusioned by Lloyd George's Irish and imperial policy was in complete agreement. In his papers there is a draft of an undated speech or possibly a letter to Edmund Bagshaw, the chairman of the Bath constituency party, in which he demolished the arguments against the Conservative Party's withdrawal from the coalition. He vigorously asserted that 'whatever happens it will not support the coalition presided over by that politician' – meaning, of course, the much-reviled Lloyd George.[33]

On 19 October, the parliamentary party met at the Carlton Club in London and voted by a decisive majority to quit the coalition. Parliament was dissolved a week later, and an election was called for 15 November. Bagshaw was delighted and congratulated Foxcroft on supporting the anti-coalition movement. As far as the subsequent election was concerned, he advised him that 'the most necessary feature of your campaign here must be to deal with industrial questions – the conditions between employers and employed and the relations of the trade unions to their legitimate object and politics'. Although

Foxcroft would win the votes of those who wished 'to balance the books', Bagshaw emphasised that he would 'have to educate the weekly wage earner AND his wife' in economic reality.[34]

Foxcroft was formally adopted by the Bath Conservative association as their candidate on 30 October. At the last minute the distinguished Liberal author and journalist, Harold Spender, accepted the invitation to stand against him. Although he lived in London, he was a Bathonian and had been head boy at Bath College, an independent school which closed in 1909 – during the election campaign he met his old nanny, whom he had not seen since his schooldays. The Labour candidate, Herbert Elvin, was General Secretary of the National Union of Clerks. The *Times* observed that 'the Bath contest is one of uncommon interest' as 'the politics and personalities of the candidates suggest a fight of the sort before 1914', with Foxcroft being a traditional Tory diehard and Spender a Gladstonian Liberal. The *Times* correspondent anticipated that the contest would be 'severe and searching', for, although Foxcroft was clearly the favourite, on account of 'the deeply rooted Conservativism of a very large number of Bath electors', his criticism of the Irish Treaty would lose him votes, while Spender would win the votes of both wings of the Liberal Party.[35]

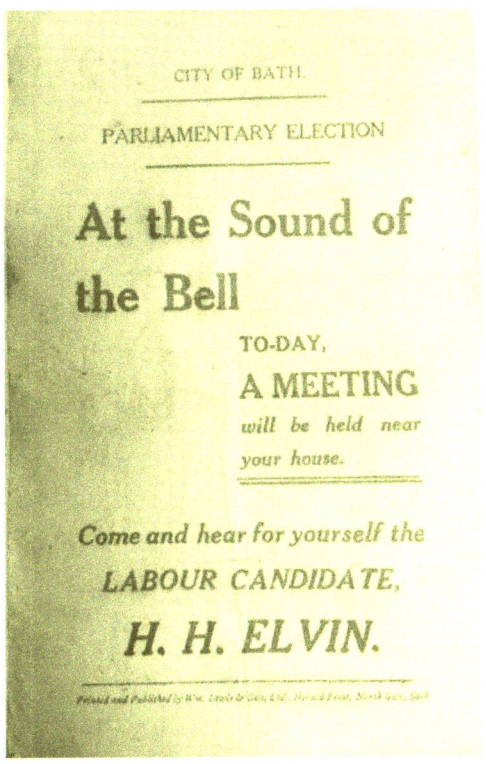

Poster announcing Herbert Elvin's campaign in Bath in the 1922 general election (Bath Record Office)

Over the next three weeks the election campaign was fought strenuously but by and large in an atmosphere of good humour. One evening, for instance, Elvin and Foxcroft bumped into each other at the British Legion club house as one was arriving and the other leaving. Much to the amusement of their supporters they stopped 'for a hearty handshake and patted each other on the shoulders'. Meetings were held all over town; on one day alone Spender addressed meetings in Morford Street, Snow Hill, Lambridge (after a football match), Moorland Road and Kingsmead. By Armistice Day the Conservatives were so confident of victory that, out of respect for the dead, they did not campaign for 24 hours. Spender, on the other hand made a telling point when he said that the dead were best commemorated by the freedom to campaign politically for a new government. Spender, as the *Times* had anticipated, did manage to mobilise the Liberal vote. At a meeting at St John's Parish Room, Bathwick, he made a good humoured but effective attack on Foxcroft, which went down well with the audience:

> He did not know that there was such a dear old crusty Tory living on earth (laughter). He thought that these dear old crusty Tories were rather ornamental in private life, but in public life they were a nuisance, and they could not be quite sure whether Captain Foxcroft would not become more and more crusty as time went on (renewed laughter). [36]

A rather more hard-hitting criticism was made by Councillor Withy, who compared Foxcroft to the Bourbons of France who had 'learnt nothing and forgotten nothing'.

The *Westminster Gazette* commented that Elvin, despite 'the uphill task he had in front of him … was keeping a stiff upper lip'. Elvin's line of attack was that the two old parties were as bad as each other, since both supported the existing capitalist system, and only conceded reform when forced to. The core of Labour's support came from Twerton and Weston, where Elvin could rely on packed meetings. One evening he was particularly feted by the children of Weston, who 'thronged around him and cheered him and ran with the taxi as far as they could'. Just days before polling day the general good humour of the election was marred by Countess Temple descending with her estate manager, Tarrant-Bailey, in tow, on Elvin's committee room, which was in a house belonging to the Temple estate. She had received an anonymous tip-off informing her that the house was covered with election posters. When the tenant refused to take them down, they were removed by Tarrant-Bailey and the Countess's chauffeur. Menacingly, she told the *Chronicle* that she would prosecute any Labour man who dared dispute her action. Not surprisingly this aroused 'considerable feeling' among Labour supporters, particularly those in Twerton. Elvin declined to start legal proceedings, but warned that 'during the election day her friends should restrain her, otherwise he would be compelled to take action'.

On polling day, 16 November, the weather was clear and sunny and there was a large turnout of voters. In contrast to previous general elections, the polling booths were surprisingly busy with voters during the morning. At the Oldfield Boys' School on Wells Road, about a quarter of those registered to vote had already voted by midday. Numerous cars carried voters to the polls, mainly in the Liberal and Conservative interest. In the city itself, many women as well as pet dogs were wearing blue rosettes, scarves or violets, although out in the suburbs the colours of the other two parties were more in evidence. Two dogs wearing rival party colours were spotted by a journalist having a scrap; one retired with its tail down, but the journalist coyly avoided saying which colour it sported. Spender's two youngest sons, one of whom was Stephen, the future poet, had taken the day off from their prep school, the Hall, in Hampstead, to help their father. They drove round the city in a donkey cart covered with slogans such as 'Vote for daddy and a happy family life'. Stephen held aloft a hand worked banner made by himself and his brother, which bore a horseshoe for luck. As usual, local newspapers reported humorous incidents, including the rumour that a dead man had voted and the attempt by a cow to enter the polling booth in Long Acre. When the election results were declared the following day Foxcroft won with 50.2% of the vote (13,666), Spender polled 32% (8,699) and Elvin 17.8% (4,849). It was a clear victory for Foxcroft and the Conservatives, but the combined votes of the two losing parties added up to 13,548, a mere 118 votes behind Foxcroft.

It looked as if Britain's political future was now settled for five years, but only 13 months later there was another election in which the Lib-Lab candidate in Bath would defeat Foxcroft. To understand how this occurred it is necessary to look at the interaction of economic, political and international factors, which were as evident in Bath as elsewhere in the country. 1923 saw an improvement in the unemployment situation. In March, there were 607 fewer unemployed in Bath than there had been twelve months earlier – a reduction of 20% - yet the total was still just under 2,000.

By the end of September, the number had declined still further to 1,634. Economically, some green shoots also seemed to be appearing. In September, for example, Hortsman Cars was planning to break into the Australian and New Zealand markets, although high tariffs and American competition made it an uphill task.[37] However, there were worrying signs over the coming winter that unemployment would increase due to the prolonged Franco-Belgian occupation of the Ruhr having destablised the German economy and disrupted trade across Europe. At a meeting on 12 September 1923, the BTLC warned the council that 'there would be a dearth of employment and urged that steps should be taken above all to feed the children'. By the autumn, Stanley Baldwin, who had become prime minister in May when throat cancer forced Bonar Law to resign, had come round to accept that the only answer to the country's economic problems was the introduction of a general tariff to protect British trade from foreign imports. This was a radical innovation and flew in the face of what since 1846 had been the traditional policy of free trade. In the absence of any mechanism for a referendum, Baldwin decided to appeal to the electorate for a fresh mandate, and parliament was dissolved on 13 November 1923. The threat to free trade united the Liberal Party and made de facto cooperation with the Labour Party a practical proposition.

In Bath. the political consequences of Baldwin's decision were quickly seen. The Labour Party decided not to fight the election on financial grounds. The Liberals chose an experienced candidate, Frank Raffety, a barrister from High Wycombe, who the previous year had been a candidate in the Bristol west constituency. The news of the dissolution of parliament reached Foxcroft when he was in Palestine. While driving home, he badly pulled a leg muscle, and for the first few days of the campaign was forced to rest at home. The argument that free trade would result in a steep rise in the cost of living proved in the end to be very persuasive. The majority of Labour votes went to Raffety, which resulted in a Liberal victory with a majority of 644 on a 79.1% turn out. Waiting for the results on that cold and foggy evening of 6 December a good-natured crowd greeted the news of Raffety's victory:

> It was just after 10.45 when the first sharp fusillade of clapping was heard through the closed doors of the banqueting Room. It was a momentous sound –a sound destined to be heard in Westminister. The Town Clerk ... came into the corridor with the momentous news of Bath's choice. Two minutes more and the Mayor had announced the news to the waiting throng. Another chapter in Bath's parliamentary history had been written'.[38]

For the first time since 1906 a Liberal had won the Bath seat. With the election over, Bathonians were able to get back to Christmas preparations, but throughout the next year politics were to intrude. The Conservatives remained the largest party in Parliament but lost their overall majority. On 21 January, a minority Labour government was formed, backed by the Liberals. As it was not a coalition, the Liberals could at any time force its resignation and precipitate a fresh election.

A whiff of revolution

As Labour voters in Bath and throughout the country were to discover, the problems of unemployment and industrial unrest stubbornly persisted.

Foxcroft succinctly commented at a meeting of Conservative women in the South Walcot Ward in March that Labour was 'in office but not in power'. Even though numbers were declining, there still remained a hard core of unemployed in Bath – in the first week of April 1924, for instance, the total number of people out of work was 1,330. On 4 March, a meeting of the 'men of the scrapheap', as they called themselves, was held in the Guildhall, resulting in the formation of the 'Committee of the Bath Unemployed'(CBU). It was supported initially by a coalition of the left in Bath, including moderate Labourites like Councillor Barrett of the BTLC, Mrs Alma Brosnan of the more radical Independent Labour Party and members of the National Unemployed Workers' Movement (NUWM), whose leader Wal Hannington was a founder member of the Communist Party of Great Britain. James Lowe, G Pointer and several other local members of the NUWM joined the CBU and were able to exert considerable influence on its policy and tactics in the coming months. At mass meetings in Sawclose, they were supported by fellow members of the NUWM specially brought in from Bristol.

Inspired by the success of the campaign in Poplar, east London, to increase the relief fund for the poor, the issue the CBU chose to concentrate on was the rules set by the Board of Guardians of the Frome Road Workhouse, which judged each request for poor relief on the individual's circumstances. It demanded that this should be replaced by a generous fixed scale of relief per week for all supplicants regardless of their circumstances. On 7 May, Lowe and Pointer visited the Poor Law offices in Charlotte Street, but the board refused to change their mind and declined to receive any more deputations. Two weeks later, Lowe harangued a crowd of about 200 men and women on Sawclose with inflammatory language telling them,

> you are letting a certain class of people in this town tread on your neck; it is time you were up and doing [sic] and got it off . Never in my life in all my travels through the country have I ever come across such a class of people as there are in Bath. Why don't you join yourselves together in one big body and demand help and your rights?[39]

Lowe and Pointer then proceeded to walk to the guardians' office in Charlotte Street, where they encountered 'the stalwart figure of Mr J Burgess', the caretaker, behind a locked gate, and were firmly told that the guardians had not changed their mind. After threatening to break down the gate with a sledgehammer, the two men. returned and incited the crowd to march to the guardians' office and, if necessary, use force to obtain their demands. A dangerous situation was only prevented by the intervention of the police and the grudging agreement of the caretaker to deliver a note to the chairman's office. According to the *Chronicle,*

> the crowd waited until about one o'clock when Councillor Hunt [chairman of the Board of Guardians] appeared at the main entrance, looking very cool and collected and smoking a cigarette. His appearance was the signal for shouts and derisive remarks and the crowd surged forward. About ten policemen formed a bodyguard for the Chairman, and he walked into Queen Square with a large crowd following. Here Councillor Evans was waiting in his motor car. Mr Hunt quickly stepped into the car, the while surrounded by his escort, and was quickly driven home.[40]

When the guardians again met on 4 June another demonstration took place in Sawclose. Initially, persistent rain kept the crowds down, but shortly before midday Wal Hannington, and several members of the NUWM arrived from London. Hannington jumped onto his soap box and urged his Bath 'comrades' to take direct action against the guardians stressing that 'it depends upon your determination and spirit as to whether you finally drag down the barrier placed in your way by these individuals calling themselves guardians of the poor'. Just at that moment the guardians left their office in Charlotte Street. The mood of the crowd was tense, and a stone was thrown by one man, but his prompt arrest by the police averted further violence.

Two days later, the more militant members of the CBU exploited the sad death of William Golledge, who had committed suicide by throwing himself in the Avon, to make a further political demonstration. It portrayed him as a martyr, who had taken his own life through fear of starvation, even though the inquest indicated that he 'was extremely well nourished'. The hearse was followed by about 40 men and youths with two banners from the St Pancras and Deptford branches of the NUWM. After the priest had presided over the committal and left the graveside, two verses of the 'Red Flag' were sung under the beady gaze of Inspector Denning, a police sergeant and a constable,

The overtly Marxist politics of the NUWM were rejected by the moderate majority in the Labour Movement in Bath. When the BTLC met on the evening of 11 June, it refused to participate in a joint demonstration because it feared that the NUWM would turn it into a communist rally. Stanley Gould, secretary of the Bath branch of the Building Trade Cooperative Workers and prominent member of the BTLC, warned that 'representatives from outside districts' were coming to Bath 'with the intention of stirring up strife' and he hoped that 'if the unemployed thought they were going to attain their ends by preaching [communism], the BTLC would refrain from having anything to do with it'. He also pointed out that the guardians could not simply offer the proposed flat rate, which in some cases would be way in excess of a labourer's wages. His colleagues agreed and accepted a motion that there should be 'a round table conference 'of representatives of both the BTLC and the CBU with the guardians to establish the facts and ascertain if there were injustices.

Two months later, on 13 August, the BTLC put their proposal for a round table conference 'in abeyance' as the members of the CBU 'had had a bust-up between themselves'. A month later the *Chronicle* observed with some satisfaction that 'the star of Mr James Lowe is on the wane'. This became clear when he was accused at a meeting on 16 September in Sawclose, by no less a person than Mr Grant, the secretary of the CBU, of a string of misdemeanours. The *Chronicle* reported the following acrimonious exchange:

> One question led to another, and Mr Grant asked what had become of the £68 which he alleged had been collected on behalf of the organisation. Why, he demanded, did not the books of the organisation show a correct state of affairs?
>
> Mr Lowe promptly and emphatically repudiated the suggestion that the books did not show a correct state of affairs. His denials involved lengthy explanations regarding the finances of the organisation.
>
> Mr Grant presently declared that the organisation had only been run for the benefit of four or five, and incidentally touched, ever so lightly, on the question of politics.
>
> [Lowe] was quick to notice the suggestion of politics, and reminded Mr Grant that it had been agreed to keep politics out of the affairs of the organisation.
>
> Mr Grant: Then why did you sing the Red Flag over a grave the other day?
> Mr Lowe was understood to say that that was a different matter.
> A voice: A fat lot of good the Red Flag will do us.
> Mr Grant said he had seen a red flag outside Mr Lowe's house.
> Mr Lowe: I haven't got a Red Flag.
> Mr Grant caused much laughter by remarking that it was 'a piece of red something'.
>
> Eventually, Mr Lowe took up a collection on behalf of his 'missus' and children, while Mr Grant took up a counter collection to defray the expenses of an indoor meeting for the unemployed on Friday.

Mr Lowe announced during the evening that he was going to London as soon as his Labour Exchange money came through.[41]

Despite declaring his intention to leave Bath, Lowe was still in the city a month later, when he represented the CBU at the funeral at Locksbrook Cemetery on 11 October of John Thomas Reed, a young ex-serviceman who died at the RUH. This time, out of respect for the feelings of Reed's relatives, there was no singing of the Red Flag, but defiantly Lowe dropped the deceased's red membership card into the grave, explaining to the reporter that this 'is the only red thing we have on us'.

Foxcroft triumphant
The demonstrations in Sawclose played into the hands of the local Conservative party. Captain Wills, the party's candidate for Frome, remarked that the next election would be a battle between the Red Flag and the Union Jack. The events leading up to the dissolution of parliament at the end of September appeared to endorse this view. On 5 August the editor of the communist *Worker's Weekly* was charged under the Incitement to Mutiny Act of 1797 for publishing an appeal to soldiers not to shoot if called upon to suppress a strike, but on the advice of the prime minister the prosecution was dropped. This gave the Conservatives the chance to accuse the government of interfering in the law and to table a vote of censure, which was supported by the Liberals. MacDonald resigned and for the second time in nine months the country was plunged into a general election.

The Bath Conservatives fearing a repeat of the last election where they were confronted by just one opposition candidate, had worked hard over the summer to improve their organisation. What the *Chronicle* called a' body of Bath stalwarts' – or as they called themselves 'bulldogs' – were recruited to ensure that Foxcroft's meetings were not intimidated by militant socialists and communists. A 'flying squad' was formed, which drove around the city to hold a series of impromptu open air meetings. The new Labour candidate, Captain Walter Scobell, like Foxcroft, was a minor landed gentleman, coming from a family who owned Kingwell Hall near Timsbury.

He had lost a leg on the Western Front, and was converted to socialism largely as a consequence of a book lent to him by one of his nurses. He believed that ultimately communism and socialism shared the same objectives, but, to achieve them, 'communism applied force and socialism persuasion'. In a city where the middle classes were convulsed by fear of communism, such a message was not calculated to win many new votes, but he had the enthusiastic support of traditional Labour voters. The BTLC fought enthusiastically on his behalf, arranging meetings and also organising their own 'flying squad of speakers or "Scobell's nightingales" to stump the districts in the interests of Labour especially from the Trades Unions' standpoint'.[42]

Shortly before polling day there was an ominous indication that the electoral tide was running against Labour, when an eminent Bath Liberal, Herbert Mathews, wrote to the *Chronicle* announcing his attention to vote Conservative for the first time:

> To break what has become the habit, apart from the convictions of a lifetime, is a considerable wrench, but I am convinced that the present election is a crisis of our time only comparable with the late war and that if the Socialist party, permeated as it is with Communism, is returned to power, it will be the greatest misfortune that can happen to the integrity of the British Empire.[43]

The following Saturday there appeared on the front page of the *Daily Mail* the banner headline: 'Moscow Order To Our Reds. Great Plot Disclosed'. There followed a detailed description of a letter allegedly from the chairman of the Communist International, Grigori Zinoviev, urging British workers to rise up against the bourgeoisie. The *Mail* went on to claim that Labour's leaders had received copies of this letter several weeks ago. The letter may well have been a fake, but it was enough to alarm Bath's bourgeoisie. At the same time there were disturbing reports in the *Chronicle* about an incident in Twerton on the evening of Wednesday 22 October, when a crowd of over a thousand people pressed around Foxcroft's car after he had just given a speech in the village hall. The blue ribbons were torn to shreds, the car's side lamps damaged and there were attempts to overturn the vehicle. One of his team was struck hard in the face, and Foxcroft could only get into the car by climbing 'in over the back'.

Election day on 29 October was wet, but despite the rain there was an 84.5% turn out. An impressive list of the great and the good lent their cars to the transport department of the Conservative campaign office, amongst whom were members of the Fortt family, Alfred and Ernest Pitman and Sir Percy Stothert. For a time, polling stations in North Walcot were hit by a power cut and the presiding officers had to go out and buy candles until the power could be restored. The polls closed at nine o'clock and the results were declared in the Guildhall at 11.30 where the usual crowd had assembled. Foxcroft, as indeed did the Conservatives nationally, won by a landslide. The figures were: Foxcroft (Unionist) 16.067; Raffety (Liberal) 8,800; Sobell (Labour) 3,914.

For Foxcroft the rest of the evening, stretching into the small hours, was a triumph of rejoicing while both the Liberals and Labour Party licked their wounds and had little option but to put on a brave face. Bath had reverted to being a Conservative city, which it remained until 1992.

3
BATH: HEALTH RESORT, CITY OF CULTURE AND SPORT, 1920-24

IN JANUARY 1921, David Evans, chairman of the Bath Chamber of Commerce, succinctly observed:

> In the baths we have the linchpin of the whole of the city's activities. It is the bathing establishment which brings the visitors; it is the visitors who largely support the business establishments. It is on the success of the business establishment that the city depends for its prosperity and the greater the prosperity of Bath, the better the lot of each resident'.[1]

In November 1920, John Hatton, Director of the Bathing Establishments, published a small book, *The Hot Springs of Bath*,[2] which was aimed principally at the medical profession. It described the treatments on offer such as the Douche Massage and the Liver Pack as well as various methods of electrical therapy, including the Greville system of hot air treatment and the Dowsing system, which used a radiant heat and light bath. It also explained the intricacies of the solarium or electric-light bath and of mechano-therapeutics, which used mechanical appliances to strengthen tendons, muscles and bones. Hatton's booklet contained a list of complaints ranging from rheumatism and arthritis to 'disorders of the digestive organs', which could be effectively treated in Bath. Ambitious plans were drawn up to expand and modernise the baths, but the economies imposed by the recession of 1921-22 inevitably caused delays in their implementation. For instance, the reconstruction of the tepid swimming bath was halted by the council in July 1921, and it was not completed until March 1923.

Hardly a meeting of prominent Bathonians would pass without ideas being put forward for the advertisement of city and the development of its amenities. In November 1920, at a dinner celebrating the reopening of the City Club in enlarged premises, the town clerk conceded that 'the problem of what was needed to be done to promote the prosperity of the city was a deep one, and he had not fathomed it'. It seemed to him that most of its citizens 'were engaged in the process of plucking wool off each other's backs'. He suggested that the council could generate more revenue from the baths by such schemes as bottling and selling mineral water – a proposal which had already been recommended back in October 1919 (see page 40). He also welcomed the suggestion put forward by the Chamber of Commerce that the methodical collection of statistics would enable the city to identify potential sources of prosperity. A month earlier, Hatton had pointed out that it was not only invalids who came to Bath, even though they were still numerous. In fact, 'a larger proportion ... came for enjoyment, possibly for rest, people who were drawn by the entertainments and by the beautiful country all round'. To cater for them, he urged the opening of more hotels, apartments and boarding houses.

In November 1921, at Hatton's suggestion, what came to be called the Civis Committee was formed by the Baths Committee to 'investigate the whole question of Bath as a spa'. As the *Chronicle* observed,

> it was not merely the bathing establishment, it was not merely the amusements: it was the hotels, the shops, the way people came here, their motor tours, the gardens, the appearance of the streets, the sport and everything else – they were all very closely interwoven and all acted and reacted upon the success or failure of each other.[3]

The importance of publicity was again underlined by no less a person than Gordon Selfridge, who in February 1922 urged the Chamber of Commerce 'to make fashion come again to Bath' and to ensure that a visit to the city was as necessary for any foreign tourist as a trip to Oxford and Cambridge. The president of the chamber assured 'the greatest retail distributor in the world' that Bath was already taking measures, which if successful 'would bring the city to the highest eminence'. The Chamber of Commerce was cooperating with its Bristol counterpart to revitalise trade in the West of England and had attracted the interest of the American consul in Bristol, who had requested 'a representative selection of literature descriptive of Bath's modern activities, including hotel prospectuses'.

Meanwhile, the Bath Medical Advisory Committee produced a detailed report at the end of March 1922 on the steps needed to improve Bath as 'a healing centre'. It called for more detailed research into the city's mineral waters 'to ascertain whether the radioactivity of our thermal water, or its chemical constituents, or a combination of these qualities are responsible for the cures effected in such a large number of cases'. Once this was established and acknowledged, doctors all over the country would, it was hoped, send their patients to Bath. It also outlined a plan for setting up a special laboratory for diagnosing diseases under the joint control of the Royal Mineral Water Hospital and the RUH, probably on the Combe Park site, where a workshop would also be opened for producing orthopaedic appliances. To make the spa more accessible to greater numbers of patients, the committee advised the council to lower the costs of taking the waters and the fares for wheel chairs and carriages. It also recommended the provision of comfortable seating in the Pump Room and the reinstatement of its orchestra (see page 89). It was highly critical of the number of beggars and street musicians in the streets, observing that Bath had become 'a dumping ground for undesirables'. The report was enthusiastically backed by Alderman Chivers, who, in his inaugural speech on becoming mayor in November 1922, declared that his main aim was to make Bath a centre for discovering a cure for the ravages of rheumatism. He pointed out that more rheumatic patients were concentrated in Bath than in any other place in the world 'and the opportunity for study and research should not be lost. £10,000 spent in this work would probably have greater and more blessed results in relieving human suffering of the most acute and terrible kind than the same amount spent in any other way'.[4]

A major step towards this goal was taken in February 1923 when the Royal Mineral Water Hospital and the Baths Committee jointly decided, as far as financial resources allowed, to supplement spa treatments where appropriate with 'all proved and established advances in surgical and orthopaedic knowledge and practice', and to conduct further research into possible cures for rheumatic diseases in the hospital laboratories. A sub-committee was set up to appeal for the 'moderate sum of money necessary for the immediate requirements'. Chivers generously agreed both to pay the salary of a biochemical assistant for a year and to provide funds to purchase for the hospital a basal-metabolism apparatus for measuring body energy. By May 1924, there was enough money in hand to finance six months research. Following the advice of Sir Herbert Barker, the famous manipulative surgeon and osteopath, in May 1925 Hatton had installed eight arc-quartz lights so that patients would enjoy 'the dual advantage of the radioactive properties of the water and the ultra-violet rays of the sun, which can, of course, be produced quite successfully artificially'. As the *Chronicle* observed, such a combination would make a reality of Bath's old name 'waters of the sun'.

BATH AS A TOURIST CENTRE

AT THE END of April 1922, under the auspices of the Chamber of Commerce, George W Kettle, managing director of the Borland Advertising Agency in London, gave Bath's businessmen yet another 'wake-up call'. He urged them to raise £20,000 annually to finance an ongoing advertising programme of all that Bath could offer and scolded them for having neither an advertising policy nor an advertising manager. In a recent newspaper controversy about which was the most beautiful city in the world, he noted that Edinburgh did not hesitate to push its claims, but from Bath there was only a sepulchral silence. Kettle's proposal sparked a considerable debate. When asked for his opinion by the *Chronicle*, W Charles of Charles & Charles, the footwear specialists in Milsom Street, reckoned that £10,000 was a sufficient budget. He thought that Bath should regularly advertise in papers such as the *Daily Telegraph* or *Morning Post*, observing snobbishly that some of the other papers 'appealed to a class of people who would be less likely to benefit Bath'. This view was echoed by WE Mallet of Mallet & Son, the well-known antique shop in the Octagon, who also advised targeting 'the cultured class' and not the 'people who would be able to spend a happy holiday at, say, Blackpool'. However, Mallet emphatically did not believe in collective advertising, arguing that each business could best draft its own publicity programme. His own firm, for example, supplied customers both locally and at its London shop in New Bond Street with a tasteful booklet giving a brief history of the Octagon together with positive references 'to the bathing establishment and the general distractions of the city'. Alderman Jackman, chairman of the Advertising Sub-Committee of the Baths' Committee, stung by the implied criticism of its record, argued that they were 'getting capital value for the money now being spent in advertising Bath'. He pointed out that 'much thought and attention are devoted to the question how best to reach the various types of people, who would be likely to come to Bath', with advertisements placed in the press at Monte Carlo and Nice and in 'the Paris papers most read by Americans and wealthy cosmopolitans'. He dismissed a budget of £20,000 as beyond Bath's means but hoped for some help from the government – and from the railway companies, 'seeing the income they would derive from a large stream of first-class passengers'.

Kettle's speech inspired the formation of the Bath Spa Attractions Week Committee which drew up plans for a shopping week. It was opened by the mayor, accompanied by councillors and a band, on 26 May. Clusters of gas balloons were released, to each of which was attached a coupon entitling whoever found it to a prize. The streets were decorated with flags and triumphal arches, there were bands in the parks and gardens, and, as an added bonus, the shopping week coincided with the County Cricket Festival. Above all, the weather was glorious. The committee set a short essay competition, inviting 300 words on 'How would I make Bath more attractive?', to be judged by Frederic Harrison, Bath's most famous 'public intellectual'. There were 41 entrants and Harrison was struck by how many of the writers had suggested more should be made of the river, as in Richmond or Cambridge. The winners were Mrs Lillian Andrews of 4 Sydney Buildings, Mrs Florence Altman of 5 Junction Avenue and Charles Craik from Clifton. Harrison commented that in most of the essays there was 'a cry for open-air restaurants, dancing platforms and music halls more or less on the continental pattern'. Further suggestions included a public lending library, an 'adequate winter garden, open and covered restaurants in the park and the abolition of the tolls on the bridges over the river'.

How effective was the Bath Attractions Week? Financially it just about broke even, but it pulled in crowds from the surrounding area and generally acted as a magnet for tourists and visitors. The Birmingham Chamber of Commerce was interested in following Bath's example and was supplied with copies of the Bath booklet and official programme. At the end of June, the chairman of the Attractions Week's Executive Committee concluded his report with the rousing words: 'In 1905 the general cry was 'wake up Bath'. In 1922 the Bath Spa Attraction Week did 'wake up Bath'.

The following January, a joint meeting of the Chamber of Commerce and the Attractions Committee decided to hold another shopping week in mid-October. By June preparations were well in hand. There were plans to print 25,000 copies of the handbook and to offer a prize for a poster design. Yet at the end of July, it was suddenly cancelled, after it emerged that it did not enjoy sufficient support. Although it would draw people into the city, the considered opinion of many of Bath's retail traders was that it would not justify the cost.

Not deterred by this setback, in December 1923 John Hatton launched an ambitious publicity campaign to attract visitors to Bath for the Christmas break. He produced a brochure entitled *The Bath Christmas Book*, which included details of seasonal festivities not only in the Pump Room but also throughout the city. The central message was that Bath was 'not a place of healing only but a holiday resort where young and old alike may spend a Christmastide of joyous gaiety'. The festivities ranged from concerts, recitals and lectures to tours of the historic city. Strikingly- designed advertisements

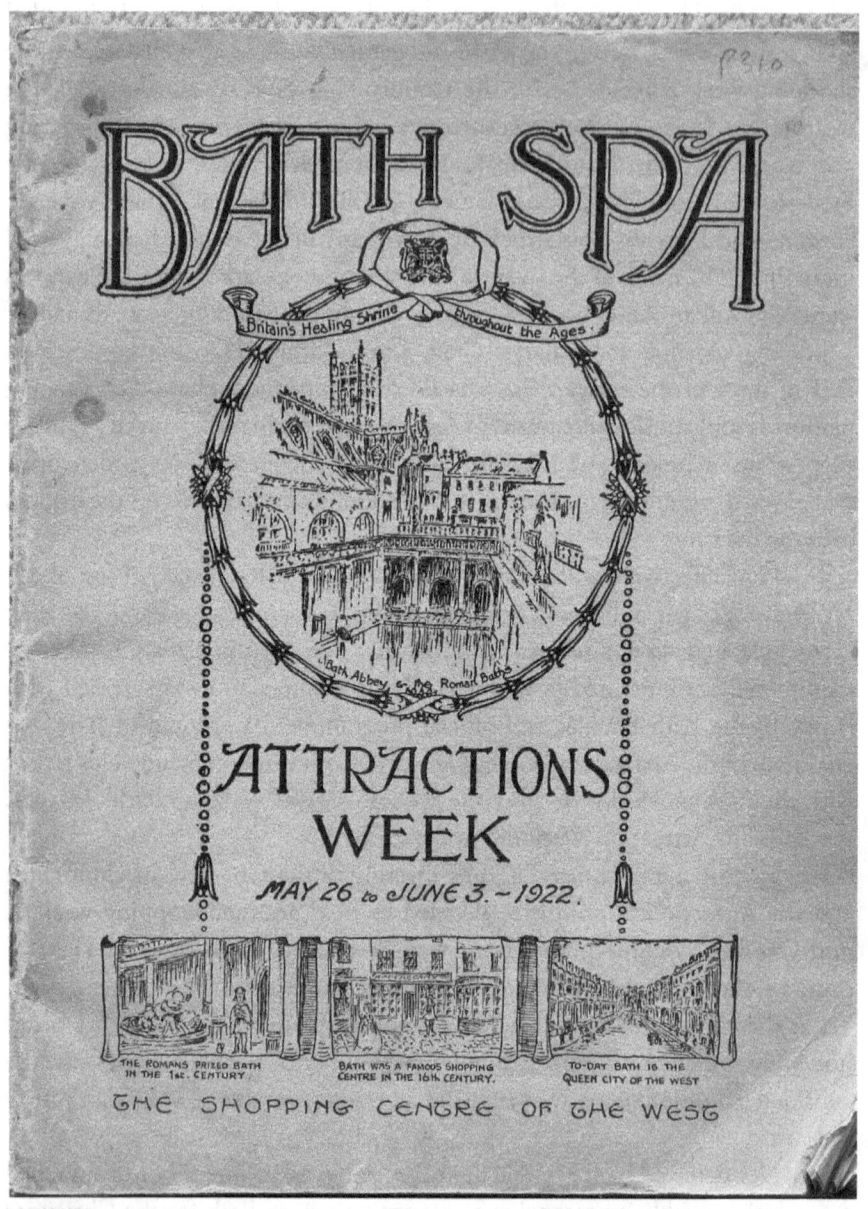

Front cover of the Bath Spa Attractions Week pamphlet, 1922 (Akeman Press)

were placed in national and leading provincial dailies. In the words of the *Chronicle*, 'the centre of the design was a jet-black silhouette of the stonework over the King's Spring ... In the steam issuing from the hot mineral water were shown brightly coloured bubbles conveying the idea of gaiety and holiday making'.

The advertisement featured three slogans: 'Spend Christmas at Bath', 'Hot Springs for Health' and 'Festivities for your Delight'. Coloured posters featuring the same design were displayed on the London Underground and at all main GWR stations. Despite the political uncertainty and the Ruhr crisis, the Bellman observed just after Christmas that

> not during the past ten years… has Bath been so festive. Every hotel has been a scene of jollity; every amusement house has been crowded by happy audiences and day by day the Pump Room has been thronged by delighted gatherings.[5]

The Empire Exhibition at Wembley also gave Bath a chance to project its image right across the empire. Bath was fortunate in securing a position for its pavilion on the 'Golden Way' which led up to the British government pavilion, and opposite a sunken bandstand with space for 10,000 people. The plot was small – only 55 square feet – but a good deal was packed into it. The pavilion was designed by the leading Bath architect, AJ Taylor, in the style of a typical eighteenth-century Bath building. It was built by by Jacob Long & Sons using stone from Monks' Park Quarry at Corsham. On a paved forecourt stood a model of the King's Spring from which, thanks to AE Jones, the chief engineer of the baths, ran a continuous flow of water water heated to at 120 degrees Fahrenheit – the same temperature as the hot water spring. To either side of it were herbaceous borders planted by Twerton Hill Nurseries. From the roof flew a flag bearing the arms of the city, while the interior was dominated by a model of the Roman baths, with photographs depicting the principal methods of treatment in the spa and places of interest in the town displayed on the walls. The pavilion was essentially a tourist information centre promoting the city, with brochures available for visitors, who were left in little doubt that it was 'the Premier Spa of the Empire'.

Aside from the razzamatazz of Attractions Week and the Empire Exhibition, Bath received positive publicity in numerous ways. Its charms were often lauded in up- market weeklies. In September 1921, for example, the *Sphere* published an appreciative article by Frederic Harrison, who had temporarily decamped to a house on 'one of the wooded hillsides' around Bath while his home in the Royal Crescent was in the hands of the workmen. He waxed lyrical about sitting in 'the shade of beeches and limes' and gazing down on Bath, feeling 'the breezes from all over the Mendips and Cotswolds', while pitying the 'holiday makers who are grilling in many seaside resorts'. In *Nash's Magazine*, HG Wells presented Bath with a superb bouquet of publicity in a short story whose main character, Sir Richmond Hardy, motored to Bath from Nailsworth with his young American girlfriend, Miss Grammont. After driving through 'unattractive and unworthy outskirts', they reached the centre of the town, garaged the car at their hotel and, after some extensive sightseeing, realised 'the charm of the place'. In the evening,

> they went to the parapet above the river ... Miss Grammont was moved to declare the Puletney Bridge with its noble arch, its effect of height over the swirling river, and the cluster of houses above more beautiful than the Ponte Vecchio in Florence ... Dear England, said Miss Grammont, summing up the gracious spectacle: 'how full of homely and kindly things'.[6]

The most fulsome tribute to Bath's beauty came from the Prince of Wales when he visited Bath in July 1923 and remarked that its lovely setting and magnificent architecture were 'the wonder of the world'.

It is difficult to assess what impact all this publicity had. At Easter 1924 the *Chronicle* reported that the city was 'flooded with visitors' and that several hotels had to refuse bookings. The visitors' book in the Bath Pavilion at Wembley was signed by guests from all over the world – Bombay, Chicago, Australia and Berlin – but how many of these visitors actually visited Bath is not recorded. However, at Christmas 1924 there was such a great demand for accommodation that the hotels again had to turn guests away. The well-known journalist and father of the House of Commons, TP O'Connor, failed to find a room at the Grand Pump Room Hotel and instead took himself off abroad. Bath was also a popular city for conventions, whether they happened to be gatherings of the medical profession, the Grocers' Association or Antiquarian Book Sellers. After a particularly enjoyable lunch at Fortt's, the chairman of the latter organisation presented Bath with another glowing compliment:

> From whatever standpoint we regard it: health, pleasure, education, we should say to the man or woman in the street: 'Go to Bath, you will be able to find there all you want in this life and opportunity to prepare for the next'.[7]

CULTURE, IDEAS AND PHILANTHROPY

CRITICS OF BATH perceived the city to be a quiet backwater predominantly for rentiers, retired officers and old India hands. Yet, paradoxically, the Lord Mayor of the dynamic city of Bristol reassured the Bath Chamber of Commerce in February 1923 that the city was something more than a mausoleum of the great men of the past; it was a metropolitan city, to which Bristol came a good second. In some respects Bristol was more provincial than Bath, which came near to the heart of London by reason of the men of note who graduated here'.[8]

Did Bath deserve this encomium as a great city of culture and the arts, or was the Lord Mayor speaking with his tongue in his cheek?

Music and Drama

As we saw in the last chapter, the council enjoyed a somewhat stormy relationship with the Pump Room Orchestra. In January 1920, it decided to economise by engaging military bands to play during the summer season, and to replace the full orchestra with a septet. The council attempted to disguise the fact that this would make over half the original orchestra redundant by informing the press that the musicians had voluntarily decided to go to Margate to play in the orchestra there. The decision was met with a storm of criticism. Tarrant-Bailey, as an accomplished and well-known banjo player, accused the council of pursuing a vendetta against the orchestra and called for the dismissal of the city entertainments manager.[9] The BTLC believed the council was more interested in weakening the Musicians' Union than in providing music for the city. In October, the council received a magisterial reprimand from Percy Scholes, the music critic of the *Observer*, who accused it of 'demobilising its winter orchestra' and denying its citizens access to high-class music. In its defence the council argued that the concert room had a seating capacity of 300 but was often only ten percent full. Nevertheless, two years later, in preparation for the 1922 winter season, the septet was augmented by a further four musicians, and in 1924 five more were added, bringing the size of the orchestra up to 16. These decisions may have been influenced by Bertram Fortt, one of the city's leading estate agents, telling the council that the lack of a good orchestra was deterring prospective purchasers from moving to Bath.

In January 1920, in a lecture at Bath's New Empire Club, Norman MacDermott, the director of the Everyman Theatre in Hampstead, left Bathonians in no doubt that the British theatre was in trouble because it was run by philistines for mere profit. He argued that it was too commercial and lacked the cutting edge of avant-garde continental drama. He believed passionately in the role of the theatre as 'an essential factor' in society, providing people with the inspiration they once received from the churches. A couple of weeks later an interesting debate, organised by the Bath Playgoers Society, took place at Fortt's restaurant. Speaker after speaker echoed MacDermott in their criticism of the commercial theatre, and the motion that 'the present-day theatre is a failure' was enthusiastically carried.

Bath had two main theatres: the Theatre Royal and the Palace Theatre. At the latter, musicals were the staple fare, while at the former Shelford Walsh specialised in producing middlebrow plays from the West End such as Elinor Glyn's *Three Weeks* and old favourites like *Charlie's Aunt*. In the Bellman's opinion, Shakespeare was not popular with the British public, and attempts to stage his plays 'spelled ruin for many a manager'. In April 1920, however, Henry Baynton, one of the last of the actor-managers, showed that Shakespeare could indeed be made accessible when he had a very successful week presenting *The Tempest* and several of the comedies to packed houses at the Theatre Royal. Arguably, Baynton's success was the exception that proved the rule. In November 1921, the Bath Licensing Justices displayed their cultural conservativism – or, as some would argue, philistinism – by rejecting an application from the writer and dramatist Lechmere Worrall for permission to open a repertory theatre in the Assembly Rooms, a decision much criticised by the Bath Playgoers Society on the grounds that the repertory movement had breathed fresh life into the British theatre.

Yet it would be unfair to dismiss the theatre-going public in Bath as complete philistines. In June 1924, the Theatre Royal hosted the Lena Ashwell Players, a newly-formed repertory company, for a five-week season which was a brilliant success. Its programme included the melodramatic *Witness for the Defence*, AA Milne's *Mr Pim Passes By* and the Restoration comedy *The Country Wife*, as well as Shaw's *The Devil's Disciple* and a more gritty play, *Diana of Dobson's*, which dealt with controversial issues such as homelessness, sweated labour and sexual double standards. As the Bellman observed, 'to attract audiences to a theatre on fine summer evenings is no small achievement'. On the Tuesdays and Fridays a late bus ran from Sawclose to Lansdown. Lena Ashwell was a passionate advocate of municipal theatre as it existed on the continent and worked hard to establish theatres in what she perceived to be the culturally barren wastelands of Greater London. In a talk at the Bath Rotarians' weekly lunch on 10 June she lamented its absence in England, where drama was taxed like whisky and tobacco and not viewed as 'essential to the civilisation of the race'.

Arguably the best productions of avant-garde drama in Bath could be seen at Citizen House, which claimed to be a 'folk house' or meeting place for citizens of all classes. Consuelo de Reyes, one of its founders, produced a series of interesting and provocative plays throughout the year, which received national – and sometimes international – recognition. They were performed by the Citizen House Players, a community theatre group which was rigorously coached by de Reyes. In 1920, three works – a phantasy, a comedy and a ballet – made up the 1920 Summer Spectacle.

Many of their productions contained hard-edged social comment. The ballet, for instance, was called *A Poet, Organ Grinder and a Dancer* and, according to the *Chronicle,* featured 'a vivid description of the sordid surroundings of ordinary working-class life'. For Christmas 1920, de Reyes produced *Shadows of the Wind*, where the nativity story was transposed to modern times, with Christ born in an attic room to working-class parents. It attracted the attention of several prominent people in the London Theatre world, such as the theatre critic, Harold Child, Anthony Ellis of the Kingsway Theatre, and the actress Ellen Terry. The *Times*' theatre correspondent paid a striking tribute to the quality of the drama produced at Citizen House, describing it in April 1920 as 'beautiful, bright and gay from top to bottom'. In March 1924, Miss de Reyes produced an adaptation of *The Beggars Opera* for children.

Among those who saw it were GK Chesterton, who had written a book of plays which de Reyes hoped to produce. Two months later, Percy Allen, the drama critic of the *Christian Science Monitor* spent a weekend as guest of Citizen House and wrote enthusiastically about its various productions, including a 'simple, ethereal moonlight fairy drama, full of lyrical beauty'.

Cinema

By 1919, at least half a million people in Britain visited the cinema twice a week. Bath was no exception to this trend. Already before the war it had three cinemas –the Picturdrome, the Vaudeville and the Electric Theatre. In December 1920, the Electric Theatre in Westgate Street was re-built and renamed the Beau Nash Picture House by its proprietors, who claimed that it was one of the most luxurious and up-to-date cinemas in the West of England. It seated nearly 800 and had managed to secure the services of the former manager of the Holloway Picture House, the second largest cinema in London. The most up-market cinema in 1921, however, was the Assembly Rooms Cinema, which claimed in its advertisements to be 'the Cinema that's *so* different'. In September 1921, the city's first suburban cinema, the Oldfield Park Picture House in Shaftesbury Road, was opened by the mayor, Alderman Colmer. In his inaugural speech he conceded that the cinema had the potential to educate people, but added 'that in many parts of the country and occasionally in Bath, there were pictures exhibited which he would not call advisable for all people to see'. He also suggested that on Sunday evening after the Churches and chapels were closed, services could be held in this new picture House, which would benefit the 'crowded neighbourhood of Oldfield Park'.

Critics of the cinema were resigned to the fact that picture houses had come to stay but were anxious about their potential impact on the nation's morals. Essentially, the thrust of their campaign to sanitise the cinema was to demand a more effective form of censorship. The British Board of Censorship had been set up in 1912, but it did little more than issue guidelines for producers. At the Conference of the West of England Women Citizens' Associations, which was held in Bath in October 1921, the representative of the Newport branch conceded that 'it might be a great force for good, but in her opinion the balance at the present time was on the side of evil'. She went on to move a resolution for the creation of a board of censors, of which half should be women, to review films where children under 16 were admitted. A letter from Alderman Dr Preston King was then read out, in which he argued that the proposal to ban children under 16 from certain films rather missed the point,

> since if films are of such a nature as to be unfit for children, they are also ... unfit for anyone. The pictures to which special exception should be taken are, of course, those that deal with sex emotions, and which too often make immorality attractive. [10]

A week later, Preston King returned to the subject when he read a paper in Cambridge to the Pembroke College Medical Society on 'the Influence of Picture Houses on Child Life'. He mentioned the possibility of eye strain and the danger of catching germs, but 'far more important' was 'the mental and moral damage'. Yet even he realised that the clock could not be turned back and so he asked rhetorically, 'what can be better, for instance, than films showing nature studies, or travels and big game?'

There was a widespread assumption that films were a bad influence on children. In January 1923, for instance, a twelve-year-old London boy, Percy Chilwell, who had absconded from Prior Park Industrial School, was caught by the police placing a sizeable plank of timber, which he had stolen from a nearby gangers' hut, on the railway line at Claverton. Had the police not found him in time, the Cardiff to Brighton Express, carrying some 200 passengers, would have been derailed, possibly with fatal consequences. When he appeared at Weston County Police Court on 20 January, the solicitor representing the GWR believed that he may have 'wished to reproduce a train wreck scene such as was depicted in certain films'. He was found guilty and sent to the remand home on Frome Road, until other arrangements could be made.

On the other hand, such was the pedagogic potential of film that many clerics and teachers in Bath embraced it enthusiastically as a positive contribution to education. The head of East Walcot Girls' School, for instance, sent ten of the 'elder girls 'to see the film of the Prince of Wales' Canadian tour in January 1920. A few days later they went to 'see the pictures of Shackleton's expedition to the Antarctic seas'.[11] In October 1921, at the autumnal gathering of the Bath Sunday School Union in the Argyle Congregational Church, the Rev Carey Bonner, Secretary of the National Sunday School Union, was asked whether Sunday School teachers should warn their pupils not to attend cinemas. He replied that, 'they might warn as much as they liked, but that would not keep the scholars away'. They should instead 'make the cinemas a medium for teaching things'. In 1923, the Argyle Congregational Church's newly- appointed pastor announced plans for three cinema shows a week in the chapel on such topics as travel and science, and no less a person than the chief constable of Bath gave his seal of approval to the cinemas in an article in the weekly film magazine the *Bioscope* in May 1923:

> I am of the opinion that the City of Bath has suffered no ill effects since the introduction of cinemas into the city of which there are five, all apparently doing well. The class of picture as now shown affords healthy recreation to a large number of residents and others.[12]

The joy and excitement that a film could afford children was touchingly evident when, on Saturday 12 January 1924, Mr J Lewis, the proprietor of the Assembly Rooms Cinema invited 600 children from Bath's elementary schools to see *Robin Hood*:

> When they were admitted there were not many vacant seats, and the chatter of excited youngsters was deafening ... Many of them had been told about the picture by grown-ups who had already seen it. Others had picked up from books a good deal about the romantic life of the well beloved robber ... while a few of more tender years were a little uncertain as to whether they were about to see 'cowboys and injuns', Charlie Chaplin, Mary Pickford or some other film star whose genius is best displayed in modern or comic productions.[13]

Societies and Clubs
The cream of Bath society belonged to the Bath & County Club, whose annual ball was one of the great social occasions of the city. Less prestigious was the Harington Club, which catered predominantly for those white-collar and

skilled workers who could afford the annual fees. The club had billiard and card rooms as well as a bar and a reading room where a large selection of newspapers were available. It was an eminently respectable club where close attention was paid to the behaviour of its members. In December 1919, for example, one member was sent a letter of complaint about his use of foul language in the presence of the manager's wife. A year later in November 1920, another member was accused of assaulting a fellow member in the skittle alley, and on 18 December, as he did not resign voluntarily, his name was removed from the register.[14] There were also Working Men's clubs in Widcombe and Bathampton, which were part of the National Federation of Working Men's Clubs and Institutes. Unlike the local Labour Party or the BTLC, the Widcombe Club was essentially a social club for local working men, who would meet to play cards or skittles and drink a pint of beer, although occasionally a federation speaker would turn up to give a talk. On 14 April, its committee risked the anger of the righteous by deciding to open on Good Friday as well as Easter Sunday.[15]

In the city there was an impressive number of societies catering for a wide range of interests. A Bathonian could go to a reading of one of the Bard's plays at the British Empire Shakespeare Society or a lecture on John Galsworthy at the Playgoers' Society. On a more specialised level, there was the Bath Literary and Philosophical Association, which in December 1921 offered a lecture on 'Bath Surnames'. If interested in the cut and thrust of debate, one could attend the YMCA Literary and Debating Society. Regular talks were also offered by groups such as the Beekeeping and Photographic Clubs. One of the most successful of Bath's many societies was the Bath Dickens Fellowship, a branch of the National Dickens Fellowship. Its guiding spirit was councillor T Sturge Cotterell, who presided over its inaugural meeting on 16 March 1921. Cotterell was adamant that its subscription should be low so that membership was open to all who were interested. He also stressed that, besides exploring the world of Dickens, attention would be 'devoted considerably to philanthropic work, and generally to the remedying of social evils'.[16] A year later the Society decided to admit local schools to meetings and lectures on the payment of a subscription of one shilling per school.

Over the next three years there were lectures and discussions on all aspects of Dickens, from his 'portrayal of women' to a paper on 'Dickens as a reformer' in February 1924 given by Miss Violet Gandy, a prominent local Poor Law guardian, who argued that 'as Dickens' public read of the social evils which he pilloried, it dawned on them that these things should not be in a civilised land'. Two days later, at the society's annual dinner at the Red House

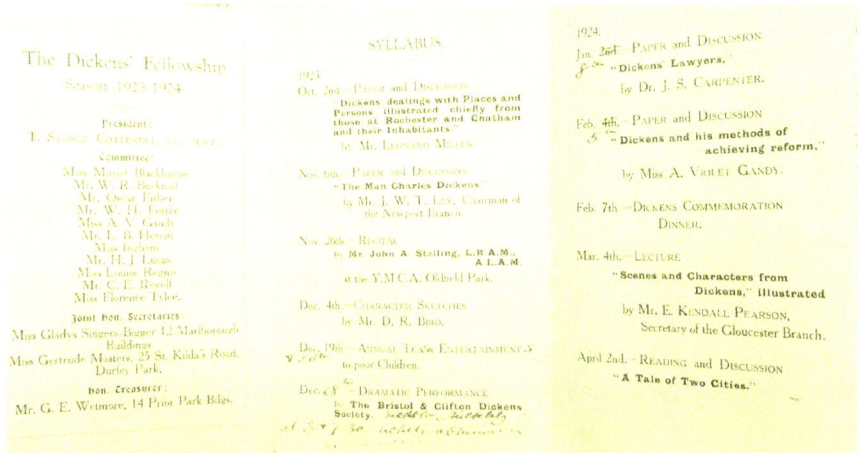

The proof of the Programme or 'Syllabus' of the Bath branch of the Dickens' Society for 1923-24 (Bath Record Office)

in New Bond Street, the Rev JC Harris of the Argyle Congregational Church, referring to the recently-formed Labour government, claimed that 'Dickens, perhaps more than any writer of English', had put it into power by showing 'the glory of the grey masses and the greatness of the commonplace'. [17] In October, the society marked the opening of its new season with a meeting in the Pump Room, attended by about 80 members and friends, with a bust of Dickens in a position of honour in front of the mineral water fountain. Sturge Cotterell gave an introductory talk entitled 'If Dickens returned to Bath', concluding that,

> save for a few changes in the city's streets and architecture, he would easily find his way about, but it would be the people, the methods of administration, and the modern traffic that would bewilder him. [He] was not sure that Dickens would not now condemn the excessive pleasure and ostentatious exhibition of wealth which he would see on every hand. [18]

The fellowship also honoured Dickens' memory in a more practical way. At Christmas 1923, parties were held in the Walcot Mission Room on Snow Hill and in the Milk Street Mission Hall for two groups of 200 children selected by the Salvation Army. These became annual events, and the following year 600 children were entertained at Snow Hill, Twerton and Milk Street. Vilven and Sons, Cater, Stoffell and Fortt and AE Rawlings of Brook Street supplied the oranges, and Fyson and Co printed the tickets, all free of charge. The *Chronicle* commented that the 'fellowship was not unmindful of the true Christmastide message of the great novelist'. [19]

The oldest and most distinguished of the city's cultural centres was the Bath Royal Literary and Scientific Institution on Terrace Walk, which had been founded in 1824. Initially in the post-war world it had a struggle to survive: its membership was dwindling, and it was forced to sell off items from its collections. Its museum was in a poor condition, the roof was leaking and its valuable collection of stuffed birds was threatened by the damp. FE Shum, the society's chairman, lamented at a meeting in April 1921 that 'a large number of the class of residents who would have been patrons of the institution in former days, now probably find their recreation in bridge or golf'. However, over the next two years the fortunes of the institution did improve. The corporation agreed to make an annual financial grant, and by March 1924 the chairman reported that membership was steadily increasing and that £160 had already been collected towards the £500 target for the centenary fund. The Institution was the home to the Bath Literary and Philosophical Society, which had struggled to survive during the first two years of the war and had to close temporarily in 1917. When it was revived in November 1921, it seemed as if it had become an anachronism. Its chairman, Dr Curd, did not hide the scale of the challenges it faced, telling those who turned up to its first meeting to listen to a lecture on the 'Sprit of the Aeneid', that

> in the hey day of its prosperity the society stood alone with, perhaps, one exception, but at the present time there were so many societies of varied sorts in Bath, which catered for many and varied tasks that there hardly seemed room for such a society as theirs.[20]

Over the next seven years it continued to provide a series of interesting lectures on literary topics, but in May 1928 lack of interest forced it to cut these back to one a month instead of every fortnight. The *Chronicle* welcomed this, observing that 'it is one of those organisations we really cannot afford to lose', but regretted that it was not better supported.

The Workers' Educational Association (WEA) differed from many of the other societies in Bath, which catered primarily for the interests of the educated middle classes. Its aim was to promote 'the higher education of the working man'. Before the war the WEA had been primarily a coordinator of affiliated societies. After the war the number of these societies declined, and the WEA began to organise its own classes. This proved an increasingly uphill task. Membership in Bath peaked at 170 in 1921 before falling to 55 by 1925.[21] At the annual meeting of the Bath and District Branch in May 1920, the chairman said he wasn't satisfied that 'the workers were taking advantage of the opportunities offered to them'. They were, with the notable exception of the inhabitants of Oldfield Park, 'standing aloof from the Association in a manner that was to be regretted'. Nevertheless, he advised the Bath branch to keep on 'pegging away'. The local Inspector of Education, who had the marvellously Dickensian name of GH Grindrod, suggested that the WEA should send 'apostles' to the other working-class areas of Bath to make the Association better known, 'especially among those who did not seem to be aware of its existence'. This prompted another member of the committee, George Long, to point out that 'not all the intelligent people lived in Oldfield Park. There were others – at Walcot, for instance, and on Odd Down'. Over the next four years, the WEA did indeed 'peg away', providing a wide choice of lectures and activities, ranging from a course on 'the landmarks in Western Civilisation' to a visit to Oxford in two charabancs, where the indefatigable Mr Grindrod showed them around his old college. In 1924 there were well-attended lectures on 'Somerset' and 'human life and sociology' as well as a tutorial class in English Literature. The president of the Bath branch was Miss Hope, one of the wardens of Citizen House, where the WEA had held its committee meetings since its foundation in 1912. On her death in 1922, the lease of Citizen House passed to Consuelo de Reyes, whose commitment to drama was far stronger than her interest in the WEA. One contemporary complained bitterly that Citizen House 'gradually became void of citizenship' and, feeling that it was no longer welcome, the WEA, moved out in 1930.[22]

The Churches
Superficially the Churches still appeared in the early 1920s to be an influential force both nationally and in Bath in particular. In February 1920, the *Chronicle* devoted a whole page to an article by the rector of Swainswick on the arcane subject of 'the future government of the Church of England'. However, church attendance was in decline, especially amongst the working classes. The vicar of St James, for instance, in a sermon in September 1920 lamented that now the Sabbath was just an excuse 'for holiday making', while the Rev Shapcott, the Metropolitan Secretary of the Church Army, observed during Church Army Week in Bath that well over a million demobilised men had 'been captured by organisations and societies, whose aim was revolution'. In failing to counter their arguments, he declared, 'the Christian people and the Christian Church in this country had lost the most golden opportunity it had had for fifty years and would have for another fifty'. The churches seemed increasingly out of touch and old fashioned. In July 1922, the Rev Thomas Hayward of Manvers Street Baptist Church was highly critical of the London County Council's

decision to allow games to be played on Sundays, while in December 1923 the vicar of St John's, Lower Weston severed his links with the Church Missionary Society in protest at what he saw as 'a refusal to accept the absolute truth of all the utterances of Christ recorded in the Bible'. In September 1921, Alderman Wills provocatively suggested that it might well be a good thing if churches were to close for six months so that people would learn to appreciate them more, but the Bellman perceptively pointed out that 'a six months enforced abstinence from church going would serve still further to attenuate the congregation', and that the root problem confronting the churches was that they 'expound today exploded beliefs of untutored times'.

In early January 1923, the charismatic figure of Gipsy Pat Smith arrived in Bath where he conducted a four-week-long mission. Rather like Billy Graham in the 1950s, he appeared to carry all before him. He was born in a gipsy caravan in the Vinegar Hill encampment in Glasgow, fought in the war, rising from private to captain, and became a charismatic evangelist on both sides of the Atlantic. In his first week, the *Chronicle* reported that nearly 13,000 people attended his meetings. At three separate meetings on Sunday 14 January the Theatre Royal failed to accommodate all who wished to hear him, and when he spoke in the Argyle Congregational Church on the evening of Tuesday 23 January, the choir stalls and the steps to the gallery were tightly packed with people. Although most of his audiences consisted of practising Christians, the *Chronicle* remarked that 'there were those among the congregation, who may be described as "the man in the Street type" [who] are not usually found among worshippers at church, even on Sundays'. Gipsy Pat's charm lay in his youth, humour and sincerity – he seemed to possess 'the baptism of the Holy Spirit'. After the meeting at the Argyle Congregational Church on 11 January, around 70 young people entered his 'enquiry room' to find out more about his message. Two months later, the Young People's Fellowship of Oldfield Park Baptist Church invited 40 young converts to a social gathering in the Sunday School room. A more lasting legacy in Bath was the establishment, by men who had been inspired by him, of a weekly Sunday afternoon meeting at the Beau Nash Picture House.

This mass enthusiasm was not without its critics. At the annual meeting of the supporters of the RUH in February 1923, Forbes Fraser, the eminent surgeon, commented bitterly, in view of hospital's £6,400 deficit,

> that thousands and thousands of people were going to the meeting of this revivalist, and that hundred and hundreds had changed their mode of living, and had been what was called converted ... When he saw the money falling

into the exchequer of the Royal United Hospital, when he saw the elementary Christian principle, 'Love one's fellows, succour the sick, care for the poor' being followed in Bath, when he knew that this disgraceful deficit had been wiped off the hospital, which was a shame to Christian civilisation, then he should know that this religious revival had been of some real effect.[23]

Controversies and debates

Bath was no stranger to intellectual controversy and debate, as we have seen with the impressive list of visitors who regularly visited the city to lecture on current events and issues. There were frequent lectures and debates on temperance reform, eugenics, teaching methods and the role of the new woman. In her occasional articles in the *Chronicle*, Dorothy Penrose would discuss social problems such as 'equality of pay', 'the unmarried mother and her child' and 'child assault'. In November 1922 she urged housewives to start discussion groups to come to grips with these topics. A more controversial issue was euthanasia. After the City Medical Officer of Health had presented his report to the Health Committee on 18 September 1922, the question of cancer arose, which led Councillor Cook to give notice that he would move a motion at the next meeting in October urging the Government to legalise euthanasia provided that each case was initially approved by a medical tribunal. Movingly, he said,

> he could only regard the matter from the working-class standpoint. He had heard the friends of people who were down with cancer say, 'It's a pity the Lord doesn't smile on them and take them away'. He had known people afflicted, pray to die, and yet they had to linger in agony ...What cancer in the working man's home means, only those who have experienced can realise. No hospital will take these cases, and supposing the man is the one afflicted, they probably get him upstairs, and the wife has to look after him day and night.
>
> With him in constant pain it is a terrible picture, and it would be a great blessing if he could be saved this suffering.[24]

Cook's emotional speech was received 'without comment' by the Health Committee, but it was quoted in the Bath press and resonated across the British Isles and beyond, and he was deluged with a large number of letters. The great majority were in varying degrees sympathetic, although one from London asked, 'how are you sure that what some doctors diagnose as cancer is cancer? There are tumours which are not and cannot be known to be malignant till removed'. The correspondent ended with a thunderous salvo:

Such a proposition as yours is in itself so ignorant, unthinking, and conducive to such evil and wrong doing that it is you who ought to be put in a lethal chamber as a danger to others.[25]

One letter from County Dublin, however, written by somebody who had spent over 20 years in Bath, enthusiastically endorsed Cook's proposal and felt pride in having been a Bathonian when such 'progressive men' were on the council. Another correspondent from Gloucester urged Cook to keep up his campaign, which, if successful, 'will give occasion for the blessing of the innumerable sufferers of cancer and their friends'.

However, running through some of the letters was also a note of caution and an awareness of how euthanasia and eugenics could combine to produce what a later generation was to witness in Nazi gas chambers. A letter from Chelsea pointed out the obvious danger in legalising 'lethal chambers' as some people would want to put 'extremists there' and others would also want 'that class, who insist upon breeding most undesirable stock, who eventually fill the prisons, etc.', liquidated. A lithographic printer from London was even more emphatic:

From working at my trade, I have been slowly poisoned and have been under a London hospital for years. Whilst under their care I have heard quite sufficient of what doctors and students would like to do with Labour men. Do not put any easy means in their way of getting rid of workers. They want no prompting.[26]

When the motion was debated on 16 October, Cook dealt with the argument that life is sacred head on, and pointed out that 'on the battlefield millions of lives were destroyed on the altar of patriotism and that on the industrial battlefield they had millions of workers going to their graves years before they ought to go'. In a lengthy discussion the Health Committee reviewed the whole question. Dr Preston King agreed that the Ministry of Health needed to engage more urgently with patients suffering from incurable cancer and recommended setting up what were in effect hospices. He pointed out how undesirable and paradoxical it would be if the London press announced 'that Bath, a health resort, was going in for killing people'. In a disturbing aside he confessed that he himself had been 'in favour of euthanasia' and had advocated 'a lethal chamber for certain so-called human beings'. In the end, Cook withdrew his motion and agreed to support efforts by the Health Committee to persuade the Ministry of Health to develop a more compassionate and effective way of dealing with terminally-ill cancer patients.

SPORT

IN BATH THERE were many who had little time for or interest in the arts. Sport, on the other hand, enjoyed great popularity. Traditionally horse racing appealed to all classes. Three race meetings a year were held on the Lansdown course with the summer meeting usually being the most popular, as it included the historic Somerset Stakes, which was originally a trial run for the Derby. Provided there was no rain, 'the northern plateau' of Bath was at its best in May. On race days Lansdown Road was gritted to prevent great clouds of dust being caused by the increased traffic. The Bellman somewhat cynically observed a week before the race meeting in May 1922 that despite 'the hard times' it may be anticipated that considerable crowds will throng the course; the same old cosmopolitan crowd ranging in social degree from the aristocrat on the stand to the humble, though not at all modest, 'follower' of racing. [27]

In early summer, with the football season safely out of the way, Bath Cricket Week took place, during which Somerset played a series of county cricket matches on the Recreation Ground. Although Somerset's home ground was at Taunton, it had strong links with Bath – its captain, John Daniell, was born in Great Pulteney Street. Like so many sporting organisations and clubs, Somerset was suffering financially, and in 1921 had to appeal for support to 'all lovers of cricket'. By December 1923, after rigorous economies, the club had managed to pay off much of its debt, and in February 1924 launched a campaign to increase the number of members. For a guinea they would have admission to the ground and pavilion at all county matches in Somerset. By the end of the summer of 1924 finances had recovered sufficiently for the club to be able to contemplate signing up one or two young players.

Even the prestigious Lansdown Cricket Club, to which many prominent citizens belonged, was not immune to financial problems. It managed to raise £70 from its members in 1919 to reopen, but by the end of 1920 was again facing an acute lack of cash. An emergency meeting under the chairmanship of Sir Percy Stothert was held in the Red House in January to consider the situation. Its secretary, General Aitken, painted a most negative picture, and saw no prospect of the club surviving unless members could raise what he considered to be the unattainable sum of £200. Rather than see the club deteriorate, he resigned. Fortunately, the rest of the committee was ready to battle on and a resolution was passed which combined economies with limited financial guarantees from members, who would be asked to contribute sums between £1 and £5. This proved effective, and by 1924 the finances of the club had fully recovered. In August, it played a formidable team of London intellectuals, composers, actors and authors captained by the playwright, writer and critic, Clifford Bax. The game was depicted in an amusing sketch by a *Chronicle* journalist - one RLP. Initially, he imagined Bax's team to be composed of highly-strung romantics sitting all night writing and composing in garrets 'barely furnished by table, chair and carpeted with neat little bundles labelled "returned with thanks"'. The author's illusions were quickly exploded by finding that the team was composed of practical and capable people, who beat Lansdown.

As is still the case today, the most prestigious of Bath's sports' clubs was the Bath Rugby Club, which had a formidable reputation. In 1920, for instance, it won eleven matches, drew one and lost six. Bath was defeated by Gloucester on 18 September 1920, but in the eyes of the Gloucester *Citizen*, they deserved to win. Rugby in Bath was encouraged by the Bath and District Supporters' Club, which gave small financial subsidies to local clubs. A typical recipient was the Bath Schools' Rugby Union, which in 1923 was given a grant of £13. The Union was strengthened by the entry of the West Central and Widcombe Schools, but its attempts to attract more schools were unsuccessful. During the 1923-24 season the supporters club contacted the headmasters of 13 junior schools, but none of them replied.

Soccer was a more popular sport if measured by the number of its supporters and clubs in the Bath area. Indeed, it was a sport played almost everywhere, especially by children in the streets. The principal football team was Bath City. Nationally it was seen as a nursery for young talent especially for Bristol Rovers. In 1920, one City player was chosen to play for Wolverhampton Wanderers, and another for Huddersfield Town. In July 1920, the club was taken to court for infringing entertainment tax regulations. The case was heard by magistrates at the Weston Petty Sessions where Bath City was defended by the eminent local lawyer, WF Long, who despite being a 'Ruggerite' was one of the financial guarantors of the club as well as a loyal supporter. The case gives an interesting insight into the finances of the club and its somewhat haphazard methods of crowd control. On Good Friday 1920, Bath City played Welton Rovers at the Horse Show Ground at Lambridge. The gate amounted to £103 9s 1d. on an attendance of 2,845, and £24 3s 8½ d. was duly paid out as entertainment tax. Unknown to the club officials, Walter Swain, the local entertainment tax regulator, decided on that day to make a tour of inspection. At the main entrance everything was correct, but, as the *Chronicle* reported he noted that,

> at the enclosure entrance men were collecting money from some of the people going in, and the latter were receiving no tickets in return. Some went in

without any challenge owing to the rush, so that tickets were not collected. At the stand soon after his arrival he saw the men in charge leave, and there was no one in charge for quite half an hour during which time people went into the stand unchallenged.[28]

In the club's defence, Long did not mince his words. He ridiculed Swain's suggestion that the 'uncollected stamped tickets could be made use of again' and accused the Customs and Excise department of wasting money by pursuing such a 'paltry case'. The bench agreed and dismissed the case on the grounds that, while 'there had been a little irregularity … there had been no intention to defraud', leaving the club to pay the legal costs of two guineas.

Financially, 1921 was a difficult year for the club, as it was for almost every other organisation in the country. It managed to join the Southern League, but this put its finances under strain, as travelling further afield involved extra expense. It also needed to sign 'tip top players' since it now faced formidable competitors. Inevitably, this involved further expense because, as the chairman of the club explained in December 1921, 'they could not go into the back garden' and just dig them up. His appeal to the citizens of Bath and the Bath City Football Supporters Club for financial support met with only moderate success, and in the year ending June 1922 there was a deficit of over £390. At the end of the 1923-24 season the club was only kept in the black by £1,000 being raised through a lottery. However, despite the travails of Bath's leading soccer club, soccer was a flourishing sport in the city and in surrounding towns and villages. In June 1924, nearly twenty local teams applied for admission to the Bath and District League for the next season.

Bath also had a ladies' football team. Its creation was inspired by the famous Dick Kerr's Ladies' team, which had been formed in 1917 by workers at Dick, Kerr and Co's Armaments Factory in Preston to raise money for the care of the war wounded. All over the country, ladies' teams sprang up with similar charitable aims. By July, the members of the Bath City Ladies' FC were playing regularly on a private ground in Bath. Their first fixture to be reported in the pages of the *Chronicle* was a charity match on Wednesday 22 September 1920 against Caerau FC in Maesteg, Glamorgan. It was played in front a good-natured crowd composed mainly of miners and raised about £200 for the local hospital. As the *Chronicle* remarked approvingly, the Maesteg players never once forgot 'they were playing against ladies'. Since the match had been a success, the Bath Ladies drew up plans for matches against several other clubs, including Blackpool, and a French ladies team. This later fixture was in some doubt because the French team were to visit Bath after a tour of Ireland, but

*Bath's Ladies' Football Team, 1920 (*Bath Chronicle*, 11 September 1920)*

given the unrest there, the likelihood of cancellation was high. In the event, it seems that the match never took place, as no report appeared in the *Chronicle*.

By early 1921, the Bath Ladies were doing so well that they were ready to form a second team, and their captain held two recruitment evenings at West's Commercial Hotel & Dining Rooms on Upper Borough Walls on 7 and 8 January. A week later their team went up to Manchester where they were soundly beaten by the best ladies' team in Britain – Dick Kerr's, which had never been defeated. The match drew an enormous crowd of 31,000 and raised some £2,000 for the unemployed of Manchester.

The Bath Ladies had a busy early spring schedule. On Good Friday 1921 they played an away match against the Atlanta Ladies' team in Huddersfield, which they lost 1-0. The date of the fixture had been sharply criticised in a letter to the Mayor of Huddersfield from a Bath woman, who signed herself AG. She complained about the game being played on that most holy of days, Good Friday, and asked provocatively, 'what are women coming to these days?' The letter drew a sharp response from Constance Waller, Atlanta's football Club's chairman, who pointed out that, as the game was to be played at a quarter past five, there was plenty of time left to attend a church service in the morning. Constance Waller went on to defend female participation in sport:

> By playing football and other sports we are coming into a new age physically. When girls realise the great pleasure that playing football and cricket gives,

there will be less girls spending their time idly walking the streets or reading sticky [*sic*] novels ... Add to these the household and personal duties that most of them have, and it does not leave much time in which Satan can find work to do, does it?[29]

On Wednesday 20 April the Bath Ladies defeated the Southampton Bramtoco Ladies Team at Ashton Gate in Bristol,. Three days earlier, they had visited the ground in their full football 'rig-out' to sell tickets for the forthcoming match. On Wednesday 11 May they played at Southampton against a combined team representing Bramtoco and Pirella, and lost 'at almost the last kick of the match', but the fixture raised £3,000 in aid of St Dunstan's Hostel for servicemen blinded in the war. Further matches followed over the Whitsun weekend at Plymouth and Yeovil.

In December 1921, in common with ladies' teams throughout the country, their progress was rudely interrupted by the Football Association's sudden ban on ladies' teams playing at its members' grounds. Allegedly this measure was to 'protect' the frail female body from the rigours and dangers of football, but in reality, the decision was motivated by the need to protect the financial takings of the men's clubs, since the ladies, who were usually playing for charitable causes, often drew bigger crowds. This edict was a serious blow to the financial viability of the Bath Ladies' Club. Even so, in July 1922 it decided to struggle on for a further year, but its matches, if played at all, were no longer reported and the team faded into obscurity. It would be another hundred years before a new team – Bath City Women FC – was formed in summer 2022, with the Football Association's backing and to huge local acclaim, to play their home games on the same ground as Bath City – Twerton Park.

4
AMBITIOUS PLANS FOR BATH
THE 1925 BATH CORPORATION ACT

IN 1915 THE COUNCIL commissioned Robert Atkinson, an architect who specialised in the Art Deco style, to draw up designs for the ambitious *Bath Improvement Scheme*, the centrepiece of which was the construction of a sunken forum next to the Abbey and Roman Baths. It also included plans for a concert hall, a Roman museum, winter gardens, libraries and a remodelled Grand Parade, as well as a new bathing establishment, all of which consciously evoked Bath's classical heritage.[1] The economic context of this grandiose plan was the boom Bath experienced as a result of the war, which had made continental spas inaccessible to British tourists. Atkinson's scheme was never realised because the post-war recession meant that scarce resources were diverted to house construction. However, in 1924 the debate about the future of historic Bath revived with the government's plans for a town planning act, which would give the Minister of Health (who was still responsible for housing) power to compel cities of historic interest to draw up schemes to protect their ancient city centres. To pre-empt government intervention, Bath council drafted a bill, which would enable it to develop its own town-planning schemes and measures to preserve the city's historic identity. When it received the royal assent in August 1925, it marked a crucial stage in the modernisation of Bath, giving the council sweeping powers to build roads, demolish houses and dictate the design of new buildings.

It had its genesis the previous October, when the council's Finance Committee authorised the town clerk to employ the parliamentary agents, Messrs Sharpe, Pritchard and Co, to draw up a bill to be presented to parliament during the coming session. This was duly approved by the full council on 7 October and a special parliamentary committee was appointed, which was presided over by Sir Harry Hatt. It consisted of the chairmen of the other committees whose responsibilities would be affected by the bill, as well as Frank Sissons, the city engineer, Basil Ogden, the town clerk, and Aldermen Bush and Spear. On 20 October. the Surveying Committee considered the proposals that would ultimately be included in the bill. Its chairman, Alderman Wills, declared that the council

> wanted to take power to enable them [sic] to do anything which might be of advantage to them in the years to come. It did not follow that they would carry out what was proposed immediately; it meant they were taking a vision, a wider view of things and trying to look into the future as to what was likely to be required. ...They wanted to take powers so that if and when the council decided those things were necessary, they would have the necessary powers to carry them out.[2]

After weeks of detailed deliberations, an 'Omnibus Bill' was agreed upon by the council on 19 November. To the alarm of some ratepayers, the *Chronicle* observed that 'the powers, which the bill is intended to confer, are extremely far-reaching, and indeed appear to the lay mind practically limitless'. Street improvements were its key component, the aim of which was to improve the main traffic routes through the city.

Numerous streets – along with the historic Old Bridge – would be widened. Several new streets were also planned for the south-west quadrant of the city centre – Avon Street would be extended east from Milk Street to the south end of Westgate Buildings; a new road would be built from Green Park Buildings East to Southgate Street, providing a 'riverside thoroughfare' between the GWR and LMS stations; St James's Parade would be extended south to meet Southgate Street at its junction with Somerset Street; a new street would be built from Kingsmead Terrace, running east to the junction of Peter Street and Corn Street. South of the river, at Twerton, the widening and improvement of Brook Road and its bridge over the GWR were 'contemplated'. Most of the buildings which would have to be demolished to make way for these improvements were either commercial properties or dwellings likely to removed anyway as part of civic improvements. Indeed, the 'slum clearance' aspect of the scheme was seen as one of its major benefits. There was one proposal, however, that threatened one of the city's best-known and best-loved buildings – a new road linking Orange Grove and Pierrepont Street, so that traffic would no longer have to negotiate the bottleneck of Terrace Walk. This entailed not only the acquisition of part of Institution Gardens, but also the demolition of the Royal Literary & Scientific Institute.

The corporation also intended to acquire the six toll bridges in Bath: of these the Grosvenor, Cleveland, North Parade and Victoria Bridges needed to be 're-conditioned'. The remaining two, the Widcombe and the Weston

Bridges were structurally sound – for the time being at any rate. Ultimately tolls would be abolished and, where necessary, the bridges and their approach roads widened. The bill would also give the council the power to control pollution from factory chimneys, determine the height and general design of new buildings, pass bylaws to regulate maternity homes and tighten its grip on public utilities. To facilitate the financing of these ambitious schemes, it intended to consolidate the rates – that is to combine the inner city rate with the outlying general district rate covering villages such as Bathford and Bathampton. On 13 December, the council approved the bill overwhelmingly, with 38 in favour and 3 opposed, and four days later it was deposited at the Private Bill Office in the House of Commons. The council now had to call a statutory ratepayers meeting within 28 days. This was arranged for Wednesday 7 January.

Commenting on these proposals the *Chronicle* observed that they were

> convincing testimony to the sincere desire, which actuates our Body Corporate to do all in their power to provide for the better government and progress of the city… Few, if any, of the present generation will probably witness more than the bare inception. But the good seed has been sown.[3]

Not everybody agreed with this encomium. Amongst many ratepayers there was a suspicion that the bill would simply give the council a license to overspend and raise the rates yet further. The local branch of the National Citizens Union (NCU) was particularly suspicious of the council's intentions. Its secretary, in a letter to the *Bath Chronicle* on 30 December, explained the NCU's position: although it supported consolidating the rates and freeing the bridges from tolls, it nevertheless regarded the improvement scheme in general as ill thought-out and ultimately so expensive that it that would inevitably cause a steep increase in the rates. It would also affect those whose properties were to be demolished and for good measure destroy many historic buildings. The secretary pointed out that there was no provision for rehousing 'the inhabitants of the so-called slum areas' and urged NCU members and all those worried by the proposals to contribute to a campaign fund and attend the statutory meeting at the Guildhall on 7 January 1925.

The meeting was 'lively', and there were nearly three hours of discussions under the chairmanship of the mayor before votes were taken. The NCU was soundly defeated on two motions. The first was a rejection of the street improvement plans, which it lost by the relatively narrow margin of 112 to 94 votes. The second was an impromptu motion from the floor that the bill should be approved as a whole, which was carried by a much larger majority of 158 votes to 89. The NCU was still not ready to accept defeat. A week later it petitioned the mayor to hold a special poll of the city's ratepayers, but offered to withdraw this demand if the council dropped those sections of the bill dealing with redevelopment.

Confident that it enjoyed the backing of a majority of the ratepayers, the council decided to call the NCU's bluff and drew up plans for a snap poll, or local referendum, to be held on Saturday 24 January.

The poll was a 'general election in miniature'. The customary polling stations in each ward were open from 8am to 9pm, and the week leading up to it was a period of frenetic activity with meetings in every ward. The

Alderman Alfred Wills (1872-1949). Mayor of Bath 1918-19 and chairman of the Surveying Committee (Bath Record Office)

NCU attracted many middle-class voters, but the opportunity of clearing the slum areas won over the BTLC. Councillor Walter Barrett told its members in no uncertain terms that they should 'seize that opportunity to clear a blot from the city. It was their moral and bounden duty to do what was right and just'. A major boost for the council was the endorsement of the bill by the Bath branch of the National Women Citizens' Associations, whose members were invited by the mayoress, Sarah Grand, to a meeting in the Banqueting Room in the Guildhall on Friday 16 January where the mayor and Alfred Wills would explain its contents. Many of its members arrived determined to oppose the bill, but the mayor told the *Chronicle* that, 'as soon as it had been fully explained to them, they were one and all in favour of it'. He believed that 'much of the opposition was due to sheer ignorance of its proposals'. On the day of the poll, Bob Hope, an influential member of the Bath and Twerton Cooperative Movement, the WEA and the congregation of the Ascension Church, pointed out in a letter to the *Chronicle* that the bill would help find work for the hundreds of men who were still unemployed. He urged the workers 'in their own interest' to vote 'in their thousands for the Bath Parliamentary Bill on Saturday next', arguing that there has always been opposition to progressive measures, as when the Bath Gas Co. applied for a Bill to light the city with gas in 1817. A form of petition was placed in the Guildhall by a body of citizens for signature against the Bill on the ground of terrible things that would happen (these citizens preferred the smelly oil lamps).

It is the same spirit working to-day through the National Citizens' Union, a spirit that, if it had always prevailed, where now is beautiful Bath, would have remained a swamp, and Bladud's swine would still have been wallowing in its mire.[4]

The vote was won decisively by the council, with 6,185 votes against 4,191, on a relatively low turnout. Making the best of their defeat, a spokesman for the NCU observed that, 'we are satisfied that the whole subject has been ventilated, and we feel certain that the council cannot now go blindly forward with any section of the Bill'.

After the poll, the town clerk received eleven petitions from bodies including the Bathwick and Widcombe Bridge Companies, the railway companies, Georges' Bristol Brewery, Bush's Grocers, and St John's Hospital, which would be potentially affected by the bill. The NCU also decided to force the 'closest attention' to it before it became law by mobilising sympathetic MPs in parliament. By the time it came before the Private Bills Committee in the Commons in May 1925, however, the opposition had been largely appeased. The bridge companies were offered generous terms by the council, while the railway companies were satisfied that their interests would be protected. On 7 April, the council discussed the question of negotiating and compensating those whose properties would be affected. After considerable debate its parliamentary committee was empowered to negotiate with interested parties and draft agreements, which would have to be approved by the full council before demolition and street improvement work began. At first the Labour members were suspicious that the committee might overcompensate commercial property owners such as the powerful Georges' Brewery Company at the expense of people who 'were not so powerful', but Alfred Wills

> pointed out that the properties under the Bill could be compulsorily acquired but that would be a very costly matter, and very undesirable . . . The position was somewhat of a jig-saw puzzle. If they could move A at less cost than B, they would try to move A.[5]

GAINING THE APPROVAL OF PARLIAMENT

IT COULD NOT be assumed that parliamentary approval would automatically be granted. When the Ministry of Health, which had taken over the work of the Local Government Board in 1919, prepared a report on the Bath bill, it was particularly concerned by the powers that Article 118 would grant the council to determine the general design and height of new buildings. The Royal Institute of British Architects (RIBA), which had given evidence to the Ministry of Health's departmental committee on building by-laws back in 1918, had advised strongly against vesting too much power in local authorities. It feared that local councillors – such as Alfred Wills, perhaps, who owned a large building firm in Bath – would be tempted to use their position to nudge plans in a direction that would benefit their businesses at the expense of the historic beauty of their cities. The ministry had agreed and proposed that an independent committee composed of a member of RIBA, as well as a member of the Royal Institute of Chartered Surveyors and a JP, should advise councils on these questions.[6]

The Commons Private Bills Committee was due to start dealing with the bill at midday on Thursday 14 May, but because discussions over the Walsall and Wolverhampton Bills overran – due to 'a heated "scrap" between the rival authorities' – it was postponed for nearly a month. The Bath delegation, which consisted of Sir Harry Hatt, Alfred Wills, the town clerk, the city engineer and the treasurer, returned home that evening empty-handed. Eventually though, the 218-clause bill had an easy passage through the committee in just three days, largely due to the expertise of Sir Lynden Macassey, KC, the leading counsel of the parliamentary agents, but also as a result of preliminary negotiations in Bath having appeased the opposition. The street improvement schemes were first to be considered, on 9 June. The city engineer, Frank Sissons, with the help of a map and photographs explained their importance and cost. Congestion was so bad, he told the committee, that 'there were 3,138 tons of traffic at Terrace Walk per square yard per day, exclusive of tramcars'. Andrew Maclaren, the Labour MP for Burslem, one of the more vociferous members of the committee, after glancing at a photo 'of the slum area', facetiously asked whether it 'represented part of the Roman remains'. Sissons 'hinted in reply' that 'the Romans had left nothing so discreditable'. Prompted by Macassey, Sissons gave an assurance that the corporation would carry out its obligations with regard to housing people displaced by the construction and widening of roads. The clauses concerning the bridges over the Avon gave rise to considerable discussion. The corporation wanted a period of ten years before they became toll free, but the committee shortened this to seven years. According to the *Chronicle,* Maclaren showed 'his antipathy to private proprietorship of the bridges by diverse satirical commentaries' and made the 'facetious suggestion' that the corporation should specially rate the bridge companies 'for the privileges they had so long enjoyed'.

All in all, the 'progress of the bill was 'highly satisfactory, if monotonous'. During the second day, the hot weather, combined with the fact that the MPs on the committee were recovering from an all-night sitting of the Commons, had its effects, as the *Chronicle*'s reporter observed:

> Sir Robert Newman, the member for Exeter ... had forty winks both before and after lunch, and even the alert chairman, Sir Thomas Robinson, displayed signs of drowsiness towards the end of the sitting, almost going off once ... and a [Bath] city Alderman of ample proportions inclined his head in the late afternoon. But he stoutly denied that he had been asleep, and attributed his restful attitude to the process of deep and searching thought.[7]

The final hearing of the bill in its committee stage, on Tuesday 16 June, took just 110 minutes. There was a light hearted exchange between Maclaren and Macassey over the insertion of a clause forbidding the erection of any buildings which would be out of scale with Pulteney Bridge. Looking at a picture of the bridge, Maclaren noticed the hideous wooden addition to it on its northern side and asked:

> Have you no power to prevent vandalism of that sort?
> Counsel: No.
> Maclaren: Does it belong to a member of the Council?
> Counsel: No, a councillor would not do a thing like that.
> Maclaren: I am not so sure about that (laughter).[8]

Alfred Wills was also questioned closely about Article 118, which sought to regulate the height of new buildings erected in Bath. The committee agreed to the appropriate restrictions and to others regulating the height of chimneys to avoid spoiling the city's skyline. In return, the Bath delegation had to accept the input of an 'independent advisory committee' along the lines proposed by the RIBA in 1918, which was incorporated in Article 128. At the end of the proceedings, Wills expressed himself delighted with the speedy progress of the bill, telling the *Chronicle* that 'we have got everything we wanted, and in half the time we expected. If the Bill had been fought, it would have dragged on and cost thousands of pounds to both sides'.

The bill went before the standing committee in the Lords and received its second reading on Tuesday 7 July. A petition from the Salvation Army requesting that its maternity home in Bath should be exempted from council inspection was accepted. On 23 July, a select committee of the Lords considered the clause permitting the corporation 'to purchase and provide and let for hire but not manufacture electric fittings' and to 'wire the houses of their consumers'. Sir Harry Hatt, the chairman of the city's Electricity Committee, pointed out that the number of electricity consumers in Bath had risen from 1,000 to 3,000 since 1914, and would continue to grow. Currently, the corporation could not lay a mains cable in a street unless it received advance payment or a financial 'guarantee' from each householder. In working class areas this was often impossible, and consequently no cable was laid. To avoid this, Bath, in company with Burnley and Barrow-in-Furness, had drafted clauses which would allow house owners to pay their councils by instalments rather than having to put down a lump sum. This was hotly contested by the Wiring Contractors Association, but the Lords dismissed their petition, and the bill received its third reading on 30 July. On 7 August, the Bath Corporation Bill received the Royal Assent.

THE TOLL BRIDGES

WHEN ALFRED WILLS was interviewed by a *Chronicle* reporter a week later, he was emphatic that the city was 'now in a position to take advantage of the powers conferred by the bill', adding that, 'if we fail now, the opportunity may be lost for ever'. The proposals outlined in the Corporation Act would, of course, take years to implement. The most straightforward item was the purchase of the bridges and the abolition of their tolls. Ownership of Cleveland, North Parade, Widcombe and Victoria Bridges was transferred to the corporation at midnight on 30 September 1925. The transfer of Grosvenor and Weston Bridges followed shortly afterwards. As the act laid down that the tolls did not have to be abolished until 7 August 1932, the council continued to levy them for the next four years, since it needed the money to help finance the refurbishment of the bridges. At a council meeting on 6 October, Wills, aware of the cost of implementing the Bath Act, warned his colleagues that he would 'be bringing forward a proposal in a month or two which would make them' need 'all the money they had'. A revised list of toll charges was drawn up and the toll-keepers were now employed by the council. The fees they collected ensured that the bridges paid for themselves, and in the financial year 1928-29, the last full year of tolls, made a net profit of £512.

Slum properties in Bath: (above) Milk Street and (below) the area around St George's Place off the Upper Bristol Rd (Museum of Bath at Work)

Both Cleveland and North Parade Bridges needed extensive work to make them strong enough to allow heavy traffic, including lorries, to cross them. Cleveland Bridge was the key to the future development of Bath's road network. In December 1926, the corporation decided to apply for government loans to strengthen the bridge and 'to improve the roadways between the London Road and the new Warminster Road and the east end of Pulteney Street'. In the subsequent enquiry, presided over by a Ministry of Transport official, the town clerk outlined the significance of this project for Bath stressing that:

> Cleveland Bridge was important from the point of view of traffic as it enabled the heavy traffic between London and Bristol to be diverted from the centre of the city. Numerous cars passed through Bath from the north, which in many cases did not wish to stay in Bath.[9]

The ministry approved the scheme and granted £10,500 towards its cost as it formed a link in what it categorised as a 'first class road'. The City Improvements' Committee advised the council to apply to the local government department of the Ministry of Health, for permission to borrow £8,000 to finance work on North Parade Bridge. Grosvenor Suspension Bridge was also scheduled to be replaced by a reinforced-concrete pedestrian bridge. As it would carry a water main to supply the Warminster Road area from Monkswood Reservoir, the committee recommended that the Waterworks Committee should contribute £500 towards its total cost of £2,750. After a survey of Victoria Bridge, the city engineer also advised that a new footbridge was needed to replace the current dilapidated structure at the cost of £2,000, and the Ministry of Health was again asked to sanction the borrowing of this sum.[10]

These expenses did not go unchallenged. At a council meeting on 13 December 1927, dire warnings were issued by Alderman Bush that work on the bridges would push up the rates by an extra 4d in the pound, while councillor Kitley proposed saving money by limiting access to North Parade Bridge to pedestrians. After an hour and a half of heated argument it was decided by a majority of four to refer the plans back for further consideration. Three months later, on 6 March, the question of the bridges returned to the agenda. Kitley was annoyed to hear that the Ministry of Transport had insisted that North Parade Bridge should be open to vehicles, and testily observed that the ministry should not 'dictate to the corporation how the bridges should be dealt with'. Arguably a weightier argument was put forward by Councillor Cook, who feared that the expense of the bridge schemes would 'hinder a much more important matter –slum clearances'. In the end, however, both the North Parade and Grosvenor Bridge proposals were carried by a narrow margin, but the following month the decision on North Parade Bridge was reversed and its future was again 'in the melting pot'. In July 1929, however, after the government offered to pay 75% of the cost, the decision was at last made to upgrade North Parade bridge and open it to unrestricted motor traffic. Even so, it was not until July 1936 that the bridge, encased in ashlar stone and with its foundations strengthened by reinforced concrete, was finally reopened.

In May 1929, the city engineer submitted a plan for replacing the old Victoria toll bridge with a reinforced concrete structure to take 'unrestricted modern traffic', which was accepted by the council. Yet long delays occurred and costs escalated. In December 1936, the council received a letter from Stothert and Pitt pointing out that Victoria Bridge Road ran through their works and that the volume of traffic which would use the bridge, once it was opened, would create an unacceptable level of congestion. As a result, in January 1937 the project was abandoned in favour of building a new bridge to replace the Destructor Bridge on Midland Road, which dated from the 1870s. Not until October 2020 was a new Destructor Bridge finally opened; Victoria Bridge, meanwhile, survived, without significant repairs until 2010, when it was reconstructed to the original design and reopened five years later

The Grosvenor and Cleveland Bridge projects were completed much more quickly. Both were carried out by Lotz and Kier of Stoke-on-Trent. The new Grosvenor foot bridge, which opened in the autumn of 1929, was a minor project compared to the renovation of Cleveland Bridge. Work began on Cleveland Bridge, along with the widening of Bathwick Street, in the spring of 1928. The Surveying Committee was informed by the city engineer that, as 3,000 cubic feet of concrete had to be laid, 'unless he was provided with a new concrete mixer, the job would not be finished in under 100 years'. The committee put his mind to rest by giving him permission to buy a mixer costing £354 from Stothert and Pitt. Widening Bathwick Street on the approach to Cleveland Bridge involved cutting down a number of mature trees. Some residents protested, but were mollified by widening the grass verges and pavements on either side of the street. With the arrival of autumn, however, came further complaints that the verges were so 'churned up so as to resemble a miniature ploughed field' and that the pavements were too high. Work on the bridge proceeded slowly over the winter of 1928-29, and completion was delayed for some weeks by exceptional frosts and snow after Christmas. It was not until the end of April that two steam rollers were able to test the strength of the reconstructed bridge. One of the *Chronicle* journalists, possibly the Bellman, light-heartedly described his impressions of the work involved:

> Such industry – and such a din! The constant clatter of the motor as it produces compressed air for the drills, the hissing of the oxy-acetylene plate-cutter, causing a thousand sparks to fly into the placid waters of the Avon; the rhythmical clanging as sledge-hammer meets crowbar first from one man, then from his mate. Yes, this bridge building is a warm job.[11]

Despite reservations by the City Improvements Committee and the opposition of five councillors, the council decided on 4 June to abolish tolls on all six bridges on 20 June, rather than waiting until August 1932. This was an important landmark in the city's history, and was welcomed by the *Chronicle*, which claimed that visitors regarded the tolls as 'an archaic survival as well as a blot upon the hospitable welcome the Spa desires to give'. The *Daily Express* described their abolition as setting 'an admirable example to the whole country'.

Lord Bath, who had just been granted the freedom of the city, opened Cleveland Bridge in the presence of the mayor and aldermen. Afterwards, celebrations were held in Sydney Gardens where the band of the Gordon Highlanders gave a concert which was followed by a dance. In Widcombe, the ward's three councillors laid on a treat for 520 school children. After the children had assembled in the school playground at 4.30pm, their teachers led them, each clutching a teacup, across Widcombe and North Parade Bridges to have tea in the Old Cricket Field. They were entertained by a Punch and Judy show and the Bath Post Office Band, and at 6.45 were addressed by the mayor, Aubrey Bateman, who explained the significance of the day. When he asked them how they would spend the halfpenny they would no longer have to spend on the toll, he was met with a loud chorus of 'sweets'. One Bathonian remembered decades later the bar of chocolate he was given to mark the occasion.[12] On Friday and Saturday evenings North Parade Bridge and Institution Gardens were illuminated, the illuminations being given added impact by the rise of the 'clover moon', which, to quote the *Chronicle*, ' came up in all its fullness and majesty from behind the rim of the hills, gilding the gentle slopes and furnishing an extra spectacle for sightseers'.

The abolition of tolls had important social and economic consequences for Bath. It physically helped unify the city. Toll free access over Victoria Bridge, for instance, enabled the inhabitants of Twerton to make greater use of Victoria Park. But, as the *Chronicle* pointed out, it had an even more fundamental impact on the lives of thousands of Bathonians:

The opening of the bridges is altering the habits of years of many people. Some admit that they were accustomed to going further round to escape the toll – no inconsiderable burden on a labourers' home where there was a large family. Now they take the route directly. [13]

THE CITY IMPROVEMENT SCHEME

THE REPAIR OF the bridges and the abolition of tolls were relatively straight forward in comparison with the complex process of street widening and road building which was planned for the south-western quadrant. The city improvement scheme involved large-scale slum clearance in Kingsmead, Avon Street and Milk Street, as well as in Dolemeads area of Widcombe. By January 1927, the Housing Committee had drawn up an initial list of some 40 properties to be compulsorily purchased. This was a lengthy and time-consuming business, which tested the patience of those eager to bulldoze Bath's slums. When the committee met in February 1927, Alfred Wills complained testily of attacks from those clamouring for the work to get under way immediately, who had

> no conception of the enormous amount of work involved in the schemes passed in the last two years, Some thought it was only necessary to hold up their hands, and Hey, presto! Next week it was an accomplished fact. The work thrown on the Engineer's Department was simply phenomenal. [14]

In July 1928, the City Improvement Committee approved a detailed plan for the street improvement work authorised by the Bath Corporation Act and for rehousing those made homeless as a result. To keep costs down, the committee recommended cancelling work on six sites, including the Old Bridge, which reduced total expenditure to £459,980.

Nevertheless, the plan was still ambitious, as it involved work at Westgate Buildings, Sawclose, Monmouth Street, Kingsmead Square, Westgate Street, Peter Street, Corn Street, Kingsmead Terrace, New Street, Riverside Road and St. James's Parade. At least 208 houses were to be be demolished – home to 1,500 people – with a further 60 houses earmarked for demolition later. To rehome those affected, 88 one-, two- and three-bedroom flats would be built on the site of the Corporation Depot in Dog Lane. The blocks would form three sides of a square with an open space in the centre, while the south side of the square, fronting the river, would be left open 'so as to provide the maximum amount of sunlight'. Further flats were also planned for adjacent sites, with businesses and shops on the ground floor.

After being scrutinised by the Finance Committee, the plans were available for public inspection in the Guildhall for a month. On Tuesday 25 July, when they were debated by the council, Wills announced that, for the first time, his fellow councillors 'faced realities, and were up against a practical proposition to deal with the slums'. He pointed out that the Dog Lane Flats would 'only solve a quarter of the slum problem' and that further building would be needed as further slums were cleared. Even if the council proceeded with the whole scheme as quickly as it could, it would take ten to fifteen years to implement. When the proposals were put to the vote on Thursday the 26th, 31 councillors backed the scheme, but five remained sceptical if not openly hostile. A few days earlier they had written a highly critical letter to the *Chronicle*, with one of them, George Hughes, claiming that the plans would saddle the ratepayers with a debt, from which it would take a generation to recover. Councillor Long, another of the sceptics, told Wills that the proposals had won the support of 'every profligate gambler in the city, all slum clearance enthusiasts ... reckless motorists; the Labour Party who saw in it a method in the direction of more employment, whether economic or not, and the Socialist Party'.[15]

Such a tirade had little effect in blunting Wills' message that the proposed scheme would not only eliminate the slums but would also be a sound investment in the future of Bath. Apart from a few diehards, public opinion in the city realised that the slum problem had to be 'fixed'. The severe floods of January 1926 and 1927, which had caused so much hardship to slum dwellers and been fully reported in the *Chronicle*, had awakened the social conscience of the city. On 2 January 1926, for example, many families in the Dolemeads spent the night huddled together in their top rooms. Relief agencies set up in the flood-hit areas distributed free milk, bread, cheese, tea sugar and butter.

THE BACKLASH:
REVIVAL OF THE OLD BATH PRESERVATION SOCIETY

THE MINISTRY OF health eventually approved the Dog Lane Flats scheme in 1929, and in 1931, when work on them started, their name was changed to Kingsmead Flats. Elsewhere, though, discontent was growing. The road widening and slum clearance schemes had stirred up the old debate about the nature of Bath and in whose interests it was being administered. Was Bath a Georgian shrine or a modern city with a thriving industrial sector, or could it be both? Since the Bath Corporation Bill had become law the main thrust of the council's plans had been to clear the slums and bring the city into the age of the motorist. Inevitably, its street widening plans threatened gems of Georgian architecture. To many traditionalists, the corporation appeared to show no commitment to the preservation of its Georgian heritage.

Their worst fears seemed to be confirmed when in 1929, two years after the celebrations marking the bicentenary of John Wood the Elder's return to Bath, the Council served a legal 'notice to treat' on the Tenement Venture Trust, which provided flats in Chandos House. This was effectively a compulsory purchase order because of plans to widen Westgate Buildings and raised fears that Chandos House, one of Wood's first buildings in Bath, would be demolished. In fact, the Trust did not move out until 1935 and Chandos House survived. Three years later it was taken over by the Salvation Army as Bath's 'Slum and Good Will Centre'. Nevertheless, it was this 'veritable bombshell', to quote councillor Knox, that triggered the re-emergence of the Old Bath Preservation Society, which had originally been formed to halt the demolition of the north side of Bath Street in 1909. [16] On Monday 10 June 1929, it was relaunched at a meeting presided over by the Archdeacon of Bath, reaffirming the role of its members as 'guardians of the city', which was essentially "a Georgian shrine and national possession"'. Knox gave an impassioned speech pleading for the preservation of Chandos House. He told his audience that a friend who often visited Bath 'bitterly regretted that nearly every time he came ... he found some well-known landmark had gone' and wondered whether the council wanted to make it 'more like an ordinary town'. Knox concluded by emphasising that, 'if they lost the charm of Bath, they would destroy its interest not only to the residents but to the visitors'.

The significance of the beauty of Bath for the tourist industry was not a new message, but in some parts of the city, where many of the inhabitants worked in factories, workshops or on building sites, tourism was not seen as particularly relevant to their lives. An active proponent of this view was Ernest Crawford of 2 Rosehill Terrace, Larkhall. He was a local eccentric and controversialist, who was described by the Bellman as 'a versatile epistolarian'. In March 1928, he wrote to the *Chronicle* arguing that the number of employees who looked after the city's visitors probably represented only five per cent of Bath's workforce:

> Think of all the persons employed in the engineering works, corset works, cabinet works, soap works, cloth works, etc, also the tradesmen in the outlying

districts who only do a local trade in their shops. To most of those I have indicated a visitor to central Bath is about as welcome as a bum-bailiff in a dwelling house.[17]

There was, of course, a divide between industrial Bath and tourist Bath. Yet, despite Crawford's special pleading, tourism did generate both revenue and jobs in the city.

5
THE IMPACT OF THE GENERAL STRIKE AND THE COAL STRIKES, 1925-26

THE PROSPECTS FOR international peace and economic recovery for Britain and Europe in the New Year of 1925 were promising. The London Agreement of August 1924 had ended the prolonged standoff between France and Germany over reparations and terminated the Ruhr crisis. At home the Conservative landslide, however unwelcome to the left, ensured that there would be no more general elections for the next five years. After two years in which there had been three general elections there was at last the prospect of political stability. However, despite these reasons for cautious optimism, there hovered over the country the ever present threat of industrial strife possibly escalating into a general strike.

The number of people out of work was declining, albeit far too slowly. Unemployment remained an uncomfortable reality, and competition for jobs was fierce. For instance, in 1925 the Rector of Combe Hay, Rev CM Becker wrote personally to Owen Keevil, the works manager of the Fuller's Earth Union at Midford and Combe Hay, to see whether there was any work for 'a willing and industrious man who had been in the army'. The man, Mr Allen of Peasedown, had hoped for a job as an underground carter, but he was offered instead employment as a miner, which involved a 48-hour week filling 16 'trams' or trucks every weekday with fuller's earth and another 10 on a Saturday. Desperate for work, another Peasedown man informed Keevil that Allen had been working on farms, while drawing unemployment pay. This annoyed Keevil who reprimanded him by pointing out that 'it was foolish to try and run another man down and that if he had a genuine grouse, he should contact the Labour Exchange'.[1]

Bath's industries showed some modest signs of recovery in 1925. Owing to the widespread depression in the engineering industry, Stothert and Pitt's was unable to pay a dividend on its ordinary shares for the financial year 1924-25, but by July 1925 all its departments were fully occupied. A whole array of cranes was under construction for various harbours and gasworks.

The Fuller's Earth Union was also active in winning contracts in 1925. Keevil clinched a deal with the Celtic Collieries by offering to reduce the price on the fuller's earth used for coal dusting, and also secured a six month contract with Guest, Keen and Nettlefolds at the Dowlais-Cardiff Colliery.[2] At the *Exposition Internationale des Arts Décoratifs et Industriels Modernes* in Paris, Bath Cabinet Makers, who were exhibiting in the British Pavilion, won the *diplome d'honneur* for four pieces of furniture designed by CA Richter – an honour given to only one other company in this class.

The Horstman car company, Lazarus-like, staged another fragile recovery. On 24 October 1924 it had gone into receivership but struggled on under a manager appointed by the receiver. It still manufactured a small number of cars, but its principal income came from servicing and supplying spares for older models, which just about kept the firm on 'life support' until a rescue operation was mounted by the Grosvenor Financial Trust. In the summer of 1925 a number of local businessmen subscribed to the capital of the new company and purchased the assets, lease and goodwill from the receiver. Sidney Horstmann was appointed managing director with full powers to 'employ and dismiss all sub-managers, foremen, clerks, accountants, draughtsmen, servants and other persons employed by the company'.[3]

THE APPROACHING CRISIS

During 1925 the TUC, under the influence of Fred Bramley, its General Secretary, and Arthur Cook, the Secretary of the MFGB, moved politically to the left. There were fears shared both by the government and many voters that it was being penetrated by the communist-dominated Minority Movement, of which Cook was a member. In January 1925 Charles Foxcroft warned a Conservative women's social at Bathwick that

> soon there would be big strikes engineered by the extremists, which would turn a lot of people out of employment and make private enterprise impossible so as to bring in a soviet government in place of the present one.[4]

To many Conservative voters in Bath there was disturbing evidence of socialist activity in the city, which seemed to confirm Foxcroft's dire warnings. The local branch of the ILP, for example, was expanding and announced that it would support measures for the redistribution of wealth beginning with a massive capital levy on individual fortunes. Yet with Bramley's death in 1925 and his replacement by Walter Citrine, the TUC once more fell under the control of the moderates, even if that did not always appear to be so.

The crisis in Britain's out of date and inefficient coal industry threatened to be the catalyst for a general strike or even revolution. Coal production had been in steady decline since 1921. The paralysis of the German mining industry caused by the Ruhr occupation in 1923 gave British coal a brief respite, but the end of the occupation the following year meant that export markets were again flooded with cheap German coal. At the same time, sterling's return to the gold standard in April 1925 at its 1914 parity of one pound to four US dollars forced British exporters to increase their prices way beyond their rivals. In May 1925 Bath's Rotarians were told optimistically by the Director of Studies of the Institute of Banking, that this 'would affect favourably the welfare and happiness of at least two generations' in this country', but in reality it had a devastating impact on coal exports. Locally this could be seen in the Somerset coal fields, where in 1925 unemployment rose and the Dunkerton Colliery was closed. Ripples of the crisis in the Rhondda coalfields also reached Bath, when the GWR, which drew a considerable revenue from transporting Welsh coal to London and the rest of the country, closed the passenger lifts at Bath station as a temporary economy in early April, just as the Easter tourist trade was gathering momentum.

To regain prosperity the coal industry needed to rationalise and modernise, which would involve large scale redundancies and massive investment. The mine owners bluntly informed their men that they must choose between less pay and longer hours, but the MFGB rejected both options. When the union turned down a pay deal, which would have reduced their pay by 2sh a shift, either a coal strike or a lockout by the employers seemed inevitable. On 23 July, with the full support of the transport unions, it announced that a strike in the coal fields would start on the 30th. In anticipation of this, the council's Parks Committee decided to order a reserve supply of anthracite coal for its greenhouses and the same policy was followed by schools and other premises owned by the council. The BTLC drew up plans for setting up a council of action to support the miners. However, at the last moment on 31 July the government blinked and offered to subsidise the miners' current wages for a nine- month period, while at the same time setting up a royal commission under Sir Herbert Samuel to consider the future of the industry. The following day the *Chronicle* reported that

> after a day of great anxiety in which hopes and fears have strangely alternated, the coal crisis is over, a provisional settlement being announced at 4 o'clock yesterday.[5]

The MFGB suspended the strike notice for a fortnight, and then after consulting its members accepted the offer. During these deliberations the BTLC continued plans for establishing a council of action 'to deal with contingencies as they arose' – in other words, if the miners rejected the government's offer. It proposed making the council a 'permanent institution' to deal with 'trouble locally', and on 31 July this was 'confirmed unanimously' subject to ratification at the council's annual meeting in January.[6]

The government's concession met with a mixed response. On the left it was initially seen as a victory for the miners, but Herbert Smith, the President of the MFGB, was quick to point out that 'it was a mere skirmish', adding that 'the main battle has still to be fought and won'. In the Conservative party there were influential politicians such as William Joynson-Hicks, the Home Secretary, who argued that sooner or later the question had to be 'fought out by the people of this land'. In the Bath and Frome branches of the Conservative Party there was some sympathy for the lot of the miner. Pauline Peto, the wife of the Conservative MP for Frome, told a Conservative women's meeting at the Assembly Rooms in April that she had been down a mine in Radstock and found that 'the conditions are very hard and difficult under which these people work'. When she added that, 'if there is any means by which they can be helped by legislation, it ought to be taken seriously', her remark was met with applause.

In a letter to the *Morning Post* in August, Charles Foxcroft called upon the government

> to separate the economic from the revolutionary factors. Miners and mine owners should be alike reminded that their suicidal strife is killing the industry upon which both depend – an industry which can only continue to exist if both parties work their hardest and work together ... Finally, the Reds must be warned in no uncertain voice ... that if 'you ... attempt a political strike to paralyse the nation, the government and the nation will meet you with their utmost resources – and there can be no doubt of the issue'.[7]

What this threat might entail could be glimpsed in Bath when Brigadier-General Blakeney, the Director General of the British Fascists, addressed a meeting in June at Rudloe Park, near Box, which led to the formation of two companies of volunteers who wore the distinctive black shirts of the Italian Fascist movement. Company No 1 was commanded by Lieutenant Ernest Chapel, who had 'a long and distinguished army record' and was 'an expert in physical training', and its members came for the most part from his physical training classes. Company No 2 was led by LJK Blake, a worker at Stothert and Pitt, and recruits came from among his fellow employees. Each company was intended to consist of three troops or platoons with a minimum of six officers and 63 men, and they were to be trained specifically in patrol work, signalling and jujitsu.

The British fascists or *fascisti*, as they were originally known, had been founded by Miss Lintorn-Orman, the grand-daughter of a field-marshal, two years earlier in May 1923. Their inspiration was the Italian Fascisti, who were widely admired. Charles Foxcroft, for example, spoke warmly of Mussolini, painting him as a romantic hero who had saved Italy. Mussolini was also presented as a romantic hero in a popular film based on Hall Caine's novel of 1910, *The Eternal City*, which was shown at the Assembly Rooms in March 1925. Mussolini even made a brief appearance in the film, in which the fascisti were portrayed as the saviours of Italy. According to Robert Benewick, the historian of British fascism, at this stage the British fascists differed markedly from their Italian counterparts, tending to regard fascism as 'the adult growth of the Scout movement'.[8] In September 1925, Chapel, one of the local commanders, took pains to stress how moderate its aims were, pointing out that

> the idea of the force is to act as auxiliary police force in the case of a revolutionary movement. We should only act when called upon by the police. The Fascisti is to help protect the public against the Communists. There is, of course, no intention of the force being armed.[9]

Not everybody in Bath viewed the formation of what was potentially a paramilitary force with equanimity. Bob Hope, a leading member of the congregation of the Ascension Church in Oldfield Park, after listening to an anti-communist tirade in a sermon by the Vicar of Twerton, remarked pointedly in a letter to the *Chronicle* in early October that

> he makes no mention of the British Fascisti ... I saw in your columns the other evening that there were two companies ... being formed in Bath, but I have yet to learn of any Communist Party in the city, so I suppose the Rev. gentleman will be able to sleep in peace as far as Bath is concerned.[10]

Three weeks later a mysterious incident occurred in Box, which some attributed to the local fascisti. Early on Wednesday 28 October, three masked men attacked Tom Coles, an agricultural labourer, who lived with his parents on the Devizes Road, as he was bicycling to work at Hatt Farm. When he turned into the lane, he noticed a large 'saloon type closed-in car standing with the engine purring pointing towards the main road'. He was not particularly worried as vehicles of all sorts would often park there while their drivers had a nap. Suddenly, in Tom Coles' words,

> the door of the car was opened and a man came out straight to me and put his arms around my body leaving my arms and hands free on the handlebars. He tried to lift me off the saddle ... As soon as I saw his motive, I tried to tear his mask off and knocked him in the mouth with my other fist as hard as I could. [Then] another taller man over 6ft high came out of the car. He was wearing glasses. Before he could knock me I knocked him in the glasses as hard I could. I ran back towards the main road in order to have a better chance when the chauffeur who was in livery came out, and as he passed me, he threw something in my face which burned my face and eyes. He then kicked me in the stomach, nearly winding me. I fell to the ground over a ditch into which I rolled, buckling my left arm under me. In case my assailants should again come for me I stopped quiet there pretending to be unconscious.

Then, quite extraordinarily, one of the men pinned onto Coles' prostrate body a note – 'in printed form, but like that of a schoolchild' – with the following message: 'We are sorry. We had the wrong man. We had to do it. He fought like a madman. Will the finder take him home and he will be greatly rewarded.' Coles managed to stagger up the lane to the farm where he fainted in the farmer's arms. He was duly taken home and then to the doctor, 'who ordered him to take things quiet for a day'. The police were mystified by the motive for the attack. There was speculation that it might have something to do with the 'racing fraternity', but, as the *Chronicle* speculated,

> perhaps not unnaturally, in view of the prominence which has been given to the activities of the fascists in the Box district, rumour also connects that movement with the outrage. It has even gone so far as to suggest that an attempt was being made to kidnap someone who was either prominently identified with the movement or against it.[11]

The police apparently did not 'attach much weight to this theory', but they did not dismiss it outright. After all, in March 1925 fascists had kidnapped Harry Pollitt, the general secretary of of the National Minority

Movement, when he was on a train en route to Liverpool. The incident in Box remained a mystery, but the mere fact that this suggestion was made shows that some people in Bath were aware of the potential for fascist violence. A further reminder of the essentially violent nature of fascism, in Italy at any rate, came in March 1926 when the *Chronicle* reported that a Cambridge Rugby Blue and old boy of Downside School had been beaten 'black and blue' by the police at Genoa.

The Royal Commission deliberated on the problems of the mining industry throughout the winter of 1925-26, but to many this was merely the lull before the storm. At the annual meeting of the National Citizens' Union in early February 1926, Councillor Colonel the Hon HS Davey of Lansdown Ward painted an apocalyptic picture of what a general strike would entail:

> There would be no coal, no gas, no electricity, no transport ... There would be no petrol either after a fortnight ... no food in the shops and no milk ... above all there would be the constant probability of dangerous rioting and looting. [12]

To prevent this doomsday scenario, the Organisation for the Maintenance of Supplies (OMS) had been formed in September 1925 with government backing. Its initial task was to prepare for the government a list of volunteers for a range of services and duties. Councillor Davey, the chairman of the Bath branch, appealed for volunteers to present themselves to the OMS office in Broad Street, stressing that their services would be required only in an emergency. In November 1925, England and Wales were divided into ten areas, each under a civil commissioner with a staff of civil servants, who, if an emergency arose, would be called into action by telegram with the code word 'Action'. The OMS was non-political and British fascists were explicitly barred from joining unless they changed their manifesto. In the event, many of them, including General Blakeney, defected to join the OMS.

The Royal Commission's report on the coal industry appeared on 10 March. It rejected nationalisation and longer working hours but did recommend the acquisition of mineral rights by the state and the amalgamation of smaller concerns. More controversially, it also recommended wage cuts as the quickest way to reduce working costs. The first reaction of Fred Swift, the agent of the Somerset Miners' Association, was to compare the report to the curate's egg – 'good in parts' – but it was also the opinion of 'various interests' in the Somerset mining industry that the question of wages would be 'the great bone of contention' – and so it was to prove.

For the next six weeks, mine owners and miners deliberated without result, even though it looked at times as if they might reach a compromise. The sticking point was, as anticipated, the question of wage cuts, which the miners rejected outright, while the owners stubbornly refused to make any concessions. At midnight on 30 April, the General Council of the TUC took over the negotiations on behalf of the miners, and the following day the government declared a national emergency. Unless some last minute solution could be found, a general strike would start at 11.59pm on 3 May.

In the meantime in Bath the council had been preparing for such an eventuality. A committee was set up in April under Thomas Wills with a remit to deal with food supplies in the event of an emergency. Wills aimed to make the committee as representative as possible by inviting the Bath and Twerton Cooperative Society to appoint a representative, and they nominated their general manager.[13] The council also began in January 1926 to stockpile some 1,500 tons of coal in the corporation yard in Dog Lane. This was done on the orders of the mayor without consulting the councillors – or at least without consulting the Labour councillors. The first that Sam Day and AE Cook, both Labour councillors, knew about it, was when the secretary of the Bath branch of the National Union of Railwaymen (NUR) alerted the BTLC that the council had bought an 'enormous quantity of house coal', and urged it to take some action as 'we as ratepayers, have a right to know who is responsible for this, and on whose authority it was purchased'. The BTLC discussed the contents of the letter on 31 March, and Cook declared he knew all about the 'notorious' OMS circular of November, but was not aware of any other instructions. Sarcastically he suggested that the 'mayor was going to run a big social function and intended having a little bonfire on Sham Castle'. The BTLC decided to write to the town clerk, who replied on 9 April that the coal had been ordered on the mayor's instructions 'under the authority of the city council for the benefit of the citizens of Bath'. This, of course, did not satisfy the BTLC, as the coal was obviously intended to counter the effects of an increasingly likely miners' strike. WW Clarke, the Labour candidate for Weston Ward, angrily asked his fellow members at a meeting on 28 April:

> Are we going to allow the Mayor to stand on his dignity, and tell us he bought 1,500 tons of coal? Out of our money he tries to beat our own workmates working in the pits ... He should be made to fetch coal.[14]

The other side of the argument was put by the Bellman, who called the measure an act of 'prudence'.

For Bath's industries, stockpiling coal and coke was far from easy. By the end of January 1926, for example, the Midford works of the Fuller's Earth Union received two months' supply of coke from the Old Silkstone Collieries in Yorkshire. It was offered more but Owen Keevil was unable to accept it because he had nowhere to store it. Three months later, however, he was desperate for further supplies. He had just negotiated a potentially lucrative deal with the Anglo-Persian Oil Company for supplying 150 tons of fuller's earth on a regular basis and had been requested to provide a trial order of five tons, but just at this juncture the growing threat of a general strike threatened to cut off all supplies. On 27 April, Keevil wrote to the coal factors, Dinham Fawcus and Co, enquiring about the dispatch of two trucks of Old Silkstone Coke, and stressing that his business would be in 'an awkward predicament' if they did not arrive. Optimistically, he also asked Fawcus & Co whether the collieries they dealt with possessed any coal and coke reserves, which would enable deliveries to continue 'for a time at any rate'. Although the two trucks of coal were duly dispatched, Keevil was bleakly informed by the company the following day that, 'in the event of a stoppage', it would be impossible to move any coal from the collieries.[15]

THE GENERAL STRIKE

Throughout 2 and 3 May, last-minute talks continued between the government and the TUC, but the chances of success, slim as they were, were effectively torpedoed by the strike of compositors at the *Daily Mail* who refused to print a strongly pro-government leader entitled ' For King and Country'. Baldwin told the TUC that the 'work of the peacemakers [had] been killed by hotheads'. He then handed its delegation what was essentially an ultimatum demanding the miners' acceptance in full of the recommendations of the Royal Commission chaired by Sir Herbert Samuel. Since these advocated pay cuts and the reorganisation of the mining industry, it was rejected by the MFGB, leaving the TUC no other option but to support the miners. Ernest Bevin observed that its duty was now 'to fight for the soul of labour and the salvation of the miners'. The strike began, as planned, at one minute to midnight on 3 May.

The last two days before the strike were a painful reminder to the Bellman of the war years when crowds waited outside the *Chronicle* offices in Westgate Street to get news hot off the press. On Sunday evening, 2 May, Westgate Street was again 'thronged with people' avid for up-to-date information. When a special edition of the *Chronicle* appeared early in the evening 'there was 'a frantic scramble' for copies as newspaper boys rushed up and down the street selling them. The following evening, after the crowds gathered again,

> just before half-past eleven came the dolorous news ... that the strike could not be stopped [and] it was a dejected throng of people who made their several ways homeward, many unwittingly faced by days of inactivity, the number of which no man could with certitude estimate.[16]

On Monday there was a sudden spike in the dispatch of telegrams from the post office, no doubt informing recipients of changing plans. One macabre consequence of the imminent strike was that the inquest on a Peterborough tradesman, who had died under anaesthetic in a Bath nursing home, had to be held on Sunday 2 May, if the body was to be safely conveyed back home by train. It was the first Sunday inquest the city coroner had presided over.

Nationally about one and half million workers went on strike. In Bath some 3,000 people, belonging to 18 trade unions, had downed tools. Transport workers, railwaymen, motor-vehicle builders, construction workers, carpenters, joiners and cabinet makers, as well as builders, tramway staff and typographers, all joined the strike. Most building activity in Bath ceased, but unions allowed work to go ahead at the Royal Mineral Water Hospital where new baths were being installed, and, although all work ceased in the city's railway stations, the dray horses used for deliveries were still cared for by their stablemen. By and large, those on strike throughout the country behaved with forbearance and avoided violence, but tempers flared in the East End of London where food was transported from the docks in convoys guarded by armoured cars and troops with fixed bayonets. In Aberdeen, buses driven by student volunteers were attacked and one bus was forced onto the pavement killing a pedestrian. Even in Bath, there was at least one potentially serious incident. Most of the tram and bus staff joined the strike, but on Wednesday 4 May Mr Withers, a union member, dared to brave the picket lines, and was instructed to drive a bus on the Lambridge-Devonshire Buildings route. On his return journey a gang of strikers decided to intercept the bus at the Old Bridge. Another group had apparently taken a taxi up to Devonshire Buildings where, posing as bona fide passengers, they boarded the bus. When it reached the Old Bridge, 'they were the first to act in stopping it in connivance with the main body of strikers, numbering some hundreds'. What happened next was graphically described in the *Chronicle*:

As it came down the Wells Road, the strikers formed a cordon across the road with a view to bringing it to a halt. The driver, however, did not heed this obstruction. and went straight ahead [over] the Old Bridge. As the human line gave way to it, men clambered on to the bus, turned off the petrol ... and then not too gently hauled the driver out of his seat and left the vehicle by the side of the road. [17]

*Strikers rushing the Bath Tramways Bus in the Wells Rd on Wednesday 5 May (*Bath Chronicle, *8 May 1926)*

Inevitably, the incident 'caused much alarm' to the passengers, but the situation was dealt with by the speedy arrival of a police car containing three constables, a police inspector and a tramways' inspector. The bus was then driven off. There were no arrests and the strikers returned via Southgate Street to the Guildhall 'in very high spirits'. The driver was given another bus to drive, but this time he worked under police protection, and during the course of the day carried nearly 700 passengers.

There was a further incident in Walcot Street that afternoon when 'booing strikers' attempted to intercept another bus, but, before they succeeded, the Chief Constable himself 'drove up in his car and the men beyond booing did nothing'. On Friday, another driver, who was also a member of the TGWU, reported for duty at the Kensington garage, which was being monitored by pickets. A crowd of nearly 200 strikers rapidly assembled. Again, the police were alerted, and three constables were detailed to sit in the front seats of the bus to guarantee the driver's safety. The manager of the Bath Electric Tramways

Co, WE Hardy, responded to these incidents by presenting his workers with an ultimatum. A notice was posted on the depot gates announcing that any man not reporting for work by 12 noon, Saturday, 8 May, would not be guaranteed his job. Volunteers, protected by special constables. would be used instead to run the buses and trams. This ultimatum had some success, with some drivers returning to work the following day, and on the Monday a regular service was reinstated.

Like their colleagues in the national press, the typesetters, stereotyping and machinery staff of the *Bath Chronicle* walked out on the night of Monday 3 May. The management was particularly incensed that they had broken their contract with the paper by not giving two weeks statutory notice. James Tarrant, the secretary of the Bath Council of Action, who was himself a typesetter, justified the walkout by pointing out that the *Chronicle's* staff had come out in support of the miners, and, when the trouble was over, 'they would go back to their places'. The stereotyping and rotary machine staff soon returned to work, but the typesetting staff were made of sterner stuff and remained on strike. To keep on printing the special emergency newspapers, the editorial staff had to set the type themselves. Even the services of veteran journalist 'Uncle Fred' were called upon.

On Wednesday 5 May, the *Bath Chronicle* appeared in a 'reasonably complete form', but the most reliable source of news was the BBC, whose bulletins were exhibited in often incoherent and badly-spelt summaries posted in shop windows. Meanwhile, the sale of wirelesses boomed. The Earl and Countess Temple had an elaborate wireless set installed at Newton Park in March, but it took nearly three months before the reception was deemed satisfactory by their agent.[18] Most people had to make do with more humble models bought, for instance, from Bentley-Hunt and Vanstone in Wood Street. So many 'wireless poles or aerials were erected in the Oldfield Park district', however, that it 'was then aptly nicknamed 'Pole-field Park'.

Each union had its local strike committee, which controlled the activities of its members. The local branch of the Amalgamated Union of Distributive and Allied Workers initially called out the Co-op's drivers, but, after the intervention of the chairman of the Bath and Twerton branch, permission was obtained from its strike committee for transport workers to deliver milk and foodstuffs to the Co-op's customers.[19] The activities of the various unions were coordinated by the council of action at the Labour Party headquarters in Green Park, which sat every day during the strike from 9am until midnight. It threw open its doors to workers who had been laid off to use its premises as a club. It became so crowded that the Woodworkers moved to Foresters'

Hall, the Railwaymen to the Adult School in Oldfield Park and the Tramway workers to the Trades and Labour Institute.

Apart from the incidents on Wells Road and in Walcot, the strike was conducted in Bath in an atmosphere of restraint with occasional flashes of humour on both sides. On Wednesday 5 May, a speaker at one of several meetings in Sawclose assured Mayor Chivers, who presided over the meetings, that he would have no trouble with the strikers. He even went on to say that, 'I think the police and our people will work well together ... in keeping order'. This was a message echoed by several of the leading members of the Bath Labour Party, and many strikers simply retired to their allotments. Fred Swift appealed to the Somerset miners at a meeting in Midsomer Norton 'to conduct the fight in a quiet and orderly manner'. Even the conservative-minded Bellman conceded that it was only fair to the strikers 'to say that being on strike, they generally exercised a restraint, which was commendable' The fire-eating MP for Bath, Charles Foxcroft, while describing the strike as the event 'for which England's enemies have been hoping and working for many months', was also careful to stress 'that none of us [should] say anything which can in any way embitter strife', while doing 'everything we can to help the government carry on'. By the end of the first week of the strike, Bath's chief constable was reported in the *Chronicle* as 'being very pleased with the general behaviour of the strikers and crowds in the city'.

A crucial role in defeating the strike right across the country was played by volunteers. Attention focussed on what Roy Hattersley has called the 'celebrity strike breakers' or the 'plus four brigade', of which there were a few in Bath. A photo of CE Pitman, the Oxford stroke in the 'Varsity race' and member of Pitman family, on the footplate of an LMS locomotive, featured prominently on the front page of the *Chronicle* on 15 May. Another sportsman, Edward Collings, the Bath and Somerset bowler, volunteered to drive mail from Bath to various outlying towns. However, the great mass of volunteers came, to quote Hattersley again, 'from the usually reticent middle classes'.[20] Despite the fears of many, the local fascist movement played no part in countering the strike. Nationally, fascism was weakened by the defection of its leader, General Blakeney, to form the British Loyalists, who cooperated fully with the OMS.

At the start of the strike a recruitment office for volunteers was immediately opened in the Guildhall, and within days 'fully a thousand' had enlisted. Volunteers were classified according to their suitability for particular types of work, and it was left to employers to take up the offers. Many of the volunteers wanted to drive vehicles, but the *Chronicle* also reported that offers of clerical assistance are abundant, and many, both male and female, are willing to engage in canteen work. There are also volunteers for railway, tram and postal duties and general labourers by the score are willing to put their hands to anything.[21]

Road transport was the key to countering the impact of the strike. During previous railway strikes, the country had been crippled within days, but now independent non- unionised road hauliers could transport vital food supplies, and car drivers could rapidly learn how to drive buses, vans and lorries. This combination of independent haulage firms and volunteer drivers was able to keep Bath supplied. One 'old school' volunteer caused some amusement by driving a lorry while wearing spats. The *Chronicle* reported on fifth day of the strike that

> nothing could be smoother than the passage of food into the city. It is coming out of Bristol and other centres to Bath with surprising ease, and the transport arrangements are more than sufficient. The position is better than in any previous strike. 'Not a single hitch anywhere' is the verdict of the Food Controller.[22]

When the Strike began, there was a month's reserve of meat in cold storage in Bath. Initially there was a run on sugar, but grocers were ordered to allow families or individuals only what they usually ordered per week, and prices remained at their normal level. There was inevitably a temptation to stock up on luxuries such as alcohol. One woman was reported to have entered a wine merchant's shop in 'a hurried state' and told the shopkeeper that

> now that the strike is on things will be getting very short. I want six bottles of gin, twelve bottles of port, twelve bottles of whisky and enough syphons of soda ... 'Will that be all, Ma'am, asked the shopman?' 'Yes for today', said the woman.[23]

Many local shopkeepers and publicans made their own transport arrangements. 'One leading grocer' personally unloaded supplies from a railway wagon in the sidings at Mangotsfield, while a publican hired a lorry labelled prominently 'Food Only' to deliver beer from Trowbridge. Bath bakers sent a car to Harwich to collect a load of yeast. Canteen committees were set up to make arrangements for feeding long distance lorry drivers. At Calne, meals were provided for some 300 drivers, while nearly 7,000 meals were produced at Chippenham. At Marlborough, sleeping facilities were laid on for 100 long-distance drivers. Buses and charabancs were able to provide a skeleton service. Coaches for Bristol left New Bond Street at 8.15, 8.30 and 9am each day, while the Lavington Company, whose drivers were non-unionised, provided a regular service from Devizes, Steeple Ashton and other Wiltshire towns to Bath. An occasional charabanc could be seen in Bath heading for Birmingham, London or Bournemouth, but the local White Line Company was ordered by the regional commissioner to send its coaches to Bulford camp for possible emergency troop movements. Commuters from Trowbridge to Bath were helped by the establishment of a special bus service which ran three times a day between the two towns.

Petrol rationing was avoided by giving priority to vehicles required for essential services, and petrol dumps, guarded by volunteers, were established. In North Wiltshire 'a strike comedy' was reported after two volunteers spent the night mistakenly guarding a water cistern rather than a petrol dump. Nationally, the police were given instructions to exercise discretion if a car did not have an excise license, and parking rules were 'considerably relaxed'. Cars could be parked anywhere in a street, provided they did not cause an obstruction. Motorists driving longer distances who were ready to share their journey with a passenger were asked to inform the volunteer bureau at the Guildhall, where those needing lifts could register their requests. It was from there, too, that the post office enrolled owners of private cars to fetch mail. Locally, pedestrians facing long walks did not hesitate to hitch a lift from passing vehicles. One evening, two Bathonians walking home from the Bristol tram terminus at Brislington, decided on the off chance to hail a passing motorist, who turned out to be a Keynsham doctor returning from seeing a patient. After calling into his home to check that there were no more urgent cases, he drove them on to the Globe Inn at Newton St. Loe, from where they continued their journey on foot. Another Bathonian, a clergyman, was stranded in Monmouthshire and managed to hitch a lift almost as far as Bath in a motor hearse 'complete with corpse'.

It was much easier to drive cars and lorries than run trains. Nevertheless, with the help of the 30 volunteers who were assigned for work on the railways in Bath and the few staff not on strike, a skeleton service could be organised. On Friday 7 May, the GWR ran 15 trains to Paddington, Salisbury, South Wales and the West of England. On the afternoon of Wednesday the 5th, Mr J Davis, the stationmaster at the LMS station in Bath, took a light engine from the sheds to Westerleigh sidings, and after dropping some consignments of perishable goods off in Bristol, returned to Bath with five wagons. According to the *Chronicle*, however, by the end of the first week of the strike, Bath's LMS station had 'assumed a comparatively normal appearance'. A regular timetable was in force on both the Midland and Somerset & Dorset lines, and 'the only exceptional feature was the absence of the daily papers on the book stall'.

Crucial to the maintenance of morale in Bath, as elsewhere, was the normal functioning of the gas and electricity works and an adequate supply of coal being available to meet the basic needs of the population. There were no stoppages at either the gasworks, which had sufficient coal for three months, or the electricity generating station. Coal was strictly rationed for both the general population and industry.

Permits were issued by the coal controller for Bath, the city engineer Frank Sissons, under the direction of the Coal Emergency Office in Bristol. Householders were limited to receiving one cwt (51kg) per week, and only then if they had less than 5 cwt in their cellars, while industries were entitled to only half their normal supply. All shop window lighting and illuminated advertisements were also banned. Owing to the demand for coal permits, the office issuing them had to be moved from the Guildhall into the Market where it was open from 9am to 9pm, with a one-hour lunch break. On Wednesday 5 May, 1,200 permits were issued. On the following day, a further 1,800 were issued, with 500 being handed out in the space of just two hours. Rationing ensured that Bath had sufficient reserves, but one problem was the unseasonable cold, which led to greater consumption. The logistics of supplying rural areas proved more difficult, but a separate coal control office was set up by the rural district council in Queen Square.

What impact did the strike have on the people of Bath and the neighbouring towns and villages? Apart from the Somerset miners, those most affected were commuters and workers in industries which were forced to shut down or reduce their hours because of logistical problems. Bath and Portland Stone Firms Ltd, for example, had to close down temporarily because of transport difficulties. At Bradford on Avon, Spencer Moulton's rubber mills had to close on 6 May and during the following week only worked half time for three days. This was due not to lack of fuel but to the inability to transport goods. Up to 6 May, the situation at the Bradford Labour Exchange was 'normal', but the following day extra staff had to be employed to meet the increased demand caused by the mills' closure. Otherwise, life in Bath and the surrounding countryside continued much as normal. William Chun, who was still living with his parents at 3 Cork Terrace, Lower Weston, mentioned the strike only once in his diary, when on 6 May it led to the cancellation of his scouting activities. Despite the strike, he continued to work daily from 8am to 6pm at Eyres & Sons, milliners and court dressmakers, in Milsom Street. The entries for the following two days, however, read as if there were no problems with the world:

> Friday 7 May: 'Work 8am till 6pm. Wolf cub games from 7 till 8.45. Went over to Mr Davis and had my hair cut and a shave.
> Saturday 8 May: Work 8am till 1pm. When I reached home, I cleaned my boots then had my bath.[24]

The spa worked right through the strike, and it was calculated that overall there were only 10% less visitors than normal. On the evening of Saturday 8 May, at the end of the last pump room concert of the season, the audience 'instinctively' joined in singing the first verse of the national anthem. Yet there was nevertheless an undercurrent of fear and apprehension as to where the strike might lead. After all, a light cruiser had been moored at Avonmouth and a destroyer in the Cumberland Basin in Bristol as rather sinister precautions against possible revolution. As an antidote to this anxiety, the manager of Bath's Palace Theatre went to enormous lengths to put on a show to replace a revue cancelled due to the strike. He 'literally scoured the country by motor' and managed to assemble a company of artistes who performed a series of individual turns which the theatre critic of the *Chronicle* judged to be 'surprising for their variety, their all-round excellence and effective appeal', observing that good humour is always a necessity, but 'especially so in times of stress like these'.

The churches and the mayor attempted to create a climate of moderation and peaceful debate. Many churches were open for prayer and intercession during the strike. Beginning on 7 May, inter-denominational services of intercession were held every day in the Abbey for the duration of the strike. The mayor, who was an old-fashioned Liberal, chaired a meeting of several hundred strikers in Sawclose on both Wednesday and Thursday afternoons. He listened to speeches by James Tarrant, the secretary of the Bath Council of Action, and the organising secretary for the South West branch of the NUR, JW Brown. Chivers was emollient and good humoured, and stressed that he had every sympathy with efforts to better the conditions of the miners, but 'wanted to know the facts'. When another large meeting of strikers congregated in Sawclose the following day, there was a measured and good-humoured exchange of opinions. Chivers provocatively posed the questions,

How are you going to help the miner by leaving your employment and making yourselves all the poorer and so less able to help him, instead of making a levy upon yourselves and helping him in that way?' and 'If the strike was to be a universal one, which would bring paralysis on the body politic, how would the miner benefit?[25]

Chivers' arguments were rejected but the atmosphere of the meeting was 'of an exceedingly friendly character' and concluded with a vote of thanks to the mayor.

The aftermath

The TUC had backed the miners, but it was as wary as the government of a state of prolonged political chaos that could lead to revolution. Once it was clear that the government was able to move essential supplies, it could see no solution but a resumption of negotiations. It responded favourably to Herbert Samuel's proposals for setting up a national wages board for the coal industry and an advisory committee on reorganisation, and, contrary to the miners' wishes, called off the general strike on the evening of Wednesday 12 May.

Meeting in Sawclose that afternoon, supporters of the strike were unaware that the TUC was about to withdraw its support. Malcolm Hardyman, a prominent member of the local Labour Party, rashly claimed that 'victory was in the air' and that 'the TUC would not submit to any condition short of victory'. Replying to rumours that the police had taken over the TUC headquarters in London, he issued just the sort of the clarion call to revolt that the TUC was so desperate to avoid:

> If that has happened, other trade union headquarters will be taken over. If it is so, remember this: When one Council of Action goes, another can be formed, and there are sufficient men on strike in Bath today to make sufficient Councils of Action to keep every special constable they can enlist busy, until they are released. That's all I have got to say.[26]

By the evening, wireless bulletins had made it clear that there had been no victory, and that the TUC had effectively abandoned the miners. Orders were immediately given by Earl Stanhope, Civil Commissioner for the South Western district, to the volunteer service centres to cease recruiting, although the rest of the emergency arrangements would remain in place for as long as the coal strike continued. Meeting again in Sawclose the following day, the local council of action tried to come to terms with the TUC's decision. Winding up the proceedings, George Ward, the prospective Labour parliamentary candidate for Westbury, attempted to put a brave face on the TUC's surrender by stressing that 'the whole Labour movement both politically and industrially was fifty percent higher in the estimation of the people than it was a fortnight ago'. While distancing himself from the communists he lashed out at the 'British fascisti', who 'ought to go with all speed to the homes established for the mentally deficient'.

The next day, several hundred miners from the Somerset coalfields trudged into Bath for another political meeting. The febrile atmosphere of the time is indicated by an incident at Odd Down on the afternoon of Friday 14 May, a vivid description of which was given in a letter from Owen Keevil, the manager of the Fuller's Earth Union, to J Lambern of Woodside Cottages:

> At 4.45 yesterday afternoon as two of my men Mr S Densley and Mr E West were passing along the main road near your house, they were grossly insulted by your wife. I cannot put into writing the filthy language she used towards these two men without provocation, but amongst other things she called them blacklegs. Densley and West were close behind a procession of several hundred miners who were passing over the hill en route to a meeting in Bath. Had these colliers overheard your wife's remarks it is almost certain that there would have been a serious breach of the peace because the colliers were naturally not in a very amiable frame of mind, and they would undoubtedly have retaliated against men whom your wife publicly proclaimed as blacklegs. Densley and West are not blacklegs and never have been. [27]

Keevil demanded a written apology from Mrs Lambern to his two employees. If she refused, he threatened to take out a summons against her for 'foul language on the public highway' and 'for conduct calculated to create a serious breach of the peace'. As there is no record of such a summons in Keevil's correspondence, one can but assume that an apology was offered and accepted.

In Bath, amongst the middle classes, the collapse of the general strike was met with a feeling of profound relief that, to quote the Bellman, 'the long awaited thunderstorm' had broken and 'the long anticipated electrical discharge ... taken place'. Amongst the working classes, feelings ranged from anger at the TUC's alleged betrayal to resigned acceptance. The immediate problem facing the strikers was the refusal of some employers to re-engage them on their original terms of employment. The government had called upon both masters and men to resume work in 'a spirit of cooperation' and to avoid 'victimisation'. Initially the railway companies ignored this plea and insisted that the unions should acknowledge their liability in respect of their broken contracts, which would enable the railway companies to claim damages from the strikers and unions. The unions rejected this and in Bath and elsewhere most railway staff remained on strike on Thursday 13 and Friday 14 May. On the Friday afternoon, a compromise was negotiated and there was a general return to work the following day. Building workers also began to return to work, on Friday joiners and cabinet makers took up their tools again, and on Monday, masons and plasterers. By Friday afternoon all *Bath Chronicle* staff had also resumed work.

The return to work by former tram and bus employees did not proceed so smoothly. WE Hardy, the managing director of Bath Electric Tramways, was adamant that the company would not rehire any of its former staff unless they renounced their union membership. By the end of June, the majority had accepted this ultimatum, hoping that the prime minister's pledge that no worker would be victimised for taking part in the strike would eventually ensure that the company's ban on union membership would be lifted. Thirty-four employees, however, refused to comply and were left to tramp the streets. Neither Labour councillors nor the BTLC could persuade the company to change its mind. Despite initial assurances from some unions that their members would not return to work until the tramway men had been reinstated, there was little enthusiasm in the city for further strike action. In July, the BTLC passed a motion recommending a tram boycott, and a month later on 12 August organised a sparsely attended protest meeting in Sawclose, which in torrential rain was addressed by the Swindon representative of the TGWU. By the end of October the dispute remained unresolved. The tram boycott proved ineffective, and at its meeting on 27 October the BTLC could only promise to explore further channels of assistance, although on a more practical level it had paid out £84 to the men affected. [28]

It took several weeks for disruption to the railways and the docks caused by the strike to be overcome, and this resulted in considerable logistical problems. At the Bathford Paper Mills, for example, Henry Tabb, the managing director, shortly before the general strike had ordered ten tons of sulphate of ammonia from Henderson, Craig and Co, but the day after the strike ended the company told him they had no idea when it would turn up 'as so far everything here is at a standstill'. A fortnight later, the best they could say is that they hoped to get the order to Bristol 'in about two weeks hence' and pointed out that 'transport both by rail and shipping is terribly slow – congestion being met at every point'. They did, however, offer to send two tons from their London stock, as long as the 'GW Railway will accept the traffic', but even this was by no means certain, as several GWR goods stations had refused to accept any more consignments. At the end of May, work at the paper mills was placed in jeopardy when 40 boxes of starch failed to turn up. The London firm of Sir John Francis Ltd explained to Tabb, what had happened:

> We have now heard from our London Office ... They had no idea the starch had not left London, as they were told on May 3rd that it was on rail [sic]. It appears now that it was put back in the warehouse to make way for foodstuffs, and the wharfingers say that, owing to congestion at the wharves and the fact that foodstuffs are, even now, given preference over any other goods, it has not been possible to forward this consignment. It is scandalous business even taking into consideration the strike difficulties. [29]

THE MINERS REMAIN ON STRIKE

THE COAL STRIKE did not end on 12 May as the miners defiantly continued to reject any settlement that involved a cut in their pay, and the employers responded with a lockout. On 14 May, the government offered the miners a new deal which involved rationalisation of the pits, a temporary increase in working hours, and financial assistance to redundant miners coupled with increased welfare benefits. They insisted, however, that there had to be pay cuts, and the proposal was rejected by both the miners and the mine owners. The Somerset miners supported their union, but had no issues with their own employers, who had offered them, as one miner pointed out in August in a letter to the *Chronicle*, 'the old hours and the old pay'. Nevertheless, they loyally rallied to the support of their colleagues in other coalfields. The *Chronicle* reported on 26 June that, 'in the Somerset coalfields ... circumstances remain exactly as when work ceased on April 30th. The men are still firm in their resolve not to commence work pending the national settlement.'

As the strike dragged on, the suffering of the miners became more acute, awakening widespread sympathy across the country. In Bath, efforts were made to raise money to ease the impact of the strike on the Somerset miners' families, not only by the cooperative movement and the BTLC, but also by the churches. The Prince of Wales, who was a large landowner in the Somerset coalfield area, gave £10, but was easily outdone both by Mayor Chivers who gave £50 and the Bath and District Free Churches who raised the large sum of £100. The BTLC organised a series of concerts and dances to raise money for the miners, and at their weekly meeting on 27 October the secretary of the Somerset Miners' and Children's Distress Fund

> explained in detail the mode of procedure for distributing the monies received and reported how they were endeavouring to replace boots and shoes of men, women, and children in the area. He also gave in detail the procedure adopted for distributing the gift of clothing and footwear, which showed [that] an up-to-date organisation and methods were in evidence.[30]

Many in the Labour movement felt that the TUC and Labour party had betrayed the miners and been instrumental in the failure of the general strike. Walter Scobell, the prospective Labour candidate for Bath, resigned from the party in protest. At its meeting on 25 August, the BTLC decided to boycott a conference in Bristol organised by the TUC to consider ways of raising money for the miners, and instead donated what it would have cost to send two representatives to Bristol to the Miners' Distress Fund. Stanley Gould, a prominent member, observed that it would be 'far more to the [TUC's] credit to first of all make it public why they let the miners down'.

Throughout October a steady trickle of miners returned to work. By 13 October, 218,000 out of a national workforce of 1.25 million had returned, despite every effort by the MFGB to stop them. At the end of September it had defiantly called out the safety men in the pits, an action which the chairman of the Labour Party described as 'the sightless Samson feeling for a grip of the pillars of the temple'. In the Somerset coalfield, work at Norton Hill Colliery resumed on 12 October, and over the next five weeks miners began to return to the other pits. Possibly in protest at these developments, at about 9 o'clock on the evening of Thursday 28 October an incident occurred at Middle Pit Colliery, Radstock, which could have had disastrous consequences. The night watchman, George Short, told the *Chronicle's* reporter that he had noticed a figure behaving suspiciously near the colliery's winding tower:

> Thinking he was looking for coal, I shouted to him, 'Now then old man, that won't burn'. No sooner had I said this than the man dashed away in the darkness around the back of the pit, and up the incline towards Clandown.[31]

Short immediately went to the spot where he had seen the man and discovered several canisters of high explosive together with detonators and a fuse primed for lighting.

Had they been detonated, the destruction of the winding tower would have led to the flooding of two pits, and the neighbouring gasworks would also have been severely damaged. Extra police were immediately drafted into the coalfield and billeted at South Hill House, Radstock, which belonged the colliery owner, Sir Frank Beauchamp. The police superintendent stressed that the behaviour of the miners had in general been 'exemplary' during the long drawn-out dispute, but 'that it was no longer safe to leave things to chance'.

Dunkerton Colliery, one of the mines in the Somerset coalfield. It ceased working in 1925 but many of its miners moved on to work in other pits.(Museum of Bath at Work)

Meanwhile, support for the coal strike was waning. In early November, the Nottinghamshire miners formed their own union and the TUC refused to place an embargo on the movement of foreign coal. Finally, on 20 November, the national strike ended, and four days later representatives of the Somerset miners recommended that those pits still on strike should resume work. After meetings throughout the coalfield, the recommendation was accepted, the men went to the colliery offices to sign up and work resumed in many of the pits on Saturday 27 November.

The Impact on Bath

In early October, the *Chronicle* observed that over the summer Bath had escaped the worse effects of the coal stoppage, except for the impact on local investors of their 'vanished dividends'. At the end of May, coal stocks in the city, thanks to the contingency supplies at Dog Lane Yard, were more than sufficient for domestic use.

While Bristol had had to cut its ration per household to half a cwt per week, Bath was able to provide the full ration of one cwt both to the city and the outlying villages. In June the number of permits issued had fallen dramatically partly because a small amount of coal (28 lbs) could be still picked up without a coupon, but also because households were increasingly switching to cooking by gas. The prolonged coal strike initially posed far greater logistical problems for local industries than it did for individual households. Stothert and Pitt, for instance had won an impressive number of contracts for cranes for Calcutta (Kolkata), Karachi and Santos in Brazil, in the teeth of German competition, but, as Sir Percy Stothert told a meeting of shareholders in the Grand Pump Room Hotel in October, the strike prevented the factory from obtaining the material to carry out those contracts, and consequently, 'instead of men working full time, they were able to work only four days'. Stothert accused the miners of causing an 'enormous amount of difficulty and trouble' for their fellow workers.

For the duration of the coal strike, businesses were required to apply for permits from the local coal controller before they could order coal in any quantity. This was a complex, bureaucratic and often stressful process, which tested the patience of Owen Keevil, the plain-speaking manager of the Fuller's Earth Union. In his efforts to obtain the coal needed to heat the steam kilns at Tucking Mill, where the fuller's earth was dried after it had been mined, he had a series of acrimonious exchanges with RH Whittington, the clerk to the council, who had been appointed coal controller for the rural district council. On 26 May, Whittington was at first willing to issue a permit for only 3½ tons which would have kept the kilns going for just over a day. In a letter of 26 May, Keevil argued trenchantly that this was an uneconomic use of coal:

> We seriously suggest that the allowance to us of 7 tons per week, thereby enabling us to maintain our employees in full work, is a more economical proposition from your standpoint than allowing us 3 ½ tons of coal per week, fully two tons of which would be wasted in raising heat, and in the end giving our employees 1 to 1 ½ days per week only.

Whittington was persuaded, but approval for the full seven tons had to be obtained from his superior at Bristol. Keevil duly telephoned the Bristol office and finally gained permission to take possession of a truck of coal which was due to arrive at Midford 'any day now', but was warned by Whittington that 'the issue of the present permit would not be taken as a precedent'. [32]

Keevil ran into further difficulties in an attempt to obtain coke from the Bath Gas Light and Coke Company. On 27 May an order for 24 tons of coke for the Fuller's Earth Union had been accepted inadvertently in the absence of the manager, who on his return tried to cancel it. To avert this, Keevil dangled the possibility of future orders in front of him after the strike had ended, and implied that he also had a moral, indeed patriotic, responsibility towards thousands of Yorkshire mill workers:

> After speaking with you yesterday we got into touch with the Coal Emergency Officer. Our material is essential to upward of 100 cloth mills in Yorkshire and these cloth mills probably employ close on 10,000 hands. It is certain that if we have to close down for want of fuel these cloth mills in due course will have to do the same thing because they cannot get Fuller's Earth anywhere but from us. This fact so impressed the Coal Emergency Officer that he gave us straight away a permit and suggested that we should get in touch with you again and urge you to take a national view of our requirement rather than merely a local view. It is in the hope that you will do this that he has granted us one week's permit only, and we are to communicate with him again after we hear finally from you.[33]

This letter won over Wesley Whimster, the engineer and manager of the Bath Gasworks, and at the end of May Keevil obtained a delivery of gas coke.

Keevil had been told wrongly by the Bristol office that firms could buy as much imported coal as they could obtain without having first to get a permit from the local coal controller. Consequently, on 1 June, the day before the truck containing his seven tons of coal finally arrived at Midford, he somewhat rashly vented his frustration about the red tape involved in securing a permit on Whittington:

> We do not anticipate having to approach you again for coal supplies and we shall certainly try to avoid doing so. Upon the two occasions when we have had to speak to you, you have treated us with scant courtesy and extreme curtness. The regulations have compelled us to approach you as the official responsible for the control of fuel, and we certainly think that an official who takes on these duties in difficult times like these should treat manufacturers with more courtesy and tact than you have accorded us.

This clearly stung Whittington, who wrote back by return of post: 'You have no justification in making [these] remarks and until you withdraw them and apologise, I decline to hold any further communication with you.'[34]

He also accused Keevil of claiming a permit for the delivery of coal on 'a misstatement of the facts' with regard to the Yorkshire Mills. In reply, Keevil conceded that he had been offensive and 'withdrew the statements' to which Whittington had taken offence, but 'was horrified' to hear that Whittington thought he was deliberately exaggerating the possibility of unemployment in the mills to obtain a permit. On the contrary, he stressed that 'it was correct in every sense'. Oil was poured upon troubled waters by Whittington's assistant who diplomatically wrote:

> I feel certain if Mr Whittington were here, he would accept your withdrawal of the statement to which he took exception. In view of the particulars you now furnish and your emergency request for a further permit to clear the truck at Midford station, I herewith enclose the necessary permit.[35]

Despite this concession, Keevil was finding it increasingly difficult to secure sufficient coal supplies, and contemplated closing the works for the duration of the coal strike, but was overruled by his head office in Redhill. He thus had no option but to continue to deal with Whittington – and relations did not improve. Whittington's accusations of 'inconsistencies' in the company's paper work, which required 'explanations', again led an exasperated Keevil to complain on 16 June that

> your attitude towards us appears to be one of suspicion that we are trying to acquire unnecessary coal, and that we are not at all particular what we say in order to get it. This is not in accordance with the traditions and principles of the firm I represent.[36]

Despite Whittington's retort the following day that 'it is evident that neither accuracy nor ordinary courtesy can be expected of you', the Fuller's Earth Union was permitted to acquire ten tons of steam coal, but permission only applied to coal released by the South Wales Coal Emergency Committee, which had to be purchased through Dinham Fawcus and Co of the Coal Exchange in London.[37]

During the next five months, Keevil managed to keep the Works open, although trade was very quiet in August. He contacted old customers and in October exported 20 tons of fuller's earth to Sydney. Despite his spats with the permit office, he bought coal, sometimes of dubious quality, from wherever he could find it. In September, for instance, he managed to secure a truck load of Westphalian coal only to find that it was 'utter rubbish'. Gradually, however,

An advertisement for fuller's earth products and an aerial view of its Combe Hay works on the Radstock Road, near Bath (Museum of Bath at Work)

local coal supplies increased, first of all from the Somerset and Nottinghamshire coal fields, but by early December Keevil was able to revive the firm's former contacts with the Welsh collieries.[38]

By early October, as it became colder, household demand for coal far outstripped supply. Normally, coal cellars were restocked in the summer, but in 1926 this had hardly been possible. Foreign coal was to all intents and purposes unavailable as it was snapped up by factories wherever possible. The Bath Gas Company sold some 7,000 tons of coke, but most of this went to industry and the city's bakeries. In October, there was such a rush to obtain permits that the coal office was moved to the former premises of the *Bath Herald* in Northgate Street so that it could handle the larger numbers of applications. In the first week of November, the number of permits totalled 7,526, and the lengthy queues that formed were depressingly reminiscent of wartime. According to the *Chronicle*, applicants had 'to pass up the side entrance and queue up towards the front door, taking their permits as they pass out'. To those living in the outskirts of Bath, the process could take up the best part of a morning or afternoon. It was, however, possible to avoid the delays by ordering several weeks' permits at a time by post. The *Chronicle* reminded its readers in early October that 'general self-denial and sparing use are a civic duty as much today as in the heroic days of the Great War'. However, in early November the situation eased as the coal ration was doubled so that each householder was allowed 2 cwts of coal and 4 cwts of coke every fortnight.

As substitutes for coal, peat was burnt in some homes, and in a number of cases businesses were reduced to burning old timber. For those who could afford it, the most effective way to avoid the use of coal was to switch over to gas or electric cookers and heaters. There was, according to the *Chronicle*, 'a practically unprecedented rush to get gas heating stoves installed'. Fortunately the Bath Gas Company had a large stock of stoves and its employees worked flat out fitting them. Not surprisingly, there were record sales of gas cookers and fires in 1926, but the gasworks was dependent on coal. In May, it had sufficient reserves to last 12 weeks, but to maintain those reserves it had to buy foreign coal, especially from America. By the autumn, coal and transport costs had risen 400% so it was inevitable that gas prices went up – initially by a penny a therm, with a further rise of a penny in November. Schools were instructed to economise on the use of coal by giving their pupils more physical exercise than normal to keep them warm and using as few classrooms as possible. Hospitals were better supplied with coal, but it was mostly poor quality 'stuff from the heaps' and not very effective in providing heat.

The coal strike hit the railways, affecting both passenger and freight traffic. The *Chronicle* reported on 9 October that one railway official had assessed the financial loss to the railways over the summer to be as high as £22,197,000, which resulted in cuts to services and economies in the autumn. The GWR works in Swindon were put on a three-day week in early November. In Bath a number of passenger trains on both the GWR and the Somerset & Dorset were suspended and emergency timetables issued. Even when the strike ended, the chief goods manager of the LMS warned businesses that the disruption caused by the strike would persist for some time.[39]

CHRISTMAS, 1926

BY THE END of a wet and dismal November, which established a new record for rainfall, the strike was at last over. The permit system ended on 4 December, and once supplies began to come in from the Somerset and other coalfields, prices fell steeply. At the Somerset pit heads there was a reduction of five shillings a ton, which was sufficient to avert another rise in the price of gas. Christmas gave Bathonians a welcome relief from politics and worrying about the next delivery of coal. Instead of issuing dire warnings about revolution and Bolshevism, Foxcroft gave a lecture on poetry at the Red House, while his former Labour opponent, Captain Walter Scobell, was preoccupied with his new bungalow in the grounds of Kingwell Hall, his ancestral home, and his Great Dane, which he was grooming to compete in a forthcoming dog show in Bath.

In the days before Christmas the hotels filled up with guests, parties were held and the Dickens' Society, which was noted for its elaborate celebrations, held its Christmas party at the Red House. Its highlight was a poem by

Florence Tylee on 'The Pickwick Family Coach', which was described taking Dickens' family to celebrate Christmas in the 'Queen of the West'. The Pump Room announced its usual Christmas programme, which, in the words of the *Chronicle*, 'involved one long round of music, gaiety and entertainment'. The post office was overwhelmed with parcels; a spokesman from the sorting office said that there had been 'a marked falling off in the practice of sending greeting cards, and presents, small and large, have to a great extent been substituted'. Amidst the usual Christmas enthusiasm, a few Scrooge-like notes were struck. The Bellman complained about children singing carols on the doorstep as 'an education in mendicancy', while the Temperance Association unsuccessfully tried to block the Licensed Victualler's offer of free beer for the inmates' Christmas lunch at the Frome Road Workhouse. The large number of applicants – about 3,000 – for the issue of vouchers by the Mayor's Christmas Fund, which entitled their holders to coal, meat or groceries, indicated, however, that poverty and hardship had not disappeared in the euphoria of Christmas.

6
EDUCATION AND HEALTH

THE YEARS 1925-1929 marked a significant turning point in the history of Bath between the wars. The Bath Corporation Act created the means for modernising the infrastructure of the city and sweeping away the slums, while the council's three-year education programme, drawn up in 1929, laid the foundation for an improved and expanded educational system. Building a new school on Beechen Cliff was as important as building the Kingsmead Flats or moving the RUH from Beau Street to semi-rural Combe Park in providing glimpses of a more optimistic future, even though the Great Depression and the Second World War would act as significant restraints.

SCHOOLING IN BATH

The education act of 1918 raised the school leaving age from 12 to 14 and obliged local authorities to open continuation schools, where former pupils who started work at 14 could study one day a week. It also introduced a new type of selective school – known as a central school – and schools for children with special needs. Local authorities also had to provide regular medical inspections for all children up to the age of 18, which parents, however, had the right to refuse. Bath council decided to set up central schools in the existing school buildings at Weymouth House Boys and Girls Schools, Central Walcot Boys and Girls Schools, Oldfield Council Boys and Girls Schools, West Twerton Boys and Girls Schools and St John's Roman Catholic Mixed School. The City Secondary School was eventually to be moved out of the Municipal Technical College and reorganised into two separate schools – one for boys, the other for girls – but the Twerton Higher Elementary School remained co- educational. Alderman Bush, the chairman of the Education Committee, warned ratepayers in March 1919 that, despite a 60% grant from central government for councils to implement the new act, 'it was more than probable that a very largely increased sum of money would be demanded' from them, and that, even then, it would be impossible to provide secondary education for all.

In 1926 the Hadow Report recommended raising the school leaving age to 15 by 1932, placing more emphasis on vocational training for non-academic children and improving teacher-pupil ratios. The government accepted the main recommendation of raising the school leaving age, and Bath, along with other local authorities, was told to make the necessary arrangements. In August 1928, Alderman Bush remarked to a journalist that an extra year at school would 'prevent boys and girls ... picking up habits of idleness on the streets', but it was not until 16 October 1929 that the education committee approved plans for raising the school leaving age with effect from 1 April 1930, while reserving the power to grant exemption to children between the ages of 14 and 15 'where beneficial employment has been obtained'. It also finalised an ambitious three-year programme costing about £172,000, which it hoped the council would agree to submit to the Board of Education for approval. The main proposals included:

- building a new secondary school for boys on Beechen Cliff and converting the former RUH into a new technical college;
- building an assembly hall, science room and lecture room at the Domestic Science College on Long Acre;
- building handicraft and domestic science rooms at Oldfield Council School and converting South Hayes House at 54 Wells Road into a domestic subjects centre where the girls would be taught 'housewifery ... from the buying of food to the preparing of it, the cleaning of the house and the making of beds';
- extending West Twerton Senior School;
- building a new infants school for 300 pupils and developing the four departments of the Junior Technical School;
- establishing an open-air school for 100 pupils suffering from tuberculosis;

Alderman Bush was adamant that if accepted by the council and the Board of Education, the programme would be carried out, but a more cautious, perhaps even critical note, was sounded by the Liberal councillor for Oldfield, George Long, who pointed out that it 'was only a programme of things they would like to do if and when they felt inclined so to do'. The council approved most of the programme on 20 November but it cut the number of teachers to be appointed. Although the cost of raising the school leaving age as early as 1930 caused considerable debate, the policy was implemented on 1 April 1930, but only included 14-15 year-olds who had not found work.

The jewel in the crown of the three-year programme was the construction of new buildings for the City Secondary School for Boys which currently occupied cramped quarters in the basement of the technical college in the Guildhall, where pupils had to work by artificial light. There had been talk of building a new school on Beechen Cliff for at least 20 years, but finally, just before Christmas 1928, the council decided to issue a compulsory purchase order for nine acres of Lyncombe Hill Farm, which was owned by Edward Tompkins of Bloomfield Road. In his annual report at the school prize day in the Guildhall the headmaster observed with relief that

> we appear to be at last within measurable distance of the possession of a new school, and this prospect is calculated to turn the sober reality of the present into intoxicating visions of the future. To have a local habitat and a name; to possess a home instead of lodgings; to occupy a site on a green hill instead of the dusty hollow of the City; to enjoy acres of windswept and sunlit playing fields at the school door in place of a few square yards of asphalt at the bottom of a well of bricks and mortar; to live and work in buildings planned especially for this great purpose, with all the latest improvements in lighting, heating, ventilation and other hygienic requirements, buildings which we can take a pleasure in still further beautifying and adorning because they are our own; are some of the things of which we dream. We look forward also with no small relief to the time when our classrooms will be free from that modern menace to health – the appalling din of the city streets – so that the pupils will be able to hear the teacher's voice without difficulty and the teacher will be able to able to make himself heard without strain.[1]

It was not until 26 February 1931 that the foundation stone was laid by Alderman Bush, and the school opened for pupils the following January. The implementation of most of the other plans was delayed by the onset of the Great Depression, but, although improvements to the Domestic Science College were dropped, the college moved into improved accommodation at the former Somerset Boys' Home in Brougham Hayes in July 1934.

For most children, winning a scholarship was the key to moving to a central school, the High School or the prestigious King Edward's School. Consequently, the work of the council's Scholarship Sub-Committee was subjected to close scrutiny, particularly from Labour councillors. Councillor Tiley voiced their concerns at an Education Committee meeting on 16 July 1924 when he claimed that there were names on the scholarship list 'which in fairness to the ratepayer should not be there'. Five years later, when the

Education Committee met on 17 July 1929, a similar suspicion resurfaced after the director of education claimed that the council 'had not a great deal of money to allocate' for scholarships. Councillor Cook challenged him, suggesting that, if parents deliberately gave false information, 'they should be prosecuted', to which the director replied rather weakly that he was 'sometimes accused of being too inquisitive'.

Private schools in Bath were by definition independent of the state school system, although they could voluntarily submit to government inspection if they so wished. They consisted of a variety of establishments ranging from prep schools, public schools, and commercial schools such as Cannings' College. The Royal School in Bath was a private boarding school for the daughters of army officers such as Margaret Cowan, who returned with her parents from India in 1920 and eventually went on to became a physiotherapist at the Bath & Wessex Children's Orthopaedic Hospital.[2] Bath High School for Girls, which was part of the Girls' Public Day School Company, was a small but fiercely academic school of only 184 pupils in 1925, the year before it moved from 4-6 Portland Place to Hope House in Lansdown. In April 1928, four High School pupils gained places at Oxford and two of these were awards – neighbouring Bristol University was usually the favourite choice for the relatively few Bath pupils from the city's secondary schools who went on to university.

There was little contact between independent schools and the state sector, although there were a small number of scholarships offered by public schools. At Monkton Combe, for instance, there were a few scholarships available. The High School also offered a limited number of scholarships to children from local schools. In July 1923, for example, three were gained in a great coup by South Twerton School. The fees of public and prep schools were such that only relatively prosperous members of the middle classes could afford them unless they were helped by a scholarship. It was entirely what was perceived to be the natural order of things that Dr Burdon-Cooper, for example, the leading oculist in Bath, who lived at 12 The Circus, should send his daughter to St Leonard's School in St Andrews and one of his sons first to Monkton Combe and then to Oundle School in Northamptonshire. For parents with sufficient means, public schools were also convenient places to incarcerate awkward teenagers. In July 1924, a 14-year-old who claimed to be 16 was caught by the police driving a car. His father, a well-known local businessman, assured the magistrates that he had given his son a 'thrashing for the first time in his life and he was going to send him away to a public school'.

Although King Edward's School was not under council control, the council provided five free places a year for children from the city's elementary schools. Much to the irritation of some Labour members of the Education Committee, King Edward's had an Officers' Training Corps (OTC). In September 1925, the Labour councillor Sam Day asked what control the Local Education Authority had over the school and whether 'pressure [was] brought to bear on scholars to get them to join the OTC'. The chairman of the Educational Committee, after seeking legal advice from the town clerk, answered only the first question by reminding Day that the committee did not control the school. The latter, however, stuck to his guns and, in shockingly antisemitic language, replied that

> he thought that whether they had control over the school or not they might pass a resolution protesting against military training in the school. He served four years in the army for the benefit of a few Jew financiers and he wanted to see the fostering of military training amongst the young done away with.[3]

Schools and Popular Memory

The reminiscences of septuagenarians and octogenarians recorded by the Bath Industrial Heritage Centre Oral History Project in the 1980s and 1990s often focused on how strict discipline was in the schools. Mr G Perry, for instance, recalled that he was frequently caned at Walcot Central School, while his namesake, Ron Perry, who attended the same school, also remembered over 70 years later how 'hard' the school was: 'You had to be there spot on 9 o'clock. If you were two minutes late, you had the cane.' Nevertheless, he added, 'it was hard days they were, but happy days'. A similar sentiment was expressed by Gwendoline Wicks, whose father worked at the Fuller's Earth Union. She attended Combe Down Senior School from the age of 11 to 14, and, when interviewed decades later, remembered that the school was well run by the popular but strict head master, Mr Collins. She recalled that she was a timid girl, 'a frightened Isaac' as she picturesquely put it, who was often day dreaming 'in a world of [her] own', and would be 'brought back to reality with a shout from the teacher'.[4]

Punishments meted out by teachers did not always go unchallenged. When Miss Winifred Love slapped Joan Atkins twice at Kingsmead Infants' School on the afternoon of 13 October 1920, Joan's mother not only reported her to the police, but went round to her house, and told her in no uncertain terms that she should never have been a teacher, allegedly calling her 'a cruel cat' and 'a hussy'. Her complaint to the police resulted in the case coming before the magistrates, where it emerged that Mrs Atkins had been round to the school on several occasions and had threatened teachers by 'putting her fist in their faces'. The court was reminded by Winifred Love's lawyer that 'the teacher's position is not an enviable one by any means'. He then asked the headmistress whether she approved of the action taken by the defendant and she replied, 'yes – I had told the teachers they might smack the children, but do not approve of any other punishment'. She went on to say that she did not think such a punishment would hurt a child and pointed out that 'for the last half hour of that afternoon's school the child was in the class knitting and was quite cheerful and happy'.[5] The magistrates agreed and dismissed the case.

Complaints about caning at Walcot Senior Boys' School nearly 17 years later were more successful. One mother, Mrs Fielding, complained to the headmaster that her son, Roy, who was a class monitor, had been 'caned by his teacher … for no apparent reason whatever' and informed him that her son would not attend school next Monday 'as it would be his turn to be caned again'. The teacher concerned was a poor disciplinarian, and, when the headmaster questioned him about the incident, the teacher told him that he 'was training them to bear pain when they became men'. He was promptly informed that this sort of thing must stop and that he must surrender his cane, which on two previous occasions he had been instructed not to use. He at first refused but when told he could take the night to think over the matter, decided to surrender the cane before he went home.[6]

On the other hand, many elderly Bathonians remembered with affection how individual teachers went out of the way to encourage their pupils and help them realise their potential. Doreen Williams, for instance, recalled how one teacher at Harley Street School, Miss Tanner, would stay behind to help prepare pupils for the scholarship exam to the central schools, while Patricia Connett, who attended the same school, recalled walking to school with another teacher, Miss Case, who would quiz her on the names of the capital cities of various countries around the world.[7] Another Bathonian, Bob King, did well at Batheaston School but did not sit the central school scholarship exam because his family needed him to find a job and help support them financially. His teacher, however, did not wash his hands of him. When he left school at 14 to work in a garage, he persuaded the Coop at Batheaston to give him a job more suited to his ability. He was proved right. Bob later passed the Coop's internal shop-assistants test with 100% marks and was sent to the provisions department in Westgate Buildings.[8] Many pupils could not wait to leave school, however. George Perry, for instance, left Walcot Central School at 14½ and started work at a blacksmith's. As his father disapproved of the job, he left after a week, but, faced with the threat of having to return to school, he managed to secure a place with Bath Cabinet Makers.[9] At West Central

School, the register of leavers records that, well over a decade earlier, one Felix William Heaton, had left in October 1918 'apparently out of parents control' and 'refuses to return to school'.[10]

Many Bathonians who were at school in the 1920s and 1930s recalled the use of slates instead of paper for written exercises, and how they had to be cleaned with a damp cloth. Others remembered the boxes of discarded clothes to be given to the parents of the poorer pupils. Empire Day was always a major event in the school calendar. Madge Logie, for instance, remembered how it was celebrated at St Luke's School with a parade in the playground with the Union Jack flying. Patriotic songs and hymns were sung, the girls 'carried bunches of white, red and blue flowers', and afterwards all the children were 'allowed to go home and have a holiday for the rest of the day'.[11]

Many parents' view of education was of necessity determined by their financial position. Patricia Connett, for instance, gained a place at the High School but had to go to the Girls' Secondary School as her father could not afford the fees. Eric Smith, a scholarly child who loved poetry and was 'top of the class from start to finish', secured a place at the City of Bath Boys' School, but his family too could not afford the fees, as his father had just been made redundant and also had four-year-old twins to provide for. Eric did manage to gain a place at the Technical College, but again his father stopped him from taking it up. Rather sadly he reflected years later that 'father had little idea of the value of education'. He believed that a 'clean collar and tie would get you anywhere'. Perhaps, after all, his father was right as his son later became provisions manager at Cater, Stoffell and Fortt.[12] Bob King's experiences reveal a bleak tale of poverty and how it could stunt a child's education in the interwar years. In 1926 his father was unemployed and suffering from the effects of a head wound after being hit on the head with a pickaxe, The family was in receipt of poor relief and given a weekly twelve shilling grocery voucher. One day, while pregnant, his mother collapsed in Kensington Road. Fortunately, a passing police car stopped and brought her home. As his parents were unable to look after their two children, Bob, aged six, and his sister were sent to the children's home at Three Ways Cottage, attached to Frome Road Workhouse, where he stayed for six months and 'hated it'. He was well looked after but the discipline was tough and he was given a 'hiding for giving bread to the birds'. Bob was so anxious to get home that he did not tell the matron that he was suffering from a lesion in his ankle, but successfully disguised his limp until he was back with his family. He was to be off school for the next six months. At the age of nine he secured a part-time job delivering parcels for a local grocer's, and a year later moved on to work for a greengrocer in the mornings before going to school. Inevitably, he was sometimes late for school, but managed to dodge the School Attendance Officer. Despite these distractions, he was often top of his class.[13]

A much easier childhood was experienced by Madge Logie, who later became a primary school teacher. Her father had a regular job as a carpenter and the time and energy to read her stories and make up elaborate tales concerning 'the adventures of a wandering mouse', which gave Madge a lifelong interest in language and literature. In 1929, at the age of five she went to St Luke's. Six years later, after sitting 'a composition and arithmetic paper and [answering] some simple questions on history', she won a scholarship to the City of Bath Girls' School. In the autumn she transferred with some 80 other girls to her new school where she studied a predominantly academic syllabus consisting of Latin, chemistry, physics, biology, maths, history, geography, scripture, art and needlework.[14]

MEDICAL SERVICES

Hospitals

With the exception of the Forbes Fraser, Pensions and Children's Orthopaedic Hospitals at Combe Park and the Isolation Hospital on Claverton Down, Bath's hospitals were situated in cramped inner city locations. The RUH in the Gainsborough building in Beau Street was particularly inadequate for its purposes. In January 1927, the chairman of its managing board, Dr Curd, reported that 'every bed was filled, cots were made up, and mattresses were even placed on the floor to accommodate patients'. Inevitably, such overcrowding resulted in long waiting lists for non-essential surgery, and this was exacerbated by the growing number of motor accidents, which resulted in an increase in emergency cases.

The ultimate solution to this overcrowding lay in the RUH's long proposed move to Combe Park. In 1920, its managing board had raised the money to purchase 20 acres there, and built the Forbes Fraser Hospital and the Children's Orthopaedic Hospital, both of which were opened in 1924 by the Prince of Wales. The former was named after the eminent surgeon, who died in 1924 of blood poisoning contracted whilst operating on a patient. The rest of the site was leased to the Pensions Hospital, which continued to nurse seriously injured servicemen. At first the prospects of moving to Combe Park seemed to be a pipe dream, but by November 1928 the complex bits of the jigsaw began to fall into place. When the Ministry of Pensions announced that their hospital would close in January 1929, the mayor, Aubrey Bateman, seized the opportunity to facilitate the RUH's move to Combe park by proposing that the council should purchase for £30,000 the hospital's original premises in Beau Street for the site of the new technical college. The City architect, AJ Taylor, and AW Hoyle, the Director of Education, both supported the purchase, agreeing that 'the main building lends itself to an exceptional degree to the work of adaptation'. The council's offer was backed by the generous promise of £10,000 from the tobacco magnate Stanley Wills. The logistics of the move were aided by the availability of the temporary buildings of the Pension Hospital, which after renovation would still have a life span of 10 to 15 years. The RUH could therefore use these premises while the new hospital was being built. The foundation stone for the new hospital was laid on 25 October 1930 by the mayor and it opened in December 1932.

With the exception of the City of Bath Isolation Hospital on Claverton Down, which was controlled by the corporation, Bath's hospitals were all 'voluntary' and depended on donations from the public. Some patients also made donations, although – according to the *Chronicle* in September 1928 – most left after being 'patched up' without making any contribution whatsoever. As a result, Bath's hospitals had large overdrafts. In March 1928, the Bath Ear, Nose and Throat Hospital at 27-28 Marlborough Buildings reported a financial deficit of £515 despite the matron exercising 'the greatest economy'. One member of its board of management, Lt Col Norman Barnett complained that 'while the public have accepted the policy of voluntary hospitals, I am afraid the public have not adopted the necessary corollary of putting their hands deep into their pockets'. The deficit for the RUH for 1927 was much larger – £ 9,034.

Voluntary hospitals were dependent on their wealthier patients paying for treatment and on donations to help those who could not afford to pay. Donations came from numerous sources and in many forms – not just money but also gifts of fruit, cigarettes, sweets, gramophone records, games, books and magazines. Hospital Friendly Societies, which were largely run by volunteers, played a crucial role in raising money. In September 1927, the *Chronicle* published an appeal by the chairman of the RUH Friendly Society for volunteers:

> The duties simply mean a lady or gentleman goes to 25 or 30 houses every quarter, opens the [collection] boxes, checks the contents, exchanges signatures and hands the sum collected to the local secretary. A few hours four times a year will be sufficient in most cases. There are now about 1,200 ladies and gentlemen engaged in this most practical and successful scheme for the Royal

United Hospital. We still want more, so it is with confidence that we ask helpers in nearly every ward in the city of Bath to come and join us.[15]

Another important source of revenue was provided by the workers' insurance schemes run by many factories and businesses. Railwaymen working for the LMS in Bath, for example, paid twopence a week to a hospital fund, to which the company added a penny. This guaranteed them and their children for up to 15 years free treatment, and in 1927, the fund paid out £152 15sh 6d to the various Bath hospitals. The previous year, the Workmen's Hospital Fund of Stothert & Pitt, Bath's biggest employer, paid out £218 18sh in grants to Bath's hospitals.

Doctors, nurses and midwives

Hospitals were places of last resort. It was to doctors and district nurses that Bathonians, like everyone else, initially turned. The treatment provided depended on the patient's income. In 1913, when the National Health Insurance Scheme was introduced, workers in insurable occupations earning less than £160 a year were covered for basic medical treatment from an approved list or 'panel' of local doctors. Sickness benefit of ten shillings per week for men and seven shillings and sixpence for women could also be claimed for 26 weeks. This was financed partly by weekly contributions from workers and employers and partly by the taxpayer. The scheme was administered by 'approved societies', usually set up by town councils, employers and friendly societies. By 1936, some twenty million people, including six million women, were covered by the scheme. Those who earned more had to pay for their own treatment, although there was provision for contributing to the scheme through voluntary payments. There was no provision for dental or ophthalmic services

More prosperous Bathonians, of course, could afford to pay for their medicines and appointments with doctors and medical specialists, many of whom lived in the Circus, which was consequently known as 'the pillbox'. Interviewed in 1992 the octogenarian, Mr Preston Jones, recalled Dr Nelson, one of the medical men who lived in the Circus, being driven around in 'a magnificent four seater Daimler with brass headlamps on it'.[16] Panel doctors earned a capitation fee, and to maximise their earnings had every incentive to enrol as many patients as possible, with some of them having over 2,000. It was fashionable to sneer at panel doctors as the hacks of the medical profession, but they could earn good money. On 25 July 1929 at a meeting of the Bath Insurance Committee, which administered the National Insurance Act, its chairman, Arthur Withy, firmly rejected the phrase 'hack work' to describe panel doctors and pointed out that one doctor on the local panel earned 'about £900' a year. Panel doctors were under constant pressure to reduce the number of medicines and sick notes they issued, and, when it was pointed out at the meeting that the number of prescriptions issued by local panel doctors had been less than in any year since 1924, it was suggested that this indicated that the doctors were short-changing the working man. This was roundly dismissed by all the committee members. Dr Fosbery said that 'personally he would not hesitate to give more expensive drugs, but in nine out of ten cases this was totally unnecessary', while another member, AS Gunstone stressed that, 'regardless of cost', expensive drugs like insulin and radium were available under the National Insurance scheme.

At a meeting on 27 May 1929, the Health Committee had reassured Councillor Cook, who in 1922 had proposed euthanasia for terminally ill cancer patients, that there was a fund of £250,000 to spend on radium for cancer patients across England and Wales, with Alderman Spear adding optimistically that 'the time was not far off when it would be within reach of everybody'. In 1931, the Bristol Radium Centre opened, but, Dr James Blackett, the Medical Officer of Health, warned that it would not provide a magic solution to cancer as the 'proportion of cases in which radium is likely to be useful is as yet very small'. Realistically, all that could be offered patients in the advanced stages of cancer was extra nursing assistance and 'the admission if necessary to special hospitals', while their families could be provided with domestic help. During 1930, special assistance was given to 24 cancer sufferers, 17 of whom died.[17] It was crucial, as the Cancer Committee stressed in its report in 1925 that

> the public should be told, and told repeatedly, that cancer, if taken in time, is curable. The Local Authority has an important duty to perform in helping to spread this knowledge, which is at once a message of hope and a warning.[18]

If a serious accident occurred either at home or on the streets, the first recourse was often to contact a GP or district nurse or to take the casualty to a local surgery. For instance, when George Cooper, a tram driver, slipped in August 1924 whilst alighting from his tram near the Devonshire Arms on Wellsway, injuring his ribs and back, he was taken to the local surgery, and then after examination driven by the fire brigade ambulance to the RUH. If the accident had occurred at home, there would most likely have been a long delay before the doctor arrived. An inquest on the death of the 72-year-old George Braimbridge, a master tailor, in September 1927, shows how long the delay could sometimes be. The *Chronicle* reported that George's wife told the coroner that, after he had collapsed and was in great pain in the backyard of his home at 6 Albion Buildings, Upper Bristol Road,

> she sent successively for three doctors, but no one came, and the deceased lay on the ground groaning for hours, as she and others could not lift him. Eventually [she] went to the Royal United Hospital in a taxicab, and they phoned for the Fire Brigade ambulance, which arrived at her home within a few minutes ... Almost simultaneously with the ambulance a lady doctor came.[19]

The *Chronicle* observed in May 1928 that 'the district nurse proceeds upon her path of succour largely unsung, doing good – one almost said by stealth, so unobtrusively does she work', and quoted a 'leading Bath physician' who stressed that 'there are hundreds of chronic invalids among the poor of this city in need of daily care, dressing of wounds, daily washing and general attention, who owe more than they can say to the regular visit of the District Nurse'. In 1927, 700 patients in Bath were attended to by six general nurses and some 24,000 home visits were paid. Given the pressure on district nurses, sometimes it was neighbours, relatives, or friends who stepped into the breach. At Midford, Gwendoline Wicks remembered a family living at Combe Hill House at the top of Brassknocker Hill where there were three daughters, one of whom acted as unofficial district nurse of the village: 'if anyone was ill, she would trudge down Brassknocker fields' and 'if at night, would sleep on the side of the patients bed'; not surprisingly she was 'in great demand'.[20]

Dr Blackett was particularly concerned about the training of midwives. At a meeting of the Royal Sanitary Institute in Exeter in April 1927, commenting on a report that one mother in 250 died in childbirth, he declared that 'if midwives were thoroughly efficient and proper pre-natal methods were adopted, the deaths of mothers ought to be reduced by 50 per cent'. He provocatively added that he would 'be sorry if the whole ante-natal treatment were left entirely to midwives in their present state of education'. This drew a stinging rebuke from a midwife at the meeting, who asserted that 'doctors showed great ignorance of maternity' and went on to claim that 'men doctors held human life rather cheaply'. Sadly, however, in the 1920s there were still a few Sarah Gamps left amongst practising midwives – Eric Smith remembered how the midwife and the 'layer out' of corpses 'were often the same person'.[21] The city health authorities ran an ante-natal clinic and a small maternity home in Rivers Street to which 99 mothers were admitted in 1929. There were four full-time midwives in the city, who in 1928 managed to pay 1,647 visits to the homes of expectant mothers. When midwives arrived to supervise a birth, they were reliant on help from the mother's relatives or friends for hot water and clean sheets. Sometimes they did not arrive punctually. Mary Dale, for instance, who was born in a cottage on Primrose Hill in Weston, remembers being told that her aunt kept 'her hand beneath her for some time until a midwife arrived on her bicycle to cut the umbilical cord'.[22] For those who could pay, there were private maternity homes such as one run by a qualified midwife and nurse, Phyllis Thorpe, at St John's House, Bloomfield Place. Freelance certified midwives advertised regularly in the *Chronicle*. One such was a Nurse Miles of 12 Lorne Road, Twerton, who only made daytime visits. What happened if the baby made its appearance in the middle of night is not at all clear. Despite all the imperfections in maternity care in Bath, during the inter-war period infant mortality steadily declined. For the progress made in reducing infant mortality, *the Daily News* awarded a prize of £25 to the City in 1925 and another of £10 in 1927. The 'vital statistics' for 1927, produced by Dr Blackett in his annual report and published in the *Chronicle* in January 1928, showed that 'excellent progress had been made in reducing infant mortality': 28 infants under one died that year compared to 49 in 1926 and 79 in 1924.

The most traumatic births were often experienced by single mothers. One particularly sad case concerned 39-year-old Dora Moore, who was staying in a bed-sitting-room in a lodging house at 1 Great Stanhope Street. She had been separated from her husband for two years and had two children, aged 16 and 18. On Friday evening, 25 June 1926, she gave birth alone to a healthy male child. The landlady heard her call out and went to the room and found the baby immersed in a bucket of water – the subsequent inquest concluded that he had drowned. Both the doctor and midwife were belatedly summoned. The latter told the Police Court on 8 July that 'there was not even a safety pin in the house by way of preparation'. Dr Scott White 'was not satisfied with the state of affairs' and reported the matter to the police. Dora Moore was charged with manslaughter but was found not guilty by the jury at the Somerset Assize Court on 23 October. The judge observed that a woman could not be convicted for 'the lack of preparations for a birth'. To avoid the trauma and stigma of an 'illegitimate birth' sometimes suicide seemed the easiest option, as can be seen from the tragic case of 17-year-old Dorothy Margaret Pow, a scullery maid in Stanley Mark's restaurant at 7 George Street. When she saw her panel doctor on 10 September 1928, she was told that she was pregnant and advised to fetch her mother so that together they could discuss the matter. Instead of going home to Charles Street, she threw herself into the river near the Midland Railway Bridge and drowned. Her suicide surprised all who knew her. The coroner described her death at the inquest as 'one of the saddest tragedies I have had to enquire into for some time'. Had she lived, she might well have been helped by the Bath Vigilance and Rescue Society, which offered sanctuary to unmarried women in its shelter at 9 Southcot Place on Lyncombe Hill.

THE HEALTH OF BATHONIANS

THE SCHOOL MEDICAL service carried out regular health checks on Bath's schoolchildren, and when necessary referred them to the hospitals for further treatment. According to the *Chronicle,* in the last two months of 1928 1,310 children attended the Minor Ailments Clinic. One common thread running through memories of childhood between the wars was the removal of adenoids and tonsils at the Ear, Nose and Throat Hospital, which was often a traumatic experience. Doreen Williams, for instance, remembers being taken there at the age of five by her mother. She took her favourite doll with her but was not told where she was going. Her initial experiences were terrifying. She was handed over to the admissions staff, the door was closed firmly behind her, and three nurses immediately blocked the way out, in case she tried to escape. She was not visited by her parents, who feared that she would want to accompany them back home. On her way up to her ward, she had the unsettling experience of seeing a man lying on a bed having his eyes and nose inspected. Gwendoline Wicks had similar memories. Aged seven, she was taken to hospital by her mother, walking from Midford to Combe Hill and then catching a tram into the city. She was bought a penny doll in Southgate, and when she was given chloroform, which she experienced as a smelly bag being put over her mouth, she thought she was being killed.[23]

Unlike children, adults in Bath were not examined regularly, and frequently preferred to rely on patent medicines such as Eno's fruit salts or Cassell's tablets, which were frequently advertised in the local press, rather than see their doctor, which would cost a good deal more. It was often suggested that cancer was more prevalent in Bath than elsewhere. Certainly the death rate from cancer was higher in Bath than in many other cities, but the city's Health Department argued in December 1928 that this was because 'we have relatively more elderly people amongst us and cancer is a disease of later life'. From 1923 to 1927 there were more deaths than births in the city, reflecting the city's large elderly population, as well as fatalities among those who had come to Bath to take the waters or visit the Royal Mineral Water Hospital. In 1927, for example, 1,042 people died in Bath – 212 more than were born –

but 136 of them were visitors. The main killer was heart disease followed by cancer, while between them. bronchitis and influenza claimed 133 victims.

Each winter, a recurrence of the Spanish flu pandemic was feared, but although seasonal flu outbreaks occurred, they were on nothing like the same scale. There was, however, a relatively short-lived epidemic in the early months of 1927. Its symptoms were described in his usual flippant vein by the bard of Batheaston, William Blathwayt:

> Last Saturday in Union Street
> Whom should it be my lot to meet But Mrs Brown, a little pale;
> 'Good morning to you, Mrs Brown. 'I haven't seen you in the town
> For weeks and weeks ...' 'Ah, Zur', she said ...
> 'I've been abed with this 'ere flu.
> Me joints and me muscles wur so sore I never thought to rise no more:
> And then me head did ache and swim Till everything looked sort of dim;
> I wur so bad that there I lay A doing nothing all the day:
> And then at night the doctor came ... He told me I must stay in bed
> And t'wur the only thing to do
> One can't stand up to this ere Flu.[24]

Although comparatively mild, the flu epidemic of 1927 disrupted several social occasions, such as the Duchess of Beaufort's luncheon at Badminton in honour of a royal visit to Bristol. It also – to quote Dr Blackett – 'picked out' some of the more vulnerable elderly people such as 85-year-old Charles Duddridge, who lived with his son-in-law at 43 Lyndhurst Rd, Oldfield Park. Already suffering from heart problems and bronchitis, he was acutely vulnerable when his whole family caught the virus. By the morning of 7 February, he urgently needed medical assistance. Since the whole

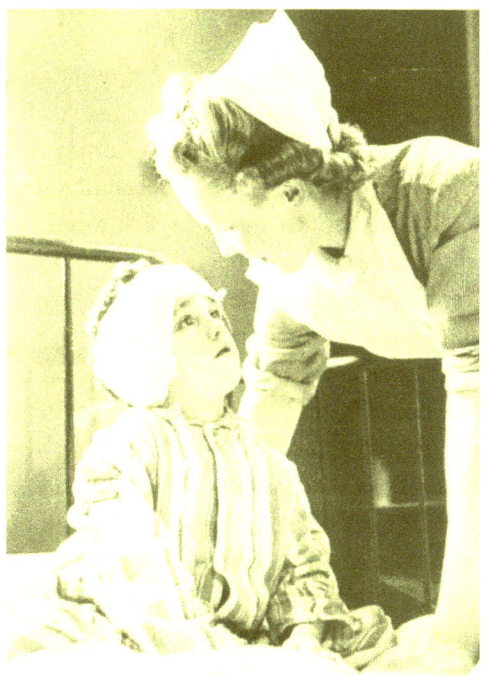

Nurse and child (Museum of Bath at Work)

household was immobilised by flu, a boy, who happened to be passing by the house, was asked to take a note to the doctor. By the time he arrived, however, some hours later, Charles was dead.

Two days later Dr Blackett was able to report to the Health Committee that, 'so far as he could judge', the epidemic was 'on the wane'. An interesting discussion then arose as to how to deal with the causes rather than the effects of the epidemic. Councillor Cook raised the question of overcrowded trams, adding that on the Oldfield route 'he saw a car packed like bloaters in a box' and wondered whether a 'disinfecting syringe could be used'. He asked Dr Blackett whether the Health Committee had any power to stop this overcrowding, but was reminded that we can 'only advise'. Nevertheless, it was decided to call the attention of the Watch Committee to the problem. The following winter's flu epidemic was mild, although several eminent residents such as Lady Bath and the playwright Arnold Ridley were reported to be bed-bound as a result of it, but the threat of a more virulent flu epidemic striking Bath in the future loomed large in the thinking of Bath's medical authorities. In April, Dr Blackett, in a lecture to the BTLC, appealed to his audience to take 'all reasonable precautions' against infectious illnesses:

> Spitting in the streets could be stopped with the best possible effect on public health, and there is another little habit which could be well dispensed with, namely wetting the finger while turning leaves of paper.[25]

There was also a dire warning issued by the 'family doctor' in his *Chronicle* column, 'Talks on Health', on 2 June that 'cats carry infections and should be banned from the sick room'. In late September, a further note of alarm was sounded when Mr Moore Hogarth, the Chairman of the College of Pestology, warned that 'the unusual plague of insects, which has been a feature of the summer [might] lead to a recurrence of the influenza epidemic of 1918'.

Nationally, in early 1929 the country did indeed suffer a severe attack of flu. London, Liverpool, South Yorkshire, Portsmouth and Southampton were all affected badly. The Ministry of Health was particularly concerned because this was the first time since January 1919 that a widespread outbreak of flu had coincided with a period of intense cold. The ministry sent a circular to all local authorities sanctioning special measures, if they became necessary, for providing nursing, visiting and extra facilities for dispensing prescriptions. Bath drew up an emergency scheme, which could be put into immediate operation, but towards the end of February, it was becoming clear that it would not be needed. On the 19 February, Dr Blackett was able to reassure the Health

Committee, 'after being in communication with medical men of the city, that there was no influenza epidemic in Bath'. This was borne out by the causes of death recorded for the four weeks to 4 March, with only five due to influenza, compared to 14 to cancer and 16 to bronchitis and other respiratory diseases.

The Bathwick typhoid outbreak of 1928

In the spring of 1928 there was a serious outbreak of typhoid centred on Bathwick Hill, which affected 32 people and led to five deaths. According to the Ministry of Health inspector, it was caused by 'specific pollution in the neighbourhood of surface springs used to supply an elevated district of the city of Bath'.[26] Bathwick Hill drew its water from springs which rose on Bathampton Down where the water was collected in large tanks at three different levels.

The first typhoid case was notified to Dr Blackett on 4 April, but it was not until the 25th that a second case was reported. By 1 May, however, after a further four cases had been confirmed, Dr Blackett concluded that the cause was water contamination near Sham Castle. The Waterworks Engineer found that the recently laid drain from the local golf club to the cesspit in North Road had fractured some 20 yards before it entered the cesspit. To avoid further contamination, the water supply from the springs to the majority of properties affected was cut off the following day and replaced with water from Monkswood reservoir. However, 34 houses on Bathwick Hill, which were well above the point where the fracture had occurred, continued to receive water from Bathampton Down, as it was assumed that it would not be contaminated. It was from people living in or visiting these houses over the next three weeks that 26 more typhoid cases were notified. The council eventually alerted these households to the danger on 18 May, advising them to boil all their water. Heavy rain was forecast, which Dr Thomas, a member of Dr Blackett's staff, feared might 'force up or remove to another place contamination that was in the ground'. Even then, it was not until 27 May, after Mowbray Green, the well-known local architect, who lived on Upper Bathwick Hill, had informed the Combe Down Water Company of the typhoid outbreak that the contaminated water supply to the 34 properties affected was at last cut off.

On 26 May, a petition demanding an enquiry was sent both to the council and Dr Blackett from seven residents on Bathwick Hill, all of whom had contracted typhoid. It accused the corporation of 'great neglect in the supervision of the water supply to Bathwick' and made three damning criticisms of Dr Blackett:

> When the water from the Bathwick springs was turned off for the greater part of the ward, no steps were taken to acquaint the householders where the water could not be turned off ... or to provide them with uncontaminated drinking water. Where it was found desirable to turn off the water ... it was clearly the duty of the MOH [Dr Blackett] to warn *all* houses in Bathwick to boil the water for at least a week. No notice was sent to *any house* until seven weeks after the first case. Further, that although the MOH has cases of typhoid notified to him, he took no steps to inform the medical men in the city that such was the case.

The sting in the tail was that the petitioners reserved the right to claim 'substantial damages from the Corporation for the expense and anxiety' caused.[27]

Arguably more important to the council than this threat was the impact that the typhoid outbreak might have on the city's tourist trade. It was therefore vital to keep the matter out of the papers. On 5 June, the council sat in private and set up a special committee to undertake a full enquiry into the outbreak. It also resolved that both the public and the press should be excluded from any meeting in which it was discussed. On 3 July, the council gave the Waterworks Committee permission to spend whatever was necessary to provide a safe supply of water to Upper Bathwick Hill. The Special Committee held its first meeting on 8 June, and at its second on 18 June resolved that 'their inquiries would be held in private'. So it was that the minutes of the crucial meeting of 22 June, when the relevant officials were interviewed, were never published.

By early June, Bath's conference season was in full swing. On the 7th and 8th the Association of Education Committees convened in Bath; a few days later, on the 11th, about a thousand members of the Incorporated Municipal Electrical Association descended on the city. So it is understandable why the council wished to keep news of the epidemic out of the press. It is also understandable why the press were not happy to go along with this. On 31 May, the *Western Daily Press* complained that 'great secrecy has been maintained in official quarters regarding the matter', adding that 'an official of the Bath Health Department yesterday told a *Press* representative that there was nothing to communicate'.[28] On 4 June, the *Morning Post* published a detailed report 'from our special correspondent', and the following day included a letter from Edward Knox, the councillor for Bathwick, in which he pointed out that 'conditions are even worse than are stated in your article' and gave a detailed report of the council's failures. In a desperate attempt to prevent this damning account from circulating widely and alarming tourists and conference organisers, the council phoned local newsagents, asking them not to display placards for a 'Bristol newspaper' and the *Morning Post*, both of which contained articles revealing the council's attempted cover-up. Some agreed while others 'indignantly refused'. The council did not stop there, however. According to the *Morning Post*, on 7 June,

> newsagents received visits from a woman who in each case asked for all copies of the *Morning Post* that could be spared. Visitors to Bath were thus in many cases prevented from obtaining copies, and only regular subscribers were able to do so. I was told however, that copies of the *Morning Post* were passed from hand to hand by regular readers to those unable to buy copies.

On 6 June, a journalist of the *Morning Post*, Mr Bell, was subjected to a 'lengthy interview' in the Guildhall by Basil Ogden, the town clerk, Councillor Hacker, and John Hatton, Director of the Baths. Bell asked why they had attempted to suppress his report and was told emphatically that he had made 'a sensation of a local matter' after assuring them that he would do 'nothing' to cause 'a scare or panic' that might frighten visitors away from Bath. Bell responded by telling them that he had been sent down to Bath by his editor because the council had been attempting to 'stifle *the Morning Post*'. Bell was then asked:

> on what grounds he could justify giving more columns on the outbreak of typhoid in Bath, as compared with the retirement of a Speaker or the prevalence of smallpox in Wandsworth ... We impressed upon him that we regarded it as entirely unpatriotic for a leading morning paper to damage

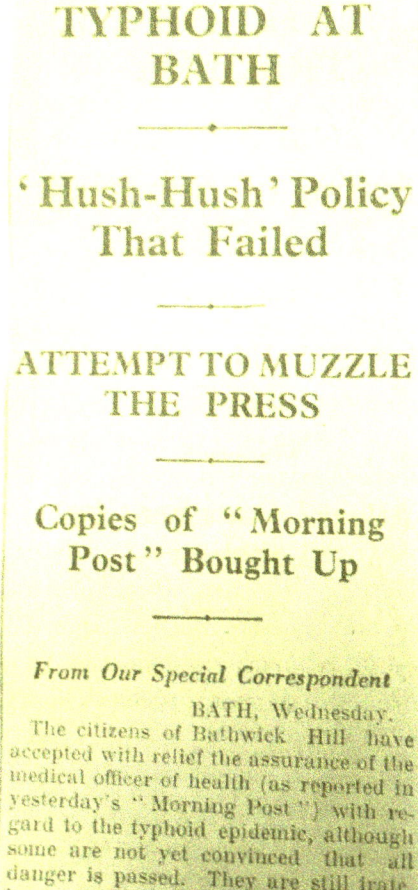

Morning Post headlines 7 June 1928 (Bath Record Office)

a health resort in this country, and that Mr Hatton was entirely justified in taking such steps as may be necessary to prevent visitors staying in Bath from being wantonly frightened into leaving the city.[29]

The council's initial response to demands for compensation for medical fees, loss of earnings and even loss of life was, to quote the historian Robert Millard, 'robust'. The objective was to avoid damaging litigation, while at the same time shielding the city from excessive financial claims. However, it was dealing for the most part with wealthy and influential people. When negotiating with Godfrey Lipscombe, JP, of Claverton Lodge and Colonel Lewis of 23 Bathwick Hill, it initially attempted to persuade them to reduce their claims to spare the pocket of the poorest of the ratepayers, but Lewis rejected this on the ground that his rates 'at all times include items on behalf of the poorest ratepayers, which are of no benefit whatever to me, but I do not complain'.[30] In the case of the seven petitioners from Bathwick Hill, a writ had to be served by their solicitors in London before the council became more amenable to their claim. After consulting its solicitors and Reginald Croom Johnson KC, the Recorder of Bath, the council drafted a letter on 30 July, which was sent to all claimants or their lawyers, inviting them to send in details of the financial losses they had suffered. The council still continued to haggle over individual claims, however. It was only after the lawyer representing the petitioners pointed out that these were the consequence of 'a very serious illness' that they were authorised a total payout of £829 7sh 3d.[31]

The most expensive claim concerned the death of Gresham Gray, manager of the Westminster Bank in Milsom Street. and treasurer of the local YMCA. Both he and his wife, as the *Chronicle* enigmatically put it, 'were among the recent cases of illness in Bathwick'. They were removed to the Forbes Fraser Hospital on 26 May, where Gresham died on 10 July. His wife recovered and in due course her solicitors claimed on her behalf nearly £12,000 in damages on the grounds that she needed to be compensated not only for the loss of her husband's salary but for his housing allowance from the bank and pension on retirement. Basil Ogden, the town clerk, consulted the claims department of the GWR since its solicitor had recently dealt with a similar problem, and was advised to offer her a round sum of £7,000. In the end, 'after prolonged negotiations', Mrs Gresham Gray agreed to accept £7,500 with the corporation also paying her solicitor's fees. What lay behind the council's thinking was made clear by a remark let slip a few months later. After the Armistice service on 11 November, the Recorder asked Ogden 'how we were getting on with our water troubles'. When told that Mrs Gresham Gray's solicitors had settled

EDUCATION AND HEALTH

for £7,500, 'after thinking for a moment', he replied 'that he thought we were well out of our troubles in that quarter, as it was likely that a Jury would have awarded her £10,000'.[32]

In most of the other cases, the amount claimed by a knowledgeable and influential litigant who used the services of a good solicitor was paid in full. For example, Dr Paterson, an Ipswich physician, claimed damages on behalf of his wife, who had contracted typhoid while staying in Bathwick Hill for over a fortnight. As a medical man, he wrote directly to Dr Blackett to obtain full details of the outbreak. Dr Blackett informed the town clerk that 'the tone' of Paterson's communication 'suggested the advisability of being reasonably frank with him', although in his reply he played down the council's culpability in not cutting off the contaminated water supply to the 34 houses on Bathwick Hill.[33] However, Patterson's claim was paid in full.

The death of 14-year-old Joan Wornham, who lived at 2 Sydney Place and died in the RUH on 19 June, was a particularly sad case. Claiming compensation on behalf of her mother, Ernest Shum, her solicitor, observed that Mrs Wornham was

> a war widow with only a small pension, and she has no other means, all her money having been expended in giving her two daughters the best education possible, and in the ordinary course of events she was anticipating some help from this daughter in the course of the next two or three years. [Joan] has always been a very healthy girl.

After the headmistress at the City Secondary School for Girls confirmed that 'she was a normal healthy child', the corporation granted Mrs Wornham her full claim of £132 18s.[34]

The council was able to persuade four claimants who had not engaged a lawyer to reduce their claims. One of them, Alice Ellis, a teacher at Widcombe School, who lodged at 27 Sydney Buildings, put in a claim for £121 17s 6d, but the council offered her only £82 17s 6d on the grounds that there was no need to compensate her for any school holidays she had missed through illness. The Director of Education was, however, ready to recommend to the Education Authority that she should resume duty with the full complement of 'sixty days leave in hand'. Despite not obtaining all she claimed, she thanked the committee for acting with 'great fairness in recognising moral responsibility in this matter without having their legal liabilities definitely established'. The council also refused to pay the probate charges for Miss SA Lawson, who died of typhoid, although it did pay her funeral expenses. The corporation did behave more generously towards Mr Holloway, a gardener, who was unable to work for two years: as compensation he received free treatment at the Royal Mineral Water Hospital and City baths and a lump sum of £800. Nevertheless, nothing could alter the fact that, when the outbreak was first reported, council officials had reacted too slowly. In the words of the solicitors acting for Mrs Slingsby-Long, whose 21 year old daughter Una died from typhoid at the end of May, it was 'a lasting disgrace on the honour of the Corporation of Bath'.[35]

Bath was spared any more major outbreaks of typhoid, but individual cases continued to be reported. In October 1932, a 'mild case' occurred in the Bath Rural District, and in February 1938 rumours of a typhoid outbreak had to be categorically denied by Walter Barrett, chairman of the Health Committee. He reassured residents that, unlike during the Bathwick outbreak, water samples 'were being taken at least four times a day, and chlorination was going on'. The Waterworks Committee paid particular attention to the report of a typhoid outbreak in Croydon in October and November 1937, which resulted in 43 deaths, and in the early spring of 1938 introduced medical checks for their employees working at reservoirs and springs. When one of the workers employed by the War Office in Corsham contracted typhoid in May 1939, Dr Blackett immediately contacted all Bath's GPs informing them that,

> owing to the large number of men with whom the case may have been in contact, it is difficult to trace the infection, but known contacts are under observation, and have been advised to consult their own doctor.

As three weeks had elapsed since the case was notified, Dr Blackett was cautiously optimistic, but nevertheless he warned the GPs 'to be on your guard in case of illnesses that you may be asked to see'. Over the next few months, there were five further notifications, all of which apparently 'did well, but the source of the outbreak was never discovered.[36]

Mental health and eugenics

Dr Blackett, addressing the Rotarian Club in May 1921, spoke of the 'new gospel of health' which proclaimed somewhere in the distant future 'a promised land' of permanent good health. This optimistic outlook was sadly missing in the realm of mental health, however. The Mental Deficiency Act of 1913 divided the mentally ill into four categories – 'idiots, imbeciles, the feeble minded and moral defectives' – and it was the responsibility of the local authority to provide asylums, institutions, hostels and schools for those affected. In 1924, 40 mental patients from Bath were sent to asylums in Bristol, Devon, Somerset or further afield, while 45 cases were kept under supervision in the Frome Road Infirmary, possibly pending removal to asylums elsewhere.

Alderman Dr Preston King, who was elected chairman of the Bath Health Committee in November 1924, was a passionate advocate of sterilisation and eugenics, both of which had considerable support in Britain. Initially, as a young doctor he had believed in euthanasia for 'hopeless, mindless idiots', but, after becoming aware of the dangers of abuse inherent in such a policy, he came round to advocating enforced sterilisation instead. In a lecture to the YMCA in January 1924 which 'created an unusual amount of interest', he explained his thinking:

> Nature's law is the survival of the fittest and we are all flying in the face of Nature in educating our mentally deficient children, because when they are educated to a certain point, they become a danger to the state.[37]

He proposed that no 'mental deficients' should be released from an asylum until they had been sterilised, and suggested that it should be a criminal offence for a couple to have a child unless they had a certificate to show they were 'fit for parentage'. The Nazi regime in Germany was to introduce exactly this policy.

Preston King continued to propagate his views on the treatment of the mentally ill at every opportunity, but at the meeting of Bath City Council on 9 April 1929 they were firmly rejected by his colleague, Alderman Thomas Vezey, the Chairman of the Mental Deficiency Committee. When it was agreed to grant £1,000 to convert the former Bathwick Rectory into a hostel 'for female defectives', Preston King immediately asked whether the patients would be kept there for 'the rest of their natural life or released as an increased danger to the community because of their seeming improvement'. Vezey firmly rebutted this view and pointed out, in the terminology of the times, that they were 'high grade defectives', needing only 'kindly homely supervision' and had every chance of recovery and of 'becoming as normal as Dr Preston King', a retort which according to the *Chronicle*, his fellow councillors 'greatly enjoyed'.[38]

By 1930, Bath had a good record in helping the mentally ill who did not need to be confined to an aslyum. It had the Magdalen Hospital School at Rock Hall House in Combe Down, the House of Help 'for Feeble-minded Fallen Women and Girls' at 112 Walcot Street, and the new hostel in the former Bathwick Rectory. Awareness of mental illness was also promoted by the local branch of the Society of the Crown of Our Lord, an Anglican society 'pledged to pray daily for mental invalids and to render active service to them where possible', as well as the Bath Voluntary Association for Mental Welfare.

In 1937, the council bought the White House in Upper Weston, which reverted to its original name of Weston Lodge and was converted to a nursing home for women suffering from 'functional nervous disorders'. Initially, local GPs were unsure of the type of patient for whom it was most suitable, but Dr Blackett informed them that it was 'essentially for borderline patients and those suffering from the less severe forms of mental and nerve trouble'. He suggested the following conditions as the most suitable for treatment there: 'mild cases of melancholia, mild delusional cases, anxiety conditions, certain forms of organic brain disease, nervous debility after childbirth, severe shock, or of post operative origin [sic]; mild drug addicts; early cases of GPI [syphilitic paresis or the onset of insanity resulting from syphilis] . . .'[39]

The 1913 Act made it obligatory for local authorities to provide schools for the education of 'mentally defective children'. In Bath this obligation was carried out by St Michael's Special School in Saxon Court off Broad Street. A glimpse of the work it did is provided by the *Chronicle's* account of an open afternoon in June 1920. Boys were observed mixing clay and weaving cane seating for chairs, while girls were engaged in sewing, mat-making and creating canvas and wool bags. Children were sent to St Michael's on the recommendation of Dr Blackett. In April 1925, a father was so alarmed by a decision to send his son there that he tried to enlist the help of the BTLC to move the child to another school, arguing that his son, while 'not keen on education' was 'certainly normal mentally'. He feared his son's 'contamination with children mentally deficient [would] be detrimental to his future ability and physique'. Sometimes, however, committing a particularly unruly child or adolescent to an institution could come as a relief to the family, as can be seen from a sad case that came before the magistrates in November 1929. It concerned Albert, aged 16, of Little Corn Street, who had stabbed another boy in a fight. The magistrates learnt that he had had a violent temper ever since being injured in an accident, and was mercilessly teased by other boys in the street. The police surgeon, who had examined him previously, attempted unsuccessfully 'to have him dealt with as a mental case' under the 1913 Act. His father was unable to control him and openly confessed that 'he could do nothing with him'. His mother offered a more robust defence but, breaking down in tears, 'sobbed out that she was willing for her boy to go away, so that he should not be taunted by other boys'. The chairman, after consulting Dr Blackett, decided to send Albert to Frome Road House (as the workhouse was now known) 'for a while'.

7
BATHONIANS AT THE TURN OF THE DECADE

An article in the Christmas edition of *Vogue* in 1928 emphasised the elegance of Bath and argued that, if Jane Austen were to return, she would find much that was still familiar. There were, for example, 'the quaint shops' in Milsom Street, which the *Chronicle* had no hesitation in calling the Regent Street of the West. Yet much of Bath was arguably more Dickensian or even Hogarthian in atmosphere. Cattle were still herded through the streets to the slaughterhouses. There were street traders like the fishmonger, Bloker Wood, with his handcart, the 'muffin lady' and the woman in Bath Street who sold pigs' feet for sixpence. Milk was still delivered by milkmen or women carrying yokes with pails attached. On Friday and Saturday evenings there was an open air market in Sawclose, where almost anything was on sale from shoes, clothes and soap to corn plasters and sweets. Some stallholders came down by train from London with 'great big wicker baskets' which were conveyed to the market in a GWR horse-drawn van. As a teenager, Herbert Cobb managed to earn sixpence a basket and a further sixpence for supper by looking after them until their owners were ready to start business. In a very 'white' Bath there was one trader who stood out: 'a darkie', as Cobb called him, who sold tooth powder. By way of advertisement, 'he grabbed the kids and cleaned their teeth for them'.[1]

Sawclose Market and Milsom Street were two very different worlds, but both in their different ways were reminiscent of the eighteenth or nineteenth centuries. There were, however, shops such as Woolworths and Marks & Spencer which anticipated more modern retail trends. The joy of these shops was that the customer could wander through them at will without the forbidding presence of shop assistants, as historian Juliet Gardiner puts it, interposing 'themselves between the customer and goods kept out of reach on shelves and in drawers'.[2] A favourite pastime of William Chun on Saturdays, after he had finished work and his scouting activities, was to go 'into town to look at the shops [and go] into Marks and Spencer and Woolworths.[3]

The 1931 census showed that Bath's population had barely increased over the preceding decade. The population had risen from 68,669 to 68,801, with women outnumbering men by 10,465. In Bath there was an average of 13 people per acre, although this figure is largely meaningless as it includes parks and rural districts within the borough.[4] In the slums off Walcot Street and in the riverside areas around Corn Street and Avon Street there were pockets of intense overcrowding. Bathrooms were non-existent and outside toilets were shared by several families. The Parkhouse family, for instance, had to cram into two rooms in Corn Street, an intensely stressful situation which led to the children being taken into care for a time. Sarah Lacy recalled how her parents lived in a small cottage in Hedgemead Park with 13 children, with the boys sleeping at the top of the house and the girls below, all of them fitted into beds 'top to toe'.[5]

Living conditions in the semi-rural outskirts of Bath were better, if only because there was more space and fresh air. After Ron Perry's family moved out from Rivers Street to Fairfield Avenue near Charlcombe, he remembered how they would sit up in 'the rear bedroom window of a summer evening and listen to the nightingales singing as it got darker and darker'.[6] Similarly, Pauline Forrest's father, who was a bus driver, decided to leave the Kingsmead area, despite his wife's reservations, and move to Primrose Hill in Weston. Pauline recalled

> how at first, I was not impressed with our new home. The bottom window was protected by bars because it was on a level with the lane, and there was an old lamp bracket above the front door. Mother opened the door with a large key and we went down four steps into a passage. We opened another door and I was totally taken aback to see such a beautiful garden, a little overgrown maybe, but nevertheless far better than anything I could have imagined. Then I looked up at the beautiful hill and the green fields all around and wondered how a couple of town kids were going to fare in the country.[7]

Life in a modest private hotel or as a paying guest in a rented room was the fate that still awaited many single people or couples of limited financial means. For middle-class spinsters or widows, Partis College offered a much coveted refuge. It could only take 30 'decayed gentlewomen', who had to be Anglicans and widows or single daughters of clergymen, officers in the armed services, professional men in law, physics or divinity, or merchants. Many applicants were the widows of men who had been out in India or the colonies, while some had been missionaries or governesses. Anna Kempson, who applied in 1934, had an annual income of between £35 and £40 and lived in a one-room flatlet in Eastbourne. She had been a governess with a British family in India and returned home with them. In 1920, she had gone to Lichfield to look after an invalid aunt, whilst spending the mornings tutoring two children. Mary Lockward, who applied in 1930 and had an annual income of £50, was the former matron of a 'home for backward girls'. A successful application was like winning the lottery, as it guaranteed security for life. Margaret Pennington, when she heard that her application had been successful, was surely not exaggerating when, on 10 July 1922, in her letter of acceptance, she wrote, 'I cannot describe to you my joy … upon receiving your kind letter this evening'. Given the popularity of Partis College and the need it fulfilled, it is no wonder that funds were raised to extend it in 1929.[8]

Many of Bath's large Georgian houses had been converted into flats or lodging houses. Mary Dale's mother, Florence Sheppard, looked after one in Green Park before the family moved uphill and 'away from the river' to 18 Rivers Street. Two tenants, Mr and Mrs Gregory, moved with them and rented a couple of large rooms on the second floor. Mary's family lived on the ground floor in a large back room behind folding doors, which were 'always closed'.

There was a lavatory on the ground floor and another in the basement, but the rest of the tenants had to share one bathroom and a third lavatory. The only hot water in the house was in the bathroom, ' where a vicious noisy geyser emitted scalding water and volumes of steam when a shilling was inserted'. Pauline Forrest, in a telling phrase, refers to the 'lost people living in lodging houses'.[9] In many ways, 18 Rivers Street was a haven for such lonely people, who were well looked after by Mary's mother. They included Miss Humphreys, a dress maker at Jolly's, and a 'tiny dwarf-like' lady, who lived separately in two large rooms on the first floor for many years. Sadly, the latter eventually began to hear 'angel voices' and had to be admitted to Frome Road Infirmary. One evening she escaped and returned to Rivers Street where she locked herself in the bathroom. Mary was sent to fetch her uncle, who had to break open the door before she could be taken back to Frome Road. When Mr Gregory was dying, Mary was sent by her mother to sit with his wife whilst she waited for her husband's death. Decades after, she recalled how

> Mrs Gregory kept feeling her husband's feet, explaining that when they had gone cold he would have died. I went up several times, [as] death [was] not so out of sight then as it is nowadays, and I was told to touch him when he had died, so I touched the end of his stiff waxed moustache.

She reflected later that 'there must have been a learning purpose in all this'.[10]

Private hotels and lodging houses were a major Bath industry. They offered their owners both a home and a potentially lucrative business. When, for instance, the farm owned by Jessica Godwin and her first husband proved to be financially unsustainable in 1928, they bought a Georgian guest house in Belvedere. Their guests were provided with full board, and hot water in brass cans was carried up to them by a maid. Jessica also nursed her guests if they fell sick, and gained such a good reputation that she had a waiting list. One lady from the Grosvenor Hotel pleaded to have the room of a dying guest once it became vacant.[11]

There was, of course, much of Georgian Bath that was still inhabited by the 'gentry'. A cursory glance through the pages of the *Bath Chronicle* and Kelly's Directory in the second half of the 1920s reveals, for example, that Lady Enniskillen, the barrister Peter de Labilliere, the mayor of Bath, Aubrey Bateman, and the Deputy Lord Lieutenant of Somerset, Major James Townsend Reilly, OBE, all lived in the Royal Crescent, the very epitome of 'posh Bath'.

WORK

AT THE ANNUAL banquet of the Bath Chamber of Commerce at Cater, Stoffell and Fortt on 6 February 1929, the parliamentary secretary to the Board of Trade, Herbert Williams, told the assembled local businessmen that, 'you have industrially an importance which is not quite realised'. For this he blamed the 'novelists and dramatists', because whenever 'Bath does appear on the stage we see the Exquisites ... and the invalids of 150 years ago'. Bath's economy, as we have already seen, was a mixture of tourism (including health tourism), retail trade and manufacturing. Although the industrial sector in Bath was a major employer, other sectors – retail, construction, office work, health care, tourism and above all domestic service – between them employed more people. The 1931 census gives the following figures for the total number of workers in each sector:

	MEN	WOMEN
Transport	2,558	56
Metalworkers	1,817	16
Makers of instruments and watches	117	13

Textile workers	71	79
Makers of textile goods and articles of dress	540	1,319
Workers in wood	1,221	45
Workers in Paper, cardboard	194	254
Printers and photographers	428	88
Builders	1,225	2
Agricultural workers	954	27
Clergymen	42	—
Solicitors	53	—
Doctors	100	9
Sick Nurses	15	505
Teachers	180	430
Architects	19	1
Authors and journalists	43	7
Accountants	18	—
Personal Service	1,228	6,147

The Medical Officer of Health's annual report for 1934 gave a more detailed breakdown of personal service:

Domestic Service	215	4,587
Hotel, lodging and boarding housekeepers	232	429
Waiters porters, barmen, etc	299	177
Charwomen, caretakers, cleaners	89	326

It also gave the total number of people engaged in commercial and financial occupations – 3,148 men and 1.627 women.[12]

Nationally, by early 1929, economic prospects – except for declining industries in the depressed regions – seemed reasonably good. Strikes had abated, unemployment had stabilised at about 4.5%, and, to quote the Parliamentary Secretary to the Board of Trade, 'world peace [seemed] reasonably established'. Stothert and Pitt benefited from this relatively benign economic climate. Besides securing several orders for harbour cranes, it also won the contract for erecting two towers as part of the Mettur Dam project in India, which at the time it was built, was the largest dam in the world. Cranes and other machinery were constructed and assembled by groups of fitters, semi-skilled men, apprentices and labourers under a charge hand. Stothert and Pitt also employed a number of girls as machinists. Holidays were unpaid, but the firm shut down for a week at the end of August. Life at the factory was regulated by a hooter, which not only marked the beginning and end of the working day but also an hour-long lunch break from one to two o'clock.[13]

The Bath Cabinet Makers Ltd experienced a modest boom helped by the demand for bespoke wireless sets. Earl and Countess Temple, for example, had, according to their agent, one of their 'beautifully finished Wireless Receiving Sets' installed in their mansion in Newton Park.[14] The firm won a large contract for the Golden Arrow and Continental Pullman cars and designed fittings for some of the great ocean-going liners, the first being two Italian ships, the *Saturnia* and *Oceania*. It also produced the interior panelling

(above and opposite page) Stothert and Pitt cranes (Museum of Bath at Work)

for London's County Hall and the new university buildings in Bristol, as well as making furniture for several Indian Maharajahs and King Faisal of Iraq. One Bathonian, George Perry, in an interview in 1989, recalled his experiences with the firm in the twenties and early thirties. On his first day as an apprentice he was taken to buy essential tools at Paisey's in Kingsmead Square by the foreman, Jack Williams, whose nickname was 'Old Hundreds'. In retrospect, George described him as a 'good cabinet maker', but added, unflatteringly and maybe inaccurately, that he was 'an ignorant old devil'. Altogether, there were several hundred people working for the firm – machinists, cabinet makers, polishers, fitters-up, as well as those in the timber yard. As at Stothert & Pitt, holidays, including the Christmas and Easter breaks, were unpaid.[15]

The Horstman Car Company continued its erratic course. One of its employees, who worked as a turner in the twenties and thirties remembered, when interviewed in 1993, that the factory was 'open plan' and at any one time only four cars could be assembled there. His impressions of Sidney Horstmann were perceptive: he was 'clever, inventive but perhaps not the best type of businessman'. Car production ceased in 1929 but work continued on the development of coil spring suspension for cars and motorbikes. The Slow Motion Suspension Company (SMS) was formed to sell the new products. Here indeed Horstmann showed his inventiveness, which could arguably be described as genius. In March 1929, the prototype of the Horstman spring suspension system was tried out by Kaye Don, the record-breaking car and speedboat racer, for the Avon India Rubber Company in a car driven at 40 mph on 'an unkempt road, which was in an appalling condition having potholes five or six inches deep in places'. He reported that 'the car had the feeling of floating over the road rather than travelling on it'. Its suitability for motor cycles and sidecars was also tested by the chief designer of the Ariel Works in Birmingham, who was ready to recommend it for mass production subject to minor modifications.

The War Office was interested in adapting 'slow motion springs' for their new 'baby tanks'. In April 1930, a tank was fitted with them in the James Street works and tested by Tank Corps personnel on Lansdown. It created a considerable stir when it was driven back down Milsom Street. The War Office was impressed with the results and in March 1931 entered into discussions with Sidney Horstmann regarding the possibility of adopting the system not only for their three-man tank but also for a 'cheaper lighter tank'. One SMS director told Horstmann that, if the company's designs met with the approval of the War Office, 'you will have your works full for the rest of the year'.

A baby tank fitted with the Horstman spring suspension system (Bristol Evening Times and Echo, Horstmann papers, Museum of Bath at Work)

The company rose to the challenge and was able to demonstrate that a tank or a tracked vehicle fitted with the new suspension system could go about 50% faster. Shortly before Easter 1932, the army sent an engineer to report on the progress being made at the James Street works in adapting the suspension system to the six-inch howitzer. He was impressed and told the directors that the very valuable assistance so liberally and frankly offered 'enabled me to compile a report which received special attention from the Chief Inspector and created the right kind of atmosphere at Woolwich for our purpose'.

The SMS design team worked flat out. The suspension systems were patented in May and were subsequently adopted by the War Office. Vickers-Armstrongs Ltd attempted to argue that they infringed their own patents, but when their claims were shown to be inaccurate, they entered into a license agreement with Horstman's 'for the sole rights to use the suspension for tracked vehicles of any kind'. In 1939, the German armaments firm, Friederich Krupp, disputed the Horstman patent for suspension systems and applied to have it revoked. It was unsuccessful, as the German Patent Office conceded in December that the Horstman invention differed 'from the prior construction advanced by Krupps'. Astonishingly, these arguments took place in the early months of the Second World War. Not surprisingly, Sidney Horstmann was told by his British patent agent that payment to the German patent agents could wait 'until after the conclusion of hostilities'. By 1940, the Horstman suspension system was being widely used in British tanks and caterpillar track vehicles. The *Gas Times* also claimed that the Russians were using it, 'but without paying royalties'.[16]

Sidney Horstmann had also been involved, back in 1903, in setting up the Bath Motor & Garage Company, a wholly-owned subsidiary of S&A Fuller, whose coachbuilding works were in Kingsmead Street. It saw very early on which way the wind was blowing and switched production to building bodies for chassis provided by motor manufacturers. The company also serviced vehicles and by 1921 had a workforce of between 50 and 60. As neither Austin nor Ford would agree that their cars should be repaired under the same roof, there had to be two separate workshops. According to one former employee, WH Usher, wealthy doctors in the Circus and Gay Street were among their best customers. Usher joined Fuller's as an apprentice in 1929 and

> often had to walk or cycle to Bowler's in Corn Street to buy things. Approximately once a week he went to buy steel, bronze, brass screws, nuts and bolts ... [The] shop had a large free moving bell over the door. Frank Bowler, the son of the firm's founder JB Bowler, would eventually appear at the counter [at which] the order [was] placed which he would duly study. If a small item was required, he would turn to one of the many unlabelled wooden drawers and choose the correct one nine times out of ten. For a special alloy such as steel, bronze or brass, he would go to the workshop and cut it. To cut the metal the steam engine would have to be started. The workshop had a stark and heavy atmosphere as if it were all about to collapse.[17]

Bowler's was one of the wonders of Bath. Almost anything that was needed could be found or made there. Its business files, which are preserved *in toto* in the Museum of Bath at Work, contain requests not only from local firms such as Stothert and Pitt, but from businesses all over the country for nuts,

Bowler's shop in Corn Street in 1972 after it had closed down (Museum of Bath at Work)

piping and illuminated signs. Frank Bowler was totally dedicated to his work and, according to Usher, in the evening would work in his potting shed at home with a light attached to his forehead. Next door to the workshop was Bowler's mineral water factory. Agnes Joyce, whose father was the grandson of JB Bowler, remembers going to the factory as a child and 'being sat on a tall stool behind the counter and given a bowl of horrible smelling paste and a little brush' to stick labels on the bottles to show their provenance and whether they contained 'orangeade, appleade, lemonade, etc'.[18]

One of the most unpleasant places to work in Bath was the woollen mill of Isaac Carr and Co on the Lower Bristol at Twerton. Ella Lucas, who was an invoice clerk there, remembered that the floors were encrusted with grease and wool fluff, and that, although the noise was well nigh unbearable, no earmuffs were provided. In Wilf Gingell's opinion, much more salubrious employment was to be found on the trams and buses, despite the possibility of picking up flu germs during the rush hour. Wilf started off as a conductor before being promoted to driver. He enjoyed wearing his uniform of blue serge, red piping and brass buttons, and loved the job, especially in the spring, when his favourite route was Bathford to Combe Down, which took him out into the open countryside.[19]

For many 14-year-old boys, their first job on leaving school was to work as an errand boy, since groceries and many other goods were delivered to customers by hand – or rather bike. After leaving school, William Burraston, for example, worked briefly on a milk round before becoming an errand boy and rat catcher at Evans & Owen. One of his duties was to climb up to the roof every evening to lower the store's flag. He later moved into the construction and haulage industries.[20] For those who passed the General School Certificate, office work was a possible option. 17-year- old John New joined the solicitors, Stone, King & Wardell, in Queen Square, as a junior in the cashier's department. On Monday mornings his first job. along with the other juniors, was to clean and fill the inkwells. Later he graduated to collecting rents on behalf of clients, often from the residents of slum properties.[21]

In Bath, as in other cities, there were a large number of small shops which employed just one or two assistants. Cyril Bond remembered that there were four grocers' shops within a hundred yards of each other on the Lower Bristol Road. He had originally intended to go into plumbing, but one of these shops – at 11 Avon Buildings – was owned by his Baptist Sunday School teacher, Frederick Batten, who in 1929 persuaded him to come and work there. Nearly 60 years later, Cyril could still vividly recall weighing sugar, tea and butter and how cheese was bought from Spear Bros & Clark, whose rep, resplendent in bowler hat and carrying a rolled umbrella, called to take orders on Thursdays.[22] There were also numerous small butchers and fishmongers. Ada Derrick's father, who lived in Avon Street, had premises across the road from his house, where he would wash and smoke kippers, mackerel and herrings after collecting them from the station early in the morning with his horse and cart. He was the only fish merchant in Bath to produce bloaters by smoking and curing herrings; he supplied them to a local fishmonger in Corn Street as well as several street vendors. Ada was given the task of taking bills round to his customers, but, as she recalled, 'a lot of people didn't pay'.[23] Independent butchers also rose early to prepare meat for their customers. Patricia Connett, who lived over her father's butcher's shop at Claremont Terrace on Camden Road, remembered her father starting work at 6am and bringing meat from the fridge outside into the shop where it was cut up and priced. He had a lucrative delivery round, extending all the way up Lansdown to the Hare and Hounds. The father of a another Bathonian, Preston Jones, owned a prosperous butcher's shop in Margaret's Buildings and a nearby slaughterhouse, while he grazed his cattle and sheep in a small field below the Royal Crescent.[24]

The spa clinic employed some 40 medical staff, as well as a plumber, an engineer, several labourers and an upholsterer to maintain its couches and chairs. The clinic was also a good customer of the Fuller's earth Union. Fuller's earth was delivered in sacks before being mixed to a paste and applied in packs to patients' swollen joints. Many of those who came to Bath to be treated at the spa were wealthy, and their needs and whims bolstered the city's economy. Local shops often sent in goods on approval for patients to buy if the fancy took them. Patients also took rooms in local hotels and boarding houses. The Grand Pump Room Hotel had a lift connecting it with the Treatment Centre, while other hotels ran private buses to the spa. All this provided employment, especially for girls and women. Margaret Powney, for instance, worked as a chambermaid in the Empire Hotel, which she much preferred to her previous jobs in private service and as a cleaner in the Frome Road Workhouse. She slept in a dormitory in the basement with twelve other girls, and remembered how the beds were infested with 'little, tiny white things' which came in from the river. Her day started at 7am. Once the staff had breakfasted, she took tea up to guests in the rooms which had been allocated to her, and, after they had come down for breakfast, she cleaned their rooms. The girls had to buy their own dresses, but were given two weeks paid holiday. Alas for Margaret and the other girls, the porters and waiters received most of the tips. Margaret's exact contemporary, Mr W Willis, also worked at the Empire where he qualified as a waiter in 1923, remaining there until 1939. Some 65 years later, he recalled the routine and strict discipline in the hotel dining room. He started work each day at 7am laying the tables and then serving breakfast. Afterwards he had to change the tablecloths and lay the tables for lunch. At 11am the waiting staff had an hour's break before beginning their lunch duties.

Each waiter was responsible for six tables and had his own sideboard for the dishes, which were carried to the guests on a tray resting on the waiter's shoulder. Dinner preparations began at 6pm for an elaborate meal, consisting of seven or eight courses. Apart from the tips, one consolation for the hard work involved was the frequent presence of such notables as Lord Nuffield, Lord Derby, Sir Thomas Beecham, Paul Robeson and the actor Jack Hulbert, who was in town while filming Arnold Ridley's *Ghost Train* at Camerton station in 1931. The waiters had just one afternoon off a week.[25]

Although Bath's reputation as a tourist centre was enhanced by the medicinal value of its waters, it was not dependent on it. There were thousands of visitors who weren't interested in taking the waters, and they provided much needed employment. A party of American travel agents visiting the city in October 1929 told a *Chronicle* journalist that, 'you've got Rome beaten'. On Easter Monday 1929, despite the cold wind, the city was inundated with tourists. The GWR brought in a constant stream of people, and Bath Tramways had a record day. All this, of course, boosted the coffers of restaurants, cafés, ice-cream sellers and the purveyors of Bowler's fizzy drinks. Bath also hosted conferences, which brought hundreds of delegates and their wives into the city. In 1928, the Royal Institute of British Architects, the Incorporated Municipal Electrical Association and the Association of

Education Committees of England, Wales & Northern Ireland all held conferences in the city. On 10 May, when a conference on rheumatism – described as 'a miniature BMA gathering' – took place, the Chief Medical Officer of the Ministry of Health declared it not only 'a great success from a medical and scientific point of view, but also as a social gathering'.[26] One can only imagine that he was unaware of the typhoid outbreak on Bathwick Hill ! In September the following year, 550 members of the Meat Traders Federation met in Bath, bringing work not only to the hotels and guest houses but also to Cater, Stoffel and Fortt, which laid on a banquet at the county skating rink (now the Pavilion).

Despite periodic complaints in the *Chronicle* that girls were no long willing to work as servants, domestic service was still a major source of employment in Bath, as the 1931 census revealed. Many girls started work at 14 in private houses. Ada Derrick, for instance, was cook-general to the curate of St Paul's for two and a half years and learnt how to make such gastronomic delights as 'jugged hare and tiny cakes'. Sarah Lacy went into 'general service at the same age with a Mrs Mannering, who lived near the Spa Hotel. She was paid nine shillings a month and was allowed half a day a week and every other Sunday off. She slept in the basement and was given no instruction in her domestic duties. Gwendoline Wicks also took up a post as a domestic servant and was paid £15 a year. As she recalled, 'after roaming the fields and woods of Tucking Mill, it was like prison', as she too was only 'let out half a day a week and alternate Sunday afternoons'. Not surprisingly she jumped at the chance of becoming a lady's maid to a 'Mrs C', 'an elderly lady, tall and willowy with a stick and a plaintive voice', whose name she unfortunately does not reveal. She was apparently a very grand lady, who travelled extensively around the country, and employed nine inside and five outdoor staff. The precise and elderly butler followed exactly the same routine every day, right down 'to lighting his pipe ... and marching to the toilet along a long passage'. Mrs C treated Gwendoline 'as a robot', never conversing with her, only telling her 'to do this or to do that'. When she went out in her large Daimler, Gwendoline sat in the front with the driver. She also accompanied Mrs C on train journeys, and at one station was ordered to fetch some newspapers from the bookstall just as the train was about to move. A porter seized her and flung her back into the carriage, and Mrs C 'never batted an eyelid'. One advantage of being a lady's maid was that there was no housework and opportunities to travel. It was this, perhaps, that explains why Gwendoline remained eight years in Mrs C's employment.[27]

HOME LIFE AND LEISURE

ONE OF THE facts of life in inter-war Britain for the great majority of the working classes – and indeed for many of the middle classes, such as priests, teachers and clerks – was a shortage of money. As Pauline Forrest observes in *Childhood Memories*,

> money was scarce and we had to make do with what we had. I realised that my character was developing around the hard times we had to endure. For even as a child it taught me how to be careful with almost everything ... I knew only too well the financial embarrassment that seemed to be lurking everywhere.[28]

John New's childhood memories illustrate this. As a child he lived in an eleven-room house and was well fed and looked after, but there was no spare money, as his father, a goods-train guard, had seven other children to provide for. John received a penny a week pocket money. When as a sixth former at King Edward's, he was selected to play in the school's rugby team in an away match against Bristol Grammar School, his father duly bought him a 1/6 return ticket, forgoing his weekly treat of tobacco as a result. The New family was able to keep its head successfully above water, but some families were overwhelmed by poverty and the children had to go temporarily into care. Others could only get by with weekly visits to the pawn shop. Some husbands drank, others gambled.[29]

The key rule for so many families was 'making do', which manifested itself in every area of life. Clothes were handed down and often made at home, and 'skirts were "turned" so that worn parts were unseen inside the garment'. Food was 'plain and wholesome', the highlight of the week being Sunday lunch. This was usually a roast, served with potatoes and greens from the allotment, and for the next few days what was left of the joint served as a base for stews or cottage pies. Mary Dale's mother 'made a delicious meal composed of boiled bones, red lentils with potatoes, parsnips and carrots'. No food was ever wasted or sent back from the table. John New remembers how surprised he was when invited to the birthday of a school friend, whose father was a company secretary, and some left-over fruit was taken back to the kitchen to be thrown away – 'that was unknown in our family', he later remarked.[30]

For many, holidays were a luxury. Cruises and continental trips were advertised by Bell's Travel Bureau in New Bond Street, but only the well-to-do could afford them. For the majority, if they were lucky, there were seaside boarding houses, whose landladies cooked food which guests bought themselves.

Those who were more affluent could stay in hotels or rent bungalows, cottages and apartments. Ernest Bowler and his family, for example, often went to Ilfracombe.[31] For those who could not afford to get away, there were day trips by train or charabanc to such places as Weymouth and Weston-super-Mare. Nearer to home, swimming at Bathampton Weir was popular, as was listening to the band in Parade Gardens. A trip by tram to the Glass House Café at Combe Down, where tea was served with strawberries and cream, was also a favourite summer excursion.

Bath was a city divided by class. Looking back at Bath between the wars, Mary Dale observed that 'we think of Bath as wealthy but to us it was them or us'. Even Agnes Joyce, a member of the Bowler dynasty, was intimidated by the 'grand ladies of Bath' when she worked as an apprentice shop assistant. 'Lots of titled people' came into the shop where she worked, she later recalled, but they 'treated most of us as dirt' and 'barked or hollered at you'. There was very much a 'them and us' attitude.[32] Yet, beneath the surface, there could often be found a common humanity or perhaps vulnerability. To take one example, Richard Butcher, the son of a prosperous GP, and Gwendoline Wicks, whose father worked for the Fuller's Earth Union at Tucking Mill, had similar problems with elderly parents. Richard remembered that it was only when his father taught him to fish while on holiday that he had any contact with him. He was 50 when Richard was born and seemed to him an old man, so not surprisingly he envied friends who had younger parents. Gwendoline also complained of the aloofness of her parents, regretting that she never had any conversation with them. All she ever heard was 'don't do this or that', while discussing births and deaths was 'taboo'.[33]

Another story that shows humanity rather than arrogance is related by Pauline Forrest. One day, she was peering into the chemist's window in St James's Square when a large car drew up driven by a chauffeur, who rushed into the post office, while his master went to the chemist. Pauline was so smitten by his little white 'Scotty dog', who was left outside, that she abducted it and carried it off to Victoria Park. After playing with it, she took it back to the address on its collar, which was a house at the top of Lansdown near the race course. When she arrived, she was met by a friendly but relieved butler and given a five shilling reward by the master for finding the dog. Later she reflected that 'it was lucky that the dog could not speak'.[34] There were, too, people who could bridge the class gap like the vicar of Monkton Combe, Percy Warrington. He was an eccentric, who walked around the village in a top hat and long cravat, but organised marvellous fêtes which featured attractions such as a roulette wheel and a fortune teller, which shocked some of his more straitlaced parishioners. In his spare time, his mission was to save the historic houses of England from demolition when their owners could no longer afford to keep them going. Thanks to his efforts as founder of the Allied Schools Trust, both the mansions at Stowe and Westonbirt became schools and survived.[35]

8
INTO THE THIRTIES

THE END OF AN ERA

IN EARLY 1929 two prominent Bathonians died: Alderman Cedric Chivers and Captain Charles Foxcroft. Chivers, a staunch Liberal who had been six times mayor, was in many ways the public face of Bath. He generously contributed money to its hospitals and, in the words of *Chronicle*, 'never tired of his birthplace'. He also ceaselessly worked to create harmony between capital and labour. Captain Foxcroft was a political, but not personal opponent, a diehard Tory, who represented Bath for the Conservative Party from 1918 until his death, apart from the brief Liberal interregnum of December 1923-October 1924. He was in many ways a 'marmite figure', disliked by many on the Left but revered by the local Conservative Association, which emphasised above all his 'consideration and kindliness'. This was particularly evident when in March 1919 he insisted that £100 of his annual donation to the association should be awarded to its faithful but scandalously underpaid secretary, Mr Strawson. Foxcroft died at six o'clock on the evening on Monday 11 February at his home in Hinton Charterhouse, and was given a feudal send-off by his tenants, with his gamekeeper, gardeners and chauffeur carrying his coffin at his funeral.

Alderman Cedric Chivers five times mayor of Bath and founder of Cedric Chivers Ltd., Bookbinders. He died in office in January 1929 (Bath Record Office)

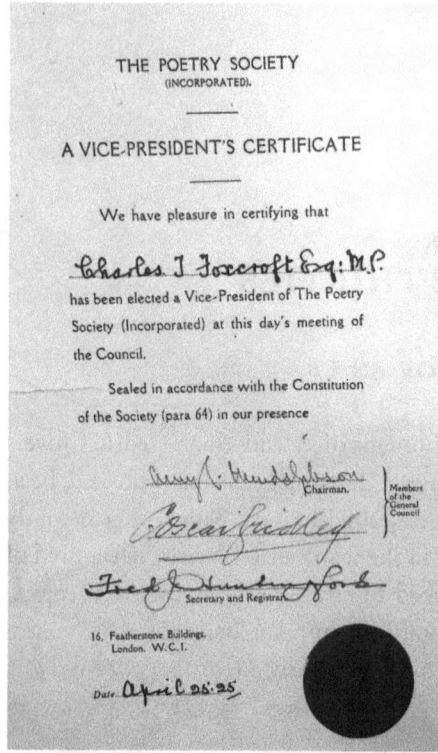

Besides being a conscientious and forceful politician, Foxcroft was also a poet and in 1925 was elected Vice-President of the Poetry Society (Bath Record Office)

His sister, Helen Foxcroft, was moved by the number of letters of condolence she received from fellow Conservative MPs, Bathonians and representatives of organisations he had supported or helped, such as the Southern Irish Loyalist Relief Association, the Friends of Italy and the Orthodox Jewish association in London. James Tarrant, the secretary of the Bath Trade and Labour Council (BTLC), told her that, despite their political differences, Foxcroft had always been ready to listen to the BTLC's concerns. He remembered particularly how Foxcroft had fully explained the workings of the Trade Disputes Bill and answered all their queries. He concluded his letter by telling Helen that 'this vote of sympathy was carried unanimously by a full Council of Delegates'.

Foxcroft's death led to a by-election in Bath on 21 March 1929, and his successor was Charles Baillie-Hamilton, who had been Stanley Baldwin's private secretary. In his acceptance speech on 25 February he gave an upbeat review of the Conservative Party's record and lauded the extension of the vote to women aged between 21 and 30, stressing that 'in common decency and common justice they should have as much say in the nation's destinies as young men of their own age'.[1]

The government, which was facing a general election within a few months, had suffered a string of by-election defeats but was determined to hang on to Bath. Baldwin himself enthusiastically endorsed Baillie-Hamilton, and Harold Macmillan, the Conservative member for Stockton-on-Tees and future prime minister, agreed at short notice to come down and address a meeting at St Peter's Hall. Although the franchise had been extended, the by-election was still fought on the old register, as there had been insufficient time to update it. The poll was down by some 12% compared to 1924, and the Conservatives held the seat comfortably, but, as the socialist Malcolm Hardyman pointed out, of the 24,785 votes cast, 13,614 were 'dissatisfied' and went to either the Liberals or Labour.

Within weeks of the Bath by-election, the general election campaign started. The country was tired of the Conservative administration, and as the *Times* commented later, 'the doom of the Baldwin administration could clearly be foreseen'. Yet, as the *Chronicle* observed, in Bath the election campaign was attended by 'a curious apathy', despite the electorate having been increased by the addition of 8,000 more female voters; at political meetings attendance was low compared to past campaigns. The most eccentric incident in a well-mannered campaign was JR Charmbury's threat to stand as an independent Conservative. In the event, it became apparent that he was mentally ill and had to be 'conveyed to an institution in Wells'. Baillie-Hamilton defended the government's record on unemployment and attempted to curdle the blood of Bathonians with frequent references to the 'Red Peril'. With the anti-Tory vote still divided between the Liberals and Labour it was no surprise that Baillie- Hamilton romped home with a majority of over 6,000. The result was declared by the mayor on the steps of the Guildhall at 11.30 on 30 May and greeted with prolonged cheers. Despite reports of 'apathy', the turnout in Bath was just over 82% – only 2% less than in the 1924 election The elected member also had his 'Hollywood moment' when his fiancée, the 'femme fatale', Miss Wanda Holden, who would divorce him three years later, joined him at the window and blew kisses to the crowd. A dissenting note was struck by Sidney Daniels, the Liberal candidate, who argued again that 'the Conservatives only owed their success to an out-of-date electoral system, which allowed 'a man to be elected against the wishes of a majority of his constituents'. Further excitement was to be had in Sawclose where the Palace Theatre was 'a blaze of light'. Its staff were receiving constant updates from the *Chronicle* office about the election results across the country, which were displayed to the crowds outside on an illuminated screen. Nationally, there was a marked swing to Labour, which with 288 seats emerged as the largest party, but failed to win an outright majority. Labour formed a government that was of necessity dependent on the support of the Liberals, who won 59 seats, while the Conservatives secured just 260 seats.

THE WALL STREET CRASH AND THE FORMATION OF THE NATIONAL GOVERNMENT

THE MINORITY LABOUR government initially appeared to be a reasonably competent administration, but was derailed by the Great Depression, which the historian Robert Boyce has called the 'third global catastrophe' of the twentieth century (the world wars being the other two). The new government inherited an encouraging economic situation, but by the autumn there were signs that 'all was not well'. The Great Economic Depression was heralded by the Wall Street Crash on 29 October 1929, when the value of US stocks and shares plummeted. This led to a sudden end to the speculative bubble in the US and a halt in the flow of American investment into Germany and many other counties. It severely damaged world trade and led to a sharp rise in unemployment in the UK, where by January 1933 there were nearly three million out of work. The Wall Street Crash received relatively little attention in Bath, although a report from 'a Bath lady in New York' appeared in the *Chronicle* nearly a fortnight later:

> The stock markets are in a terrible state over here, and things are topsy turvey in Wall Street. Being right in the heart of the business centre, we, of course, see and hear lots of happenings. The other day when there was a crisis in the financial world, there were ambulances rushing along Broadway all the afternoon: I expect heaps of people had heart attacks, and we heard of more than one suicide in the course of the day. The American people are all finance mad; money is the theme of every conversation.[2]

As the economy deteriorated, Philip Snowden, the Chancellor of the Exchequer, set up the May Committee in the spring of 1931. In July, much like the Geddes Committee ten years previously, it recommended increased taxation and a series of swingeing cuts . A month later, financial collapse in central Europe, where the City of London had invested heavily, caused a run on sterling. In reaction, foreign investors rapidly began to withdraw their deposits from the City. The fear that this would force Britain off the gold standard and trigger hyper-inflation led to the formation of a national government under Ramsey MacDonald, the Labour prime minister, which was supported by both Liberals and Conservatives. Only four ministers of the previous Labour government and eight of the party's backbenchers voted for the new government, as the majority were bitterly hostile to the proposed cuts in wages and unemployment benefits, which it was hoped would save the pound. The pound was not saved, however, and on 21 September Britain left the gold standard. Five weeks later, on 27 October, MacDonald went to the country and called for a 'doctor's mandate' to deal with the economy.

HIGH DRAMA IN BATH'S CONSERVATIVE PARTY

IN BATH, THE Conservative candidate was not Baillie-Hamilton, but the fabulously wealthy 25-year-old Thomas Loel Guinness, who was one of the first people in Britain to own his own plane. His predecessor was deselected in dramatic events which, as the *Chronicle* remarked, were 'unparalleled in the history of Conservatism in Bath'. Baillie-Hamilton had won two elections in 1929 by a large margin and was initially popular with local Conservatives. At the annual meeting of the Conservative Association in October 1929, after congratulating him on his two victories, Edmund Bagshawe, the chairman, told his fellow Conservatives that 'now they had got him, they had to keep him'. At first all seemed to go well. In December 1929, at a meeting of women Conservatives, he attacked the Labour government for producing no policies to deal with unemployment, and presented some interesting ideas on the future of Empire trade. He was popular with the Imps, as the Young Conservatives were called, and was a supporter of the Junior Imperial League. In June 1930 he held several meetings in Bath – at the Oldfield Picture House, Kingsmead Square, Southdown, Widcombe Hill, Sawclose and Abbey Green. The Abbey Green meeting attracted most attention, as he was accompanied by the young Randolph Churchill, whose provocative speeches did much to raise the political temperature.

Yet under the surface relations between Baillie-Hamilton and the Conservative Association were not harmonious. He ruffled some feathers at the annual meeting in October 1929 when he observed that the name of the Conservative Party should be changed to the Empire Party, remarking that 'to him the name Conservative represented something dead and gone'. Increasingly, complaints began to circulate about him, and he was accused of 'contemptuous treatment' of the Bath Conservative Association. Between January 1930 and May 1931 he only visited the Association offices at Pitt House four times, and when he did attend local events, he delivered very badly prepared speeches. Dr James Allen told the annual meeting of the association in May 1931 that, 'for the last nine months he had been going about the Weston ward, of which he was chairman, and conversing politically with everyone, but he had never heard one single word in favour of Mr Baillie-Hamilton spoken to him.' He had also been told in no uncertain terms by many supporters that, 'on no consideration whatever', would they vote for him at the next election. He added ominously that he had heard the same message from other wards.[3]

Baillie-Hamilton's parliamentary attendance also came under close scrutiny. His voting record was unimpressive. In the 1929-30 session he had been absent from 285 divisions. Initially, Bagshawe took no action on the growing number of complaints, believing as late as May 1930 that 'every young man should be given an opportunity to find himself', but in July he requested a meeting with him to discuss the reasons for his growing unpopularity. When the meeting eventually took place in October, Baillie-Hamilton 'professed himself absolutely satisfied' with his own conduct and argued that he visited his constituency as often as most other MPs did theirs. However, he did concede that 'one or two of his speeches' had not been well prepared.

At the executive committee meeting on 13 January 1931, Bagshawe confessed that he had been through every election since 1903 as chairman 'but had never felt so anxious about an election as I do the approaching one'. The reason for this, as Sir Harry Hatt spelt out, was that Baillie-Hamilton was 'not making himself sufficiently known and liked' by the voters. The committee therefore decided to call a special meeting to decide what the next step should be. How the announcement should be worded was left to Lord Bath. On 27 January, a meeting of the special executive committee passed a resolution, by a majority of four, baldly stating that it could not 'recommend the Hon CW Baillie-Hamilton as Conservative candidate for the next election' and requested the committee 'to take immediate steps to find a candidate'. Bagshawe warned his colleagues not to let 'what has happened tonight … go to the press'. On 17 March, a full meeting of the general committee endorsed this decision by 87 votes to 1, and on 28 April, at the annual meeting of Bath Conservative Party, the decision was decisively supported, despite 124 dissenting voices. Two weeks later, on 15 May, Baillie-Hamilton gave his side of the story at a meeting in the Pavilion. He told his audience that

> I have tried very hard – and I think I have succeeded – in banishing any bitterness from my heart over this business, but I think it only fair to say this: that while things are changing all over this country, everything seems to be stationary and static in Bath. I have tried to change it, but it does not seem to be of any use (laughter). I want you to realise that these are very dangerous times.[4]

Charles Baillie-Hamilton, Conservative MP for Bath 1929-1932 (Bath Record Office)

He did not seek to hide his bitterness when he went on to say that, 'as long as you have the same men at the head of this show in Bath, all I can say is, from the bottom of my heart, [that] I pity my successor'.

The Association did not waste time. Given the fact that there was a minority Labour government in power and an election could come at any time, in just over a month it chose Thomas Loel Guinness as the prospective Conservative candidate. In many ways he was a very similar candidate to Baillie-Hamilton: young, wealthy and well connected and he had cut his political teeth as a Conservative candidate in Whitechapel. He was also a staunch believer in empire free trade.

When Ramsay MacDonald decided to appeal to the country for a 'doctors' mandate', several well known Liberal councillors in Bath, including Aldermen Wills and Spear, immediately declared their willingness to vote Conservative for the first time in their life as this seemed the best way to support the national government and avert the threat of economic ruin and hyperinflation. Their advice found a receptive audience in Bath, and Loel Guinness was returned in October with a sweeping majority of 14,696.

DEVALUATION

STERLING'S DEPARTURE FROM the gold standard on 21 September and the devaluation of sterling by some 30% had little impact on everyday life in Bath. Unsure of its significance, the *Chronicle* immediately sought out AE Hunt, the headmaster of West Twerton School, who had degrees in commerce and economics, to explain what devaluation meant for its readers. He reassuringly told them that the British people had little to fear from paper currency, provided the Bank did not print money indiscriminately – 'the fact that the standard is one of paper does not mean that we are rushing headlong to disaster'. Mallory and Sons, the jeweller's on Bridge Street, immediately tried to cash in on the rising price of gold and announced that it would give customers 'at the moment a higher price for any gold' which they might wish to sell. Yet for some the departure from gold was a national humiliation. The vicar of Widcombe, the Rev C Lovegrove-Herman was on holiday in Switzerland on the day it occurred and, as he said later, 'he never felt so humiliated in his life'. He could not express what he felt when he received only 15 shillings, instead of 20 for the British sovereign'.

Although the general public hardly noticed any difference, for importers of manufactured goods and raw materials, there were considerable difficulties.

Bathford Paper Mills Co. Ltd. (Museum of Bath at Work)

The Fullers' Earth Union, for example. was informed that the price of Swiss silk bolting cloth was to rise by 30%.[5] The Bathford Paper Mills also felt the impact of devaluation in the autumn of 1931, when one of their suppliers, Lloyds Packing Warehouse Ltd in Manchester, bleakly spelt out the implications of the situation:

> Owing to our having now received definite advice of the intention of our foreign suppliers of paper to surcharge our invoices with the equivalent of the fall in Sterling Exchange and also as our stocks have now been exhausted, we have no option but to withdraw all quotations for materials supplied by us from stocks.[6]

The impact of devaluation was also felt by Bath's timber firms, JT Holmes and Co Ltd and the Locksbrook Wharf Timber Company. In early October 1931, a spokesman for the local timber trade described the situation as 'chaotic'. The cost of imports from the US had increased by about 25%. As Sweden and Norway had also left the gold standard, their prices remained stable. Finland, on the other hand, remained on the gold standard, and its exporters were demanding sweeping price increases. JJ Lee and Sons, the cardboard box manufacturers in Trim Street, were also facing steep price rises on imports from Holland and Germany of some 20-25%.

Amongst housewives there was an initial fear that food prices would rise sharply, but deflation actually meant that the cost of home-grown products steadily declined. JR Huntley, the provision merchant in Northgate Street, reassured his customers that that while 'everyone needs to be careful ... no one needs to be panicky'. He told them that the price of imported American, Polish, Dutch and Danish foods, such as bacon, would certainly rise, but, given that the cost of a large number of provisions had declined by some 20% over the previous two years, these rises would not be drastic. He conceded that, 'we may be compelled to put up prices later on', but added optimistically that, 'even if we do this, the public will be better off than they were last year, and much better off than two years ago'. In August 1932, a similar message was delivered by the President of the Bath Cooperative Society who reported that, although cash sales were down about 2% for the quarter ending in April, 'this really indicated an increase in the quantities of goods dealt with', since the cost of living had fallen by 7% compared to the same period last year. The decline in the value of the pound also helped local hotels because wintering abroad had become more expensive. In October 1931, the number of enquiries at the Bath Information Bureau increased dramatically and this resulted in a very busy Christmas for the hotels. As the *Chronicle* observed in its Christmas Eve edition, 'the national crisis and the period of Depression do not seem to have left any mark on Bath's Christmas booking'.

THE GREAT DEPRESSION

THE DEPRESSION HAD a greater impact on the country than devaluation. Bath was no exception, but her industries fared better than those in the great industrial regions of South Wales and the North. During the years 1931-33 almost all the city's industries faced declining orders and profits, yet most through a combination of laying off workers and introducing short-time working managed to survive. In June 1931, the shareholders of Bath Cabinet Makers were told that the company had been badly affected by poor sales. At one stage, according to George Perry, who was an apprentice with the company at the time, there were 'only about two workers still employed in the whole place', and he was out of work for 17 weeks.[7] Stothert and Pitt continued to win contracts for cranes, but by March 1932 persistent rumours were circulating around the city that the firm was about to close owing to a shortage of orders. These proved unfounded, but some employees were laid off, and – except for the fitting and machine shops – the factory went onto three-quarter time, which meant working from 9 to 5 on Mondays to Fridays and closing on Saturdays. In the financial year 1931-32 the company made a loss of over £16,000, but a trickle of orders, combined with work on the Mettur Dam in India, enabled it to survive.

The Bathford Paper Mills retained its workforce, but no new workers were enrolled. One optimistic young man from Keynsham, who had heard that paper mills were offering apprenticeships to 'young fellows, who have been well educated and wish to take up practical paper making', had his hopes dashed.[8] The Fuller's Earth Union was able to retain major customers like the Anglo-Persian Oil Co and Shell-Mex, but the demand for some of its products, like washed and refined earth, was 'dead'. As trade was so quiet, there was 'no particular hurry' in replacing Prince, one of the pit ponies, who died in August 1931. However, Owen Keevil, who had now moved to the company's headquarters at Redhill, upbraided RW Nicholds, his successor in Bath, for having the dead pony summarily removed to the knackers' yard instead of being decently and respectfully buried at Combe Hay.[9] Some firms appeared initially to buck the trend. The Bath and Portland Stone Firms Ltd, for example, had two bumper years in 1930 and 1931, but the Depression caught up with it in the second half of 1932 and its profits were halved. Thanks to rigorous economies, however, it, too, survived. Other businesses, such as Cedric Chivers bookbinding company continued to make a profit right through the recession years. In both 1931 and 1932 the number of books bound increased. The board of directors was in the enviable position in 1931 to be able to report that 'despite the adverse conditions that had existed, the Company was able to record another successful year, although the figures which appear in the balance sheet are not so favourable as the previous year'.[10]

Although unemployment did not rise as steeply in Bath as in many other areas, the *Chronicle* observed in September 1930 that 'a general increase in the country is usually reflected in some measure in the local figures'. The weekly figures published in the *Chronicle* included, besides the number of long-term unemployed, several hundred who were affected by temporary stoppages or were classified as casual workers. In the first week of November 1930, the total number of unemployed in the city of Bath was 1,770, whereas a year earlier it had been 1,264. In the whole of the area covered by Bath Employment Exchange, which included the coalfields around Radstock, the figure was nearly double – 3,321 compared to 2,498 twelve months earlier. By August 1931, the total had crept up to 2,149 in Bath and 3,660 in the whole area. In the run-up to Christmas, shops and the Post Office took on temporary workers, but in January the remorseless upward trend in unemployment set in again. By early April, there were 2,739 people unemployed in Bath and 4,618 in the whole area. The totals fell slightly in the summer, but by November they had risen to 3,080 and 5,151 respectively. Only in 1933 did numbers begin to show a steady decline; by July the total for Bath was 1,877, while in the whole area it stood at 3,991. In September, the *Chronicle* felt it safe to observe that 'the gloom of the distressing situation today hangs rather less heavily over the country than it did. There is a recovery, which, although not spectacularly big, is at least substantial'.

Behind these figures were stories of deprivation and hardship. Responding to a provocative observation from Councillor George Long that, 'they could not shut their eyes to the fact that unemployed men were able to provide themselves with cigarettes and other luxuries', Ellen Hancock, the wife of an unemployed builder, wrote to the *Chronicle*:

> Now, Sir, my husband is unemployed and drawing the dole each week. He is an ex-soldier, served 27 years; served through the Boer War and was one of the first to join up again in the Great War, served right through till Armistice was declared; is the proud possessor of five medals, does not draw any pension whatever, nor ever has had any. There he is today, down and out, looking for fag ends in the streets of Bath

Another correspondent, who went under the name of 'Still Smiling', from New King Street revealed her weekly budget. Her husband received a dole of £1-9-3 per week. Out of that she paid:

Rent	12/-
Milk	1/2
Bread	3/-
Coal	1/-
Insurance	9d
Gas	1/-
Meat	1/6
Groceries	8/-
Total	£1-8-5

In addition she managed to give her husband 'two twopenny packets of Woodbines a week'. 'So, you will see, sir,' she concluded, 'that we have not got left a lot to clothe ourselves and three children but is sad to say that thousands are in the same boat.'[11]

For those in employment there loomed the constant threat of wage cuts. The budget of September 1931 reduced the pay of all central and local government employees, including teachers and policemen, by 10%. Baillie-Hamilton, who was still the sitting member for Bath, was overwhelmed with letters of protest from teachers. All he could do was publish a reply in the correspondence columns of the *Chronicle* on 19 September. While expressing sympathy for 'a sacrifice they could ill afford', he remarked bluntly that, 'it is my opinion that the teachers of this country should be prepared to bear their share of the burden', pointing out that, 'so far there has been no question of their losing their position which is the plight of many in other professions'. Threats of further wage cuts remained until the Depression eased. The police in Bath, for instance, were reminded in November 1931 by the Chief Constable of 'the urgent need for economy'. He pointed out that 'the question of a further supplementary deduction from pay next year depends upon the amount that can be saved in other ways', and emphasised that 'this is a matter that affects everyone individually'. One economy involved the issue of new clothing; it was decreed that 'only such garments as are actually unfit for further wear' would be replaced'.[12] In October 1932 in an effort to stop cheese-paring economies. the Somerset branch of the NUT took to supplying teachers with 'information so that they [would] be in a position ... to rebut arguments against the cost of education'.[13]

One of the most hated measures introduced by the national government as part of its austerity package in 1931 was the means test. Unemployment benefit could now only be drawn as a right for six months; any further payments were dependent on a means test carried out by local Public Assistance Committees. These rigorously looked into every applicant's financial circumstances, which included the value of their house and furniture. Not surprisingly, a member of the BTLC observed at a meeting on 9 December 1931 that 'some of the things going on are abominable'. In an attempt to defuse criticism, CJ Butlin, Bath's Director of Public Assistance, and Councillor AA Hunt, chairman of the Public Assistance Committee (PAC), explained the workings of the means test to the BTLC at a meeting on 13 January 1932, which was fully reported in the *Chronicle*. Hunt joked that they were entering the 'lions' den'. Citing statistics from the *Public Assistance Journal*, which showed that Bath was more generous than other areas, Butlin wondered whether 'the question to be asked in Bath was not "are we dealing with the cases too harshly?' but rather "are we dealing with them too leniently?' Nevertheless, he conceded that administering the means test was 'a very unpleasant task', but pointed out that, although 'the result may be unfair to the applicant ... that is the fault of the legislation, not of the local authority'. Bathonians, like people throughout the country who were subjected to the test, viewed it in an extremely negative light. Some 60 years later, Rosie Maslen recalled that if you 'had anything, you had to sell it'. Bob King, who was also a child at the time, remembered how humiliating the test was, describing how 'an obnoxious man would come round from the department and hammer the door with a walking stick, so neighbours would know'. His family was grudgingly given twelve shillings a week and some grocery vouchers. Fortunately, his mother had been in service as a nurse with wealthy families, who still wrote to her and sent her clothes.[14]

In Bath, as elsewhere, the main thrust of the campaign against the means test came from the National Unemployed Workers' Movement, (NUWM), whose founder and organiser, Wal Hannington, was no stranger to the city. Under the leadership of GT Pointer, the local branch of the NUWM had about 350 members, and in early 1932 held daily protest meetings on the Seven Dials site at the end of Westgate Street and in Lambridge. In reality it could achieve little, as the TUC and many Trade and Labour Councils, including Bath's, distrusted and feared the NUWM's links with communism. The Bath branch of the NUWM was, however, allowed to send several delegations to the Public Assistance Committee in Charlotte Street, where they were politely listened to but emerged empty handed with only the promise that 'one or two points' they had made would be borne in mind. On 21 September, a delegation led by Pointer argued forcefully that the means test was 'driving our class to desperation' and had created 'a bitter class hatred' in Bath.

The NUWM did all it could to fuel this hatred, but in the final analysis it was a small group with little influence in the city. One Friday in early June 1932, it put up a poster in Westgate Street appealing to the workers of Bath to join the movement and 'fight in the struggle for work or full maintenance'. It made a vitriolic attack on Edmund Bagshawe, describing him as a 'big mouthful, who is adept on voicing the views of his party' and declaring that 'we should like to dump him in the mud of the trenches during the late war, bring him back home ... only [to] find destitution and want staring him in the face'. By the next day the poster had been removed, but the message was printed in full in the *Chronicle* on 18 June.

During the Depression years, young men tramping around the country seeking work became a familiar sight. Many of them stopped off at Frome Road

House (formerly the Workhouse) for the night as casuals, not only putting an increased burden on its facilities but also clearing off in the morning without carrying out the jobs they had been allotted. Their cause was taken up by Brother Douglas of the Franciscan Order, who in an attempt to stop them becoming lifelong vagrants and petty criminals, had opened up settlements in Somerset where a few of them could receive shelter and training for future employment. To raise money for this project he visited Bath in February 1933 and spoke at a meeting at the Guildhall, which was organised by the National Council of Women, and attended by the mayor and the leading clergy of the City.

Bath lay on the route taken by hunger marches organised by the NUWM, from Bristol and the South Wales to London, and it was where the marchers spent the first night of their trek. This caused the council a problem as it had no option but to find accommodation and provide food for them. In March 1930, the BTLC received a request from the NUWM to make arrangements for 130 men from Wales, who would be passing through Bath on 21 April. The BTLC, along with the other trade councils in the South West, had decided to have 'nothing to do with this year's proposed hunger march', and voted unanimously to refuse the request. Stanley Gould, one of its leading members, summed up the general feeling when he observed that, while 'nobody was unsympathetic, we feel no good purpose could be served by a converging march to London'.[15] This refusal meant that the council was landed with the problem, and somewhat grudgingly agreed to put them up in Frome Road. On the evening of Easter Monday, when they arrived in Bath, they were accommodated in the dining hall and supplied with 'the usual casual diet'.[16]

On 17 October 1932, another hunger march bound for London from South Wales arrived in Bath. Initially, the PAC had hoped that the marchers could be accommodated in the Drill Hall on the Lower Bristol Road, but when it was unable to hire it, the education committee made the former Somerset Boys' Home available. Two days later, at a meeting of the PAC, Councillor Adrian Hopkins complained that this was tantamount to making a financial 'contribution to the Communist Party', as they were simply marching to London to 'ferment strife'.[17] When the contingents of hunger marchers from the depressed areas arrived in London, there was indeed 'strife', with riots in Hyde Park, Trafalgar Square and outside parliament. Both Hannington and the veteran trade-union leader Tom Mann were arrested and imprisoned. While the BTLC disapproved of the march, it unanimously carried a resolution condemning Mann's imprisonment, which was sent to the Prime Minister, Home Secretary and Loel Guinness.[18]

On Valentine's Day 1934, two columns of hunger marchers numbering about 160 converged on Bath, one from South Wales and the other from Bristol. They were part of the protest against the so-called 'slave bill', as the new Unemployment Bill was called. This not only retained the means test but transferred the granting of transitional benefits from local PACs, which at least had some knowledge of local conditions, to a national body, the Unemployment Assistance Board. It also gave this board the power to make benefit payments conditional on attending a government training centre. The marchers reached Bath just before 6.30pm and were given a warm welcome by onlookers in the street. One group stopped off for refreshments at the Friends' Meeting House, while the rest marched through Orange Grove and Westgate Street to the Milk Street Mission Hall where food was provided. As the *Chronicle* observed:

> There were in the procession 15 or 16 red banners bearing various slogans in white letters … and some of the banners indicated the area from which groups of marchers had come … Not far behind the musicians – a clarinet player, a bugler, a drummer, and two kettle drummers – who led the singing of the Marseillaise, the Red Flag, the Internationale and other marching songs – walked a group of girls, whose bright red berets made them conspicuous. Most of the marchers appeared to be quite young; they were mostly miners and seamen. The oldest was a man over 60 and the youngest a girl of 17.[19]

Collecting-box 'skirmishers' dashed in and out of the crowds watching them and met a generous response. Overnight sleeping accommodation was arranged at the Milk Street Mission Hall, the Friends' Meeting House and St. Paul's Mission Room. Later in the evening there were well-attended public meetings around Kingsmead Square. There had been rumours in some left-wing papers that Bath Council intended to ban any demonstrations in the town, but wiser counsels seem to have prevailed. There were no attempts to curtail proceedings, and, according to the *Chronicle*, 'the police showed the greatest of friendliness towards these visitors', who in turn 'maintained excellent order throughout'. The next day, en route to Chippenham, Grace Tollemache, the veteran suffragette, laid on lunch for them at her house in Batheaston.

The welcome given to the hunger marchers indicates the attitude of Bathonians to the curse of unemployment. Whatever their politics, they were aware of the hardship inflicted by the Depression, even if many accepted that the means test was necessary in the interests of economy. In response to a dramatic appeal from the Prince of Wales in January 1932 to refuse 'to be paralysed' by the unemployment problem and 'to see it as a national opportunity for voluntary social service' several organisations sprang into life in Bath, as elsewhere. The most prominent was the 'Good Neighbours' Club', which was prompted by a suggestion from Mrs Haslewood, the wife of Lieutenant- Commander Haslewood. At the annual parochial meeting of St. Mary's Bathwick on 20 February 1932, she proposed opening up church halls for the use of the unemployed one evening a week. The rector welcomed the idea warmly and on 3 March the Good Neighbours' Club opened at St. Paul's Church Hall. Volunteers were recruited, funds raised and books, magazines, newspapers, writing materials and games were provided. Another organisation founded in response to the prince's appeal was the League of Voluntary Service. The president of the Bath branch was Mrs Loel Guinness, and it was supported by such eminences as the mayor and the Marquis of Bath. Although its aim was to enlist volunteers to help anybody in need – such as pensioners and hospital patients – it had a sub-committee, headed by the mayor, to assist the unemployed, which concentrated its efforts on providing occupational, educational and recreational activities. It also set up a clothing and a 'make and mend club' for unemployed women. Many people also took it on themselves to help out. Mrs Golledge, for instance, who ran a sweet and tobacco business known as the 'Better 'Ole' at 6 Cleveland Row, started a shilling fund for the local unemployed in the weeks before Christmas 1932. She managed to raise £10-11- 0, which she sent to the Mayor's Fund. The Bath Police Fund for Clothing Destitute Children was also a source of help for the unemployed. According to the *Chronicle* in October 1932 the police did 'much good work in an unobtrusive way'. From time to time, for instance, tramps would call at the police station 'footsore and weary', and would be given 'part worn but otherwise serviceable boots', which local residents had discarded.

Charity was, of course, a palliative. The only real way to tackle unemployment was to create work. At a meeting of the Bath Rotary Club on 22 November 1932 members were told of a scheme adopted in Bristol 'to induce people to ... buy things, with the double object of finding more employment and getting more money into circulation'. Alderman and fellow Rotarian, Alfred Wills, commended the scheme and criticised the government, which in 'asking for public economy had conveyed to the citizens a wrong impression' that they too should economise. Wills argued that, on the contrary, people must be told that 'spending money within their own circle' would help create work. In January, the mayor, together with the *Chronicle*, church leaders of all denominations, the Good Neighbours' Club, the League of Social Service, the British Legion and the chairman of the Local Employment Committee, acted on this advice and appealed to the people of Bath to find work for the unemployed:

> Somewhere in your house, or about the premises, in the garden, perhaps, or in the garage, no matter where, there is a job to be put in hand. You have concluded that it must be done at some time or other. Get that waiting job done now and help employment'.[20]

In April, when 'the brilliant sun [was] showing up the defects, which have accumulated since the last spring cleaning', the *Chronicle* again appealed to Bathonians to find work, however small, for the unemployed. Since much of this work inevitably remained unrecorded, it is hard to know how effective the appeal was. In February the newspaper noted that 'at least one Bath business house is circulating the customers on its books, making attractive suggestions for the "stitch in time" regarding the welfare of motor-cars'. Altogether, at various times from May to October, in the parish of Box alone, under the auspices of the League of Voluntary Service some 4,000 hours of employment were provided for 15 men, of whom three were found permanent work'. Projects included clearing one and a half acres of brushwood at Stowell Wood, between Ditteridge and Colerne, and cleaning out the big pool on Kingsdown.

In December 1932, the council drew up plans for a number of work creation projects. These included a new cemetery in Pennyquick, a miniature golf course on High Common and the construction of a storm water culvert to prevent water from Southdown and Rush Hill cascading down into the Moorfields and Oldfield Park districts. The Bath Gas Company, after taking over the Chippenham and Corsham gas works, also accelerated plans for laying a new twelve-inch main from Box to Chippenham, a distance of about ten miles. In order to employ more men, it dispensed with machinery and relied entirely on manual labour, thereby providing up to 100 extra jobs. The work commenced in November 1932 and finished the following June. However, it was building projects that provided most work opportunities for the unemployed. The first major developments were the Kingsmead flats, completed in October 1931, the new RUH at Combe park and the Boys' School on Beechen Cliff. Further jobs were created by the demolition of the Royal Literary and Scientific Institution and the subsequent remodelling of Terrace Walk, building the Forum Cinema on St James's Parade, the new central stores of the Bath Cooperative Society on Westgate Buildings and the new electricity showrooms and offices by the Old Bridge.[21] Bath was witnessing

*Work in progress building the Kingsmead Flats
(Bath Record Office)*

a building boom, and it came as no surprise that unemployment fell. Between May and June 1933, for example, the numbers out of work fell by 301.

The BTLC was understandably anxious to ensure that unemployed Bathonians were given the jobs that these projects created. However, government money for work creation projects was conditional on 20% of the workforce being drawn from the distressed regions, which in practice, as far as Bath was concerned, meant employing men from South Wales. This led to frequent complaints about Welshman rather than local workers being employed. At a meeting of the BTLC on 27 May 1931, its president, Harry Lang, complained that, where Welsh firms had secured local building contracts, they brought in their own workers, and warned that, if this was not stopped, 'there would be very soon trouble', as local labour would be 'crowded out'. Another member of the BTLC wondered what would happen to the Welshmen when the work was finished and was told that they followed the contractors around the country, 'unless any of them got entangled with some fascinating lady and settled down.'[22]

One of the Welsh contractors working in Bath, Copp Bros of Barry, was engaged on a housing project in Odd Down. A spokesman for the firm told the *Chronicle* that it had brought over only a very small number of Welshmen and that the rest of the workforce were local men. He criticised the BTLC for taking such a parochial view, pointing out that, 'if you go through the valleys of South Wales, you will find almost as many West of England men as Welshmen'. In a period of high unemployment, though, with the insecurity it created, there was inevitably intense competition to find work, and even considerable resentment that men from as near as Radstock 'were coming into the Bath district and attempting to undercut Bath workers'.[23]

Like their Welsh comrades, some Bath workers were prepared to travel to find employment. In early 1932, the Jersey Farmers' Union decided to recruit 3.000 workers in England rather than France to lift the season's new potatoes. Selection committees toured the South West. One visited the Bath Employment Office at the end of March and interviewed about 200 applicants, out of whom they selected 40 men and one woman, who were given free rail and boat tickets and told that there was a chance of permanent work on the island. Many in the Bath contingent were unpleasantly surprised by the exhausting nature of the work. Six of them, egged on by some of their fellow Bathonians, wrote a letter, which was published in the *Chronicle* on 18 June about their experiences at the hands of the Jersey farmers, describing the work as 'murderous'. However, a different spin on the situation was put to the editor by a man who had returned home because of an injury that had incapacitated him. He pointed out that the employment office had made a big mistake 'in sending out men quite unfit for the job, such as clerks, hairdressers and others, who have never had to do hard manual work'.

Throughout the developed world, the economic crisis inevitably affected the value of stocks and shares. In Bath, Stothert and Pitt, for instance, paid no dividend for the financial year 1931-32. The government added pressure on the rentier class by converting the 5% war loan to new stock, which yielded interest at only 3½%. Earl Temple, who was 'a most prolific spender', in a letter to his broker expressed the frustration which many rentiers felt and accused the government of following a socialist policy:

> I do not think much of a national government that puts the screw on the holders of government stock and on the tax payers. The same individual is hit twice, so the operation appeared more in keeping with the late [Labour] Chancellor of the Exchequer than the present.[24]

He was to a certain extent able to shore up his finances by investing considerable sums in property in and around London. Those of humbler means were hit much harder by the Depression. The owner of Bath's last pawn shop, Newman and Co. of Corn Street, reported in March 1932 that many more middle-class people were now amongst its customers. In July, a divorced man in Corsham managed to persuade the local magistrates' court to reduce the maintenance order for his wife by over a third. The chairman, Sir John Gladstone, observed that, 'you are, like many others, in an unfortunate position. Everybody today is suffering from a loss of dividends.'

However, despite the plight of many of its inhabitants, Bath never became a ghost town. As the *Chronicle* pointed out in December 1931, 'the secret of success of any places is to be always on the map'. The city was fortunate to still have, as its Spa Director, John Hatton, who ensured that Bath received more publicity that any of its rivals in Britain. Bath also had rugby, cricket and the races, all of which brought people into town to spend money. The city remained a favourite spot for both those who stayed in its hotels and for excursionists who came by train and, increasingly, by charabanc. Over the summer of 1932, so many buses and charabancs brought day trippers to Bath that the regional traffic commissioners, who had been set up by the 1930 Road Traffic Act, introduced regulations to control them. They were to set down and pick up passengers 'at the west end of York Street, on the north side of the street, by the wall of the Roman Baths'. Entering and leaving Bath, they were required to avoid the city centre. From the London and Warminster Roads, they were instructed to go via Great Pulteney Street and Grand Parade, while from the Lower Bristol and Wells Roads, they had to cross the Old Bridge and travel via Dorchester, Manvers and Pierrepont Streets. They also had to 'proceed direct to garages' after setting down and 'return to pick up not more than 20 minutes before the prearranged time of departure'.[25]

Over Christmas 1932, hotels were fuller than they had been the previous year, but guests stayed for less time. Previously, many had stayed for up to two weeks, but most now spent just a few days either at Christmas or over the New Year. On Maundy Thursday and Easter Saturday 1933, well over 1,700 people came down by train from London, and, as the *Chronicle* reported 'the Roman Baths were the Mecca of innumerable pilgrims'. Regular concerts were still held in the Pump Room, and a multitude of lectures and society meetings carried on as before. In 1930, the first Bath Spring Festival of Contemporary Arts was held. The theatre in Bath was very much alive. The Theatre Royal drew crowds with such plays as Sydney Blow's *Two Deep*, which went on to the West End. At Citizen House, Consuelo de Reyes continued to produce a series of challenging plays, several of which were transferred to the Everyman Theatre in Hampstead. At Christmas 1932, she produced a Nativity play called the 'Virgin of the Poor', which, according to the review in the *Chronicle*, featured

*The Kingsmead Flats, designed by Frank Sissons
(AW Wills, The Kingsmead Flats, Bath Record Office)*

none of the sweet softness of the old-time Nativity, but a clarion call to face the present horrible mechanical bound age. The Christ Child is not the gift, in this play, to the rich, to the religious, to the Kings – but the rabble of beggar, street walker, drunkard, and the unemployed received him gladly, a gift which passes their understanding, but leaves them with the peace that these poor souls have long sought.[26]

9
THE EMPIRE, THE DICTATORS AND THE ABDICATION CRISIS

BY THE END of the Twenties the international climate seemed to be set fair. Anglo-German relations had improved immeasurably. When, for example, a party of German students came to visit Bath in July 1927 they were warmly received by Sarah Grand, the mayoress, who in her speech of welcome remarked that 'the more the young people of the two countries saw of each other, the better they would grow to like each other'. The Kellogg-Briand Pact, which had the utopian aim of outlawing war, was signed in August 1928 by fifteen states, including Britain and was celebrated in Bath by an interdenominational service at the Argyle Congregational Church .Yet by 1936 the situation had deteriorated dramatically: Japan annexed Manchuria in 1931, Hitler came to power in 1933, Mussolini attacked Abyssinia (Ethiopia) in October 1935 and the Spanish Civil broke out the following July to be followed in 1937 by a full scale conflict between China and Japan. Phillip Hopkins, the prospective Liberal candidate for Bath aptly described the situation in August 1937:

> We are in a vicious circle of international trouble which began in Manchuria wended its way to Abyssinia and Spain, and is now back at the point of the circle where it began'-China.[1]

BATH AND THE EMPIRE

BRITAIN WAS NOT In a good situation to navigate the storms ahead. She remained a formidable power, but the Empire, which was the basis of that power, was in the process of radical change and no longer formed a coherent bloc. By the mid-1930s the Imperial ideal was still popular, and thanks to the introduction of Empire tariffs, trade between Britain and the Empire had increased significantly in the 1930s, but in reality the Empire's days were numbered. The Statute of Westminster effectively created the modern

Commonwealth in 1931 by recognising the Dominions as independent self-governing states. The King was no longer sovereign of a united Empire, but the separate sovereign of each individual Dominion. The African colonies were governed directly from Westminster and their independence seemed unimaginable. India, however, was a different matter. In 1935 India was granted a federal constitution, but London still kept control of foreign policy and the armed forces. Ultimately, however, it was becoming increasingly clear that India would eventually become a fully self-governing Dominion.

These trends were closely followed in Bath, where visiting speakers usually stressed the need for Imperial unity. As late as February 1939 John Hutton, the Development Officer of the Overseas League told its Bath branch 'that we heard too little of the Empire today …our newspapers were concerned more with what Hitler is thinking than with what the Dominions are thinking'. The Conservative party was strongly imperialistic. In early February 1934 the chief event of the 'Bath Conservative Fayre' was the presentation of a tableux, 'Dream of Empire', in which Britannia surveyed her Empire. Schools and the Young Conservatives, the 'Imps', were particular targets for Imperial propaganda. Uncle Fred in the *Chronicle* invited his readers in May 1934 to send in essays they had written to commemorate Empire Day. The answers printed in the *Chronicle* invariably concentrated on the Dominions and stressed that they enjoyed the same freedoms as Britain herself did. Little was written about the colonial empire.

The contentious issue of the future of India was to convulse the local Conservative party. In October 1929, the new Labour government, faced with growing civil unrest on the subcontinent, announced that Britain's aim was eventually to grant India dominion status. What this might entail was the subject of three Round Table Conferences which were held in London between November 1930 and December 1932. They were attended by the representatives of both the Indian princes and the nationalist parties, and at the 1931 conference Mahatma Gandhi himself represented the Congress Party. In 1933, the British Government drew up a white paper setting out proposals for a new Indian constitution. To oppose these, the India Defence League was formed. It included 58 MPs, among them Winston Churchill, as well as several former governors of Indian provinces and notables such as Rudyard Kipling. Bath's Conservative Association was also firmly against Indian self-government. At the meeting of its executive committee on 11 October 1932, a resolution was passed welcoming the government's 'firm action' in restoring order in India after a wave of riots and assassinations. It went on to say, however, that, while it was 'in no way opposed' to minor constitutional changes 'compatible with the peace of India and the security of the British Empire', it had grave concerns that that the constitution outlined in the white paper would in practice create an Indian democracy hostile to British interests. As the *Chronicle* pointed out, 'Bath was a constituency that was singularly well informed upon the problems of India', since many of its residents had worked for the Raj as administrators and soldiers, or run businesses there. To many of them, Gandhi was, in the words of Brigadier-General Roberts, the chairman of the Lansdown branch of the Conservative Association, 'a political rogue', who should never have been invited to the conferences, as he was prepared to condone the use of force to gain Indian independence. Not everybody agreed. In his sermon in September 1931 at the New Church in Henry Street, the Reverend Wall compared Gandhi to the prophet Isaiah and called him a deeply spiritual leader. He told his congregation that 'we must admire his sincerity and courage and devotion to the cause he has embraced'.

Captain Adrian Hopkins, the new Chairman of the Bath Conservative Association was bitterly opposed to the government's proposals and attended the Defence League's founding meeting in London in June. Helen Foxcroft, the sister of Bath's former MP, the late Charles Foxcroft summed up the dilemmas facing not just Conservative voters but the whole country:

> The vast and terrible importance of the India problem- the future of populations numbered by hundreds of millions – must … haunt the imagination of all who but touch the fringe of this question. But the many who are without the personal knowledge on which to base an opinion, have to face the fact that those who do know, differ, and differ diametrically. How [to] weigh opinion against opinion? How [to] balance long experience against experience less prolonged, but more recent? What reliance can be placed on official, what [on] independent opinion.[2]

Over the next eighteen months there were a series of often bad-tempered meetings in Bath on the White Paper, which according to the *Chronicle*, displayed 'a liveliness that is usually associated with general election times'. The Bath Conservative Association in April 1933 invited Lord Lloyd, the former Governor of Bombay, to talk to its members 'on the subject of India'. On 23 June at a meeting attended by some 800 people. Lloyd dismissed plans for Indian self-government as a 'mad folly' on the grounds that India was patently not ready for democracy. Loel Guinness, much to the annoyance of some party members, sat on the fence pleading that he needed more time to study the complex issues involved. The Liberals exploited his lack of leadership and compared it to the support for Indian self-government given by their own parliamentary candidate, Sidney Daniels, who had spent 30 years in India. Lilly Keir, the chair of the Bath Women's Liberal Association, wondered not unreasonably how the dithering Guinness could 'vote on this grave question in the House of Commons with intelligence as our representative'.

In an effort to achieve some sort of balance on the Indian problem, the Conservative Association invited Sir Hari Singh Gour, a distinguished Indian barrister and politician, who had been advising the Parliamentary Joint Committee on the Government of India Bill, to address a meeting at the Guildhall on 18 September 1933, where he was subjected to a barrage of frequently hostile questions. The following day he attended the Bath Rotarian lunch, where he once again discussed the Indian problem. One question went to the heart of the future of the Empire: AW Hoyle, the Director of Education asked whether it was a wise policy for Britain 'to relax the rein as far as possible between herself and her dominions. Sir Hari's telling reply was to quote the former prime minister of Canada's comment that 'our loyalty is proportionate to our liberty'. This was the crux of the issue. Should India be granted 'home rule' or should force be used to suppress Gandhi's Congress party. In December Daniels tellingly observed that the India Defence League should be called the India Domination League.

Pressure grew on Guinness to take up a definite position on the question. In February 1934 at a meeting of the Bath branch of the India League at York Villa, Kensington, which Guinness did not attend, Major Lestock Reid accused him of having 'the politician's happy knack of closing his eyes when he does not want to see', and then asked testily 'why isn't he here?'. It was not until 7 December 1934 that Guinness accompanied by Euan Wallace, the Civil Lord of the Admiralty, finally announced that he supported Baldwin's India policy 'whole heartedly' at a meeting of the Bath Conservative Party at the Guildhall. Bagshaw, the former chairman of the Bath Conservative party, with Wallace clearly in mind claimed to loud applause from the audience, that support for the bill came primarily from 'ministers, place men, (paid or unpaid) and Members of Parliament, who have received, or are receiving or may receive favours' from the government. Guinness immediately leapt to Wallace's defence, and 'speaking vehemently and striking the rail of the platform violently', apologised to Wallace and regretted that such an insinuation had been made. This led three days later to Brigadier-General Roberts announcing that he was resigning from the Conservative Association and transferring his subscription to the India Defence League. He was to have second thoughts about this and decided a day later to retain his membership by 'paying the minimum subscription only', but he did resign the chairmanship of the Lansdown Ward because, as he told the Executive Committee of the Conservative Association, 'he felt he could not continue in view of the party's Indian policy'. Bagshaw, who was now vice-chairman of the party, did not resign but he did not disguise his anger at Guinness' reaction to his criticisms of the government's policy. He wrote an angry letter to the new chairman, Adrian Hopkins, asserting that the 'fine phrenzy [sic] exhibited by Captain Wallace and Mr Guinness must have ... been displayed either from a sense of servitude or from ignorance of the common facts'. He commented, somewhat incoherently, that 'these young men would not have dared to speak of me an hundred years ago as they did last night and that their language was provocative and a breach of the peace'.[3] The acrimonious debate about India rumbled on in Bath until the Act received the Royal Assent in August 1935.

The moral dilemmas of Empire

It was a paradox that while the British ruled over an enormous empire encompassing much of Africa and Asia, so few Africans and Asians were seen in Britain's cities. Children throughout the country were taught to be proud of the Empire, but they rarely met any people of non-European ethnicity. Consequently when such encounters occurred, children were sometimes irrationally frightened. In Bath the most visible ethnic minority presence consisted of the Chinese, who ran several local laundries. Pauline Forrest, when playing in her school playground, accidently hit a ball over the wall into the yard behind the neighbouring Chinese laundry. After school she asked at the counter if she could go through the laundry with her friend to find it. As she later recalled: A Chinaman

> lifted the top of the counter up, so that we could walk through and we followed him. I was quite all right until I was confronted with a crowd of Chinamen, all working amid the steam and heat. I noticed a Chinese lady with a baby strapped to her back.... Suddenly I was seized with fright –it was as if I had been plunged into Chinatown with the mysteries of the east surrounding me ....I felt trapped with all eyes upon me. Through a second room we walked with more Chinese people surrounding us. Then I saw a back door –an escape– with fresh air blowing on our faces. I had just one thought in mind –ball or no ball. I was going to escape over the wall as quickly as possible.

Afterwards she realised that the Chinese were simply curious at suddenly seeing 'two small white girls coming through their place of work' and had no intention of frightening them.

Sometime later on a Saturday morning Pauline witnessed an extremely unpleasant and overtly racial incident outside the Chinese laundry in Kingsmead Square. A girl called Lilly, whom she knew and who worked in the laundry, was about to marry a Chinese colleague. As they came down the steps from the laundry and made their way to the taxi to go to the marriage ceremony, they ran into a hostile and aggressive crowd where Pauline heard 'a lot of unpleasant banter going on' – one comment being ' Fancy marrying a Chink, Had to, I reckon'. Then as the couple came down the steps, the crowd started pelting them with handfuls of hard rice, which was 'like a shower of hailstones'. Mercifully the couple managed to get into the taxi and drive away. Not surprisingly the sheer unpleasantness of the incident reduced Pauline to tears. She could only wish that Lily would be happy ever after with her husband.[4]

In the ethnically undiverse world of Bath 'a little black baby', who was 'a great favourite with everybody' in the nursery of the Frome Road Infirmary in July 1931, was so exceptional that it merited mention in the Child Welfare and Maternity Committee. On the other hand, there were various high profile characters of African origin who passed through the city in the 1930s. In March 1933 Paul Robeson sang at the Pavilion, moving the *Chronicle* to observe that 'not to have heard Robeson [was] to have missed an intense experience of life'. 'Prince Monolulu, or Peter Mckay, the famous tic-tac man, who was born in the Virgin Islands, played on the rarity of his colour at race meetings, one of his slogans being 'black man for luck'. He regularly attended the Bath races, and in August 1939 the *Chronicle* described him pitching for bets behind the refreshment tent:

> Strikingly attired in red and gold with a feathered head-dress... [speaking] quietly and confidentially to the crowd, which quickly gathered around him.[5]

A more serious figure to appear from time to time in Bath was Harry O'Connell, a Guyanese ship's carpenter from Cardiff, who had made a name for himself campaigning against the racial discrimination practiced by the National Union of Seamen. In September 1935 he addressed a series of meetings in Seven Dials protesting against the imminent invasion of Abyssinia by Italy. He told his audience that 'we negroes are not a selfish class of people and are in agreement that the wealth of Africa can be distributed to the world as a whole, but we say that it must be distributed by the hands of Africans not by the hand of any imperialist power'. The most influential African to settle in Bath was, of course, the Emperor Haile Selassie, after the occupation of Ethiopia by the Italians in 1936 (see below).

From time to time, as we have seen, Indian politicians, academics and barristers, like Sir Hari Singh Gour or his political opponent Amin Ali, visited Bath to address one or other of its societies, usually on the issue of Indian independence, but in June 1934 Bath was introduced to a different but more typical aspect of Indian life when an exhibition of Indian village life was opened in the Assembly Rooms. The mayor, Colonel Davey, had a garland placed around his neck by 'a beautiful young Indian lady'. In his opening speech he observed rather condescendingly that the exhibition 'was only a tiny slice from a vast Empire teeming with people who were full of ideas and political keenness' and that 'it was a mistake to think of the natives as remote people who were hardly educated'. The romantic marriage in May 1936 of Loel Guinness' first wife, Joan Yarde-Buller to Prince Aly Khan in the Paris Mosque just days after her divorce had been made absolute, was a matter of considerable interests in the city. Joan herself converted to Islam and took up the name Taj-ud-dawlah (Crown of the realm). Due note was taken when she gave birth to a son seven months later in December.

While the Empire was still perceived by the majority to be a great force for good, there was an awareness expressed particularly by missionaries that change was coming. The Bath branch of the Missionary Union was firmly told in October 1932 by the Rev Wakelin Coxill, who had just returned from the Belgian Congo, that the idea was spreading throughout West Africa that 'Africa should be for the Africans', and he was sure that in the end 'it would spread throughout the whole of the great continent'. How this 'tiger' of independence was to be ridden by the colonial authorities was not at all clear, but he, together with his fellow missionaries, was convinced that the conversion of Africans, to Christianity was the key to the future of Africa. The Labour Party was increasingly pursuing an anti-imperialist line. In March 1939, George Desmond, Bath's Labour parliamentary candidate observed that 'we must repent of our past grabbing ... and hand back the colonies to their former owners-the indigenous inhabitants of those colonies'.

The issue of slavery that so preoccupies us today, was not ignored. Its evil was readily conceded. In a sermon in 1930 at St. Mary's Bathwick

The existence of the Empire formed a backdrop to everyday life as this announcement for the BESS Bazaar shows (Bath Chronicle, 29 September 1934)

the Archbishop of the West Indies, the Venerable. D Trussell bluntly gave his audience the facts:

> It took the people of England over 200 years to realise that there was anything wicked in slavery. It had been started in 1562 by Sir John Hawkins, who transported 300 slaves from Africa on his first trip. On his return he was sent for by Queen Elizabeth, who supplied him with a ship from the Royal Navy named Jesus, for a second trip![6]

Wilberforce and the abolition of slavery were celebrated with pride. In a talk arranged by the Royal Empire Society in November 1930 FH Melland, a former provincial commissioner in Northern Rhodesia contrasted the British record in West Africa where 'the English were one of the chief offenders in the slave trade' with their achievement in east Africa. Here, he claimed, rather ingeniously 'their sole reason for entering was to put down the slave trade' –the 'last gang of slaves' being set free in 1898. Sir John Harris, a former Liberal MP and the secretary of the Anti-Slavery and Aborigines Protection Society, told an audience in the Guildhall in July 1933 that Bath's doctors, by restoring Wilberforce's health in 1788, had indirectly helped the abolitionists cause. In 1934, which was the centenary of the abolition of slavery in the British Empire, the focus of the celebrations was the campaign to liberate the five or six million chattel slaves who still existed in Ethiopia and Arabia and the child slaves in China.

THE TRIUMPH OF THE NAZIS IN GERMANY

HITLER'S SEIZURE OF POWER in January 1933 was a decisive turning point in the inter-war years. There was now a government in Berlin that was actively planning for war and systematically militarising German society. As Hitler's initial aim was to eliminate socialism and communism in Germany, it was not surprising that in Bath it was the Labour Party and the Trade and Labour Council (BTLC), which were the most vociferous critics of the new regime. As early as April 1933 a German socialist, who was described for security reasons as a 'man without a name' spoke to the Widcombe Men's Section of the Bath Labour Party about the situation in Germany. His main message was that the divisions amongst the working class in Germany had made possible Hitler's success. The trial in October of the Dutch communist, Marinus Van der Lubbe for allegedly burning down the German *Reichstag* was followed closely by the BTLC, which passed a motion expressing

Its grave dissatisfaction with the conduct of the trial now being conducted at Leipzig and is of the opinion that the real instigators of the crime of firing the *Reichstag* are to be found amongst the prominent members of the Nazi Movement, who have probably used Van der Lugg [sic] as a tool to carry out their design to stampede the country [into voting Nazi]. We demand the immediate release of the other prisoners concerned ... .[7]

Bathonians were left in no doubt about the fate of the Jews in Germany. The pupils of Oldfield School on Shakespeare Day in April 1933 were told by the vice-president of the British Empire Society that whenever he saw *The Merchant of Venice*, he was reminded of Adolf Hitler, while in September it was reported in the *Chronicle* that 'the Jewish persecution in Germany ... had cast gloom over the whole Jewish community, and that many Jewish agnostics in London were returning to their faith in protest against events in Germany'. In May 1934 a meeting of the Church Missions to the Jews in the Assembly Rooms was informed that a new organisation called 'The Friends of the Jews' would seek to raise money to help the 50,000 Jews who had already been expelled or had fled from Germany.

In June 1936 Major Thomas Grenfell, who every Saturday sold copies of the Communist *Daily Worker* in Stall Street, rashly attempted to gain access in Hamburg to the trial of Edgar André, a native of Alsace, who was accused of killing a Nazi in a street brawl. Inevitably Grenfell's interest raised the suspicions of the Gestapo, who later interrogated him in his hotel, and ordered him to hand over all his money and leave Hamburg the following morning by boat. When Grenfell insisted that he had plans to travel to Paris by train and categorically refused to surrender the money, the Gestapo attempted to take it from him by force. However, he managed to contact the British Consulate, which sent an official around to the hotel, but he was unable to prevent further

Hitler celebrating his 50th birthday, April 1939 - he was a malign influence on Bath as on everywhere else! (Das 12 Uhr Blatt)

prolonged interrogation lasting some five hours. In the end by arguing that he suffered from chronic sea sickness he was allowed to proceed to the Belgian frontier under police escort. On reflection Grenfell wondered whether he had been mistaken for the Labour MP for Glamogan, who had the same name. When news reached Bath that André had been sentenced to death on 19 July, a resolution was immediately passed at a meeting chaired by the formidable 'blue stocking' and Labour supporter, Hilda Oldham, and sent to the German Ambassador in London. Its gist was that the sentence 'was outrageously severe ... and if carried out will brand such trials as instruments of Nazi prejudice and vindictiveness'.

Not all reports from Nazi Germany, however, were so negative. The popular Bath Rotarian, Lawrence Fraser, in a talk to his fellow Rotarians at one of their weekly lunches in December 1933 gave an embarrassingly sympathetic account of Nazi Germany and

*Major Grenfell, a courageous citizens of Bath but one of its 'awkward squad' and a self-professed Communist (*Bath Chronicle, *27 June 1936)*

played down its anti-Semitism. In February 1937 Miss Patricia Horstmann, daughter of Hermann Horstmann of the Horstmann Gear Company, in a lecture to the Geneva club, summarised her impressions of Germany gained from over a decade of visits. She argued that Hitler had led Germany out of the 'slough of despond' and she

> saw improvements on all sides; streets were cleaner, trade was reviving, the people looked more cheerful and their beloved opera houses, cinemas and even churches were again crowded.[8]

More contentiously she described Hitler as 'a man of high ideals and sincere in his wishes for the wellbeing of his country'. Even more surprisingly she thought he was 'merely a figurehead whose power was considerably lessening, as he deprived the people more and more of their freedom of action and individuality of thought'. The Nazi salute was the subject of both interest and ridicule in Bath. On prize day at Kingswood School in July 1934 representatives of the 6th Form, after singing German songs, exited the stage saluting in the Nazi style. A few months later at the YMCA swimming gala at the New Baths, the *Chronicle* reported that one of the many 'amusing dives included a Hitler dive'. Unfortunately, it does not specify what this involved - presumably a Nazi salute of sorts. The salute also seems to have made an impact on Thomas Anthony Lock, who already had 14 convictions for drunkenness and was arrested on a Wednesday evening in March 1935 in Stall Street for once again being drunk and waving his arms about and shouting 'Hitler forever'.

THE BLACKSHIRTS IN BATH

THE PRESENCE OF MEMBERS of the British Union of Fascists (BUF), the Blackshirts, on Bath's streets was an uncomfortable reminder of the threat to democracy and peace presented by Fascism and National Socialism. The BUF had been founded by Sir Oswald Mosley in 1932 and was inspired by both the Italian Fascists and the German Nazis. It absorbed most of the membership of the British Fascist movement of the 1920s. In November 1933 the BUF opened an office in Bath in Monmouth Street, and there were other branches in Chippenham, Frome and Weston-super-Mare. In early October Bathonians had a chance to hear about the aims of the BUF when L J Cumings, a prominent figure in the movement, explained to a crowd of well over a thousand in Seven Dials, why it had been created and what its programme was. He told them that the BUF was a reaction to the economic crisis and the inability of the existing parties to solve it and claimed that it had already recruited a 'considerable number of adherents' in the city. How accurate that was, is difficult to gauge. Certainly in March 1934 what the *Chronicle* called a 'fair sized audience' assembled at the Guildhall to hear the BUF's director of propaganda, Wilfred Risdon, who had been born in Bath, further expound its political aims and philosophy. Two weeks later Oswald Mosley himself visited Bath *en route* for a rally at the Colston Hall, Bristol where he encountered a vociferous opposition, five members of which were so badly beaten up that they needed medical help– two even having to go to hospital. There was no violence on a comparable scale in Bath, but in Melksham in May 1934 a carload of Black Shirts was 'literally driven out of town by an angry crowd that included many women'. The following April William Joyce, later known as Lord Haw-Haw, spoke at the Guildhall. He was heckled, but there was no physical violence, and the meeting was described by the press as 'very poorly attended'.

A confrontation between the BUF and communists in Seven Dials was defused in September 1936 by Superintendent Tom Ashworth who managed to persuade the BUF to call the meeting off and go back to their headquarters. A few days later, on a Sunday evening, a group of young communists came over from Bristol with the intention of breaking up another Black Shirt meeting in Seven Dails but confrontation was again avoided, when as a result of heavy rain the meeting was held inside. The potential threat to public order in Bath posed by these confrontations led to the Watch Committee putting forward new regulations for open air meetings, which would have given the Chief Constable permission to grant or withhold meetings at will. However, at the council meeting on 2 August 1934 Alderman White described this as 'an insidious form of Hitlerism, which we have got to put a stop to', and Sam Day, a leading member of the local Labour Party, threatened to defy the regulations if they were passed. Under pressure the council retreated and dropped the proposal. It was not until January 1937 that the Bath Police in common with police forces throughout the country were given powers under the Public Order Act to counter the threat of disorder in the streets. Wearing political uniforms in public places or at political rallies was banned. The maintenance of order during meetings was left to party stewards, but the police could intervene when requested to do so by them.[9]

SUPPORT FOR THE LEAGUE OF NATIONS AND THE PEACE BALLOT

DESPITE THE MOUNTING evidence of German and Japanese aggression and Mussolini's intention to annex Abyssinia, it was still hoped right across the country that the existence of the League of Nations would prevent another world war. The Bath branch of the League of Nation Union (LNU) had a membership of over 600, and regularly held meetings, which were addressed by distinguished speakers. For example In October 1934, Gilbert Murray, Oxford professor, public intellectual, and president of the League's Committee on Intellectual Cooperation, addressed a meeting in the Guildhall , which was also attended by many groups of school pupils. While critical of the league's failures, he optimistically believed that it could still succeed, observing that 'the prospect of disarmament is not dead –it just failed the first time'.

That autumn the whole country was swept by an almost religious fervour when the LNU, inspired by its president, Lord Robert Cecil, organised a peace ballot or 'National Declaration', as it was officially called. Local branches were instructed to set up committees, and the Bath branch lost no time in organising the ballot.[10] A 'large and representative meeting' was held at the Guildhall on 22

October to discuss strategy. Rev Dr Gillie, the minister of the Bath Presbyterian Church, was chosen to be the chairman of the executive committee, and rapidly drew up plans to enroll some 600 canvassers to distribute ballot papers to every household in the city. Anybody over 18 was eligible to vote. The ballot was timed to coincide with the Armistice celebrations –an important 'psychological moment' as Gillie observed. A committee was formed, which included Alderman Wills and the chief constable, to ensure that the poll was properly conducted. Over the next few weeks nearly 17,000 ballot papers were delivered by hand. A further 3,000 were sent by post, paid for by supporters of the League. Dr Gillie informed a reporter of the *Chronicle* that the reaction to the poll

> has varied in certain quarters of the city ... Where well-to-do people reside there has been ... a limited interest, but it would be a great mistake to suppose that interest is shown only in the working-class districts. Quite a number of retired people have entered into discussion with the distributors, sometimes on the affirmative side, sometimes on the negative.[11]

The first returns were announced in Bath, Bury, Dudley and Norwich. On Monday 3 December, the results in Bath were declared at the Friends' Meeting House.[12] An overwhelming majority endorsed the League of Nations and its efforts to maintain peace. The ayes to all questions totaled 79,246 and the noes 11,969. Altogether 16,704 Bathonians voted and the answers to the five questions posed gave a clear indication of the strength of negative feeling against rearmament:

1 Should Great Britain remain a member of the League of Nations?
    Yes 15706 (95%)   No 888 (5%)
2 Are you in favour of all round reduction of armaments by international agreement?
    Yes 14644 (90%)   No 1777 (10%)
3 Are you in favour of all round abolition of national military and naval aircraft by international agreement?
    Yes 13035 (80.8%)   No 3094 (19.2%)
4 Should the manufacture and sale of armaments for private profit be prohibited by international agreement?
    Yes 14324 (90%)   No 1487 (10%)
5 Do you consider that, if a nation insists on attacking another, the other nations should combine to compel it to stop?:

(a) by economic and non-military means?
    Yes 13763 (92.6%)   No 1093 (7.4%)
(b) if necessary, by military measures?
    Yes 7774 (68.2%)   No 3630 (31.8%)

The national results were announced on 27 June 1935 to a huge crowd at the Royal Albert Hall. Altogether 11.6 million people voted, and the result was an overwhelming endorsement of the League, although, as in Bath, intervention against an aggressor commanded only moderate support. The ballot was a piece of brilliant propaganda for the LNU . Yet within months the League was to be put to the test and found tragically wanting

BATH AND THE ABYSSINIAN CRISIS

HELEN FOXCROFT OBSERVED in July 1935 in the *Chronicle*:

> Abyssinia! What is Abyssinia? At this moment she is the danger zone of the world. On her borders Italy is now said to have massed over 100,000 men and there those…'vultures' … we more politely and prosaically describe as 'Special Correspondents', are already gathering together.[13]

During the Spring and Summer of 1935 Bathonians became increasingly aware of the complexities and dangers of the Abyssinian crisis. In 1930 Italian troops had occupied an important watering hole at Wal-Wal some fifty miles inside Abyssinian territory, which led to a bloody clash between Abyssinian and Italian troops four years later. Emperor Haile Selassie appealed to the League for help, which prompted Mussolini to draw up plans for the conquest of Abyssinia as soon as he had mobilised sufficient forces. Members of the Bath branch of the LNU were given an erudite lecture on the merits of referring the Abyssinian crisis to the Permanent Court of International Justice and local politicians debated the wisdom of imposing sanctions on Italy. The Labour and the Liberal parties supported sanctions, while many Conservative politicians warned that they could lead to war with Italy. Sidney Daniels, the parliamentary Liberal candidate for Bath, stated perceptively in July that 'if Italy was allowed to go to war with Abyssinia and the other powers concerned did nothing, it would do more to discredit the League than anything which had happened yet'. Harry O'Connell, the champion of 'the cause of the coloured unemployed', was even more emphatic. He told a meeting in Sawclose in September that :

Many speakers say that sanctions mean war, but, my friends, sanctions mean peace. A victory for Fascist Italy in Abyssinia will be a victory for Fascism throughout the world. Those of you who are lovers of peace should come out definitely for the application of sanctions...[14]

'Abyssinia' rapidly became a household name, which even small children recognised. 'Uncle Fred', the editor of the 'Young Folks' column in the *Chronicle* informed his readers, for instance, that while driving his family to Aberdovey for their holidays 'our Audrey' bored by the long journey 'all at once' asked when they would 'get to Abyssinia'. By September, to quote Lilly Keir 'the atmosphere was electric with war rumours'.

The Italian invasion of Abyssinia, which began on 3 October 1935, was met with almost universal condemnation in Bath, as it was throughout the country. Bathonians were given ample opportunity to understand the crisis through lectures, summaries of which were usually published in the local press. In late November the film, *Abyssinia,* was shown in the Beau Nash Cinema, appropriately accompanying 'G. men', a story of the reign of terror exercised by criminal gangs in America. In the vestibule of the cinema stood a large relief map of the country indicating, in the *Chronicle's* words, 'the vast tracts of desert for which Abyssinia is noted, and also the many centres which have now become famous'. The phrase 'became famous' was a euphemism for scenes of carnage and terror bombing conducted by the Italians. Harar, for instance, was bombed in March 1936 and the local hospital was destroyed despite having a large red cross painted on its roof. Dr Lionel Gurney from Monkton Combe, who had previously been working with the British Missionary Society in Abyssinia, and his brother Dr Ted Gurney were part of an international group of volunteers working in the Harar district. When Ted and his wife, Molly, who was a nurse, left Bath in November, the *Chronicle* reported that he expected to be in charge of a small hospital and added ominously 'where he will be kept extremely busy'.

Like Kaiser Wilhelm before him, effigies of Mussolini were burnt on bonfire night in November 1935. RG Naish, Twerton's local historian, took great joy in setting fire to an effigy resembling Mussolini instead of Guy Fawkes on 5 November. The inscription underneath the figure read: 'Mussolini, the War Guy. So perish all the vain ambitions of the tin gods of this afflicted earth'. Others showed their disgust at Mussolini's aggression in different ways. Sidney Walton, the 'publicity expert' and press agent employed by Bath Council, told the *Chronicle* of a conversation he had had with a lady who owned a villa in

Florence. She was so appalled by Italian aggression that she could no longer bear to return to Italy. Walton sought to comfort her by inviting her to Bath in February 1936 to appreciate its late winter beauty. Not everybody, however, felt so strongly. Just a few months after the Italian occupation of Addis Ababa in 1936, Bath's Director of Education, AW Hoyle, visited Italy, and confessed later in a talk in October to the local branch of the Lancashire and Yorks Society that the behaviour of Italian youth 'led him to think that there was much to be said for the system established by Mussolini'.

EMPEROR HAILE SELASSIE IN BATH

THE ITALIAN OCCUPATION of Addis Ababa effectively marked the end of the war, although small scale guerilla fighting continued. The Emperor fled to London where he became a potential embarrassment to the British Government, which was now anxious to improve relations with Italy. He first visited Bath in August 1936 primarily for treatment at the spa, but he found time to look round Cedric Chivers Ltd, the book binders and Fortt's Bath Oliver works, as well as visiting the Bath Horse Show and the Post Office Exhibition in the Octagon. When he left the Octagon, there was 'a huge cheer' and his car was surrounded by people 'at least twenty deep' according to the *Chronicle*. Such

Hailie Selassie leaving the Baths after a visit in August 1936. Behind him is his daughter and in the inset one of his sons'.
(Bath Chronicle, 8 August 1936)

was his popularity and the disruption which the adoring crowds caused to the traffic, that during the remainder of his stay the opportunities of catching sight of him were strictly confined to the Abbey Churchyard and St. Michael's Place.

Initially Haile Selassie planned to live in a property on the edge of Putney Heath in London, but in September he bought Fairfield House on Newbridge Hill, just beyond Partis College, which had previously been the residence of the widow of the Lord Mayor of Belfast. With its high walls and two acres of garden the house afforded him privacy from the outside world. A Bath building firm, Messrs. F.J. Amery and son, was entrusted with making alterations and re-decorating. Philip Morris, who grew up in Bath in the 1930's. remembers later being told by one of Amery's workers that the Emperor's bodyguards never let him out of their sight.[15] The Emperor and the

Empress Menem moved into the house in early October together with three of their children and six grandchildren, as well as various Coptic monks and political advisors. The Emperor's younger son, Prince Makonen, the Duke of Harar, was sent as a boarder to St. Christopher's Prep School in North Road, where according to one of his contemporaries, Richard Butcher, he was a 'very good athlete'.[16] In his first week he was introduced to scouting and soccer. His father insisted, according to the *Chronicle*, that he should be treated like all the other boys: he was 'to take the same subjects, play the same games, and have the same meals, and if the occasion should arise, be punished just as any other erring schoolboy would be'. The *Chronicle* went on to observe that 'like all wise parents, the Emperor and Empress realise that there is no room in school life for social or racial distinction …' .[17] A few years later, Makonen was taught to drive a sports car by John Gait, a car salesman from Bath Garages in the grounds of Fairfield House.[18]

As Haile Selassie was short of money, he employed relatively few servants, several of whom, including his cook, were English. The fifteen-year-old Ruth Blackmore was employed as a nurse maid for the younger children. She was supposed to be paid 15 shillings a week, but in the few months she worked there she received not a penny, and her mother had to pay her daily bus fare.[19]

Richard Butcher remembered the Emperor as 'a tiny man in [a] bowler hat and cape'.[20] Each morning, weather permitting, he would go for a walk towards the centre of the city accompanied by his dog, children and a courtier, who walked at a respectful distance behind him. Apart from writing his autobiography, the Emperor's main preoccupation was to keep the Abyssinian cause alive and exert diplomatic pressure on Mussolini, which made essential the maintenance of small but expensive legations in London, Paris, New York and Cairo. To help finance this the Abyssinian Association was founded in Britain in November 1936. It was particularly active in Bath, and in January 1937 over two hundred eminent Bathonians were invited to its first reception for the Emperor at Cater, Stoffel and Fortt where they paid him 'sympathetic tribute'. The mayor, Walter Long, insisted on attending, contrary to advice from the Home Office, and to applause, welcomed the Emperor and his family as 'citizens of Bath'. In July Haile Selassie celebrated his 45 birthday with a garden party at Fairfield House to which some 80 local worthies were invited. The Bath branch of the Association organised a programme of meetings and garden parties at intervals through the year. In early October 1937 in response to ominous signs that the British government was about to recognise the Italian conquest of Abyssinia, Long, as 'chief magistrate of the city', appealed to its citizens to:

write and tell your member of parliament (Mr. Loel Guinness) that if he is a party to the gambling away of the Abyssinian Empire for the sake of any war in Spain or preserving the trade route to India –that if Ethiopia is to be made a pawn for that bargain- you will withdraw your vote for the next election.[21]

As the historian Keith Bowers observed, the Emperor was what today would be called a 'celebrity' and was arguably ' a distracting novelty amid the humdrum routine life of Bath'. Yet there was some, albeit muted, criticism of his enthusiastic welcome. The Foreign Office received a complaint in advance of a garden party in Parade Gardens, which was to be presided over by the mayor, to the effect that Bath was making too much fuss of the Emperor. He was also occasionally viewed more as a figure of fun than a celebrity. Ruth Blackmore, for instance, remembers meeting him one day with his two attendants on Newbridge Hill. She curtsied to him much to the amusement of the passengers on a passing bus, who roared with laughter. Such incidents were, however, hardly typical. In 1937 and 1938 what Lutz Haber calls the 'City Establishment' showed its support for the Emperor by organising fund raising activities. In July 1937, for instance, Dr and Mrs Marsh organised a garden party in Englishcombe at which £40 was collected. By 1939 with the growing threat of another world war, Haile Selassie was subject to less attention in the pages of the *Chronicle*, but in the winter of 1939-40 in response to his financial problems the council waived payment of the rates and the electricity bills for Fairfield House. In April 1941 with the liberation of Ethiopia by Commonwealth forces, Haile Selassie was able to return to Addis Ababa.[22]

SITTING ON A 'POWDER BARREL'

AT A MEETING of the Bath Conservative Association in May 1936, Captain Carson gave a lecture on the current European situation in which he used the dramatic phrase that Europe was '… sitting on a powder barrel'. He was referring to Mussolini's conquest of Abyssinia and Hitler's re-militarisation of the Rhineland contrary to both the Treaty of Versailles and the Locarno Agreements. Two months later civil war broke out in Spain between the Nationalists led by General Franco and the Republican Government assisted by the Spanish Communist Party. Germany and Italy intervened to help Franco, while the USSR supplied arms and specialist troops to the Republicans. To avoid this escalating into a major European war Britain and France tried in vain to persuade the powers not to intervene. The war rapidly became a struggle or 'crusade' between fascism and socialism.

In early August Bathonians were given a graphic account in *The Chronicle* of the air and sea bombardments of Barcelona by the Nationalist forces and of the fighting around Gibraltar by Alfred Wills, who had been on a cruise in the western Mediterranean. While Wills had the advantage of being on a luxury liner, there were other people with connections to Bath, whose experiences were more traumatic. Moroccan troops under the command of Franco took over the house of Colonel Brinton, the former secretary of the Bath Horse Show at San Roque, while the Scottish husband of a woman on holiday in Bath together with 37 other British nationals, who were employed by the Rio Tinto Company in Spain, was taken prisoner by workers supporting the Spanish government. A letter from an old member of Downside School to a friend in Bath gave a vivid description of a communists attack on a Carthusian monastery in Barcelona where he was staying. He reported that

> Our house ... has 'gone west'. The procurator and another monk were shot dead, and the prior, the vicar and the oldest member of the community were all badly wounded ... [23]

As the war dragged on communist atrocities were more than matched by nationalist atrocities. In Bath the political left sympathised with the Republic. In August Major Grenfell held a protest meeting near the Victoria column in the Royal Victoria Park to drum up support for the Spanish government and its supporters where a collection was taken to help finance the first medical unit to be sent to Spain. Support was also forthcoming from the BTLC, which contributed a small sum to the 'Help the Spanish Workers Fund'.

The rise of Hitler and the wars in Abyssinia and Spain fostered a feeling of insecurity throughout the country. Above all there was widespread fear of the bomber and the possible use of poison gas against civilian populations, which had been inadvertently encouraged by Baldwin's admission in 1932 that 'the bomber will always get through'. What this in practice might mean was summed up by Canon Raven, a leading British passivist, in a sermon in the Argyle Congregational Church in September 1936:

> ... one thing is certain-that the blow will be struck from a clear sky; that people will seek to shatter a possible enemy before the enemy has had a chance to make preparations. I very much doubt if any country will survive the first smash'. [24]

Two years earlier, in April 1934 Bathonians had been given an ominous taste of the future when a large number of Royal Air Force planes were involved in manoeuvres over and around the city. Most of these were bombers, which droned over the city until midnight. Loel Guinness, who was an ardent supporter of airpower in all its forms whether military or commercial, sought to minimise the threat from aerial warfare. He told a meeting of the General Committee of the Bath Conservative Association in May 1935 'that in his view ... there is nothing to get scared about' as he was convinced that the *Luftwaffe* was far smaller than the RAF. To overcome this fear and to make the people of Bath more air minded he supported forming a local branch of the National League of Airmen, whose main objective was 'to educate the British public in 'the vital necessity' of increasing the size of the RAF. As a party the Conservatives supported rearmament. Adrian Hopkins, the Chairman of the Bath Conservative Association was delighted that the defence estimates were increased by 10 million pounds after the publication of the Defence White Paper in 1935.

However, rearmament was an anathema to the Quakers and many members of the Labour Party. As early as May 1933 leading members of the Labour Party from both Bath and Bristol met at the Friends' Meeting House and decided to build up in both cities a vigorous anti-war movement. This led to the formation of the Bath branch of the Anti-War Council with Major Grenfell as secretary. He pursued a vigorous policy of writing letters to the papers criticising any public figure who advocated expenditure on armaments and organising public meetings. He also canvassed hard for support from the various trade union branches in Bath, gaining the support only of the Railway Clerks' Association. Although the BTLC refused affiliation to the Anti-War Council on the advice of the TUC as it had been penetrated by communists, many of its members were nevertheless sympathetic to its aims and in July 1934 by a majority of just one agreed to take part in an anti-war demonstration the following month to mark the twentieth anniversary of the outbreak of the Great War. In November the Bath Cooperative Society unanimously carried a motion urging the British Government to pursue a policy of peace and disarmament. Its president observed that 'there are seven million Co-operators in these islands, and if we put our back into the job we can compel the Government to take note on this issue'. Briefly it seemed that Bathonians would have the choice of a peace candidate in the General Election, which was held on 14 November 1935, A year earlier Dick Sheppard, a Canon of St. Paul's Cathedral founded the Peace Pledge Union. Shortly before nomination day for the electoral candidates it seemed that a young 23 year old graduate of Cambridge, Alfred Tanner, who had taken the pledge, might stand as a peace candidate. He was a Canadian by birth, but his grandmother was a Bathonian, and his mother had returned to live in Bath some four years earlier. She was in her own right a doughty campaigner for the League of Nations Union. However, as the *Chronicle* succinctly put it, the candidature did not in the end 'materialise'.

THE CITY'S AIR RAID PRECAUTIONS
THE PRELIMINARY STAGE, 1935-36

BATH COUNCIL was forced to consider the reality of aerial warfare in July 1935 when the Home Office asked the civic authorities throughout the country to draw up preliminary plans for 'safeguarding the civil population against the effects of air attack'. Only too aware of the peace ballot it added that these 'in no way imply any relaxation of effort on the part of His Majesty's Government to ensure the promotion and maintenance of peace by all means in their power'. In response to this the Watch Committee recommended the formation of an organising committee, or Air Raid Precautions (ARP) Committee, as it soon became known, consisting of the mayor and representatives from the other council committees which would be most affected by these preparations. These were the Education, Health, Electricity, Surveying, Watch and Waterworks Committees. Representatives from St. John's Ambulance and the Red Cross as well as the RUH and the Bath and District Nursing Association would also be called upon to attend. The council acted on this advice, and on 30 July the ARP Committee was duly constituted as recommended.[25]

On 25 July the Home Office informed the country's local authorities of its intention to organise a series of regional conferences, where county and borough councils could discuss their plans and receive further advice. Bath was invited to send five representatives, one of whom was to include the Chief Constable, to the Council House in Bristol, on 15 October. The ARP Committee at its first meeting on 2 October, decided that he should be joined by the Medical Officer of Health (MOH), the Town Clerk, the Chief Officer of the Fire Brigade and the City Engineer. The Bristol Conference was addressed by Wing-Commander Hodsell, the Assistant Under-Secretary of State in charge of the ARP department at the Home Office. Basil Ogden, the Town Clerk, drew up a report for the city's ARP Committee of the key points made by the Wing-Commander, which can be summarised as follows:[26]

While the Home Office, the Air Ministry and GPO were devising a national plan for air raid warnings, local authorities would nevertheless have to arrange their own systems for warning the public.

The police were to be responsible for enforcing the blackout or 'lighting restrictions', as they were called at this point. The country was to be divided into three zones: A, B and C; A, which comprised the eastern half, would have the most rigorous restrictions. Bath would be in Zone B.

Respirators and protective clothing were to be issued to the police, fire brigade, first aid organisations and decontamination squads. These would be paid for by the government.

Councils were to prepare plans in case there was 'a complete stoppage in telephonic communications.'

Roads and railways would be maintained by central government, but local authorities would be responsible for maintaining such services as gas, water and electric light. The highway authorities would be responsible for clearing debris from the roads.

Councils would need to recruit scaffolders and demolition workers to assist the fire brigade in rescuing people trapped in bombed buildings.

Gas schools were to be set up by the Home Office, which would train personnel to act as instructors in their area. Optimistically Hodsell observed that 'there was no new gas which could be manufactured as a lethal weapon in warfare against which we have not got a protection' adding that 'the effective range of gas bombs is comparatively small and not of long duration'.

Places suitable for shelters were to be 'earmarked for emergency' and if possible, gas proofed.

It was important to keep the public informed of these measures.

Above all Hodsell stressed that 'what the Government wanted in the preliminary stages would cost the local authority nothing ... except time'.

The pacifist movement in Bath rejected outright the effectiveness of any defence against aerial attack. In July the Bath Unemployed Association immediately condemned the council's ARP measures on the grounds that they created 'a false sense of security'. A few days later the same criticism was made by the National Union of Women Teachers, which reminded councils throughout Britain that the Prime Minister himself had said that there could be no adequate defence against air attacks. It went on to warn of its negative psychological impact on children, and how generally such proposals 'foster war-mindedness'. The Quakers, too, were scathing in their criticism of the government's policy and the corporation's intention to act on it, declaring uncompromisingly that 'we must refuse to cooperate in the prepared measures for air-raid defences'. However, there was at least one dissenting voice to this chorus of protest: a Mr Langford Hill, an ardent anti-communist, penned a handwritten note without any address to the town clerk claiming that the Society of Friends and other peace groups were in fact operating under instructions from Soviet Russia and that their hatred of capitalism had blinded them 'to every other evil and so unbalanced their minds'.[27]

Over the course of 1936 the city's ARP programme began to take shape. The town clerk was made responsible for coordinating services, and the headquarters of the ARP committee was situated in the Guildhall. In April the government set up a civilian anti-gas school for the South-west in Eastwood Park, Falfield, Gloucestershire, reassuring anxious trainees that the chances of any accidents ... would be 'extremely remote',[28] and a few months later one representative each from the city's Health and Engineer's departments and the local fire brigade were nominated to attend 'as and when vacancies occurred'.[29] The challenge involved in carrying out the government's proposed ARP measures was made clear when in April 1936 the Home Office sent councils slides accompanied by a commentary on what to expect in the event of an air raid. They were informed that 'hostile aircraft passing overhead may use H.E.[high explosive] bombs, incendiary bombs, gas bombs, gas sprays or combination of these' and warned that 'while the Air Force will try and prevent such an attack, ... it is impossible to guarantee immunity ...'. The task of the county and borough councils was to 'minimise the consequences of such an attack –a matter partly of organisation, and partly of protection' by preparing 'to deal with what may reasonably be expected to happen and providing such protection as may be possible in the circumstances'.[30]

The Medical Officer of Health, Dr Blackett, the Chief Constable, the City Engineer and the Chief Officer of the Fire Brigade all had vital roles in developing the city's ARP strategy. Blackett urged close cooperation with St. John's Ambulance and the Red Cross Society and the immediate location of suitable buildings to serve as first aid stations, suggesting that some or all of the council's schools should be used for this purpose. He also warned that adequate stocks of medical stores would have to be kept in at least two places near the centre of the city and be ready at all times for 'immediate dispatch by car to any desired first aid post'. He was confident that the Isolation Hospital, the RUH and the Frome Road House would provide sufficient beds for the seriously injured.[31] By June, Blackett had successfully located suitable premises for first aid and decontamination sites. In the city centre he suggested Blue Coat House with the adjacent Maternity Clinic, as it had 'many separate rooms and various approaches'. To the West of the city, he proposed the Oldfield Council Schools on the grounds that:

> these consist of three large buildings, each with many separate rooms, and approaches both from the Lower Bristol Road and from Wells Road. They are slightly raised above the river level and are close to Messrs Stothert and Pitt's Works, which form a likely target.[32]

In October the Chief Constable, Nelson Ashton, drew up a report for the ARP Committee outlining 'a general scheme' for the city's protection, stressing that it was still 'in an early stage of development' and that his observations were 'in many respects tentative and provisional'.[33] Financial considerations limited what could be done to organise an effective blackout system and construct bomb proof shelters. Apart from a few areas such as Audley Park Road and Weston, which were still gas lit, the city's lighting was electric. However, as the current was not controlled from one single generating station, it was calculated that it would take some 30 minutes to extinguish the city's lights, even if a partly restricted lighting system was already in force. The air raid warning, on the other hand, would give only about 15 minutes notice of an imminent attack. Theoretically street lighting could be controlled centrally but the cost would 'be prohibitive'. Construction of bomb proof shelters for the whole of the city's population was also 'impossible for financial reasons'. Consequently, there was no option but to prepare specially selected rooms at home or at work to serve as shelters. Public shelters would, however, still have to be provided for those caught out in the streets during a raid or whose houses could offer no protection. Ashton therefore ordered a census of suitable underground premises, which could serve as shelters. He approved of the Home Office's proposal to set up 'a new type of organisation' composed of persons to be known as 'street wardens' to help and advise the civil population. He considered that the warden should be 'a general friend and helper of the occupants of quite a small area- a quarter or half-mile of streets perhaps'. He should master all 'that ought to be known about household precautions' - an obvious source for volunteers was the British Legion.

At the end of 1936 the ARP Committee reported to the council on the progress made with the city's ARP defences, and stressed that, quite apart from air raid wardens, many other volunteers including boy scouts and girl guides were needed to make its plans work. It also emphasised that '… owners and occupiers of large premises should make suitable arrangements for their own staffs' and also for anybody who might be 'in their establishment during an air raid'.³⁴

In June 1936 the *Chronicle* had optimistically observed that 'air raid precautions are proceeding steadily but quietly in Bath'. Yet the council was criticised on the one hand for carrying out 'impractical' proposals from the government, which made war more rather than less likely, and on the other for not proceeding quickly enough.

THE SILVER JUBILEE

THE MAJOR FESTIVE EVENT of 1935 was the celebration of George V's Silver Jubilee on 6 May, which was declared a national holiday. Its celebrations contrasted with the grim preparations for mitigating the impact of air raids, which began just two months later. Bath put on an impressive spectacle which involved a service at the Abbey, a civic procession and the mobilisation of the city's school children, which was planned with military precision. The children first assembled in their school playgrounds at two o'clock. While the older children then processed by different routes to Victoria Park, the infants remained behind and were entertained in their own schools. At East Walcot Girl's School, for example, the infants were treated to a Punch and Judy show in the playground followed by tea arranged by the head teacher and staff subsidised by the council at 8 pence per head.³⁵ When the older children reached Victoria Park, they were addressed by the mayor on the unique advantages

Jubilee decorations: George Street in May 1935 (Bath Chronicle, Jubilee Supplement, May 1935.)

of the monarchy, and then provided with entertainment involving clowns, conjurers, dancing displays and community singing. An hour later at 4 o'clock they proceeded to the Middle Common where they had tea, which was paid for by the council and each child received a Jubilee mug. In the evening an impressive display was organised on the Rec. The King's speech was relayed to the crowd by wireless and was followed by a programme of activities, which involved military bands, a gymnastic display by the YMCA, physical training by the City of Bath Boys' School and a torchlight tattoo by guides, scouts and cadets. The city from Twerton to Lansdown flew flags and decorated the streets with bunting. The Bellman was moved to observe 'that not within living memory has there been a day of such jollity'. Thanks to what he called the 'Clerk of the Weather' everything went according to plan,

Yet there was an undercurrent of criticism. At the May Day rally in Seven Dials one speaker, a member of the Bristol Trades and Labour Council, argued that the celebrations were really aimed to deflect criticism from the National Government and create a patriotic pro Tory mood in time for the next election. A critical line was also taken some ten days later by George Desmond, the parliamentary Labour candidate for Bath , when he opened the May Fair at the Labour Institute. He argued that for some workers the Jubilee holiday was in fact a lockout as their employers would not pay for the day's holiday. The President of the Bath Unemployed Association, George Payton, another of Bath's few communists, associated himself with the Mayor of Bermondsey in South-East London, who had refused to participate in the Jubilee celebrations, and on 16 May wrote him a letter of support which was published in the *Chronicle*. At a meeting of the BTLC shortly after the jubilee, similar criticisms were made but were firmly rejected by the majority of members, two of whom had attended the Abbey service. One particularly vociferous critic of the Jubilee was told in no uncertain terms by a colleague that if he did not like this country he could go to Germany 'where before you go to work in the morning you have to lift your hand and say Heil Hitler!', and another pointed out that Avon Street, one of the poorest areas of Bath, was festooned with decorations, which was surely a sign that its inhabitants were not opposed to the Jubilee.

THE GENERAL ELECTION, NOVEMBER 1935

THE ELECTION of 14 November 1935 resulted in a comfortable win for the National Government, despite criticism from the Labour and Liberal parties of its relative failure to overcome unemployment, its decision to rearm and its handling of the Abyssinian crisis. Attendance at public meetings in Bath was lower than it had been for the last few elections, but this was put into perspective by the Bellman, who argued that rather than going out on a rainy night people preferred to sit by their firesides and listen to the leaders of the parties expound their policies on air. Despite the increased electorate the number of votes cast compared to the last election in 1931 was 2112 less. Labour, however, increased its vote by 1,505 and the Liberals by 409. The Conservatives won 4,026 votes fewer, but still recorded a comfortable majority of 12,020 over both parties combined. Loel Guinness was conspicuously not accompanied by his wife, whom he was in the process of divorcing, but his sister and father were regular attenders at his meetings and his little son, Pat, was duly sporting a blue rosette to appeal to the female voters' maternal instincts.

The *Chronicle* reported the usual string of amusing incidents which occurred on polling day. One fairly typical story concerned an ardent supporter of the Conservatives, who went to the polling booth without her glasses and voted by mistake for the wrong candidate. It also mentioned that one particularly determined old lady of 94 from the Salvation Army's Eventide Home at Bathwick Hill insisted on casting her vote in person. Violence did, however, briefly flair up at a meeting addressed by Loel Guinness in Holy Trinity Church Hall, James Street, on Wednesday Evening 6 November. This was instigated by 'a gang of hooligans from Bristol', numbering about 30, who had first made their presence known at a meeting in Green Park. They barracked Guinness and at the end of the meeting about 15 of them 'deliberately put on their hats, while God Save the King was sung. Adrian Hopkins, the new Chairman of the Bath Conservative Association, told the *Chronicle* that 'it is the first time I have seen such an incident of disloyalty in Bath' They 'hustled' Guinness as he climbed into his car in James Street. West, and according to the *Chronicle*

> ... worse befell three well known Bath ladies, two of whom had spoken in support of his candidature. The door of their car was flung open by someone in the crowd and the three occupants of the car were spat at, while there was hammering on the car windows. An unknown man, who jumped on the running board, by his courage and good sense, prevented an already ugly incident developing into a dangerous situation which might have ended in the car being over-turned.[36]

THE DEATH OF GEORGE V AND THE ABDICATION CRISIS

AN ERA CAME to an end with the death of George V just before midnight on 20 January 1936. Bath like the rest of the country mourned. Black rosettes and ties and even black hats were on sale; theatres and cinemas were closed. Functions such as the Mendip Hunt Ball and the dinner for the Bath branch of the Railway Clerks 'Association were cancelled. School children were given solemn addresses by their teachers. At Walcot Senior School, for example, the headmaster informed the children earlier that day that the King was very ill and afterwards they sang the National Anthem. The following morning the children were told that the King 'had passed away' and 'suitable hymns and prayers were taken at assembly'. After an appropriate address, two minutes silence was observed, and then in honour of the new King the National Anthem was again sung. Three days later a teacher and six senior boys represented the school at the Proclamation of Edward VIII outside the Guildhall.

At the end of the year the pupils again sang the National Anthem but this time for a new king - George VI. A terse entry in the school logbook for 14 December baldly states that 'reference was made to the events of last week and the National Anthem sung'.[37] This, of course, referred to the abdication of Edward VIII. For most of 1936 the British public knew nothing about the King's infatuation with the twice divorced American, Wallace Simpson, despite all the publicity in the American papers. During the summer the focus of attention in Bath was on the coming coronation in May 1937. There was discussion about the commemorative coins to be issued by the Royal Mint and plans for excursions to London during the Coronation week. As late as mid-November a speaker to a Conservative gathering argued that Edward was closer to the Empire than his father had been because he had fraternised with Dominion troops in the trenches. It was only on 16 November that Baldwin learnt of Edward's determination to marry Wallace Simpson. On 4 December he informed the King that such a course would inevitably result in his abdication. The following day the *Chronicle* produced a measured leader, which observed that:

> Not within the experience of any citizen of this realm, however aged, has there been a constitutional crisis comparable with that which has been disclosed to a generally astonished public concerning the matrimonial intentions of the King which threaten the stability of the Throne and rock the very foundations of national pride in our great institution of monarchical headship of the State.[38]

The *Chronicle* went on to stress that while there was considerable sympathy for the dilemmas faced by the King, there was throughout the Nation and Empire a 'great feeling of repugnance against a matrimonial alliance with a lady who, as the world knows, has twice obtained divorces and whose ex-husbands are still living'. It then posed the crucial question as to whether Edward would 'place the Monarchy before self' or whether his attachment to Mrs. Simpson was a greater force. The question was answered five days later when Edward abdicated in favour of his brother. Ironically a week later Haile Selassie announced that he had no intention of abdicating as Emperor of Abyssinia even if he was temporarily in exile.

On Tuesday 15 December the accession of King George VI was proclaimed at the Guildhall. Troops with fixed bayonets were on parade and a representative selection of Bath's population ranging from the mayor to small schoolchildren was present. The High Street was packed with people and all the windows in the buildings opposite were taken up with observers. There was a sharp shower at 11,30, but this was followed with brilliant sunshine – 'a happy omen for the new reign' as the *Chronicle* remarked. There is no evidence that there was much support for Edward in Bath. Yet the tragedy of the abdication was clear for all to see, For instance, members of the Bath Preservation Trust (BPT) attending a meeting in the Pump Room on the evening of 11 December listened to Edward's announcement of his abdication on the wireless and found it immensely moving – 'the last act in the tragedy'. Children in the school playgrounds had a simpler interpretation when they sang: 'Hark the Herald Angels sing Mrs Simpson stole our King'.

There was, however, no option but in the words of the BPT's President, 'to look forward'. Just a few days later the BTLC did exactly that when it agreed it should be represented on the council's Coronation Committee, which was to plan the local celebrations. Already Edward VIII's brief reign was becoming history. The coronation souvenirs that were now unusable were becoming collectors' pieces. Mallory and Sons, the Jewellers, were surprised that despite the abdication there was a rush for its special line in glass tankards with the Royal cipher EVIII.R. on them. With Christmas approaching yet again, the drama of the abdication could be put aside. For the hotels Christmas 1936 was a bumper year, and in the city all the usual Yuletide delights were on offer. The Pump Room again offered a special programme and there were Christmas parties galore as well as the pantomime, 'Little Bo-Peep'.

The Coronation took place as planned in London on 12 May, except of course, it was George not Edward who was crowned. In Bath the celebrations involved civic processions, a military parade and a party for school children on Middle Common. In the evening there was, music, dancing, community singing and at 10 pm a 'grand display of fireworks'. The festivities provided some light relief from the tense international situation and the growing threat of war.

10
BATH IN THE LATE THIRTIES

ON THE EVE of the Second World War Bath was still one of the most beautiful cities in Britain. It had not become, like Coventry, a predominantly industrial city. The Reverend Gillie, Minister of the Argyle Congregational Church, described Bath and its surrounding hills as 'a casket of rich jewels', but added that the 'casket was greater than the jewels'. The Old Bath Protection Society (OBPS) constantly emphasised that the city and its surroundings, 'particularly its guardian hills' were interdependent'. Town planners, such as Professor Patrick Abercrombie, were also increasingly stressing the importance of green belts and the conservation of the rural environment. John Betjeman declared on the radio in April 1939 that Bath 'was a model architecturally to the rest of England' and that people came from all over the world to see it. He described lyrically the first time he 'saw the Royal Crescent stretching out along the hill and watched from Lansdown Crescent the lights twinkling out in the evening light among the terraces and avenues of this grey stone eighteenth-century spa'.[1] Yet the city was increasingly under siege from the modern world - industrialisation, the motor car, housing estates, road widening and ribbon developments such as those along the Warminster Road towards Bathampton and the Bristol Road at Saltford and Keynsham, which threatened to make Bristol and Bath one continuous conurbation.

These developments were bitterly opposed by the Old Bath Preservation Society (OBPS) and the Bath Preservation Trust (BPT).* At the former's annual meeting in 1939, its secretary Miss Florence Tylee appealed for funds to fight the desecration of Bath telling its members that

> during this last year, we have had so many warnings of threatened mischief, which we cannot stop, except with the help of the Trust. Letters come to me telling of factories to be built in residential neighbourhoods, of cottages to be demolished unnecessarily, open spaces to be encroached upon -much of which might be prevented if funds were available ... . The guardian hills need guardians for themselves and can no longer protect the sleeping queen. She

---

* The BPT was founded in 1934 and empowered to own property and worked in tandem with the OBPS.

must wake and rise and with the help of her true sons and daughters and friends and save herself from destruction.[2]

This view was not universally shared in Bath. Mayor Adrian Hopkins, for instance, told the Chamber of Commerce in February 1938 that 'occasions may arise ...when sentiment must give way to the pressing needs of these days'.

THE BATH CORPORATION ACT OF 1937

IN 1933 BATH together with Bathavon District Council and Somerset County Council set up the Bath and District Joint Planning Committee under the chairmanship of Arthur Hobhouse, a member of the Somerset County Council, to prepare a blueprint for the future development of the whole area. Its consultant town planning officer was the illustrious Professor Abercrombie. Initially, however, the council was more concerned with the complexity of drafting what, after some drastic revision, was to become the Bath Corporation Act of 1937. On the evening of 22 October 1935 the Chairman of the City Improvements Committee, Arthur Wills, presented the council with the bill's contents. The *Chronicle* covered his speech in detail under the title 'Alderman Wills has another dream'. Its main purpose was to facilitate the re-construction of the Royal Mineral Water hospital with the new additions of an outpatients' department and private wards on the partly cleared site stretching from Westgate Buildings to the river, while the council would acquire its old buildings in Upper Borough Walls. This proposal attracted widespread support, but the bill also contained several other clauses, which were more contentious. Although some appeared to safeguard the unique nature of Bath, others threatened to sacrifice the city to the motor car. On the one hand the bill would give the council powers to purchase Pulteney Bridge, help the owners of dilapidated Georgian houses with the cost of their restoration and veto any proposed alterations to the external elevations of period property. On the other hand, conservationists were alarmed by an extensive programme of road widening, which included parts of Queen's Parade, Broad Street, Walcot Street, Old Bond Street, Burton Street and Upper Borough Walls. Above all they were incensed by plans to extend Milsom Street up to the Assembly Rooms, which would involve cutting through Edgar buildings and Alfred Street, as well as the demolition of the island site in Old Bond Street and Evans and Owen in Bartlett Street. The *Times* compared it to the vandalism in Rome carried out by Mussolini's Fascist regime.[3]

For nearly three months between October and December 1935 an epic battle was fought over the future of Bath between the BPT and the council, which attracted considerable interest in the national press. The *Daily Sketch* described it as a 'clash' in which 'architects, antiquarians, modernists and motorists are mixed up in a controversy of glorious uncertainty', while in *The Daily Telegraph* Horace Annesley Vachell observed that 'an uncivil war' had broken out in the Queen City of the West'. He was later to draw on these events and the larger-than-life figure of Alderman Wills in his novel, *The Golden House*, which was published two years later . The BPT made clear that it did not wish 'to wreck the Bill but only to secure reasonable amendments'. It supported the decision to move the Mineral Water Hospital to its new site but, mobilised public opinion against the extension of Milsom Street and the widening of Old Bond Street. It appealed to the ratepayers to contact their friends, write to councillors and hold ward meetings. If it came to a local referendum on the bill, it asked for volunteers to canvas and lend cars on the polling day.[4]

At the council meeting of 19 November Wills trenchantly defended the bill. Quite apart from the rebuilding of the Mineral Hospital, it would also revive what he called the fast-waning fortunes of Milsom Street, principally caused by the growth of a new shopping centre in the south of the city. It was approved in its entirety by an overwhelming margin of 5-33, but this support was not mirrored outside the council chamber where it was greeted with increasing hostility. Two weeks later Wills resigned both the chairmanship of the Improvements Committee, and his membership of the Special (Parliamentary bill) Committee. His resignation was partly a result of his growing unpopularity caused by his imperious manner, but he also calculated that the bill had a greater chance of success if somebody less controversial than himself took over. In the meantime as a result of the negative publicity generated by the BPT, which had launched a nationwide campaign against the Bath Bill and enlisted the support of such notables as Rudyard Kipling, the Bath and District Joint Planning Committee decided to turn to Professor Abercrombie for advice. His subsequent report was then referred to the council's Parliamentary Bill Committee. Abercrombie diplomatically congratulated 'the promoters of the bill on the many excellent clauses it contained' but did not hesitate to call the proposed destruction of the island site 'a grave mistake' and to oppose the plan for the extension of Milsom Street, which some years later in his memoirs he described as

> the sort of thing a third year student would do and would be commended for as a gymnastic exercise, but who would be told that he had quite missed the genius loci and that his details would suit Buenos Aires rather than Bath.[5]

Abercrombie cooperated closely with the BPT, whose trustees managed to persuade the council to eliminate the most contentious clauses in the bill. The proposed extension of Milsom Street and the demolition of the island site in Old Bond Street were now dropped. The amended bill was passed by the council with a majority of 26 to 5 two days before Christmas, only to be subjected on 30 December to intense criticism at a packed meeting of ratepayers at the Guildhall. To the surprise of the *Chronicle*'s political sketch writer, 'the Member for Lenswick', the meeting was not, as might be expected, carefully packed with members of the OBPS and BPT. Instead 'the men in the street as typified by Everyman' formed the overwhelming majority. Most of the councillors and majority of the members of the OBPS/BPT voted for the bill but the great mass of what could be called the floating voters ' kicked out everything'. Why was this, when the bill had, after all, been amended and its most objectionable clauses removed? Even though Wills had resigned, he did not hesitate to attack the bill's critics in the press and council chamber. He left a legacy of distrust and the perception that the bill was being railroaded through by the council without sufficient consultation. Sturge Cotterell, the chairman of the BPT, observed ,for instance,in November that 'an omnibus bill containing such varied provisions, which would have a radical impact 'on the face of the city', needed 'thoughtful consideration'. There was too a fear that such large scale works would push the rates up. Consequently the 'floaters' were already intensely distrustful of the council when they attended the meeting. They were even suspicious of its decision to move the venue of the meeting to the Guildhall, despite the fact that the water level of the Avon was rising and the Pavilion was threatened with floods. According to the 'Member for Lenswick'

> what annoyed them more than anything was the phalanx of speakers put up to speak in support of the bill. One after another was called upon by the Mayor…
> All spoke well, but the meeting began to wonder when opponents would have a chance. They tapped the floor in protest. [6]

The one opponent of the bill, Councillor WF Long, despite forgetting his dentures, made a good speech, which was enthusiastically cheered.

So shell shocked were the councillors by this opposition that the bill was rejected by 30 votes to 15 when the council met on 7 January. Its members were duly lambasted by Wills for their feebleness and told that 'never in the history of this city has the corporation cut such a sorry figure'. However, within six months the council drafted a much less contentious bill.

Its core provision was still the reconstruction of the Royal Mineral Water Hospital on the riverside site, which would in due course necessitate the demolition of the remaining slum properties there, the building of a new school to replace the existing St Paul's and Kingsmead schools and the raising of the whole area above flood level. Walcot Street was also to be widened to remove the bottle neck entrance into the city, and a new road was to be constructed from Kingsmead Square to Queen Square. Car parks were to be provided off Walcot Street and in the Ambury area by the river. The BPT was placated by regulations concerning the elevation and the materials used to build or renovate property in the city. There was, too, to be a 'schedule' of pre 1820 buildings which would be listed to ensure their survival more or less in their existing form.[7]

There was inevitably some opposition to these plans, particularly to the widening of Walcot Street and the creation of a car park in its vicinity, but in a poll of Bath's electors on 20 January 1937 the supporters of the scheme won a convincing majority of 5,791. Questions were, however, raised about where those, whose houses were shortly to be demolished, would live. Councillor Tiley had accused the council at a meeting on 16 June 1936 of dispossessing 'people and sending them into poorer class buildings unfit for rats to live in'. There was also opposition from traders in the Walcot Street. and the Corn Street. areas. In February 1937 JB Bowler and Sons organised a petition to the Lords, which resulted in the insertion of a clause in the bill committing the council to provide displaced businesses with alternative premises. At the end of July, the bill received the Royal Assent and it passed into law. Although It provided Georgian Bath with some defence against the developers, as it drew up a list of protected buildings, conservationists were worried when neither the Old Bond Street 'Island block' nor Edgar Buildings were scheduled under the Bath Act 'for perpetual preservation' and feared that that at some future date the council might yet demolish them. Councillor Rhodes Cook, who resigned when the 1935 Bath Bill was withdrawn, argued rather wistfully in January 1938 that 'with the obstruction, or perhaps one should say the block, in Old Bond Street removed', the extension of Milsom Street right up to the Assembly Rooms would create 'a very fine vista'. Not everybody supported placing Georgian Bath in aspic. In June 1938 the *Chronicle* commented that, while the Royal Crescent and Circus were inviolate, 'the circumstances are not quite the same in other parts of the city' where 'modern needs' had to be accommodated, by street widening if necessary. It pointed out that the demolition of the Literary and Scientific Institution at Terrace Walk had created a much needed open space.

The BPT and OBPS carefully monitored any threats to the buildings and beauty of Bath. The BPT regretted that the main roads into the city were still 'disfigured by advertisement signs' but realised that the council had little powers to deal with this problem. It did manage to stop the Bath Gas Company from developing the site of General Wolfe's house in Trim Street and ensured that the building was included in the list of properties to be protected under the Bath Act. It constantly checked the structural condition and appearance of the Circus and cooperated with the National Trust in clearing Solsbury Hill of thistles and stones. It also played a leading role in saving the five acre Northfields House estate from the ambitions of a speculative builder, who planned to build 40 houses on it, and donated £750 towards the cost of its purchase by the council. This ensured that 'At least two acres' ... were 'to be dedicated as a public space' and on the rest of the estate only two new houses per acre were to be permitted. In the eyes of some residents the BPT exercised too much influence on the council. The headmaster of the Art School, Clifford Ellis, observed caustically that it had 'subjected the councillors to such criticism that these gentlemen have now adopted, in self-defence, a negative policy'.[8]

THE RENAISSANCE OF THE ASSEMBLY ROOMS

BUILT BY JOHN Wood, the Younger, and opened in 1771, the Assembly Rooms were one of the great buildings of Bath, but their days of glory were long since over. During the Great War they had been requisitioned by the RAF and afterwards a cinema was opened in the ballroom, and the Tea Room became a saleroom and market. In 1931 the Rooms were bought by Ernest Cook, the grandson of Thomas Cook, the travel agent, and transferred to the National Trust, which in 1936 eventually leased them to the council for a peppercorn rent for 75 years. Initially the council planned to use the Rooms 'exclusively as a central library' but the plans were dropped in February 1936 after the Assembly Rooms sub-committee pointed out that they lacked sufficient lighting, were too damp and above all 'were not situated in a sufficiently central position' of the city to serve the needs of its readers.[9] The council then decided to utilise them for their original purpose as the city's centre for social functions, and applied for a government loan of £25,000 to pay for the costs of renovation. It engaged Mowbray Green, the distinguished local architect and founder member of the OBPS, who was the author of an authoritative book on 18th Century architecture in Bath, to supervise the alterations and repairs At the official enquiry in September 1936 the council had little difficulty in persuading the government inspector to recommend that the Ministry of Health should agree to a loan. Both the town clerk and the spa director, John Hatton, stressed how the Assembly Rooms would provide suitable space for conferences, while Alderman Sturge Cotterell, speaking on behalf of both the BPT and the OBPS argued that an ' historic building like the Assembly Rooms should be under civic control' as they were a 'distinct asset' and known all over the world.

The news of the grant was greeted enthusiastically by many Bathonians but inevitably there was some criticism of the expense involved, particularly as it emerged that £25,000 was far too conservative an estimate. At a Chamber of Commerce meeting in February 1938 a member commented that the renovation was 'the biggest financial extravagance the City Council had ever indulged in'. One of the councillors present, CB Farr, admitted that the budget had been exceeded, but that the council had now 'burnt its boats' and was three quarters of the way through the work. Completion was, however, delayed for six months by a hold up in the delivery of radiators, caused by their manufacturer being compelled to give precedence to the government's armament contracts.

Finally in October 1938 the Assembly Rooms were opened by the Duchess of Kent. The ceremonies were inaugurated on the evening of the 11th with a ball which The *Chronicle* described as being probably more splendid that even those held 'in the heyday of its old renown'. Overnight the Duchess and her party stayed at Longleat, and the following morning returned officially to open the Assembly Rooms where she was presented, as President of the Royal National Hospital for Rheumatic Diseases* with purses containing money for the hospital. Some came from schools, which were given a half holiday to celebrate the Duchess' visit. East Walcot Infants School, for example, chose Gladys Sims, from the

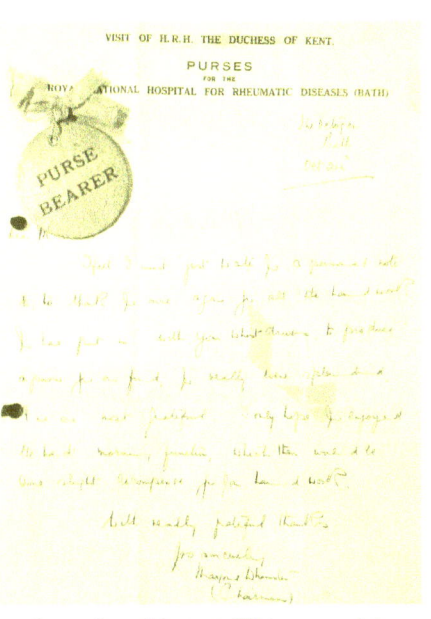

Letter from Marjorie Whimster to Mrs Florence Smith thanking her for collecting money for a purse for the RNHRD (Doreen Williams' papers)

---

* The former Royal Mineral Water Hospital had been renamed the Royal National Hospital for Rheumatic Diseases in 1936)

1st Class, to present a purse containing one guinea. Others contained money raised through whist drives and sales. Mrs Florence Smith, for instance, was particularly energetic and, through a series of whist drives held in the St Luke's school rooms, Odd Down, managed to raise £10. As a reward she was allotted a seat at the opening ceremony. The BTLC also contributed a purse containing £15.[10]

STILL A CITY OF CULTURE?

BATH WITH ITS unique Georgian townscape surrounded by beautiful countryside presented the ideal setting for the flourishing of the arts – an English Salzburg, perhaps, but in the opinion of Clifford Ellis, the headmaster of the Bath School of Art. the city in 1939 was :

> at present unhealthy from an artistic point of view, and has in fact suffered from serious debility for over a century ... [The] pale ghost from the XVIII Century was particularly out of place in the England of Queen Victoria. But Bath produced no vigorous flesh and blood to take its place. As the ghost finally flickered away, Bath as an artistic centre of national importance ceased to exist. Politics of hardly more than parochial effect, were in the hands of small rival coteries of half-pay officers, retired clergymen and their wives.[11]

Ellis conceded that some effort to reverse this trend before 1914 had been made. In 1909 the famous Bath Pageant re-enacted scenes from the city's history and the Old Bath Preservation Society was founded, but he argued that the activities of this society were 'antiquarian rather than artistic. There was no attempt to create'. Consequently 'the attempted [cultural] revival was inevitably unsuccessful'. He was only marginally more positive about the contemporary cultural scene. He admitted that 'today things are a little better; there have been performances of contemporary music and exhibitions of contemporary paintings at the Pump Room, but attendance has been disappointing'. He came to the depressing conclusion that 'though antiquarianism still persists throughout the country as a symptom of recent artistic ill-health, in Bath there [was] a specially marked lag in recovery'. He emphasised that 'it is important to realise that Bath ... is not the artistic city one might imagine, but merely a provincial town with an unimaginatively conservative outlook'.

Ellis, like many of his artistic and intellectual contemporaries, found British culture insular, but arguably he exaggerated Bath's deeply 'conservative' approach to contemporary culture. As we have seen in earlier chapters there were many cultural and intellectual societies in Bath which met regularly and enabled their members to keep abreast of current developments. In the late thirties Bath even had a branch of the 'Left Book Club', which from time to time was addressed by such eminent left-wing figures as the publisher Victor Gollancz, and the Communist Harry Pollitt. Even though the original building was burnt down in 1936, Citizen House under the direction of Miss de Reyes remained what was in effect a drama school with both a national and international appeal. Each year it held an annual drama festival. In 1937 fifty students attended amongst whom were Americans from New York, Texas and Oklahoma. In January 1936 de Reyes opened the Little Theatre, which presented alternately films and plays.

A spacious, well organised and well stocked public library is certainly the pre-requisite of a cultured city. Up to 1924 Bath lacked a lending library and was in the words of Ted Ashman, a leading figure in the Bath WEA, a' cultural desert'[12] for those unable to afford the membership of a private library. Once opened, the new lending library expanded rapidly. Between 1924 and 1933 the number of books issued nearly tripled. A children's department was established and at least five school libraries were supported with loans of specially selected books. School parties were encouraged to visit the library and receive instruction in how to use reference books, but both the lending and the reference libraries were chronically short of space. In 1934 the Libraries Sub-Committee reported that

> there would be difficulty in finding any public lending department comparable in size of stock and annual issues with that of Bath in which public service is performed under such restricted conditions. Not only is the convenience of borrowers gravely impeded, but a further disadvantage is caused by a third of the stock being housed in the basement, a division which is altogether contrary to the principles of an open access library.[13]

As the proposal to move the reference library to the Assembly Rooms was rejected by the council in 1936, the library had no option but to rent premises in the High Street where books could be stored until required for readers. Clearly Bath's public library facilities were inadequate for a city of its reputation!

The battle to save the Orchestra

In early 1936 the council once again attempted to disband the Bath Spa Orchestra and replace it with a quintet, which predictably aroused passionate opposition, and in May led to the formation of the 'Save the Bath Spa Orchestra Movement'. The *Chronicle* received an avalanche of letters criticising the council for its decision, but inevitably there were some dissenting notes struck. Marius Penel of 'Farhurst', Camden Road, for instance, argued succinctly that

> If Bath music lovers want a large band, let them draw from their inflated purses, their fivers, and if needs be their tenners to pay for the 'pipers'. It is not just to ask the vast majority of the inhabitants of this town to pay for music they never go to listen to and who, if they want music, go and switch on their wireless, should they possess a set'.[14]

When the Chamber of Commerce considered the question of re-engaging the Orchestra in May, half of its members viewed it as a business problem, which needed to be solved 'on business lines': if it did not pay, economies would therefore have to be made. The BTLC, possibly out of a loyalty to the Musicians' Union, supported the retention of the orchestra at their weekly meeting on 27 May, although their treasurer pointed out that 'they knew that some of the audiences at the symphony concerts hardly exceeded the number in the orchestra itself'. On Monday 8 June the 'Save the Orchestra Movement' organised a ratepayers meeting in the Pavilion. By an overwhelming majority of nearly 800 to 21 they voted to petition the Spa Committee to reinstate the full orchestra. The council had no appetite for a bruising and unpopular fight, and by the end of July the decision was taken to restore the full orchestra, at least, for the coming winter season. In October 'The Save the Orchestra Movement' metamorphosed into a more general 'Supporters Movement'.

The Orchestra had been given a reprieve, but its future remained uncertain, despite the appointment in September of Maurice Miles, a young conductor from the Buxton Spa Orchestra. During the first ten weeks of the 1936-37 season, it still made an overall loss. Adrian Hopkins in his usual outspoken manner asked at a council meeting in February 1937 whether 'all the agitation' had been worthwhile. He pointed out that there had been a small increase of £62 in the purchase of season tickets, but an increased loss in all the other departments. He added that it was 'lamentable that the efforts of the [Spa] Committee should be hindered by very vocal people, who were not prepared to pull their weight by paying the piper'. However, despite its reservations, the council, possibly persuaded by the Duke of Connaught's glowing praise of the orchestra, reluctantly decided in March 1937 to retain it for another season

BATH IN THE LATE THIRTIES 251

The council's penny pinching attitude to the orchestra did not prevent the Spa Committee from organising in April 1938 the fourth Bath Music Festival, which the *Chronicle* called 'the most ambitious venture of its kind' to be held in the city. It was a considerable success and provided audiences with an eclectic choice of music, which included work from Mozart and Beethoven as well as Prokofieff's *Symphonie Classique*, Gershwin's Second Rhapsody in Blue and the Saxo-Rhapsody for Solo Saxophone and Orchestra by Eric Coates. The music critic of the *Chronicle* observed that

> the festival has certainly proved that if programmes are made sufficiently attractive, public support will be forthcoming. It has been made clear, too, that there are two distinct types of musical public -one that will support Sir Henry Wood and another that enjoys Henry Hall ... the first audience consisted largely of the elderly and leisured classes and the second of the post-war generation for whom men like Henry Hall have established a new musical technique'.[15]

Henry Hall was the band leader of the BBC's dance orchestra, whose unorthodox way of conducting an orchestra was popular with his audiences. He dispensed with the conductor's podium and musical scores and 'patrolled the platform like a particularly energetic sentry.' His musicians were relaxed and 'were past masters of entertaining byplay' - more like a last night of the Proms today.

The Music Festival's success did not save the orchestra. Audience numbers at its concerts in 1938-39 continued to decline, and in March 1939 the council decided not to re-engage it for the coming season. At the final concert in May, Mrs Lilly Keir, a prominent figure in the 'Save the Orchestra Movement', in a spontaneous speech praised it for having given Bath 'a liberal musical education and very great uplift, taking patrons' minds off the tragic happenings of Europe and the continual crises ....,' and scathingly criticised the council for 'its scales of blindness' in disbanding it.

The challenge of modern art

Bathonians tended to prefer traditional landscapes and portraits, but the Festivals of Contemporary Arts of 1930, 1935 and 1936 provided opportunities for them to familiarise themselves with 'modern art'. The Bristol *Evening World* in March 1930 reported that Epstein's statue of 'Nan' was the only topic of conversation in Bath:

Cover of the Programme for the 1930 Festival of Contemporary Arts, and details of its art exhibition ((Bath Record Office)

> Every visitor to the Festival ... stops to look at Epstein's statue ... first with open-mouthed surprise and then with either scorn or uncomprehending admiration.

The *Western Daily Press* observed that some might consider it strange that 'Bath which lives to a great extent on its past is the first place to appreciate the glories of the present'. This opinion was echoed five years later by the Anglo-Belgian poet and playwright, Émile Cammaerts, when opening the 1935 festival. He congratulated

> Bath on the bold step of 'opening a window on the present and future', and after an allusion to the ghosts of the great figures associated with Bath's past, declared -'it is probably a good thing that this fine city should be shaken from her graceful complacency by the strident voice of modernity'.[16]

The 1936 Festival provided further opportunities to become acquainted with a selection of modern artists, and in 1938 there was an exhibition of modern art in the Pump Room where there were minor works of Picasso, Klee, Braque as well as Eric Gill and Paul Nash. However to Clifford Ellis, who, as the headmaster of the Bath School of Art, was arguably the leading authority on modern art in the city, these exhibitions were simply the exceptions that proved the rule. He remained sceptical about Bathonians' appreciation of modern art and in his report for HM inspectors in 1939 observed that 'One Bath lady owns a pleasant modern painting, but she now hangs it in her bedroom as she was so annoyed by the stupid comments of her friends'.[17]

Both Rosemary and Clifford Ellis were 'live wires' who brightened up the art scene in Bath. Rosemary worked as an art teacher at the Royal School for Daughters of Officers of the Army in Bath, and by all accounts was an inspirational teacher. One educational inspector judged her to be one of the best art teachers in the country, and years later a former pupil told her that she was the 'one teacher who inspired me during a rather dreary school life'.[18] When Clifford was appointed headmaster of the art school in 1937, which was on the top floor of the Technical College in Lower Borough Walls, he sought with considerable success to make the city more aware of the school by supplying the local press with information about its activities and holding exhibitions of the students' work. In September 1937, together with Rosemary ,he organised an exhibition of children's art in the city's art gallery which had already been curated in London under the auspices of the London County Council. In Bath some 4,500 children and over 5,000 adults visited it, and it was the subject of a talk by Lord Waldegrave on the BBC's West of England Programme. It led both to closer contacts between the art school and art teachers at the local schools, and a deeper understanding of modern art. Miss M. Richardson, the organiser of the original organisation in London and founder of the Child Art Movement in the UK, emphasised that even five years ago such an exhibition would never have been held. She argued that it showed that at last children were allowed to use their imagination instead of recording every detail of a scene or object as if they were engineers.[19]

Ellis' work was made easier by the support of two artists, Walter Sickert and Lord Methuen, the former being far more famous than the later. Sickert, a prominent figure among the English impressionists and leader of the Camden Town Group of artists, was no stranger to Bath. From 1918 to 1920 he rented 'The Lodge' on the slopes of Entry Hill before moving to Dieppe. He returned to Bath in 1938 when he was in his late seventies to live at St. George's Hill House, Bathampton. In March 1939 he contacted Ellis and offered to lecture at the School of Art once a week. His letter is worth quoting in full:

> It has occurred to me that when in due course of time I am gathered to my fathers, I shall be about the only witness of the work of Degas, Manet, Monet, Whistler, etc. I knew them all personally for years and worked under them. I wonder if I should not be useful by giving a morning once a week to lecturing from 10 to one o'clock.
>
> I could not accept any fees from your school. I have several dealers who buy canvasses from me at anywhere between £100 and £150. ... To add to this, I like teaching. If you have a shorthand writer, I would present your Institute

with the copyright of my lectures and they could be entitled, 'The Bath Series' or some such name'.[20]

For nearly two years Sickert arrived to talk to the students at eleven o'clock on Friday mornings 'bang on the dot', as Clifford Ellis later recalled. He was always carefully prepared and brought a portfolio of the work of his favourite artists. Kate Fryer, a lecturer at the school remembered that 'to get the ball rolling' he would display reproductions from books or back numbers of *Punch* or the *Illustrated News*. His allusions, particularly to artists he had known personally, were 'sometimes obscene' and he frequently spoke French. His lessons above all 'broadened the minds of a young and unsophisticated audience'.[21] Sickert was a colourful character who attracted the attention of the local press. *The Chronicle* described him as wearing a ginger suit and slippers when opening the Bath School of Art's exhibition in June 1939. It claimed that the presence of both Sickert and his pupil, Lord Methuen, 'emphasises the fact that Bath is gradually consolidating its position as a great arts centre of the West', and ventured to suggest that it could soon rival St Ives as an 'artists' Mecca'.

Planning The Bath Festival of the Arts, 1939

After the restoration of the Assembly Rooms and the success of the 1938 Bath Music Festival, attention turned to staging a grandiose Festival of the Arts. There was a distinct feeling that Bath was becoming dull again, and once again losing ground to Continental spas. On Sundays there were few restaurants open. In the summer of 1938, according to information from the GWR, many bored tourists returned home by an early train rather than hang around and wait for the one they had originally intended to catch. Even one of Bath's corps of honorary guides confessed to the *Chronicle* in April 1938 that the city was 'hopelessly dull'. Many remedies were put forward ranging from having a *café dansant* at the Assembly Rooms to making the Parade Gardens more attractive by providing tea and even wine. Reinforcing the feeling that Bath needed to raise its profile as a cultural centre was the current decline in patients coming to the city for treatment at the spa. A seminal report written by Alderman Wills in December 1938 for the Baths and Pump Room Committee painted a melodramatic picture in which a struggle for the survival of the fittest was taking place between the spas both in Britain and on the Continent. It baldly if inelegantly stated that 'Bath must keep up to the front or suffer in the common ruck'. For years the spa had failed to balance its books. When the council considered the report in January, Wills argued trenchantly that it needed to

1939 BATH FESTIVAL

Pulteney Bridge, from North Bridge: NATTE's *Views of Bath*, 1806

PROPOSAL:

FOR AN INTERNATIONAL FESTIVAL

OF MUSIC, DRAMA AND THE ALLIED ARTS

TO BE HELD

IN THE CITY OF BATH

17TH JULY TO 12TH AUGUST

The Proposal for the 1939 Bath Festival of the Arts (Bath Record Office)

exploit its unique assets, the mineral spring waters and abandon the various 'quack treatments', which were entirely separate from the mineral water cure.[22]

Essentially then this was the context in which the idea of a Festival of the Arts took root. Charles Cochran, the well known theatrical manager and impresario, had long advocated such a festival. After discussions with the stage designer, Oliver Messel, a plan emerged to produce a four week long festival of all the arts to rival the prestigious Salzburg Festival. The idea was enthusiastically encouraged by Bath's Mayor, Adrian Hopkins, and welcomed by the Chamber of Commerce as it would bring money into the city. In early October 1938 Hopkins presided over a meeting in the Royal Opera House in London, which was attended by about fifty people, amongst whom were Somerset Maugham, the novelist, Norman Hartnell, the fashion designer and the actor John Gielgud as well as local figures such as Lord and Lady Weymouth, Loel Guinness and his new wife and the author, Horace Annesley Vachell. An Advisory Committee was formed from which a smaller working committee was elected, which was composed of the mayor, John Gielguid, Oliver Messel, the musician Owen Mase of the BBC, Sydney Bernstein, the media mogul, Lady Diana Duff Cooper and the Hon. James Smith, a director of WH Smith.

The following month Hopkins explained to the Chamber of Commerce how the festival would be financed. The capital required would be about £50,000, most of which would be raised in London, but he was confident that Bath could raise the first £10,000. A non-profit making company would be set up, one of whose trustees was to be the banker Olaf Hambro. Hopkins conceded that 'a certain amount of money' would be lost in the first year, but the second would break even and thereafter there would be a profit. He concluded his speech on a remarkably exuberant note:

> In my opinion it is going to be the one opportunity Bath has been waiting for 2,000 years, and it is a question of grabbing it while it offers itself .... [23]

The BPT welcomed the plans and 'decided that when the Festival of Arts was finally arranged, the services of the Trust would be offered to the Mayor of Bath',[24] but some visitors and residents were appalled by the plan. Essentially, they believed that Bath should remain a quiet provincial backwater. Edgar Lister of Westwood Manor, Bradford-on-Avon, for instance, was convinced that it would 'ruin and vulgarise' the city, while Major George Benton Fletcher, the well-known London collector of early keyboard instruments, argued in a letter to the *Times* that Bath should be preserved as an oasis of peace:

> [The] truly British, insular and self-centred the city of Bath should not stoop to compete with her academic and commercial sisters nor be exploited in rivalry with Continental festivals ... . We go to Bath to escape from international turmoil, the ARP and the rush of noisy New Youth Movements. Our lost repose of mind may be recaptured through the enjoyment of intimate music

and drama in her Assembly Rooms, and our poise of body regained while wandering through the streets and squares of the Queen of the West, city of dignity and calm.[25]

The festival was provisionally scheduled to run from 18 July to 13 August 1939, but in February it was put back a year. Officially the reason for this was that the eminent conductors and artists who were invited to participate, were fully booked until the summer of 1940, but this was not the whole story. For all the initial optimism, it had proved unexpectedly difficult to raise the initial £10,000 from Bath. By March, despite donations from local hoteliers and retailers as well as individual benefactors, amongst whom were many familiar names such as Admiral Sir Richard and Lady Peirse , Horace Annesley Vachell, Lord Methuen and the Earl and Countess Temple of Stowe, the mayor's appeal stood at only £3,500. Similarly hopes of raising a further £10.000 from Bristol had not been realised.

Ultimately the outbreak of war forced the festival organisers to cancel all plans for the 1940 festival, and the changes and discomforts that swept over Bath during the Second World War were to dwarf any that the festival might have brought to its more genteel and sensitive citizens. While the flow of tourists virtually dried up, the Spa itself remained open during the war, but the shortage of hotels and boarding houses due to government requisitioning severely limited the number of patients taking the waters. The creation of the NHS in 1948 gave the Spa a new lease of life, but it closed in 1978 because of the discovery of amoebic contamination in its waters.

MIGRATION FROM THE DISTRESSED REGIONS, 1936-39

THE AVERAGE ANNUAL number of births in Bath for the years 1931-35 was 767; in 1938 it had risen to by nearly 100 to 863 and in 1939 it rose further to 952.[26] Some of this was a result of the migration into Bath of several thousand workers from South Wales and the depressed regions of northern England. They were attracted by the availability of government work in the construction of ammunition storage facilities around Corsham and were recruited by the Ministry of Labour from men who had been out of work for years. By 1934 the government was aware that the reserves of ammunition stored in Woolwich Arsenal and Bramley, near Basingstoke, were vulnerable to German bombers. After combing the country for alternatives, suitable underground storage was found in the large network of old subterranean tunnels in north Wiltshire around Corsham and Monkton Farleigh, which were approximately 100 feet below ground. The first 50 acre tunnel was purchased from the Bath and Portland Stone Company in August 1935 and over the next two years further tunnels were bought. The whole complex became known as the Central Ammunition Depot (CAD), Corsham, under the command of Major (later Lieutenant-Colonel) Minnis. By October 1936 over 600 men were already employed in Corsham, and more were recruited every week. Within two years this number had increased to three thousand. The works at Corsham set 'amid little disturbed scenes of placid rural beauty' were dependent on labour from the distressed areas of South Wales and the North, although some local men were also recruited. The work was often dangerous as the conversion of the tunnels to their new purposes involved the sinking of shafts of some 80 or 90 feet and underground excavations. Inevitably there were accidents, and the first fatality occurred in May 1938 when a young man from Pickwick, a former farm worker, was crushed to death.

Some of the first men to be employed in 1936 were able to find rooms in Corsham, but, as numbers increased most were forced to look for accommodation in Bath and its suburbs. By early 1938 nearly 2,000 men, some with their wives and families, were lodging in Bath. This was as the *Chronicle* put it in a special article in January 1938 a 'big social experiment'. Bath was now confronted with the human consequences of the devastation in the old industrial areas in South Wales and the North of England. Inevitably this had an impact on the education and health provisions for the city, as it increased the number of children in the schools and the demand for medical services. Some Bath construction workers were also attracted by the job opportunities in Corsham which in turn created labour shortages in the local building trades and drove up the price of housing.

The newcomers rapidly made an impact on life in Bath in several ways. The Welsh contingent enriched Bath's cultural life with a Welsh male voice choir, which gave its first concert at Manvers Street Baptist Church in December 1937. Alien Welsh cultural traditions bemused the citizens of Bath. For instance, when one young Welsh worker died of pneumonia in early June 1937 Bathonians were surprised by the elaborate funeral arrangements involving a long procession and a guard of honour at the Perrymead Cemetery. As many of the migrant workers were lonely young men far from home, there were inevitably frequent cases of drunken and disorderly behaviour and rows in lodging houses, which came up with depressing regularity before the magistrates. In May 1937 the chairman of the Police Court told a group of young men who had been arrested for disorderly behaviour that:

... there are a few of you who are no more than scallywags, who come here, get drunk and give the city a bad name ... Not only that- you cannot leave the girls alone. We have had pretty well enough of these Corsham cases ...[27]

In July 1938 disquiet over the 'Corsham workers' came to a head. There had been several arrests for drunkenness. Two incidents were reported in the *Chronicle*. Three young men were charged with 'maliciously damaging a motor-car ', while two other men were arrested on warrants issued by the West Hartlepool police and were ordered by the Bath City Police Court to be detained pending the arrival of a police escort from their home town. The reports of these and similar incidents concerning 'Corsham workers' prompted 'a respectable and law abiding Welshman' to write to *The Chronicle* to complain that the workers employed by CAD in Corsham were described as 'Corsham workers' as if they were an entirely different species. He asked:

Do your correspondents ever put the works' name before any other cases? For instance, should a man working at Stothert and Pitt be summoned for any violation of the law his occupation is omitted. Cannot something be done whereby the term 'Corsham worker' will cease and let the respectable chaps glory in their work instead of hating it for the bad name the works has been given through your term 'Corsham worker'.[28]

Commenting on this letter the editor suggested that the Corsham workers should set up a force modelled on the military police, which would patrol the streets of Bath at night. He somewhat pompously opined that 'a decision to organise their own disciplinary methods would not only be effective but would raise the status of the Corsham workers to the place in society to which most of them rightly belong- high in the ranks of the respectable and law abiding citizens'. The editorial provoked a heavy post bag the following week. Two correspondents appealed to publicans not to serve drinks to those who were obviously already inebriated. The other letters were divided between the fiercely critical and those who rallied to the defence of the Corsham workers. One letter from Lower Weston signed 'Working Class' condemned their behaviour and argued that the magistrates were 'far too lenient'. Walcot residents appeared to be especially critical. One pinned the blame fairly and squarely on the workers, arguing that many had misbehaved even though Bath 'had offered her beautiful self for the use and enjoyment of these men and their families'. Another resident, who signed himself 'A SUFFERER', complained of the noise made by the buses taking the men to Corsham between 4.30 and

5.30 in the morning. For him 'Bath was no longer a 'city of peace and quiet' but 'a place of horrible noise and drunken brawls'. There were, of course, those who rallied to the workers' defence. One landlady, who signed herself 'Fairplay' pointed out that many Bathonians were just as bad as some of the Corsham workers. Indeed, she went on to say that if only landladies 'made the men feel at home, and not treat them just as lodgers ... they would find the men would be willing to stay in a bit more ...' She provided her own lodgers with a dart board and a wireless and allowed them to have a friend in if they wanted. Another landlady complained that her lodgers 'threw food at each other and got into bed without washing'. Two correspondents reminded readers of the important work the men were doing at Corsham. An ex-serviceman and Bath ARP warden pointed out that they were 'helping to prevent the horrors of war by prevention first'. This theme was echoed by AW Sealy, who asked why the Churches and the local ladies, who used to sew clothes for the soldiers in the War, were not helping the Corsham workers, and remarked sarcastically that 'I suppose they are too busy playing bridge to bother about it'. In conclusion Sealy reminded Bathonians to remember that 'these men are doing the same as the men in those years did -working to keep the enemy from our homes'.[29]

Reflecting on these letters *The Chronicle* readily conceded that the men were involved in work of 'real national importance' and 'those, if there be any, who are said to look down on them, lack a sense of patriotism as well as display a despicable adhesion to snobbery'. Nevertheless, it argued that the bad behaviour of a minority of the men was threatening the attractiveness of Bath for tourists and visitors to the spa. The paper reiterated the idea of the Corsham workers policing the behaviour of their own comrades and ended by reminding Bathonians and Corsham workers alike that 'we must all wipe our shoes on the mat before we enter and realise with gratitude and thankfulness that it is a privilege beyond price to be in the drawing room of England'. A year later after further migration the Chairman of The OBPS, George Hughes, summed up the perceived threat of the presence of the Corsham workers to Bath by pointing out:

> that the incursion of any large number of new residents must necessarily destroy what is after all our staple industry, namely the beauty and amenity of the city's setting.[30]

The negative attitude of so many Bathonians towards the Corsham men provoked a stinging rebuke from John Evans of Broughton Gifford near Melksham. Although he did not work in Corsham, he, too, had fled unemployment in Wales. In a letter to the *Chronicle* he explained that he understood the need for many of the young men to celebrate their release from the grinding poverty of the valleys by singing, 'playing pranks' and becoming intoxicated, but pointed out that such behaviour 'has given the people of Bath the very weapon they most wished for, and well has it been used against you'. Ominously he warned that

> We have reached this new freedom through an exile from our beloved Wales. We are in the midst of people who from behind a racial barrier as impenetrable as any put up by Herr Hitler, have never known anything but security, prosperity and economic peace- whose economic horizon has never known a cloud… Accept the fact of Bath's implacable respectability, realise the coldness of its standarised righteousness, and act in Bath accordingly.[31]

How accurate is this stinging criticism? Did Bathonians pass by on the 'other side' or were there some good Samaritans, who offered their assistance? The Trade Unions and the BTLC did attempt to involve the Corsham workers in local activities, but, as the *Chronicle* pointed out in January 1938, there had 'been little or no help forthcoming generally from Bath or Corsham people'. In Corsham there was outright hostility to building a YMCA hut for the workers, and in Bath Councillor Major Stayner, a member of the Public Assistance Committee, feared that when their work at Corsham had ended, many of the men would elect to stay in the city with their families and be a charge on the rates. As reported in the *Chronicle* he told the Committee that since Bath was a spa it could not 'in the nature of things, expand industrially, and absorb these people'. He readily agreed that it was 'the bounden duty of the city to provide for its workless, destitute and impoverished citizens', but warned that

> by acquiescence in the present policy of the Government, we are 'sowing the wind'. The financial whirlwind will inevitably follow, with consequent lowering of our standards, and overburdening of ratepayers. It is significant that the Government pays the rail fare of workers to Bath on engagement but does not in the case of discharge extend facilities for return.[32]

A week later the manager of the Bath and District Employment Exchange corrected this alarmist picture by pointing out to the employment committee that sick men from the Corsham works were not kept in Bath but 'repatriated' to their home towns. He reassured Stayner, who attended the meeting, that 'the rejects from Corsham' had not sought aid from the mayor's unemployment scheme. He did, however, agree that Bath 'had practically reached saturation point' in providing accommodation for the men, and informed the committee that advertisements for lodgings were being placed in the Bradford- on -Avon District. Significantly he also reminded them that it was in Bath where many of the Corsham men spent their wages.

In September 1938 the Free Church Council discussed what practical steps could be taken to help the Corsham workers. Suggestions ranged from making representations to the local publicans to limit the amount of alcohol available to organising 'systematic visitations' to the workers' families. It also considered forming a leisure club, but when faced with advice that such clubs needed 'to be under the control of authoritative officials to prevent undesirable practices', it did not proceed further with this plan. The Argyle Congregational Church did offer some recreational facilities, but, as Eric Swallow, a Corsham worker himself and the Church's representative on the council observed, 'many of the men refused to attend anything on Church premises'.[33] The local Toc H branch also 'extended a hand in welcome' to them, as did the Men's Social Club in Norfolk Crescent, which organised Christmas and New Year Parties for the workers and their families. On the football, field CAD teams joined the Bath and District Association Football League. A band formed by the Corsham Workers, which was initially known as 'The Ridge Corsham Workers' Concert Party' and then just as the 'Ridge Concert Party', made quite a hit in the city. At the invitation of Mrs Hardy, who was described by the *Chronicle* as taking 'great interest' in the welfare of the workers, it even played for an hour at the North Walcot Ward Conservative social at the end of November.

A vigorous advocate of the rights of the Corsham workers was Mayor Adrian Hopkins. After his re-election in November 1938, he made a passionate speech appealing to his fellow citizens to treat them with the respect they deserved and reminding them that the 3,200 thousand CAD workers spent nearly a total of £10,000 every week in Bath:

> My complaint is ... that instead of treating these men as paying guests, an atmosphere of antagonism has arisen, and the term 'Corsham worker' has become almost one of opprobrium. The few unfortunates-among a large number of men-who get drunk, deserve sympathy, not condemnation ... and I would remind citizens as a whole of the fable of the goose which laid the golden eggs.[34]

Possibly because Hopkins was a man of the Right and had been an outspoken critic of the Hunger Marchers (see page 204), his support for the Corsham workers was received with some scepticism by the BTLC. One member, somewhat ungenerously, observed that the mayor's statement 'did not come from his heart but from the pocket of his tradesmen friends' who were 'grabbing some of the workers' money'.

When he addressed the Chamber of Commerce at its annual dinner on 12 December, even though his subject was the Bath Festival of Arts, Hopkins did not miss the chance to champion the Corsham workers. Jokingly he remarked that the prosperity of Bath depended on three words beginning with the letter C: -Cranes, Cochran (the Director of the proposed Festival of the Arts) and finally Corsham. He reminded them again of the sum that was spent by the Corsham workers in Bath every week. He then defiantly observed:

> I repeat what I said before, that these men are not getting a square deal. Under my guidance for what it is worth, they are damned well going to. Those men who have never known what it is like to get a week's money until they came to Corsham, should be treated as honoured guests, and not as social pariahs'.[35]

Hopkins was as good as his word and throughout the winter of 1938-39 he campaigned vigorously on their behalf. On Saturday evening 16 December he attended the Ridge Concert Party at Christ Church Hall, which consisted mainly of Corsham workers, where he was well received and was able to joke with the audience, about the girth of their boss, Colonel Minnis. On a more serious note he assured them that:

> I am proud of the fact that in Bath we have been able-as we call Corsham part of Bath- to provide a grand job of work for the whole host of men who had a pretty tough time until they came into these parts. Anything I can do to make your life happier shall be done.[36]

Hopkins was convinced that more leisure facilities needed to be provided on War Department property in Corsham. He wrote to the War Minister, Leslie Hore-Belisha in October asking whether the War Office would finance the construction of a temporary building 100 ft by 30 ft at the cost of about £1000. He believed the National Fitness Council would contribute to the costs and the Archdeacon of Bath had agreed to launch an appeal. He also contacted the MPs from whose constituencies the Corsham men had come, to put pressure on the War Minister. On Tuesday 6 December the matter was raised at question time in the House of Commons, but to no avail as the War Office still refused to fund the project. When informed of this by Hore-Belisha,

Adrian Hopkins, Mayor of Bath, 1937-39 (Bath Record Office)

Hopkins accused the War Office of having 'no regard for the men except during working hours', which he described as 'scandalous'.

In January Hore-Belisha invited Hopkins to meet him at Corsham. As both had been contemporaries at Clifton College, discussions were described as 'cordial' and it seemed that the War Office might at last agree to financing recreation centres in Corsham, but a month later Hopkins' hopes were again dashed. The proposal had been examined by the Treasury, which concluded that 'if liability were admitted here, a dangerous expansion of the state's obligations would be involved'. Hopkins was furious and accused Hore-Belisha of 'wiggling out of his obligations' and showing himself to be 'utterly callous' of the fate of the men who had moved to work in Corsham, often without their families. Dramatically he announced that 'There is a little war on. The matter is not yet finished. It is only just beginning'.

Hopkins' tirades did not endear him to the local Conservative Party Association, whose chairman he had been from 1933-36. When Loel Guinness announced in March 1939 that he was not going to accept the Association's nomination to fight the next election, which it was assumed would be in the autumn, Hopkins put his own candidature forward. However it was the Earl of Ronaldshay, the son of the Marquis of Zetland who was selected by the overwhelming majority of the local Conservative members in May. It was made clear to Hopkins by Robert McKeag, the Association's current chairman, that 'in his unbounded enthusiasm' he had 'given offence' to many in the local party. He had in fact 'trod on too many corns' and 'called his own leaders names'. Hopkins knew at once that this referred to his criticism of Hore-Belisha and replied that

> The real reason for my not finding favour in local Conservative circles is however, my agitation on behalf of the Corsham workers ... The fact that my honest and sincere efforts on behalf of these unfortunate men should be hurled at me is the only thing in this unhappy story, which really hurts... [37]

Hopkins did not give up and announced that he would stand as an Independent National Conservative Candidate in the next general election, but the declaration of war in September made such ambitions academic.

BATH AND MODERNITY

LIKE THE WHOLE country Bath faced the challenge of what historians call 'modernity'. Traditional culture, religion and society were being challenged by advances in science and technology as well as by new political ideologies and artistic movements. The car, aeroplane, radio and the cinema had done much to transform everyday life, while at the same time the old certainties of religion, patriotism and deference were disappearing.

The impact of the car and aeroplane

The sweeping plans for demolishing the island site in Bond Street and extending Milsom Street up to the Assembly Rooms had been defeated in December 1935, but the problem of the motor car remained. Cars blocked the city's narrow streets, which had originally been built for sedan chairs, and forced the council to consider street widening and ring roads. Apart from Bournemouth and Eastbourne, in relation to the size of its population in 1937, Bath had the greatest number of cars in the UK – out of a population of about 68,000 there were 3,166 licenses. A survey made in 1935 by the Ministry of Transport registered an increase of 65 per cent in motor vehicles in Bath between 1925 and 1935; along the London Road this had increased by 140 per cent, 46 percent of which was accounted for by cars. Horse drawn vehicles were by now in a very small minority,[38] and in the summer of 1939, the volume of motor traffic increased when buses replaced trams. Then as now car parking was a problem. Addressing the Watch Committee in November 1938, the Mayor described the situation in Milsom Street as 'hopeless' in spite of the 'very good-natured efforts of the police on duty'. He also complained about Brock Street. where 'there were cars parked on either side of the road and just room for one car to get through the middle'. Ultimately the solution seemed to be the construction of more car parks. In May 1938 the Town Planning Officer of the Bath and District Joint Planning Committee, Anthony Mealand, outlined in a paper

Southgate Street in 1938 (Museum of Bath at Work)

read at a local authority conference in Bath his plan for the creation of a series of small car parks or 'parkways' along Lansdown Road, Claverton Avenue, Brassknocker Hill and the Combe-Down-Claverton Road. Two months later the Chief Constable in a memorandum to the Watch Committee revealed that traffic conditions were now so bad in Bath that the police no longer enforced the laws relating to traffic obstruction and urged the committee to give 'direct consideration' to the harm done both to 'the reputation of the city if visitors are harried from one place to another by police officers... [and] ... to the trade of the city'. He rejected Mealand's proposal since he was convinced that drivers would not use car parks 'some distance from the place they wish to visit and then walk'. His solution, which the council adopted in August, was to provide free parking for two hours in specially zoned areas in the centre of the city. In council owned car parks the private motorist would have to pay 6d. a day.[39]

Bypasses were needed to relieve the congestion, but the contours of the 'guardian hills' dictated that they would have to be constructed a considerable distance from the city. In 1938 the Ministry of Transport conducted preliminary surveys with a view to 'the construction of a bypass on the southward side of Bath leaving the A4 at a point near Bathford passing southwards through Limpley Stoke valley ... to rejoin the A4 at a point immediately westward of Keynsham'. The BPT, ever mindful of the importance of the green belt, suggested that widening the A430 from Warmly to Chippenham would be a less disruptive option, but on the outbreak of war in September 1939 these plans were shelved.[40] In July 1939 the Ministry did, however, decide to construct the Keynsham bypass as part of the London Bristol A4 trunk road, but this was not completed until the 1960s.

Bath was often accused of not being 'air-minded enough'. As early as 1929 the Bristol and Bath Regional Planning Scheme had envisaged not only that Bristol would become a hub for international air traffic, but that 'every town and large village [would] require its "landing ground" '.[41] Speaking to the Chamber of Commerce in April 1936, the city's MP, Loel Guinness, pointed out that between 1932 and 1935 there had been nationally an increase of 4,200 per cent in air passengers, and argued that Bath was 'far too great a city to allow itself to sink backwards - to have no aerodrome and consequently no air service'. The corporation had been asked by the government in 1934 to survey possible sites for both aerodromes and landing strips. It identified potential sites for aerodromes at Charmy Down, Claverton and Lansdown, and six further green field sites dotted around Bath in the Corston- Newton St. Loe, Radstock-Camerton, Willow-Combe-Hay-Hinton Charterhouse and Limpley Stoke-Freshford-Midford regions, all of which were suitable for landing strips.[42] In early 1938 the council decided, however. that the construction of a Bath airport was unnecessary on the grounds that Bristol's airport at Whitchurch was only eight miles away and that the construction of an aerodrome at Claverton or on Lansdown would have the 'city up in arms'.

The expansion of the city and the impact of modern architecture

Physically Bath grew by nearly a third, despite the fact that its population remained 'almost stationary until the arrival of the 'Corsham workers in 1936-37. Altogether 2438 private houses were built by private developers and another 1804 by the council during the inter-war years. There were new housing estates in Englishcombe Park ,which has been called 'Bath's first garden suburb', Southdown, Rudmore Park and Avon Park, Odd Down, Shophouse Road/Innox Park, Roundhill and Whiteway as well as the startlingly modern block of flats at Kingsmead. In the city centre the Southgate area was transformed. The existing premises were demolished and to quote the historian Robin Pakes, replaced with 'a range of buildings that drew on the city's architectural traditions' while expressing 'modernity through new construction technologies [and] striking interiors'. In 1933 the Bath Corporation Electricity Department and Showrooms were opened in Dorchester Street, and the following year the construction of a 'super cinema', the Forum in Southgate and the new Cooperative department store in Westgate Buildings were completed. Work on constructing the riverside boulevard on the Broad Quay, which was to be lined with imposing modern buildings, was not started until 1939 and then, of course, had to stop because of the war.[43]

The Forum in Southgate in 2024. Arguably the most iconic building of Bath's 1930s building boom (Author's collection)

In 1934 the Bath and District Planning Committee started to prepare a plan covering the development of the city and many of the parishes in the Bathavon rural area, but it was not until July 1939 that Bathonians could inspect what the *Chronicle* called 'a product of their labours' in the auction room of Westlake, Richards and co, Princes Buildings. The outbreak of war put a stop initially to any further planning developments but the blitz of April 1942 ensured that a new plan needed to be drafted. In June 1943 the Bath and District Joint Planning Committee requested Abercrombie, Mealand and the city engineer to prepare such a plan for the city, which was unveiled in February 1945.

Wireless, cinema and television in 1930s Bath
Bathonians, like the rest of the UK, were profoundly influenced both by the wireless and the cinema. The radio effectively opened up not only the whole country but the world to its listeners When, for instance, its Parents' Association bought St Stephens's School, Lansdown a radio in December 1937, the Headmaster aptly observed that 'the world had in fact been brought into the classroom'. By 1939 the radio, or 'wireless', had become an indispensable piece of equipment in the home, clubs and works' canteens, even if many of the older generation did not understand how it worked. An incident, probably apocryphal, was reported in the *Chronicle* in July 1937 of a grandmother sternly telling her grandchild to keep away from the radio as 'the fellow that's talking has got a nasty cough'. By 1939 television had made its appearance, and local radio dealers were selling sets, even though the number of Bathonians purchasing them was small. Nevertheless *Chronicle* readers were kept up date with anything that related to Bath, which had appeared or was to appear on television. For instance, they were informed that *The Ghost Train*, a play by the local writer, Arnold Ridley had been produced both for the radio and television.

The 1930s was the decade when the cinema became a major influence in people's lives. More than the department store 'it provided a far greater scope for escapism and a compelling and increasingly global view of the modern world'.[44] It was the age of the super cinema, as epitomised by the Forum. Yet the films allowed in Bath's cinemas were strictly censored by the council, even though many of those banned in Bath could be seen in Bristol. The Forum opened every day at 1.30 except Sunday, and provided its audiences with a mixture of the latest musicals and gangster films from Hollywood as well as the Pathé news and a number of documentaries.

The decline of religion
 In common with the rest of the country Bath, was becoming more secular in the 1930s as church attendance continued to decline. A lecturer at the Friends' Meeting House in February 1938 talked ominously about 'the twilight of religion' and the 'new dark age'. This was an exaggeration but in 1930 in a country of 35 million people only about 8.3 million were active Christians. Sunday school numbers were also falling. In 1934 the Church of England lost 25,000 pupils. Arguably in Bath the situation was slightly better, at least in

some churches. Services at St. John's and Emmanuel at Lower Weston were well attended in 1939 apparently because, according to the Vicar, they gave 'the people what they want, which is a simple warm and hearty service, one that has no frills and which gives them the help they need'. The Bath Sunday School Union actually reported an increase in both teachers and pupils in 1938.[45]

The decline of organised religion moved the Vicar of Ascension Church in Bath to lament that :

> ... the sound of the church bell is no longer a summons to the majority of people to attend the House of God. Sunday observance is fast falling into abeyance on the part of the great majority. Instead of being a day of rest and quietness it has become a time when the surplus energy of week days is expanded in a great rush of pleasure.[46]

It was over the nature of Sunday that the battle lines for the soul of Bath were drawn. After his election as Mayor in December 1937 Adrian Hopkins made clear his support for Sunday games, 'so that people of limited means can occupy their Sunday afternoons and evenings in a less dreary and more health giving way than they do now'. The Bath County Recreation Company decided in January to open their tennis courts on the Rec on Sunday afternoons, despite concerted protest by the Churches and the Lord's Day Observance Society. Bloomfield Park Tennis Club followed suit, and in July Stothert and Pitt's cricket club began to play matches on Sunday afternoons. The council managed to avoid taking any decision on this divisive issue until October 1939 when it permitted games in its parks 'for the benefit of billetees and citizens'.

It was not just sport that threatened the sanctity of the Sabbath. In October 1937 the Spa Committee applied for a licence to play music in the Pump Room from 3-5 on Sunday afternoons in addition to their evening concerts. This was met with a barrage of protest from the Churches. The Free Church Council, for instance, decided to write to each magistrate and councillor in an attempt to dissuade them from granting permission.[47] The council voted overwhelmingly against the proposal, but the following May there was a majority for holding Sunday afternoon concerts in Parade Gardens initially for a two month trial, despite there being dire predictions that when the city's lido was built, it too would be open on Sunday afternoons. Sunday concerts continued in the Gardens until 18th September.

Female emancipation

Central to an understanding of 'modernity' is female emancipation. Nationally there was a large preponderance of single women. In Bath many were impoverished gentlewomen, who lived in lodging houses or bed sits., and who looked forward to a lonely old age. Every week there were advertisements in the *Chronicle* from single women seeking rooms, but the availability of cheap accommodation was progressively diminished by the conversion of houses to expensive flats. Both the Stead Hostel in Pierrepoint Street and the Bath Tenement Trust tried to fill the gap. The Stead Hostel was able to offer some shelter to women either short term or permanently. In the year 1937-38 some 350 women and girls used the hostel -165 of them for the first time. It was also used as a club for girls, who were working as domestic servants, on their days off . The Bath Tenement Venture Trust had been founded to provide accommodation predominantly for single mature ladies. In 1938 the Trust managed to acquire no. 7, Beaufort East off the London Road. and to convert it into three two room and five single room flats. The rents ranged from 5s. to 9sh 6d a week. At the Trust's annual meeting in April, Miss Tweedy, who was a founder member of a similar organisation in London, the 'Over Thirty Association', gave the scheme her blessing and hoped that it would provide more accommodation 'for those women who are hidden away in back rooms, working long hours for a small wage and who have so little comfort'. The Bath Vigilance and Rescue Association (BVRA) was still there for local girls, who were experiencing problems varying from pregnancy to violent homes. At its annual meeting in March 1938 it

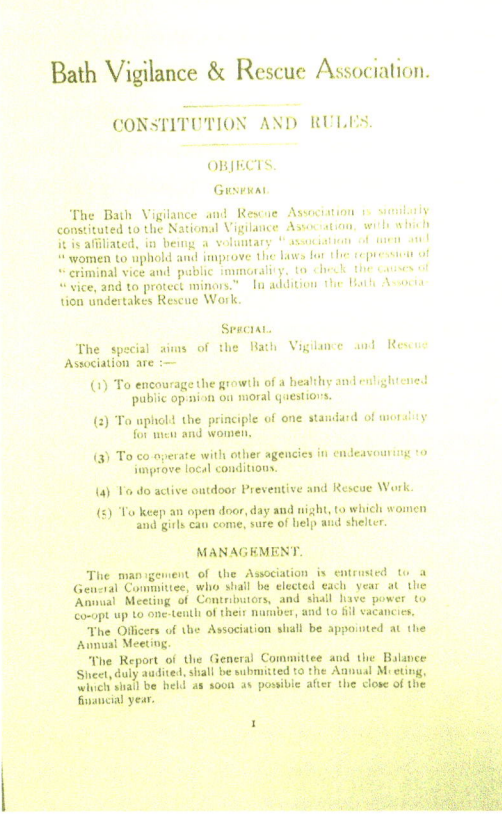

The Rules of the Bath Vigilance and Rescue Society (Bath Record Office)

reported that in 1937 238 cases had been dealt with out of which 66 girls were given places in the home on Walcot Parade.

In 1916 four police women had been employed on the streets of Bath, but two years later the force reverted to its pre-war all male status. The BVRA attempted to persuade the Council to reinstate women police officers in 1928, but it was not until December 1938 that two female officers were appointed.[48] Women were heavily represented in teaching, but in council schools, as soon as they were married, they had to resign. For instance, at the East Walcot Girls' School, Miss Audrey Luckham, who was 'shortly to be married' was presented with a Parker-Knoll arm chair as a leaving present at the end of February 1936.[49] When this issue was discussed at a special meeting of the Bath NUT in November 1938, a motion proposing that 'except in special circumstances ... married women teachers should not be appointed to the teaching service ... was carried 'by a large majority'. Ironically it was a man who opposed the motion and 'raised the point ... of women's emancipation'.[50] Married women could, however, sometimes find temporary posts in schools as supply teachers.

Relatively few married women 'worked'. The wives of working men were expected to toil in the home and look after the family. Mary Dale remembered how so many women 'at that time had leg ulcers and varicose veins caused by their long hours standing to do the housework'. She recalled further that as 'men went out to work and brought home the money, ... it was taken for granted that my strong mother was the one to carry heavy buckets of coal'.[51] Many married middle class women invested their considerable energies in running voluntary organisations. In 1936, for example, a branch of the WI was opened at Bathampton where talks on a whole range of topics from the ARP to life in the Falkland Islands, alternated with such practical activities as apple tart baking. Sometimes, as on New Years Day 1938, there was a sumptuous tea provided – 'sugared cakes, plain cakes, ginger bread, biscuits and bread and butter ...'.[52] The arts also offered an environment where both single and married women could find a creative role. Clifford Ellis' wife, Rosemary, for example, taught art at the Royal School and also cooperated closely with her husband on various artistic projects. Another prominent lady in Bath's cultural life was Consuelo de Reyes, one of the Wardens of Citizen House and an indefatigable play producer.

In the organisation of the local political parties, charities and societies, women also played an important role. Helen Foxcroft was an influential voice in the local Conservative Association as well as a contributor of informative articles on current issues in the local press. She was also a JP and president of the Bath branch of the National Council of Women, which campaigned for equal rights for both sexes. All in all, she would probably have made a better MP for Bath than her brother, Charles. On the Left there was Dr Hilda Oldham, a supporter of the Labour Party and the Bath Peace Council, who had both a Ph.D. and a BSc as well as an MA. For its social activities the Conservative Party, especially, was dependent on its female members. One such person was Mrs Florence Smith, who was active in the Odd Down Conservative Party Association. As organising secretary she arranged parties and other events, often leaving her husband to look after the children. She was a live wire, who in her daughter's words 'helped people enjoy their lives'. A friend in an affectionate poem called her 'a very good Conservative' and joked that when

> ...asked to organise any big function
> She might have sorted out Clapham Junction.[53]

By and large the inequalities between the sexes were accepted as the inevitable order of things, but sometimes the thinking behind this assumption was challenged. At Winsley Sanatorium in March 1938 the production of the monthly magazine was handed over temporarily to the women patients, who did so well that the *Chronicle* observed a month later that 'the men who now resume control do so conscious of the fact that any fall in the standard will lead to the return of women in control'. In September the *Chronicle* approvingly reported a scheme in Ohio whereby for a number of weeks the boys learnt domestic science and girls the skills which 'a handy-man has so often to be called in for'. Arguably a local role model for professional women, regardless of their politics was Mrs Tate, the Conservative MP for Frome. As a girl, according to an article in the *Daily Express* she had wanted to become a solicitor or doctor, but 'when her father heard this, he took her away from school. He said it was a woman's business to marry, not to work. Mrs Tate has done both'.[54]

Any definition of modernity would surely include sexual freedom, vital prerequisites of which are easy access to contraception and abortion on

The weekly advertisements in the Chronicle *about which the BVRA objected*

demand. In the 1920s books on birth control by Dr Marie Stopes and others were regularly advertised in the *Chronicle*, but the editor was persuaded to drop them in 1931 by the Bath Vigilance and Rescue Association, which viewed them as 'undesirable' and inappropriate reading for young unmarried girls. Nevertheless the 1930s were tiptoeing in the direction of a more permissive society. At the Lambeth Conference of 1931 Anglican bishops endorsed birth control for married couples in special circumstances. Gradually birth control clinics were opening up throughout the country. A birth control clinic under a lady doctor was opened in the Paragon in 1931, but the council's maternity and child welfare committee were of the opinion in February 1932 that the Ministry of Health regulations did not allow 'the work to extend far enough' as attendance was confined only to married women who had to have a referral from their doctor before they could go to the clinic. Not surprisingly very few women were able to attend the clinic. In the dry words of the MOH's Annual Report for 1937:

> Seventeen cases were referred to the Clinic and 15 attended. All who went were considered suitable for instruction in contraceptive methods. In every case the patient was suffering from severe debility, or anaemia, or varicose veins, usually following too frequent or too many pregnancies.[55]

The clinic was controversial and condemned in Bath by the Catholic Church and many clergy from the other denominations, as well as by those who feared that it would lead to smaller families, particularly amongst the most intelligent members of society. Dr Langdon Down, who was a member of the BMA's Committee on 'Mental Deficiency' was reported in the pages of the *Chronicle* in November 1930 as saying that the 'owing to the practice of birth control by the more intelligent members of the community, the number of the mentally deficient were increasing alarmingly'. The BVRA also opposed the establishment of the clinic. At a meeting in January 1931 its committee carried a resolution by 12 to 2 with one abstention to the effect that the clinic was 'detrimental to the best moral interests of the city'.[56]

Abortion was, as the historian Juliet Gardiner observed, a 'de facto response to inadequate birth control methods' [57] but legally this could only be achieved if a doctor agreed that the birth threatened the life of the mother. Many women were therefore driven to use back street abortionists. In December 1937 an example of the potentially lethal consequences of this was reported in the *Chronicle*. The 18 year old daughter of a former manageress of 'a multiple firm of costumiers' in Union Street, after having had her baby illegally aborted in Bristol, died of septicaemia. The abortionist, a 71 year old woman, was arrested and sentenced to prison for three years. In 1937 the Government set up a committee of inquiry into abortion under the Chairmanship of Norman Birkett K.C. It concluded two years later that there was no need to change the law, a view fiercely challenged by Mrs Tate, who herself had for medical reasons undergone an abortion. She told a conference organised by the Abortion Law Reform Association that

> A well- to- do woman was always able to pay fees of 80 or 100 guineas to doctors and specialists, who would be prepared to say the operation was necessary for the life or health of the patient. A poor woman could not obtain this service, so she had to resort to the illegal [sic].[58]

Sex

The 1930s did witness a greater willingness to be franker about sex - or at least heterosexual sex. There were regular lectures on sexual matters by the Bath branch of the British Social Hygiene Council often to packed halls. In October 1930 in a crowded meeting in the Banqueting Room of the Guildhall one speaker, Dr. Griffith, stressed that it was 'highly important that people should realise the creative aspect of sex and get rid of any negative views regarding it'. Sex education was strongly endorsed by Mayor Hopkins, who told the Bath Branch of the British Social Hygiene Council in February 1938 that 'it is only because we don't give that education in schools that we get these sordid, beastly cases which come into the courts and which ruin lives all over the country'.[59]

In 1937 the socialite, diarist and MP, Chips Channon, was told by a young police constable that it was below stairs amongst 'servants, coiffeurs, chauffeurs' rather than above stairs with 'the grand people' where the most uninhibited sexual activity took place.[60] In Bath the accuracy of this observation is hard to assess. In July 1935 there were reports in the words of the Chief Constable of 'absolutely disgusting behaviour' in one of the staff dormitories in a local hotel. To move to the other end of the social scale there was the case of Joan Guinness, who had deserted her husband, Loel, for the Aly Khan with whom she was living

Joan Guinness née the Hon Joan Barbara Yarde-Buller (Source unknown)

openly in the Paris Ritz in April 1935. Neither case really sheds much light on 'sex in Bath'. Miss E. Evans, the lady superintendent of the BVRA told its annual meeting in March 1938 that Bath was 'one of the cleanest places' she had worked in; there is not the number of cases of immorality among young people of Bath there is in other towns' . Yet Bath was populated by mortals and had its share of patients suffering from venereal diseases -in 1937 1,218 attended the out- patient clinic, and the number of children born out of wedlock were about equal to the national average: in 1938 46/863.[61]

In the 1930s for the great majority of the population sex was an intimate and private matter. Sex between males was illegal and therefore not openly acknowledged, but in London and some of the larger industrial towns there were well established homosexual networks. In Bath there were homosexuals and no doubt homosexual couples, but as long as their private, sexual life was discrete and behind closed doors, no questions were openly asked. The Garrick's Head was known by word of mouth as a gay pub in the 1930s and, as in other cities, 'cottaging' probably took place in some public toilets. Occasionally a case of 'gross indecency' would come before the magistrates, but otherwise the subject of homosexuality was shrouded in silence. In the 1930s in the pages of the *Chronicle* the only overt mention of homosexuality is in a talk to the Bath Rotary club in October 1935 on Lawrence of Arabia by the Rev Archibald Parsons, who briefly refers to Lawrence's rape by the Bey of Dera and his body guards. Essentially to survive as a gay male it was vital to escape detection by exercising the utmost discretion and keeping no incriminating diaries, and this, of course, meant escaping from history.[62]

11
WAR DRAWS EVER CLOSER

Throughout the winter of 1937-38 the international situation continued to deteriorate. The bitter civil war in Spain showed no signs of ending, while a major conflict between Japan and China had broken out in July. On the Saturday before Armistice Sunday 1937 the Bellman commented on the prevailing atmosphere of disillusion and remarked that 'with two great wars in progress and an atmosphere of constant tension and crises, it is hardly surprising that so many gloomy prophecies as to the future of modern civilisation should be current'

THE SPANISH CIVIL WAR

With Italy and Germany supplying Franco and the USSR supporting the Republican government, the civil war in Spain had become a template for the struggle between fascism and socialism. However, what concerned many in Bath and in the country as a whole, was the misery that the war inflicted on Spanish civilians, and above all on the children There were frequent appeals for money and clothing to help them. In 1937 the local Cooperative movement, the Quakers, the 'Save the Children Fund' and the League of Nations Union were particularly active in their fundraising. The Bath Cooperative Society sold nearly 838 milk tokens in its shops and raised £20.[1] In February 1937 the Quakers launched the Bath Refugee Fund, stressing that it was strictly a humanitarian organisation which 'knows no political discrimination'. It was chaired by the mayor, Councillor Long, who declared that 'I have nothing to do with politics or what is right or wrong in Spain. I should not be here if it were not to help the children'. Two years later, in February 1939, shortly before the war ended, a project was organised in Bristol to send a food ship to Spain. This received widespread support in Bath where 'The Bath Committee for the Spanish Food ship' was formed. Appeals were made for volunteers to knock on doors and to do clerical tasks. £327 in cash was raised in addition to gifts of food from a wide variety of donors, which included various church congregations, Combe Down Infants School, the Young Communist League, the Pump Room Orchestra and supporters of Bath City Football Club. The ship duly sailed from Bristol on Monday 21 March, picked up a load of potatoes in Liverpool and reached Spain the following week.

It was, however, the cinema that brought home the reality of the war in Spain to many Bathonians. In early February 1937 a dramatic film of the bombing of Madrid was shown in the New Cooperative Hall, Moorlands Road. It gave 'civilisation' as the *Chronicle* observed:

> … a foretaste of the destruction and havoc which the bombing plane would be capable of producing in a major war. Seven-storey buildings shorn completely through by a single bomb, huge craters in the capital's "Piccadilly Circus", an appalling mass of fallen masonry and timbers, fires still raging in mere shells of what were once architectural gems … [2]

A few Bathonians, or in some cases their relatives, personally experienced the perils and reality of the war. In the summer of 1937 a couple of British steamers were impounded for several weeks by Franco and forced to dock in Bilbao. The Third Mate of one of the ships, the S.S.Molton, came from Bath. A few months earlier in March Violetta Thurstan, the daughter of Dr. Thurstan in Lambridge, travelled to Spain to organise a British ambulance station in Almeira. She had a distinguished wartime record as a nurse in Belgium, Russia and France and later as a supervisor of refugee camps in the Middle East. In a letter to her father, the gist of which was published in the *Chronicle*, she described her fraught journey, which involved packed trains and long delays. When she changed trains, she was fortunate to find a restaurant open. During her meal she gave 'a lump of sugar to a child, a crumb of bread to a dog and a cigarette to a soldier'. In retrospect Violetta was convinced that these 'trifling kindnesses saved her life' since a member of the Anarchist Militia, which was fighting Franco, suspected her of being a hostile foreign agent and

> insisted on her going into town with him to show her papers. In the confusion of the moment, she lapsed from Spanish into Italian, and this increased his suspicion. Had she gone, she would probably have been shot at sight. However, the people in the restaurant backed her up, and the amateur policeman and his comrade departed glaring.[3]

For the last leg of the journey, she managed to hitch a lift to Almeria in an army lorry, which was packed with refugees from Malaga. Before returning home in June, she had arranged for the dispatch of food from Gibraltar on a British destroyer and the setting up of two children's hospitals.

In May 1937 nearly 4,000 Basque children arrived in Britain and were initially given shelter in a temporary camp near Southampton. They were then divided up into smaller groups and sent to camps and hostels throughout the country. One group of 50 children were sent to the 'Old Grange' in Street, which belonged to Clark's shoe factory, and had been placed at the disposal of the Independent Labour Party. After the fall of Bilbao and Franco's capture of northern Spain, many were repatriated from the UK, but some whose parents had been killed or in prison remained. They were later joined by a fresh wave of child refugees from Barcelona. In July 1938 there were still 40 Spanish children remaining in the 'Old Grange'. The following January the Old Grange arranged a concert tour of Somerset and Dorset for a group of Basque children in their early teens to raise funds to help pay for their maintenance. Their first performance was in the Pump Room where they sang and danced traditional Spanish dances.

Amongst the audience were 'big Bill Leakey', the son of the proprietors of a fish restaurant in Kingsmead Street, and his friend Joe Blair, both of whom had been employed at the CAD works in Corsham. The previous summer the two men had volunteered to join the International Brigade in Spain, which was composed of socialists, anarchists and republicans all united by their hatred of Fascism. As soon as they arrived in Spain, they were sent to the Catalonian Front, and fought as part of the government army at the battle of Ebro. Bill crossed the Ebro and then took up position at an observation post when an enemy machine gun opened fire. He told the *Chronicle* what subsequently happened :

> I jumped for [sic] a shell hole ... There was somebody else in it, and in trying to avoid him, I fell awkwardly and broke my leg. Later I was carried back across the river and with 17 others was lying on a stretcher waiting for the arrival of the ambulances when Franco's bombers came across. I was wounded in the heel of my broken leg by a piece of shrapnel.[4]

His wound turned septic, and he was in hospital for a month. He returned home one wintry afternoon in the week before Christmas, when 'he came limping from the 2.57 train on to the bleakness' of Bath's GWR station. When asked why he had volunteered to fight in Spain, he conceded that his views incline to the left, but probably the real reason was because he had read so much of conditions in Spain; because of his disagreement with all things appertaining to Fascism; and because he had a highly developed sense of that spirit of adventure and sympathy with the oppressed, which is the proud possession of every Englishman.

Whilst sympathetic to the plight of the refugees and the civilians in the war zones, there was a deep distrust amongst many of the more prosperous Bathonian's of the anarchists and communists fighting on the side of the Republic. Alfred Denville, Conservative MP for Central Newcastle and Dr. W J O' Donovan, former Conservative MP for Stepney, and a leading Roman Catholic publicist, speaking in the Pump Room on 28 April 1937 firmly put the case for Franco and criticised the BBC 'for having shown a certain selectivity in its news bulletins'. Denville accused the Spanish government of failing to stop the massacres of priests and nuns and believed that the majority of Conservative MPs favoured Franco. Loel Guinness was more circumspect. When speaking in October to the women's branch of the Conservative Association in Lansdown, he said that although he understood the attitude that 'we should not push our noses into other people's affairs,' he argued that the more our Government ... could do to stop the war, the 'better for all concerned'.[5]

THE SINO-JAPANESE WAR

ONCE JAPAN OCCUPIED Manchuria in September 1931, it was almost inevitable that it would eventually lead to a full scale war with China. A month later the wife of a British businessman in Hankow described in a letter to her friend, Helen Foxcroft how 'the grim menace of war between China and Japan loomed large' and how Japanese and Chinese patrols with fixed bayonets confronted each other across the road which marked the border in Hankow between the Japanese concession and the Chinese controlled area of the city.[6] After nearly six years of uneasy peace, in July 1937 the Japanese exploited a minor incident at the Marco Polo Bridge some nine miles south west of Beijing to launch an all-out war against China. Beijing was occupied in August, and after extensive bombing both Shanghai and Nanjing fell.

The savagery of the war and its impact on civilians was not ignored in Bath. At the Harvest Festival at Hay Hill Baptist Church on Sunday 26 September 1937 the pastor vehemently denounced the 'unprecedented savagery' of the Japanese bombing and declared that every Christian Church should ring with indignation. There were also frequent reports in the *Chronicle* ,which kept Bathonians well informed of the conflict. It published, for instance, on 9 October a letter from Fred Poole to his brother, the proprietor of Poole's Restaurant in Southgate. Fred worked for an oil company in Shanghai where he lived in relative safety with the other Europeans in the International Settlement, which was not occupied by the Japanese. He described the fate of the 20,000 Chinese refugees who sought asylum in the Settlement many of whom had no option but to 'sleep under any shelter they find in the streets'. On 26 October the daughter of Wellington Koo, the Chinese Ambassador in Paris, who was studying Physics in London spoke to the Bath Peace Council in the Friends' Meeting House. She mentioned with particular affect the experiences of a foreign observer in China, who after a bombing raid spoke to a Chinaman standing by the mat in the doorway of a house. He lifted the mat to reveal a pile of blood and bones . 'That', he said, 'was my wife'.

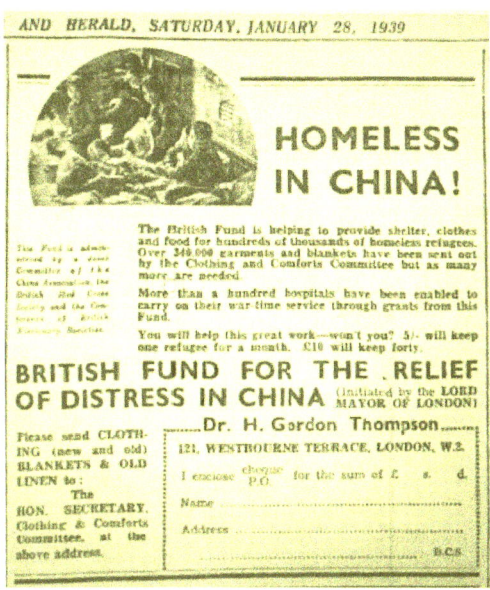

Appeal for help for the Chinese victims of war (Bath Chronicle, 28.January 1939)

As the war intensified the options facing the British government were constantly discussed by the various church and the political groups in Bath, but as Phillip Hopkins, Bath's Liberal parliamentary candidate, feared, there was a real danger that 'the public might blow off steam by making protests without endeavouring to secure any action'. The usual calls for the League's intervention in the conflict were made, but without firm backing from the US, Britain and France could hardly support such a policy at a time when they were facing a growing challenge from Germany and Italy in Europe. More practically the Bath Group of the 'Left Book Club' called for an embargo on Japanese imports and in November 1937 the local Cooperative Society as a protest against the bombing in China instructed its buyers to boycott Japanese goods. In May 1938 the BTLC also passed a resolution recommending a boycott of Japanese goods.

There were, too, appeals for money to help mitigate the suffering in China - by January 1939 there were millions of Chinese homeless and on the edge of starvation. In September 1938 Wendy Harthan, the wife of the Vicar of Cheddar wrote to the *Chronicle* appealing to its readers to mark China's National Day on 10 October, by eating 'a simple dinner' and sending the money saved to the China Campaign Committee for medical supplies. Bathonians responded generously to the Lord Mayor of London's Fund for the Relief of Distress in China. Gordon Thompson, its secretary, told a meeting in the Guildhall in January 1939 that even 'the old pensioners living in St. John's Hospital in Bath had denied themselves and sent sums of money, with which to buy food for the refugees'.

AUSTRIA AND CZECHOSLOVAKIA, 1938-39

THE *ANSCHLUSS*, the German annexation of Austria, on 13 March 1938 was in the opinion of the historian AJP Taylor, the moment that 'the pre-war' period began . It was welcomed by most Austrians and merely strengthened Prime Minister Neville Chamberlain's desire for a settlement with both Germany and Italy 'once we had all got past this unpleasant affair'. The reaction in Bath was muted. Geoffrey Strutt, a well known local Conservative, who had returned from Austria just ten days before 'the fuss' happened, told the Bath branch of the League of Nations Union' in late March that he had not seen 'the slightest sign of anything untoward taking place'. Yet he was clearly shaken by how 'in a short space of ten days or a fortnight the whole situation was changed and people whom he knew were anti-Nazi might be in prison'. A month later a meeting in the Cooperative café in Westgate Buildings heard at first hand what the *Anschluss* meant for anti-Nazi and Jewish Austrians in a talk given by Rudolf Liebmann, the former head of the Austrian Press Department in London. He explained that the policy of 'protective custody' was 'a particularly diabolical piece of Hitlerism' whereby 'the victim of this custody was actually imprisoned in his own house with a loaded revolver lying temporarily on the table'. This or worse would have been Liebmann's fate, had he returned to Austria, but he was allowed to remain in the UK as an independent journalist.

While the politicians wrestled with the deteriorating international situation, the travel industry attempted to minimise the danger and uncertainty in Continental Europe. The leading passenger shipping and insurance agents Messrs W W Bell and Co in New Bond Street, informed potential customers in April that they would receive 'a grand welcome and cordiality' in Germany and especially Innsbruck. Dina Dobson, the noted Bristol archaeologist, took her family to Germany at Easter for a tour down the Rhine and told a meeting of the Bath Soroptimists in May that she found much less 'Heil Hitlering' compared to their last visit eighteen months ago. Ominously, however, when her daughter talked to a young Germans about the possibility of war breaking out in the future, he remarked 'I suppose there will be war, but we shan't be asked'.

The *Anschlus*s increased Czechoslovakia's vulnerability to German aggression. Phillip Hopkins in his usual clear and forceful style pointed out to the Larkhall Liberal Club two days after the *Anschlus*s that 'the same technique could be used to overthrow Czechoslovakia as was used in the case of Austria'. During the summer Hitler's agents worked to inflame the nationalism of the three million ethnic Germans in the Sudetenland, the German speaking region of Czechoslovakia, in order to engineer the state's disintegration and ultimate absorption by Germany. The situation was so tense at the beginning of September that in the words of the *Chronicle* 'a mere incident might apply a torch to the powder barrel'. Tension rose still further after Hitler's speech at Nuremberg on 12 September, in which he promised the Sudeten Germans his full support. Three days later Chamberlain flew to Berchtesgaden to meet Hitler in an attempt to find a peaceful solution. Many in Bath would surely have agreed with James Van Sommer, the former Conservative councillor for Lansdown, who wrote in his diary in September 1938 : ' I am quite sure that a month ago, at most one in 10,000 … would have had 'a definite idea where Czechoslovakia was or who [sic] they were'.[7]

At Bechtesgaden it was decided that Germany was to be awarded the Sudetenland, provided Hitler agreed to make no aggressive move while the complex process of its separation from Czechoslovakia was taking place. After discussions with the French and Czechs Chamberlain returned to Germany on 22 September only to hear that Hitler now demanded the immediate German occupation of the Sudetenland. War was now the likely outcome of the crisis. All over the country 'safety trenches' were dug in parks to provide protection from air raids and gas masks distributed to regional centres. Reservists were a called up and the fleet mobilised. Phillip Morris, a Bathonian, remembered over eighty years later that as a child living in Larkhall, he was in bed when the police knocked at the front door to tell his father, a former gunner in the Royal Navy to report immediately for duty at Davenport.[8] In Bath, too, trenches were dug in parks, recreation grounds and school playing fields (See below), and the hospitals put on an emergency footing. At the Royal National Hospital for Rheumatic Diseases(RNHRD) admissions were stopped on 26

September. On the following day patients, except those from the London area, were sent home, and emergency ARP measures involving the construction of a gas proof chamber and blacking out of windows were put in place.[9]

Inevitably the crisis caused intense anxiety in Bath. The churches were full as people prayed for peace, One recently widowed woman, Mrs. Perkins of Odd Down, placed her trust solely in the Almighty. In a letter published in the *Chronicle* shortly before Christmas she advised her fellow readers not to 'worry about gas-masks or ARP shelters . The only safe shelter is in Him [God]'. In her grief she apparently viewed the possible outbreak of war with equanimity:

> A few months ago, my little boy aged 6 said, 'Mummy when is Jesus coming?' I told him I did not know, but I thought not long now. He clapped his hands and said, 'I'm so glad because when I see Jesus, I shall see Daddy'. God grant us all such a childlike faith'.[10]

Not everybody, of course, could find repose in such innocent faith. It was likely that the tragic suicide of Raymond Ford, a railway ganger on the main line at Bathampton, was triggered by the Sudeten crisis. Ford met his death by crouching in front of the 12.18 from Bathampton to Bath on Tuesday 27 September. His brother, Albert, told the Coroner two days later that Raymond had suffered ' a terrific [sic] experience during the War, and was wounded several times'. He had won the MC but had never told anybody what he had done or what horrors he had witnessed to merit the award. Not surprisingly Albert was convinced that the international crisis and the threat of another war had adversely affected his brother's mental health.

To prevent panic buying the manager of the Bath Coop emphasised that 'only normal quantities of food stuffs' would be available for sale.[11] James Van Sommer in a caring grandfatherly way thought it wise to send his grandson, Jim, who had just won a scholarship to Wellington College in Crowthorne in Surrey, 10 shillings Just in case war were declared, and the money needed in an emergency. Jim duly thanked him but did not, however, think that

> there was much danger of anything happening here as we are thirty miles east [sic!] of London. The only thing that might happen is that they might get us instead of Aldershot which is ten miles away, and they might get just that much out in a fog. We have all been fitted up with gas masks which was rather fun although their meaning is not quite so cheerful. There has been a trench dug in the field in front all zig-zag.[12]

Most, to adapt the slogan used two years later, stayed calm and carried on. For instance, when Helen Foxcroft opened a bazar in Combe Park, Lower Weston on Wednesday 28 September, the Vicar quoted the King's advice that the country 'should keep cool heads and brave hearts' and added that 'by keeping steady we were helping to break down the biggest piece of bluff the world had ever seen …'. In many ways life continued as normal: the new minister of Walcot Methodist Church condemned football pools, detailed plans were being laid for the big ball to mark the Duchess of Kent's opening of the Assembly Rooms, and above all, as the *Chronicle* reported on 1 October, in spite of wars and rumours of wars the boys of Widcombe were already preparing for bonfire night.

On 28 September in the words of the historian Professor Kershaw, 'the unthinkable happened'.[13] Hitler accepted Mussolini's mediation and agreed to attend a conference to be convened at Munich the following day. Chamberlain flew out and the 'electrifying announcement' was immediately communicated to the *Chronicle's* office in Westgate in time to have it published in the 'stop press' column. On the evening of Thursday 29 September the paper sold like 'hot cakes' and large crowds collected outside its office where up to 10.30 pm regular bulletins were posted about the progress made in the Munich negotiations. Their optimistic tone was greeted with prolonged cheers. It was not until 2 am on Friday 30 September that the Munich agreement was announced by the BBC, and shortly afterwards, the Press Association telephoned the details to the *Chronicle's* office. Hitler had agreed to give up his demand for the immediate annexation of the Sudetenland, but in practice he had achieved his aims since the Sudetenland was to be occupied by German forces in stages between 1 and 10 October, and an international commission would map the new Czechoslovakian frontier, and if necessary organise a plebiscite. For most Bathonians it was not until the morning news bulletin of the BBC that the results of the conference were heard. Those going to work early spread what seemed at the time to be the good news and one journalist 'while in bed overheard at 7 am a workman saying to his mate, "it's all right, they have patched things up'.

The leader writer of the *Chronicle* on 1 October expressed relief that another war had been avoided, but rather uneasily reminded readers of the sacrifices made by Czechoslovakia in 'the cause of peace'. 'Uncle Fred' delphically assured his young readers that 'there are times when it is right to give way and there are times when it is imperative to stand firm'. A month later the Archdeacon of Bath in his monthly letter claimed that through Chamberlain

'God had worked a miracle' and saved the world from a catastrophic war. James Van Sommer simply described the agreement as the 'Miracle of Munich'.[14]

Although most members of the Conservative Association supported Chamberlain's appeasement policy, seven members of the Association dissented and a highly critical letter signed by them was published in the *Chronicle* on 13 October. Most of them lived in Lansdown Ward. At least three enjoyed a high profile in local affairs: Janet Law was active in local charities and had managed to collect a 'purse' for the opening of the Assembly Rooms, Brigadier-General Murray often chaired branch meetings of the Conservative Association in Lansdown and Captain FH Storr had been secretary of the Bath and West Show and was currently Treasurer of the Bath branch of the YMCA and the Royal Literary and Scientific Institution. The most telling point they made was that Chamberlain had

> ... acquiesced in the humiliation and dismemberment of a small but progressive and cultured democratic country, under the threat of war, in order to secure ... a temporary and precarious peace for ourselves, and perhaps for France.[15]

The Labour and Liberal parties did not dissent from this view. Victor Gollancz, the left-wing publisher, in a talk on 23 October to the Bath Left Book-Club Group warned that 'far from the crisis being over, we were now faced with the greatest crisis England or modern civilisation had ever faced'.

A force of 1,200 volunteers from the British Legion was recruited to police the Sudetenland during the plebiscite. Amongst them were three Bathonians who duly made their way to Olympia on 6 October where they were sworn in. On the following day they embarked at Tilbury to sail to Bremen, but at the last moment the International Commission meeting in Berlin decided that the plebiscite was no longer necessary. Another Bathonian, fluent in German and French, was reportedly unable to go to Olympia because his employer refused to give him leave.

JEWISH REFUGEES IN BATH

THE TRUE NATURE of the Nazi regime was again revealed a mere six weeks after the Munich Agreement, when in response to the assassination of a German diplomat in Paris on 7 November by a 17 year old Polish Jew, it instigated during the night of 9-10 November a violent pogrom (*Kristallnacht*) against the Jewish community in Germany. 91 Jews were killed, 20,000 sent to concentration camps, and immense damage done to their property. In Bath on

Sunday 13th there was a special intercession for the Jews at the service in the Abbey marking the first Sunday in the municipal year. Two days later a national delegation of Quakers, Church leaders and Jews appealed to Chamberlain to allow some 15,000 Jewish children, who would be unaccompanied by their parents, into the country. Parliament agreed on 21 November, but the cost would have to be funded by the Jewish community and sympathetic charities. On 25 November an appeal was broadcast on the BBC Home Service by the former Home Secretary, Lord Samuel, for volunteers to enroll as foster parents for the children. On 2 December 196 children arrived at Harwich and were followed over the next nine months by nearly 10,000 more. Initially they were sent to a holiday camp in East Anglia, which acted as a central clearing house, where they would learn some English and have their needs assessed.

Bath responded positively to the request for foster parents. On the evening of 14 December, a meeting of those interested was held in the Rotary Room in the Red House, which was addressed by the Venerable Marshall Selwyn, the Archdeacon, and James McColl, a London barrister, representing the Central British Fund for German Jewry. It was so well attended that many were forced to listen to the proceedings from the doorway and passageways. The meeting started on a curiously ambiguous note when the Archdeacon reminded the audience that they should not forget the needs of 'our own unemployed', but nevertheless should be prepared 'to do a little bit extra' to help the child refugees. James McColl then spoke for about twenty minutes outlining how the scheme would work. He told the meeting that 'Bath had given a definite lead to the rest of England' and was making 'the biggest effort of its kind outside London' to help the children, who were suffering from psychological traumas and needed above all the 'personal interest and personal affection of individual people'. Their foster parents would receive assistance and advice both from the Central Committee in London and the local Guardian Committee in Bath. McColl advised that the children should be steered towards a technical education as it would be easier for them to stay in this country 'if they had a trade to their name'.

It was initially planned to send about 30 children to Bath. As the nearest synagogue was some distance away in Bristol, children from liberal, rather than orthodox Jewish families would be chosen. There was a greater willingness to foster girls rather than boys. Offers of foster care for as long as necessary had already been received for fourteen children – four boys and ten girls; another 20 offers were made from families who were ready to look after a child or children for an initial period of a year. Several farmers had offered to take girls for the payment of 6 shillings a week, so that they could be trained to settle in the colonies. Two weeks later the foster families met up for tea to get to know one another, and afterwards the children were shown the sights of Bath. One foster parent remarked that 'we have had the happiest Christmas we can remember with this young man', Each child had a 'godfather' or 'godmother' on the end a telephone to help with language difficulties.

In the 18th and 19th centuries there had been a small but active Jewish community in Bath with its own synagogue and cemetery in Combe Down, but by the early 1900s its members had either been assimilated or moved out of the city. However from 1927 to 1946 Nathan Kerstein kept a Kosher hotel at 10, Duke Street where regular synagogue services were also held. The influx of German Jews in 1938-39 created a new Jewish presence in Bath. The refugee community did not consist just of children. On Whit Sunday, 1939 a club for the German refugee girls and women resident in Bath, was opened at 21, High Street, and welcomed members on Tuesday, Wednesday and Sunday afternoons. It fulfilled a vital need since it provided, as the *Chronicle* explained:

> a meeting place for the many girls and women who have few friends here, feel desperately lonely and are worried by thoughts of the lot of their relatives who are still in Germany (many in concentration camps), or in some cases, have managed to get to America or Palestine. ... Most of the refugees are business and professional women- several had their own businesses in Germany and are now engaged in domestic service. Some are married and their children are in different homes in England.[16]

Within two months the club had a membership of about 80 and attracted members from neighbouring towns, and in early August a party of about 100 German refugees 'of both sexes' was held at the Church Army Work-Aid Home in Sydney Wharf.

Many Bathonians went out of their way to help individual refugees. In July The *Chronicle* related the story of an elderly Jewish lady, who had sufficient funds 'to take a house on the south side of the city' to provide 'hospitality to less fortunate enforced exiles'. When she visited the city's police station to show her immigration papers, she was advised by a policeman to look in the paper's property pages, where he actually marked a selection of relevant properties for her. Mary Dale remembers her mother, who ran a lodging house in Rivers Street generously providing accommodation for a young Jewish refugee in 1939:

> We had bedrooms right at the top of the house where servants had formerly slept. Mine was the smallest room but when my mother performed yet another

of her very kind acts just before the Second World War started, I moved into a 'cupboard' over the stairwell with a little skylight for air and light. This was to accommodate Gisella, a Jewish refugee from Austria. Apparently, she had been to the Guildhall where she was advised to call on Mrs. Sheppard [Mary's mother], who would be sure to take her in. This poor young woman was about 20 years old and had somehow managed to flee from the Nazis' occupation where she had been made to scrub lavatory floors. She stayed with us several years and after the war corresponded with my mother. She always kept a candle burning in her room for the family she never saw again.[17]

Despite the generosity of individual families, Britain's record for granting refugees asylum was relatively poor. In a challenging sermon in February 1939 the Rev. WR Miller reminded his congregation in Manvers Street Baptist Chapel that France had accepted several hundred thousands refugees, while Britain had taken in an infinitely smaller number. He then dealt squarely with the issue of 'our own unemployed' by pointing out that a Home Office regulation ensured that nobody could be supplanted in his work by a refugee. 'So that bogey could be dismissed'. He also stressed that amongst the refugees 'were some of the cleverest people in the world'.

CHRISTMAS, 1938

AFTER THE ACUTE anxiety caused by the Munich Crisis, Christmas in Bath was a time of relaxation. It was the second snowiest Christmas for 32 years with a snowfall actually on Christmas Day. The hotels were full, and most guests arrived by train, rather than car, to avoid the slippery roads. The usual festivities, balls and concerts took place in the Pump Room and Assembly Rooms, and on Boxing Day at 11 am Alderman Sturge Cotterell conducted his traditional tour of the city. The annual pantomime at the Theatre Royal was Cinderella, Father Christmas surrounded by some rather shy children was seen to have arrived by train in the city, staff dances were held, and charities wrapped up the usual 'parcels of good things for poor Bath homes'. Yet the spectre of war did not entirely vanish: in the Saturday edition of the *Chronicle* on 17 December there was a brief note informing readers that Bath chemists were attending a course of lectures 'in connection with gas and high explosives with a view to arranging in all local pharmacies a first aid point'. Nevertheless on New Year's Day Mayor Adrian Hopkins felt sufficiently optimistic to pronounce that there was 'every prospect that the New Year may bring more happiness and peace'.

THE EUROPEAN CRISIS INTENSIFIES, MARCH-APRIL 1939

BY MARCH EVENTS were to cast a great shadow of doubt over that prospect. The month started with 'Spring in the air' as a result of sub-tropical air being wafted up by the southerly winds from Africa, but on 15 March Hitler exploited Slovak-Czech tensions to annex Bohemia and to turn Slovakia into a satellite state. One reader of the *Chronicle* asked in despair two days later 'where, when and how is this devouring wolf-like process to stop?' Further blows to peace followed in quick succession: on 22 March Germany annexed Memel from Lithuania, which resulted in, as the *Chronicle* put it, 'Mafeking Nazis and weeping Lithuanians'. In response to fears that Germany would seize Danzig, Britain and France committed themselves on 31 March to defend Poland against external attack. A week later the Italian annexation of Albania prompted Britain and France to extended their guarantees to Greece and Romania. The Munich settlement was in ruins and war was once more a real likelihood. The only way to avert it, as all parties urged, was to build up 'a peace front' or anti-Nazi coalition. George Desmond, Bath's Labour parliamentary candidate, announced his support for such an international coalition at a meeting of the local Labour Party provided this 'absolutely and emphatically' included Russia, which he naively described 'as a great democratic country more pledged to the cause of freedom than any other country'. Whether this was possible, would become clear over the summer. RH Mckeag, the chairman of the Bath Conservative Party's Association, in a talk to the Junior Imperial League at its Bristol Week-end Political school predicted that

> .... if there is a war, our enemies would be Germany and Italy, with probably Hungary and possibly Japan and Bulgaria as their allies. Spain would probably remain neutral in theory but would be as dangerous to us as she dared. On our side would be France, Poland, Rumania [sic], Greece and possibly Russia and the United States.[18]

He concluded that In the meantime 'It is up to us to do our best, be it in the Regular Services, or in home defence or even in our normal job'

'BE PREPARED'

IT WAS THE constant refrain of ARP lecturers that their audience should 'be prepared' for the worst eventuality, while hoping and believing that it would not happen, but by the end of 1937 Bath, like the rest of Britain, was nowhere near to completing its ARP preparations. According to the *Times*, 'not half a dozen cities in the country could at the moment put into motion an adequate scheme of protection and rescue for their populations'.[19] A major reason for this delay was disagreement between central and local government about who should finance the cost of these preparations. In March 1937 the Association of Municipal Corporations, argued that it was the government's responsibility to foot the bill, and recommended that no further expenditure should be incurred until a decision had been reached.[20] It was not until November that the Home Office at last agreed to pay the local authorities 75 per cent of their ARP expenditure as well as the cost of providing the whole population with gas masks.[21] 1937 was not, however, an entirely wasted year. In Portsmouth in July a major civil defence exercise was conducted to test out the effectiveness of its blackout, air raid warnings and air raid wardens. Its results were communicated to councils, and it was particularly noted that air raid wardens were essentially the lynch pin of the ARP, and that they needed 'to be trained to a high degree of efficiency'.[22]

Given lack of public interest and government parsimony, it was not surprising that Bath in 1937 made only modest progress in recruiting personnel, educating the public and preparing its own ARP schemes. Offers from such firms as Low and Bonar of Dundee, which was trying to secure a contract for the supply of sandbags, or Nu-Swift, for fire-fighting equipment were simply ignored.[23] When the council's ARP Committee in December 1936 advertised for volunteers for the special constabulary, fire fighting, first aid, gas decontamination centres and demolition work, the response was poor. The Town Clerk received just one letter from the wife of the vicar of Kelston, who offered the use of a car and a room in the vicarage 'suitable for a first aid dressing station'. The Chief Constable was rather more successful in enrolling special constables. By June he had recruited 50 with the prospect of a further 40 from the British Legion, but in the absence of an instructor from the Home Office, he could not begin to train them.[24] It also proved difficult to recruit wardens, and by mid-1937 only about 35 had been recruited.

When Councillor Amblin discussed this inadequate response with the BTLC in November, he was roundly criticised by the redoubtable Major Grenfell, who claimed that 'all that had been done was eye-wash', and 'far from satisfactory'. Grenfell told him roundly that the aldermen and councillors should attend ward meetings and keep the public informed. Clearly there was scope for more publicity and lectures, yet for anybody remotely interested or concerned there were many opportunities to listen and learn about the ARP.

The Red Cross and St. John's Ambulance gave first aid classes. A Home Office official, Colonel Garforth, gave a lecture to the Chamber of Commerce, which was held in the Guildhall on 31 May 1937 so that a wider public could attend. He covered all aspects of air raid precautions. Despite initially announcing that he had not come to frighten his audience, he nevertheless informed it that 'the weight of bombs which might be expected to be dropped in half a day in the next war will be greater than the total weight dropped in this country during the last war', and urged them 'to get down to it and get out your schemes'. In late November the Chamber of Commerce organised another ARP lecture at the Guildhall on the subject of 'how to gas proof one's own house', which was delivered by Sergeant-instructor SC Whittle of the Somerset County Police. Whittle reassured his audience that 'fortunately we are able to defend ourselves against these poisonous chemicals'. Indeed, it was the 'only form of warfare where we can'. In proposing the vote of thanks, on behalf of the Chamber, Mr R W Pearson observed that 'a knowledge of what to do would have a psychological effect in preventing panic', but added pointedly that 'a large proportion of the population ... were indifferent to the benefit of these precautions'.

To illustrate the truth of this remark, one need look no further than Bathavon Rural District Council (RDC) where ARP precautions proceeded at a snail's pace for most of 1937. At a council meeting on 16 June the RDC's ARP Committee on the advice of the Chief Constable , recommended that its plans should be coordinated with Bath's, and, to lessen the administrative burden on the city, Keynsham, Saltford and Whitchurch should be linked up with Bristol. Each Parish Council in cooperation with its district councillor should also organise the necessary ARP measures in its own area and provide a hall for lectures. Finally it proposed that Miss Witham, the commander of a Red Cross detachment in Somerset, who was a qualified lecturer in chemical warfare, should be invited to deliver a series of four lectures. The committee's chairman Mr E H Morgan, went on to tell the RDC:

> I am not an alarmist, and I don't believe we are going to have any trouble for a very long time, but I do think we should take some steps to do what we can in case a certain event might happen.[25]

Miss Witham's request for the eventual reimbursement of her travel expenses led to a considerable argument on the RDC. A majority insisted that her expenses should not be paid. The chairman pleaded in vain that it was only a matter of a few shillings, but Councillor Geoffrey Strutt spoke for the majority when he argued that until the government had decided on the subsidy it was prepared to advance to the local authorities, Bathavon should refuse to spend a single penny. In the end the council agreed to invite Miss Witham, but that no expenditure should be incurred. The issue of her travel expenses was solved by one of the councillors offering to fetch her in due course by car.

A month later on the RDC considered a letter from the Somerset County Council urging its local authorities to continue preparing their ARP schemes, but in view of the expense involved it was agreed that the council should let the preparations 'slide for a month or two'. It was only when the government was about to make it mandatory for local councils to draw up their ARP schemes that Bathavon RDC consented in December to implement in full the measures recommended by its ARP committee and grant a sum 'not exceeding £25' to finance them.

On 22 December the government's Air Raid Precautions Act received the Royal Assent. Schemes were to be submitted by local authorities to the Home Secretary outlining their plans for protecting 'persons and property from injury in the event of hostile attack from the air'.[26] Bath had now not only to draw up its own ARP schemes but to mount more vigorous campaigns to inform the public of the need for such measures, arrange demonstrations of gas proof rooms and bomb shelters, recruit more volunteers and begin to stockpile gas masks. It had also to counter criticism from passivist and left-wing groups.

To draw up and then to implement these schemes, the council needed to appoint a full time ARP officer. Advertisements for the post were placed in the national press in February 1938, which attracted 192 applicants, amongst whom were generals, admirals and baronets. As the advertisement announced that clerical assistance would be provided, there were also a few applicants offering their services as clerks . One from John Hodges, an old boy of Clifton College, who was about to move from Hounslow to Bath conceded disarmingly that if he applied for the post, he would be 'flying too high' but observed that the new post would create much clerical work 'and that is just the duties I could satisfactorily carry out'. However, his hopes were dashed when he was informed that there were no current plans for appointing a clerical assistant.[27] The Council chose Major H Pickard, who had held a commission in the Royal Artillery for 17 years and then served a further ten at the Chemical Defence Experimental Station at Porton, where he was responsible for conducting large scale gas trials as well as ensuring the safety of the station's personnel. Pickard made his public debut when what was called a 'gas chamber' was set up on

Monday 21 March in the yard of the Drill Hall in the Lower Bristol Road, to inspire confidence in the effectiveness of gas masks. Together with Stothert and Pitt's anti-gas officer, the head of its Red Cross units, and the chief officer of the Bath Fire Brigade, he helped fit those members of the public, who were brave enough to venture into the 'gas chamber', with gas masks.

On 14 March 1938 the Home Secretary broadcast a national appeal for ARP volunteers and urged the local authorities to organise training courses for them.[28] Pickard lost no opportunity to raise the ARP's profile in Bath. In early April he was given permission to organise meetings in St Saviour's Church Hall, Twerton Parish Hall, St. Luke's School room and St Stephen's Church Hall. The Director of Education advised him to invite to each meeting the resident aldermen, clergy, heads of schools and 'other leading citizens', as well as parents.[29] Pickard followed this advice, and when he presided over the meeting in Twerton on Friday 29 April, he had the satisfaction of seeing Councillor P E Bence volunteer for ARP service. Pickard informed his audience that the city was to be divided into nine equal districts consisting of a population of about 8,000, each of which would be placed under the control of a head warden. Nine days earlier he had told a meeting of nearly a thousand ex-servicemen in the Guildhall that about 870 air raid wardens would be needed and that

> The instruction they would undergo [would be] quite simple and would take about ten hours ... There would be no written examination and no sergeant-major stunt (laughter).[30]

Special constables and volunteer firemen were also urgently needed. Women too had an important role to play. At its summer meeting on 29 June at South Stoke the Bath branch of the National Council of Women was told by Pickard that:

> The service of ladies would be very welcome. Quite a number were already helping in the fitting of masks and a proportion of the warden service could be undertaken by ladies.[31]

To make the public aware of the need for air raid precautions, posters were prominently displayed on all public and municipal buildings including the public libraries and Pump Room as well as in all 'conveniences, school premises and parks'. The City Engineer informed Pickard that 'it had thirty vehicles running about the streets' on which small posters provided by the Home Office could be placed. ARP Films were also available to heighten awareness of the menacing state of the world. One such film considered was the 'World in Revolt' which, according to a flyer from Film House, Wardour Street, was 'an engrossing picture dealing with current topics... introducing unscreened shots of the world's economic and political upheavals'.[32]

In July Pickard presented a report to the ARP Committee. He had made considerable progress in enrolling volunteers, who now numbered:

525 Air Raid Wardens
492 Casualty Service personnel
112 Rescue and Decontamination personnel
30 Volunteer firemen
Total 1,159

Major Geoffrey Lock, the president of the Bath branch of the British Legion was appointed chief warden and the nine head wardens under him were also selected. Most of these were retired ex-servicemen, although one, Rev. J H Davies, the head warden of Oldfield Park and Wells Road was a clergyman. Apart from the Auxiliary Fire Service (AFS), which remained right up to the outbreak of war the weakest link in Bath's ARP preparations, the numbers enrolled were about 70 % of the number required, and Pickard allowed himself a gentle pat on the back, observing that these figures were ' quite satisfactory, and show that the appeal for volunteers is meeting with a ready response'.[33] Despite the 'lack of equipment, no suitable training centre and insufficient qualified instructors', he managed to organise eight training courses for these

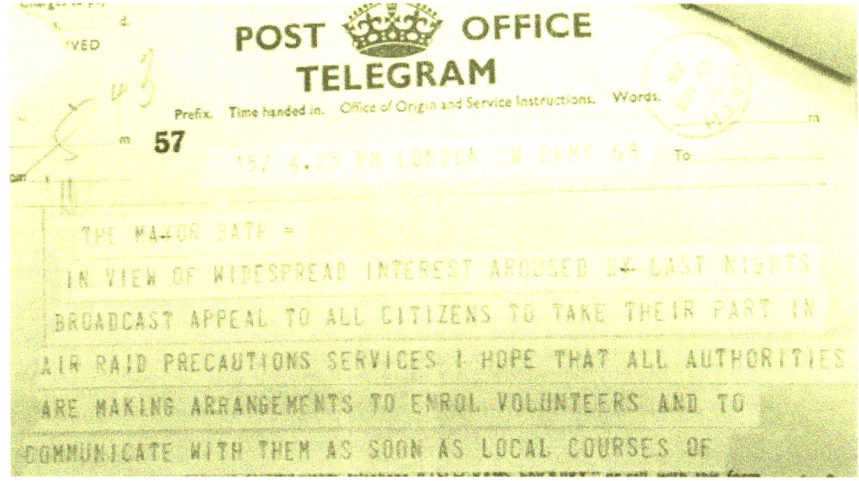

Telegram from Home Office 15 March 1938 following up on the Home Secretary's appeal on the 14th for volunteers for the ARP (Bath Record Office)

volunteers during June and July, and plans were also drawn up for training personnel in the city's utility services in rescue and decontamination work. After a preliminary survey had been made of potential sites for air raid shelters, Pickard concluded that 'the best solution' would be 'to adapt existing arches and cellars so far as possible', but if those were to prove insufficient, then digging trenches in the city's parks and squares would have to be considered.[34] At Ealand's Corner in New Bond Street where Pickard had his headquarters, a gas proof demonstration room was opened for the general public on 28 July.

Some ARP exercises resulted in embarrassing and very public failures. For instance on 6 September a fire in a derelict property at 49, Avon Street. which had been used as a demonstration for dealing with incendiary bombs, was not put out properly, and Fireman Jones had to be sent out at 4.25 pm with a hand pump to extinguish it.[35] Another failure involved the testing of an air raid siren or 'hooter', which was installed in the electrical sub-station in Bradford Road, Combe Down. As the *Chronicle* observed:

> Widespread inquiries made by our representatives, both personally and by telephone establish clearly that over a very wide area... the siren remained unheard...Policemen who were on duty in the centre of the city, in Kensington, in Oldfield Park and Englishcombe Park didn't catch so much as an echo of it...[36].

Sirens were, however, tested with rather more success on 1 October. Businesses and department stores were urged by the Home Office to draw up schemes for protecting their own employees. Pickard told a meeting of businessmen at the Guildhall on the 25 April that employers would have 'to look out for suitable places of refuge in their premises' and that large firms should organise their own schemes within their own premises to be run by 'a responsible employee'. The railway companies according to the *Chronicle* were also 'alive to the necessity of instructing their staff in the all important subject of air raid precautions'. On Wednesday 25 May 1938 a travelling ARP instruction unit arrived at Green Park station, and two lectures each lasting three hours was arranged for the local staff. It then moved on to Bristol, Gloucester, Cheltenham and Bromsgrove. Hospitals, too, were required to draw up their own ARP plans. The RNHRD's matron arranged for her nurses to attend a series of lectures, which the Ministry of Health was intending to organise in early 1939, while some of the hospital's male staff were enrolled on courses for air raid wardens. Cellars not required as shelters for patients and staff were to be made available for use by the local ARP wardens.[37] In November the Ministry of Health decided that in the event of war the RNHRD would become a general hospital, but it would not interfere in the hospital's administration except to regulate the admission of patients.[38] Trained nurses who were married or had retired were also asked to return to service by Mrs Forbes Fraser, the Hon. Secretary of the Bath Branch of the College of Nursing.

During August there was a lull in ARP preparations. Pickard himself was exhausted and on the 9th was ordered to bed by his doctor and was not fit to return to work for over a week.[39] The following month, as a consequence of the Sudeten crisis, the ARP and the emergency services faced what in hindsight can be called a dress rehearsal for war. 'Safety trenches' or air raid shelters, were dug in the following parks, recreation grounds and school playing fields:

> Twerton Roundhill, south side
> Englishcombe Park Housing Estate
> Odd Down Housing Estate
> Alexandra, Rudmore and Hedgemead Parks
> Northfields Estate, Lansdown
> Recreation Grounds, Larkhall and Innox Park
> City of Bath Girls' School Playing Field
> Horseshoe Walk -green triangle opposite Abbey view
> Sydney Gardens
> Lower Common
> Queen Square

Other measures included securing the local gas works and electrical generating stations. 'Purely as precautionary measure' the managers of the Bath Electricity Undertakings and the Bath Gas Works were ordered 'to ensure that no unauthorised person' should gain entry to their works, and special pickets were appointed to enforce this order. The Government meanwhile began the complex process of distributing 38 million gas masks to regional centres. In Bath plans were drawn up to store them in Frome Road House.[40]

On Wednesday 21 September on the eve of Chamberlain's second flight to Germany the council's Education Committee met and recommended as a matter of urgency that children should be trained in the use of gas masks and that if war broke out, schools should immediately be closed. The Education Department in consultation with the city's teachers would draw up schemes for pupils to work at home. The Director of Education could only guess how long the schools would remain closed but assumed that it would just be for a week or fortnight. He advised the committee that once the schools reopened,

The ARP enrolment card of Clifford Ellis, the Headmaster of the Bath Art School (Bath Record Office)

initially at any rate, parents should 'have freedom of choice' as to when their children should return, and the bylaws enforcing attendance should be suspended. It was, he stressed, important to cooperate closely with the children's parents so that the authorities would have their goodwill when they re-opened the schools and put in place 'such protective measures as they could arrange'. The children would, of course take their gas masks to school, and 'such protection as was possible' would be provided if they were caught in an air raid there.[41]

Despite the apparently peaceful resolution to the Sudeten crisis at Munich, there was no let-up in the city's ARP preparations. On 31 October 1938 Major Lock, while congratulating a meeting of ex-servicemen for having provided so many volunteers for the ARP services, observed ominously ' I think we have a serious time ahead and it is … possible that war will come'. The construction of shelters was a task of such 'magnitude and urgency' that the city engineer loaned four of his architects to the surveyor of corporate property, whose department in cooperation with the ARP Committee was responsible for locating shelter sites. As a survey of some of the underground cellars in the city had shown that structurally they were not strong enough to offer adequate protection against bombing, it was essential to locate safer sites for shelters elsewhere. The ARP Committee recommended that the trenches, which had been started in the parks and open spaces during the Sudeten crisis, should be finished and that provision should be made for public shelters in the new buildings being constructed or planned on the following sites:

> Boots, Pure Drug Company Ltd., 24-26 Union Street, 1 and 2 Union Street, 1 Union Passage and 1 Cheap Street
> The Christopher Hotel, High Street
> New Bond Street Corner
> The Seven Dials site
> Walcot Street car Park
> Oldfield School Extensions
> New Kingsmead School
> Municipal Buildings Extension.

It also proposed that on their completion the swimming baths at Wood Street could serve as a decontamination centre, and that a model Anderson garden shelter should be set up on a suitable site for the public to view.[42] As the Treasury paid 75 per cent of local government's expenses, Pickard discussed these proposals with the Home Office, when he was in London to attend a course at the ARP Staff School in January. The Home Office approved them in principle, but much to Pickard's surprise refused to pay for the purchase of the Anderson shelter 'for demonstration purposes'. Describing this as 'a ridiculous situation', Pickard confessed that he 'was rather rude about it', but he reassured the town clerk that 'we will dodge them somehow'.[43] The provision of shelters was also included in the plans for the construction of the new RNHRD, which could accommodate up to 300 stretcher cases during a raid. Ironically in view of the April blitz of 1942, the Ministry of Health did not consider this necessary on the grounds that Bath would not be a likely target for bombing and would instead serve as a reception centre for evacuees. However the Ministry did inform the hospital that if there were 'any obvious precautions' that 'could be undertaken without great expenditure of money', it would consider them. Initially it seemed that the council would step in and provide £2000 to pay for the shelters, but in May 1939 it decided not to in view of the escalating costs of its ARP programme.[44]

There was a host of other tasks to be completed ranging from insuring volunteers, establishing wardens' posts, to siting decontamination centres and installing lighting in the larger shelters. Furniture for the control centres in Green Park and at the Central Police Station needed to be ordered, as well as ARP signs, maps and householders' register forms. There were, too, frequent questions from the public that required answers. Mrs Haysman of 16, Green Park who owned three houses in Bath imperiously demanded that the Town Clerk, should send round 'a gentleman who will have the necessary knowledge' both to advise her on the safety of her properties in Walcot Street, Green Park and Prior Park Road and on the provision of new gas masks for her tenants. She also asked whether it was 'essential to have an 8ft hole dug in the garden of her Prior Park property 'to insert a steel shelter'. At least Mrs Haysman was requesting information and not proposing to dig her own shelters. As a member of the Peasedown Parish Council pointed out in July 1939, digging a shelter could be a 'death trap' for 'people with no technical knowledge' since it could well collapse and bury its occupants alive.[45]

The Ministry of Health's Circular No 1779, which requested information in March 1939 from local councils about their plans for the disposal of the bodies of those killed in bombing raids, was a stark reminder of the ultimate consequences of the impact of war on civilians. The committee of local undertakers, which was appointed by the council, on the assumption that the mortuaries attached to local hospitals and funeral parlours would be full up, recommended that the Walcot Closed Burial Ground Chapel, the crypts of Walcot Parish Church and St. James Church, the city mortuary near Old Bridge and St. Peter's Church Gymnasium, Twerton, should all be made available. The city mortuary was to be reserved exclusively for gas cases. The committee recommended the appointment of four mortuary superintendents and provided a list of 21 volunteer assistants, who all worked for local undertakers.

It proposed that in the event of an air raid the superintendents and their assistants would report to their respective mortuaries to receive the cadavers, which would be transported there by ambulance. To train the volunteers for their new role Pickard agreed to lay on a course of three lectures.[46]

On 18 April 1939 Government Circular No. 86/1939 ordered the local authorities to prioritise civil defence measures over all other business.[47] Right up to the outbreak of war in September the recruitment of wardens, drivers, fireman and special constables continued, courses of lectures were arranged, and appeals made to the public, especially to ex-servicemen. The Education Department organised voluntary courses for teachers in first aid and anti-gas measures. The Bath branch of the NUT, many members of which were strongly committed to the League of Nations and internationalism, had at the height of the Sudeten crisis 'a lengthy and animated discussion on air raid precautions' and decided that the question of volunteering 'was one for the individual teachers' own decision'. In fact a considerable number of teachers did volunteer for the ARP. Clifford Ellis, the Head Master of the Bath School of Art, noted, for instance, that fewer teachers were attending his courses in the winter of 1938-39 because of their ARP commitments.[48]

There was, too, a constant demand for lectures not only from parish councils in the villages outside Bath, but also from parents' associations and mothers of young children. The Parent's Association of St Stephen's School, Beacon Hill, wrote to the director of education to request a series of lectures, preferably on a Tuesday evening between 7 and 9 pm.[49] On 11 May when the Milk Street Baby League held their monthly meeting, Pickard gave, according to the *Chronicle* , 'a most helpful and instructive talk , to which the audience listened 'with deep attention in spite of the little one's chatter, laughter and tears'. Many of the mothers expressed their intention to visit the gas proof room in New Bond Street.

In January 1939 the scope for voluntary service widened when the government introduced the national service scheme for the voluntary enrolment of citizens not just into the ARP but the Territorial Army, nursing, the Women's Voluntary Service (WVS), the Land Army and the ambulance and fire services. To organise this in Bath the National Service Committee, with Mayor Hopkins as chairman, was formed. Initially enrolment was disappointing. In the first month there were only some 450 applications and very few for the Territorial Army, but over the course of the next two months numbers did pick up. The German occupation of Bohemia and Moravia and the subsequent heightening of international tension caused the number of volunteers to climb to 950 by the end of March. In July, although the National

Service Committee reported that overall 'satisfactory progress' was being made, more recruits were still needed for the territorial battalion of the SLI, nursing auxiliaries and auxiliary firemen.

In April 1939 local authorities were required by the government to appoint a Civil Defence Controller, and an emergency committee, which would assist him in overseeing ARP operations. The council on the recommendation of the ARP Committee, nominated the Chief Constable as Controller and decided that the elected mayor of the time should be one of the committee members. The other two members, who were nominated later, were Councillors Barrett and Lock, the Chief Warden. Some councillors were wary of delegating so much power to the committee, and when the council met to approve the appointment, Dr Carpenter who represented St Michael's Ward, wanted to know what powers the emergency committee would have, as he feared that it would have *carte blanche* 'to govern the city'. He told his fellow councillors that he was a 'constitutionalist' and did not ' like to see the constitution of this city or the country being abrogated'. He was reassured that the Controller's task was to carry out the instructions of the government only in relation to air raid precautions. In the opinion of the historian George Scott the Emergency Committee concentrated too much power in the hands of just three councillors and ultimately failed to protect Bath adequately from the German firebomb raids of April 1942.[50]

During the last few months of peace efforts were made to demonstrate the effectiveness of the city's ARP services. In March the Fire Brigade and AFS were deployed to tackle a simulated fire at the Empire Hotel. An operation on a larger scale took place on Middle Common on the evening of 23 May. Bath's ARP workers 'came out into the open'. Not only was there an exercise involving a house set on fire by incendiary bombs, but every branch of the ARP was on display from gas contamination squads to casualty stations. The evening started with a long column of ARP volunteers including members of the Red Cross, St. John's Ambulance and the boy scouts marching past the mayor, who then addressed them. On Sunday 2 July there was a large National Service rally in London's Hyde Park involving representatives nominated by councils right across the country. Bath was awarded four invitations, two of which Pickard allocated to ARP wardens and one each to the City's Engineer Service and to the casualty services.

In July a major ARP exercise was organised in Bath and the surrounding counties: from Midnight on Saturday the 8th to 4 am on Sunday the 9th there were to be heavy raids on Bristol, and at least two 'enemy' squadrons would attack Bath at regular intervals, thus testing the effectiveness of its ARP preparations A rigorous blackout was to be enforced. The owners of cigarette machines and illuminated signs were warned to have their lights extinguished. As far as possible motorists were to keep off the road, and doctors, who might have to drive at night to an emergency, were required to cover their lights with a thin strip of blue tissue paper. According to reports in the *Chronicle* the following day 'hundreds if not thousands came out to see what the city looked like in total darkness'. Viewed from Beechen Cliff 'there were still a few lights visible here and there' especially around the Western Gasworks, but by 3.30 am there were 'only 12 bright specks ... visible throughout the whole city. The centre was in complete darkness'. The most dramatic part of the exercise was a simulated attack on Seven Dials where a house had recently been demolished. According to the 'narrative' four people were trapped in a refuge room and two others were injured by fallen masonry. To the amusement of the crowd, who had gathered, despite it being well past midnight, the auxiliary fire brigade was slow to arrive, but it then put out the fire 'with little more than a couple of squirts'. The report centre at the central police station, was in the words of the *Chronicle,* 'the scene of well-ordered activity' where messages were received by phone, 'docketed and appropriate instructions given out'. The site of every incident was marked by flags on a large map on the wall. Casualty stations were kept busy with volunteers simulating broken limbs, lacerated faces and symptoms of mustard gas poisoning. Inevitably there were lighter moments during the night. One volunteer attended a casualty station with a label attached to him indicating that he was suffering from severe face wounds, but he had to wait so long that he took off his label and wrote on it 'bled to death' and then went home. At the last moment the RAF's role in the exercise was cancelled, but on balance the exercise was deemed a success. Pickard told the *Chronicle* that 'the communications and the functioning of various services' were operating efficiently, even though at some casualty clearing stations there were long delays, and a few householders and car drivers did not bother to extinguish their lights. Alarmingly the white stone of the new houses on the heights around Bath and the greenhouses on the outskirts of the city stood out very conspicuously when the sky was clear.

These exercises confirmed the role of the warden and the special constable as the work horses of the ARP. It was they who ensured that lights were extinguished and reported incidents to the control centre. When in the first week of August some 70,000 gas masks were assembled in boxes in James Street West and Frome Road House, it was again the wardens, who played a key role in instructing people how to use them and ensuring that they had a mask that fitted them. Inevitably at times their officiousness encountered hostility. At Bradford-on-Avon in July, for instance, there were occasions when doors were slammed in their faces.

PREPARING TO RECEIVE EVACUEES

IN EARLY JANUARY 1939 the Town Clerk's Department received a circular from the Ministry of Health giving details of its plans for evacuating children in the event of the outbreak of war from London and the other large conurbations. Preparation for this eventuality required a detailed house-to-house survey of available accommodation in Bath and its surrounding villages. Householders in many parts of the city were informed by the mayor that voluntary registration officers would be calling to assess 'how many children each house can reasonably accommodate' if war were to be declared. They were warned that:

> While the scheme is at present purely voluntary, ... Householders who do not now offer to take children may be required to take other persons in time of emergency.[51]

Initially, however, it proved difficult to find volunteer registration officers, but ARP wardens and the public spirited people who regularly made house to visits to collect money for the local hospitals, were targeted, and by the end of the month a full complement of 200 people had been enrolled, and a temporary office opened at the Guildhall. By and large, as the *Chronicle* reported on 4 February registration proceeded smoothly, but inevitably there were hesitations, subterfuges, and objections. Some pleaded that they were saving rooms for friends from London or elsewhere, only to be told that they had to give the names and addresses of 'these friends'. At the national service rally in the Pavilion two weeks later Adrian Hopkins remarked sarcastically to great applause that:

> 'Some people he knew had objected to housing children from other cities, and those people he classed as yellow and as defeatists. If war came and the citizens of Bath had nothing worse [to endure] than billeting children, it would not be war at all, but a holiday.[52]

Nevertheless, the ultimate threat of compulsion did cause some unease and hostility. The Reverend Rowe, the vicar of Englishcombe voiced the concern of his parishioners in a letter published in the *Chronicle* on 13 May, after they had been told that 100 evacuees would to be sent to their parish in an emergency 'whether they have expressed themselves willing or not'. He complained that there seemed 'to be emerging a mailed fist, rather like a dictator'. He pertinently observed that the tasks of the volunteers who would be picking up the children from the station and taking them to their destinations would 'be far from pleasant', as frightened children would be delivered in some cases to flustered and even hostile house owners. He appealed to the council to publish a list of premises subject to compulsory billeting, so that plans could be drawn up in advance for finding alternative accommodation in the event of mishaps. The WI was certainly aware of the problems raised by the Rev. Rowe. Its Somerset County Secretary sent a note in April requesting each of its local branches 'to ask for names of volunteers who would help in various ways ... those who were selected to take several children refugees in the event of evacuation'.[53]

By the beginning of July the Director of Education had a clearer idea of the number of child evacuees who would be sent to Bath in an emergency. He told a meeting of rural clergy at the Deanery that possibly some 7,000 children would be billeted in Bath and an additional 13,000 in the outlying rural districts. Initially four trains a day were expected to come to the city on four successive days with 800 children on each train. There was little he could do reassure the householders faced with compulsory billeting, but he was reported as taking 'the opportunity to refer sympathetically' to the problems this might cause. At the end of the month Mr T Tyler, the head of the sanitary inspectorate, was appointed chief billeting officer, and head teachers were made responsible for billeting children in the areas served by their respective schools.

'THERE'S GOING TO BE A WAR .... MY SON'

DESPITE THE LOOMING threat of war, holidays were still taken, as in any other year. Bathonians visiting the Continent tended wisely to keep clear of Germany, but Italy and France remained popular. Some, despite the tense international situation, went on cruises, often to the concern of their friends and relatives, but these were assured by the *Chronicle* as late as 26 August that there was no need for alarm since the captains of the 'cruising liners' had received instructions 'to alter their itineraries at a moment's notice'. The paper also noted that one ship still had plans for calling at a port 'not far from Danzig'. The uncertain situation did not stop the council's key officials going on holiday. The mayor went to the Isles of Scilly for the whole of August,

Pickard was at Bude for two weeks, Hoyle, the Education Director, at Torquay and Ogden, the town clerk, at Cardigan, but work pursued them. Ogden, for instance, was forwarded by his deputy two memoranda from the Home Office concerning ARP arrangements in individual factories and businesses.[54]

On August Bank Holiday Monday, Bath enjoyed good weather and a big influx of visitors brought to the city by packed excursion trains and buses. Bathonians meanwhile were still preoccupied with familiar peace time issues and projects: in August an American visitor warned against the vandalisation of Milsom Street in a letter in the *Chronicle*, while car parking in Bath remained a controversial subject. Plans were also announced in July for Queen Mary's visit to Bath to lay the foundation stone of the new RNHRD. The hospital's Reception Sub-Committee met regularly throughout July and August to discuss the construction of the 'largest grandstand possible 'with room for over a thousand people and further details concerned with the Royal visit.[55] There was still room in the correspondence columns of the

Pile driving on the site for the new RNHRD (Bath & Wilts Chronicle & Herald, 9 August 1939)

Chronicle on 28 July for a letter from 'a dear little old Bath lady, who finds modern "progress" so incredible' that she was beginning to wonder whether she was dreaming. At the end of July 900 'poor Bath children' were taken to Bristol Zoo in Clifton in a major logistical operation involving a fleet of buses, the distribution of balls and comics as well as 930 buns and other treats.

However the news grew increasingly ominous as the daily headlines revealed. Hitler was demanding the return of Danzig to the German Reich, while the Poles, strengthened by the Anglo-French guarantee, argued that its continued existence as a 'free city' under the protection of the League of Nations, was vital for their country's independence. Sir Evelyn French, the founder of the English speaking Union and frequent visitor to Bath, after returning from Berlin at the end of July, warned readers of the *Chronicle* that 'all Germany seemed mobilised behind the Fuehrer'. Yet there were chinks of light: Britain and France were still hoping for an alliance with the USSR, which would deter German aggression. Mayor Hopkins told the BTLC on 26 July that he 'was absolutely confident ... that there is not going to be a war', but wisely added that he would be 'the world's biggest fool' if he let such optimism impede the necessary defensive preparations being made. In Bath these precautions could, of course, be seen all around the city and air raid shelters continued to be dug. Nothing could bring home the ominous threats of air raids more than the advice given to parents of schoolchildren in Midsomer Norton. In the event of an air raid during school hours children would be kept at school until the danger had passed, but if an air raid warning occurred while they were on the way to school 'they should either return home or proceed to school, whichever is the nearer'.[56]

On 29 March the government announced that it proposed to more than double the size of the Territorial Army and allotted the Bath area the goal of recruiting a further thousand men to bring the numbers of local volunteers up to the target set. The 4Bn of the SLI with its depot in the Lower Bristol Road was by far the most popular territorial unit for local volunteers. Stothert and Pitt paid a week's wages to volunteers who attended territorial camps, and the Bath Coop also agreed to pay the wages 'less cash payments received by the Army authorities'.[57] At the beginning of August the *Chronicle* sent a journalist to cover the activities of the battalion while under canvas at Exmouth. Its report was cloyingly enthusiastic, as it described 'a world of music, of laughter and a world of discipline that was never harsh'.

In May 1939 the Royal Assent was given to the Military Training Act. All males between 20 and 21 would eventually be called up for six months service in a new conscript army anachronistically called the militia. On Saturday and Sunday 3 and 4 June all young men who were born between 4 June 1918 and 3 June 1919 were required by law to register as militia men. In Bath some 400 were registered at the employment exchange in St. James Street West. A few passivists and communists stood outside distributing leaflets, but according to the manager they made little impression. Apparently 'the general feeling among the men seemed to be, it's our job and here we are'. Medical examinations began on 15 June and were completed by 23rd. The recruits were seen by an interviewing officer, who allocated them to the service for which they were best fitted. The first draft of 35,000 selected from the 200,000 who registered in Britain in June reported to their units on Saturday 15 July. Reports from the militia camps were mixed. On the one hand there was an article in the *Chronicle* on 15 August stressing how impressed parents were by the sons' bearing and confidence when they came back for a brief leave on the Bank Holiday. On the other hand it was widely reported that 360 reservists had refused to report for duty at Yeovil Militia camp as instructors in protest at the poor quality of food and low pay, which led to questions being raised in the House of Commons about the situation in the militia camps.

To some of the more discerning Bathonians of military age, the infantry was a branch of the army to be avoided. Ron Perry, for instance, who was a mechanic at Widcombe garages, recalled over fifty years later being advised by a colleague, a former recruiting sergeant, that:

> There's going to be a war .... My son. You don't want to be gun fodder, do you? So get down to the recruiting office and see the Recruiting Sergeant to tell him you are an MT [Mechanical Transport] fitter.[58]

He took this advice and duly became a Reservist in the RAOC. Another young Bathonian, nineteen-year-old Bob King, was working in the Coop store in Westgate two days before the outbreak of war when an army sergeant came into the shop and advised him to report for a medical at the Drill Hall as a volunteer for the territorial army. When he did so, he was given £5 for being called up and a further £5 as territorial army bounty, £3.10 as payment for the initial training course and 10sh for underclothes. As he observed in retrospect, 'he had never seen £14 before'. On 3rd September, the day war broke out, he entrained to Salisbury and joined the Royal Engineers, eventually becoming a bomb disposal expert.[59]

Conscription marked the return to the militarised society of 1918. Reflecting this, advertisements for Capstan cigarettes featured soldiers lighting up, and even the weather forecast for Friday 4th August in the *Chronicle* illustrated its prediction of 'local thunder' with a sergeant-major bellowing orders at recruits. However, the Military Training Act contained a clause exempting conscientious objectors, subject to the rulings of a specially constituted tribunal. Dr. Hilda Oldham, an ardent passivist and socialist, suspected that the government would incite public opinion against conscientious objectors, but in fact the tribunal which sat in the Senate Room in Bristol University in August was humane and tolerant. On 9 August, for example, it heard the cases of 28 Objectors from Bath, Somerset and Wiltshire. Six men were placed on the register of conscientious objectors unconditionally. Twelve others were exempted from military service provided they continued in their existing employment, a further four were put on the register but were subject to six months work as prescribed by the Ministry of

Labour and the remainder were put on the military list for non-combatant duties.

THE LINK

Until 23 August when the Nazi-Soviet pact was signed, there was still hope that Russia would join the peace front against Nazi Germany and that Hitler might yet be deterred. The *Chronicle* on 10 August compared the volatile situation in Poland to the British weather and observed perceptively that the Nazis were 'trying to test our nerves'. This uncertainty and increasingly remote chance of averting war formed the background to the debate in Bath about the activities of the pro German organisation, The Link, which had been founded by the distinguished but rabidly anti-Semitic Admiral Sir Barry Domville in 1937 with the aim of bringing together the British and German peoples. In Parliament the Home Secretary had described The Link as an instrument of German propaganda. It was an offshoot of the defunct Anglo-German Fellowship of which several large firms and a few Conservative MPs, including Loel Guinness had been members.

Several branches were formed all over the country, which kept in touch with their counterparts in Germany, and arranged exchange visits. A branch was formed in Bath at the end of May and the first of what was hoped to be regular monthly meetings took place at Foresters' Hall on Tuesday 27 June where films were shown of the Rhine and the Black Forest, after which members spoke of their exchange experiences. The Treasurer, Mrs Roberts of 9, Mount Beacon, informed the *Chronicle* that its members were 'simply ordinary private citizens who hope for and believe in understanding and friendship, instead of war- between the British and German people'. Its secretary, was a young girl 'apparently' in her teens. Her membership of The Link was strongly supported by her mother 'until', as she told the *Chronicle*, 'we know that the Movement is in any ways opposed to British interests.

More research by the *Chronicle* unearthed two further committee members, one a businessman and another a retired judge from the Raj, both of whom wished to keep their names a secret. The judge was apparently 'a man of charming personality who is deeply interested in the many problems connected with world affairs' and held 'very pronounced views on the shortcomings of democracy'. He informed the *Chronicle* that

> I am a great admirer of Hitler. When I retired I eventually came to live at Bath, I have been astounded at the financial control, which the Jews have over many

essential phases [sic] of our life, including politics and the press. It always seems to me ridiculous that Mosley's name is never mentioned in the Press. The very name democracy is loathsome to me.[60]

The *Chronicle* found out that Bath and Salzburg were to be linked in an exchange partnership through The Link. In an article on 12 August it observed that Bath was a city full of retired people, 'who had occupied important positions in life and whom Nazi propagandists would very much like to convert to their point of view'. It sarcastically added that in view of the publicity 'for the mooted 'Festival of All the Arts', it was doubtless ... purely coincidental that Bath and Salzburg should be linked'. The journalist went on to report a conversation with Lieutenant-Colonel C D Roe, the Chairman of the Wells branch. Although Roe was not very 'communicative ' about The Link's membership , he did say that the county organiser, A C Streatfield of Shepton Mallet, was the acting chairman until a more permanent appointment could be made. He explained that the essential business of The Link was to get 'Herr Schmidt linked up with the British Mr Smith'. Above all he stressed that the 'Link' was apolitical and consequently he refused to condemn Germany's treatment of the Jews on the grounds that this was a matter for the Germans themselves to deal with. He did, however, concede that he 'went by what a fellow does. There are good Jews and bad Jews, good gentiles and bad gentiles'.

More information was to be gleaned at the meeting at the Little Theatre on 13 August, which Roe chaired. He was supported by the Chairman of the Bristol branch and C H Hewitt, a prospective West Country Fascist parliamentary candidate. The audience were subjected to a tirade against politicians, financiers and the national press. The meeting was well attended by about 150 people, who included Phillip Hopkins and George Desmond, respectively the Liberal and Labour parliamentary candidates for Bath, as well as S R Gould, the former President of the BTLC. Roe was subjected to searching questions about The Link's attitude to the Nazi persecution of the Jews, Hitler's aggressive foreign policy and its own political views. One woman asked outright whether The Link was 'Hitler's Fifth Column', a prominent member of the Peace Pledge Union, Mr. D. Oldham, tellingly remarked that he would 'gladly' join The Link if he could be sure that it let the German people know 'how the English people abhor the terrible treatment meted out to the Czechs'.

The reports of the meeting led to a flurry of predominantly critical letters, which were published in *Chronicle* on 19 August. Desmond quoted with great effect what 'the gallant sailor' (Domville) said about Czechoslovakia in 1938 -namely that it was 'a tumour in the heart of Europe'. Herbert F. Cole, a volunteer teacher at the Christian Adult School in Grove Street, and a devout Congregationalist, pointed out that the Boy Scouts and Workers' Travel Association helped foster international friendship, and feared that The Link was just an attempt to make Fascists and Blackshirts respectable in Britain. As long as Hitler persecuted minorities and was intolerant of dissenting opinions, Cole failed to see how reconciliation with Germany could take place. Another correspondent mockingly dismissed the aims of The Link as 'just a little vague and dream-like -a sort of wish fulfilment'. On the other hand there were some letters in support. One, not surprisingly, was from Mrs Mitchell, the local secretary of the Fascist Party, another from a 'Linker' and a third from Eleanor Kennedy of Shepton Mallet, who argued that The Link presented the 'only way out of the mess the world is in today'. Once war broke out on 3 September, The Link was dissolved and in August 1940 Domville was interned.

WAR AGAIN

CHANCES OF AVOIDING war receded dramatically on 23 August when Stalin signed the Nazi-Soviet Pact. Captain Guy Fanshawe RN, the prospective Conservative candidate for Frome was quick to point out that now the 'black cloud of war was obviously hanging over us' and that 'the situation had changed ... to our disadvantage in a most startling manner...' To Hitler's surprise Britain retaliated by signing the Anglo-Polish Alliance on 25 August.

Even though some clung to the hope that war could still be averted, preparations for the expected 'Emergency' were accelerated. Information about street lighting was updated and owners of factories and large businesses were informed of what precautions were to be taken. The PDSA also circulated information to pet owners about how to protect their pets. The ARP released information as to where public shelters and safety trenches were situated. On Friday 25 August squads of workmen were busy clearing the entrances to the outdoor shelters, and in Pulteney Road and other major thoroughfares trees were painted with white rings to help motorists in the blackout.

Bath's Cooperative shops were effectively put on a war footing on 25 August. At a special meeting the General Manager issued orders that the food departments were to discourage hoarding by only accepting orders from customers for 'normal supplies'. The windows of the bakery and dairy shops were to be blacked out immediately while 'the remainder of the premises were to be dealt with if war comes'. Suitable supplies of paint, sand for sandbags and torches for each department were also to be ordered. The meeting also recommended that the Dispatch and Outfitting Room in Westgate should be strengthened to serve as a shelter for the 162 employees working there. The procedures to be followed if an air raid occurred during business hours were also agreed on:

> During Business hours -Manager of Shop or Department to be responsible for securing premises.
> Cash to be transferred to safe.
> Customers to be given opportunity to leave shop or stay.
> After Business hours- Manager to visit shop after safety signal is given to see that premises are in order.
> Gas and electric and water ... supplies to be switched off every day at closing time.[61]

On 28 August Pickard made arrangements with the Bath Gas Company to organise five repair squads each consisting of an inspector, four men and a car, which would be based at the Bath Gas Company Showrooms and other premises in the city.[62] Four days earlier the RNHRD received the 'stand-by order' from the Ministry of Health, which involved halting the admission of new patients and preparing the operating theatres for emergencies. Classes of nurses were also 'drilled' each day in the action to be taken in the event of air raids.[63] The RUH meanwhile was also calling for 1000 blood donors.

The *Chronicle* observed on Saturday 26 August that 'greater calm is noticeable than a year ago'. Although there was a rush to buy blackout blinds, which a representative of one of Bath's departmental stores compared to the first day of the sales, there was little panic buying. A number of grocers' shops told a reporter that they 'were only laying in slightly larger orders than usual'. There was, however, a large demand for sugar, and shops were limiting the amount their customers could buy. Tinned goods, tea, coffee, beans and candles were also sought after, but surprisingly there was little demand for soap. When the Autumn term began on 28 August, the entry in East Walcot Infants' School's log book made no mention of the impending war. Instead it recorded that during the holidays seven new windows had been made in the classrooms.[64] The *Chronicle* leader for the same day was entitled 'Keep on Keeping Calm', and, against all the odds, it still believed that 'war may yet be avoided', but on Friday 1 September it was clear that this would not happen when German troops crossed the Polish frontier.

It was assumed that Bath was far enough away from London to be relatively safe from air raids. Consequently, both Government ministries and private firms were eying up premises in and around the city. The Air Ministry, the GPO, the Home Office and the Food Controller's Department had all inspected property which was potentially suitable for offices. Viewed from the perspective of the local estate agents, the situation in late August 1939 was 'more satisfactory', according to a report in the *Chronicle* on 31 August, than it had been during the Sudeten crisis. Then, those who could afford it and who were living in vulnerable areas, merely rented property in Bath 'to watch at a safe distance what was going to happen', but now given the gravity of the current crisis 'a number have decided to make their permanent homes in our city'.

However, these prosperous new residents were dwarfed in number by the number of child evacuees from London. On 28 August rehearsals for evacuation were held in London and other cities such as Edinburgh, Leeds and Portsmouth. The possible destination of London children was not disclosed to the general public but the *Chronicle* informed its readers that 'they may be anywhere south of a line from the 'Wash to the Bristol Channel'. On the 30th it warned that 'thousands of children may come to live among us' and would only bring with them hand luggage with one change of clothing. If new clothes or shoes needed to be purchased and the childrens' parents could not be contacted, the city's welfare committee would meet the cost. Shops were laying in extra stores of bedding and blankets, but if these proved insufficient, the council would request neighbours to lend blankets and spare bedding. It was also hoped that volunteers would step in and help with mending and washing clothes. Payments of 3sh. a week per child and 5sh. per adult would be made to householders billeting evacuees. Plans for how this large influx of children would be educated were still rather vague but it seemed that schools would adopt the 'double shift' method whereby local children would attend school in the morning and the evacuees in the afternoon.

Over the next two days preparations for war continued. Volunteers were called on to fill up sandbags and to be ready to accompany evacuees from the station to their billets when they arrived. The council put the city's water supplies on a war footing.[65] Information about the whereabouts of public shelters and what to do in the event of a raid proliferated in the local papers, and all over the city in schools, church halls and clinics demonstrations were given in the use of special gas masks for babies and toddlers. The German invasion of Poland triggered the decision to hand over control in Bath to the Emergency Committee 'in all matters relating to defence'. In Bristol the regional Commissioner and his Deputy for the South-Western Region were appointed by Royal Warrant and the following day ARP personnel throughout the country were mobilsed.[66]

Babies Protective Helmets

Demonstrations in the use of **BABIES' PROTECTIVE HELMETS** will be given at the following addresses at the times stated :—

Warden Group	Place	Times	
A	Widcombe Junior School.	Tues., 29th & Wed., 30th	5—7 p.m
	Church Army Home.	Thursday, 31st	5—7 p.m
	Bathwick Junior School.	Friday, Sept. 1st and	5—7 p.m.
		Saturday, Sept. 2nd	5—7 p.m.
B	St. Mark's Parish Room.	Tuesday, 29th, to Monday, Sept 4th Daily	6—8 p.m.
C & E	Oldfield Park Clinic. Baptist Church Rooms.	Tuesday, 29th to Monday, Sept. 4th Daily	6—8 p.m.
D & L	Southdown Clinic. Southdown Schools.	Tuesday, 29th to Monday. Sept. 4th Daily	7—8 p.m.
F	St. John's School. Lower Weston.	Tuesday, 29th, to Saturday, 2nd Sept. Daily	5—7 p.m.
G & K	Snow Hill Hall.	Tuesday, 29th to Monday, 4th Sept. Daily	6.30—3 p.m.
H & J	Blue Coat Clinic.	Tuesday, 29th to Monday, 4th Sept. Daily 2.30—3.30 p.m.	6.30—7.30 p.m.
M	Odd Down Clinic, New Hall Odd Down	Tuesday, 29th, to Monday, 4th Sept. Daily	6—8 p.m.

All persons responsible for young children who cannot take a small-size Civilian Respirator are advised to attend one of these

Times of demonstrations in the use of 'BABIES' Protective Helmets
(Bath & Wilts Chronicle & Herald, *30 August 1939*)

When the news was received in Bath on the last day of August that the first five train loads of London school children were to arrive on Friday 1 September, the local Schools were closed, as they were to serve as reception centres. At 12.57 pm the first train was full of evacuees, who came from the Ealing area of London, rolled into the GWR station. The mayor and mayoress met them on the platform, and outside there was a large crowd, 'including hundreds of Bath youngsters to welcome their "brothers and sisters"'. Later children arrived from Barking, Limehouse, West Ham and Victoria Dock. The evacuees seemed happy, perhaps thinking that they were on holiday. As the *Chronicle* observed, 'probably few of the arrivals realised the real significance of the departure from their homes'. They were initially taken by bus or on foot in groups of not more than 50 to the reception centres where they were fed prior to being dispatched to their billets. The

WAR DRAWS EVER CLOSER

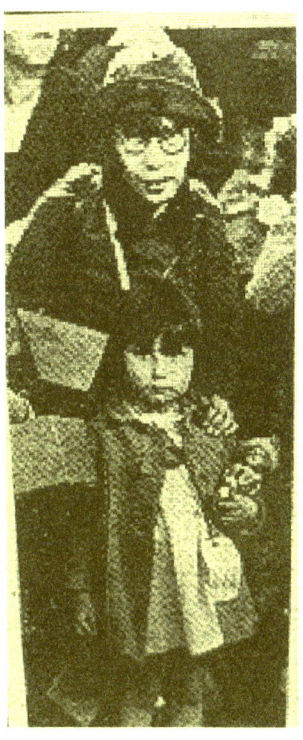

This picture indicates how bewildering many children found the evacuation process. Very much in the words of the time the B&WC&H has added the caption: 'This little London girl has not forgotten her golliwog' (Bath & Wilts Chronicle & Herald, *2 September 1939*)

exodus of evacuees from London continued through the weekend. The first train on Sunday 3 September consisted of about 800 mothers and young children. This time there was no cheering as the mothers were exhausted and when they were told that war had been declared 'there were some pitiful scenes on the platform'.

The log book for Walcot Senior School gives a clear account of how events unfolded: The head recorded:

31 Aug 1.30 Received news that the Government had decided to commence evacuation of school children from London, tomorrow. Dismissed children at 2.45 pm. Staff remained at school until 4.30 making final preparation for the reception of the children.
Head teacher attended a meeting at the technical College at 4.30. Staff met again at 7 o'clock for the discussion of future plans.
Sept 1 All staff at school whole day, received 80 children and five adults
From London
2 Saturday. All staff present all day
3 Sunday. Received nine mothers and 16 children.
Britain declared war on Germany at 11 A.M. today

On 11 September those 80 London children attended Walcot Senior School to register their names and details, and two days later returned for regular tuition - the local children returned on the 12th.[67] At the other schools similar procedures were followed. East Walcot Infants' School, for instance, closed on 31 August 'to enable staff to visit billets in readiness for evacuation', and 'during the first four days of the evacuation' 69 mothers and children were directed to their billets by the teachers. On 12 September its log book recorded:

School re-opened this morning. All children under five to be excluded for the present. No child to be admitted without gas mask. Attendance not to be pressed. ARP and gas mask drill once a week. Children who lived too far to take shelter in houses near if there is an air- raid warning.[68]

Despite the foreboding and the frenetic preparations, some aspects of normal life continued as usual during the last few days of peace. The Ladies Boating Club held its regatta, Trowbridge Carnival attracted large crowds, and at the opening of the shooting season, it was reported that there were abundant quantities of partridges. There was even a notice in the *Chronicle* on 1 September that the Bristol Coach Company was running excursion trips to Barry Island, Minehead and Dunster leaving from the Grand Parade on Sunday 3 September. At the RNHRD, however, there were no illusions of normality. On the afternoon of 1 September the hospital received the following order from the Ministry of Health: 'State of Emergency- clear hospitals'. This entailed sending home as many patients as possible and sending Dr Blackett, Bath's Medical Officer of Health, a daily statement of the number of beds vacant, as well as ensuring all ARP protective measures were in place. Unsurprisingly it was also decided to postpone the ceremony of laying the foundation stone for the new building by Queen Mary 'indefinitely'.[69]

As the expiry time of the British ultimatum to Germany approached at 11 o'clock on Sunday 3 September, most Bathonians listened intently to their wireless sets. The *Chronicle,* however, printed a special edition, which motorists arriving in the city ignorant of the news, were quick to buy. At the Abbey as at St. George's Chapel Windsor, a wireless was placed in the pulpit, and not surprisingly the announcement that war had been declared created a 'profound impression' on the large congregation. Afterwards the Archdeacon told the congregation that it was now inappropriate to conduct the traditional Sunday morning matins and a brief service of intercession was held instead. Ironically a few hours later the Bath Branch of the Old Contemptibles -the men who had faced the German attack in Belgium in August 1914- held their annual Church parade at the Abbey on the very day that another war with Germany had broken out.

CONCLUSION

By 1919 Bath was the leading spa in the British isles, despite the claims of Buxton and Harrogate. Its Georgian architecture gave it a unique character, only rivalled by Edinburgh. It was the Athens of the South West, no less. It had theatres, cinemas and a large number of societies, which could attract eminent people to speak from all over the country and Empire. Bath was no university city, but for all its staid image, it was a city of debate and free speech where minority arguments for pacifism, atheism and euthanasia could be voiced even if not agreed with. It had, too, its dissenting eccentrics such as Major Grenfell, a *soi disant* communist. What happened in Bath received attention in the national press. Admirers of Georgian architecture, especially the London cultural elite, perceived Bath to be a gem of national importance. Its beauty, spa and the surrounding countryside attracted guests from all over the world, as the weekly list of hotel visitors showed in the pages of the Saturday edition of the *Chronicle*. Patients taking the waters and tourists enjoying the city were so vital to Bath's economy that in 1928 the Corporation unsuccessfully tried to hide the news of the Bathwick typhoid outbreak.

It was not, however, just a cultural centre for the highbrow or a spa for those afflicted by arthritis, rheumatism or gout. In its own right the city was also an industrial centre with a working population with its own traditions and interests. It had a clutch of important industries, which in the cases of Pittman and the Bath Cabinet Makers were household names. Stothert and Pitt had a global reach and exported cranes throughout the world. It was, too, a city where a wide range of sports could be enjoyed, Its rugby team was famous and the Spring Race Meeting was sometimes called the 'Ascot of the West'. While Bath City Football Club was not a First Division team, it encouraged soccer in and around the city where there were numerous local teams, not least the Bath Ladies' team in the early twenties.

Nevertheless Bath's genteel and cultured image could inspire vitriolic hatred, as was sometimes displayed in demonstrations in Sawclose. The city had a large middle class population, many of whom were ex-officers in the armed forces or colonial administrators or their widows, as well as a sprinkling of aesthetes of whom, Horace Annesley Vachell, Frederic Harrison and Mowbray King were the best known, Yet there were other Baths such as the one inhabited by lonely spinsters in private hotels or bed sits., and the slums around Avon Street, the areas of working class housing in Twerton and Oldfield Park as well as the new housing estates springing up on the outskirts of the city. Class divisions were deep but could at times be bridged. The drive to provide work during the Great Depression of 1931-3 met with an enthusiastic response and Mayor Adrian Hopkins, a staunch Conservative and enthusiastic Imperialist, was also a doughty champion of migrant workers coming from the distressed areas to work in Corsham, many of whom lived in Bath.

Bath's economy weathered the tempestuous inter-war years. Although the city did not suffer on anywhere near the same scale as the old industrial areas of Britain, successive economic and financial crises took their toll. Unemployment rose in Bath during 1921-24 and 1929-33. Yet throughout these crises the spa, the Roman baths and the matchless Georgian architecture continued to attract tourists and money into the city. At the same time Bath adapted to the modern world. Progress was made in slum clearance, modern flats were constructed in Kingsmead, which would not have been out of place in Weimar Germany, and council houses were built in the outskirts of the city. The council also sought to come to terms with the potentially destructive age of the motor car but its controversial plans for street widening were often opposed by the Bath Preservation Trust.

In the late thirties Bath, like the whole country, was experiencing rapid technological change, growing secularism and increasing demands for the equality of the sexes. Its relatively static population was confronted between 1936-39 with a substantial influx of workers from the distressed regions. It was also exposed to the challenging ideologies of socialism, passivism and anti-imperialism, even though these were inimical to most well off Bathonians. Yet its essentially traditional nature survived. It was still packed with retired imperial administrators, colonels, admirals and distressed gentlewomen. It remained predominantly a patriotic 'Red, White and Blue Town', which regularly returned a Conservative MP.

Neither was Bath insulated from global events. The course of the Russian Revolution was followed by some with fear and loathing and by others, who viewed it as a blueprint for paradise. An alternative model for peace and harmony was seen by many Bathonians to lie with the League of Nations. The brief lull in international tension after 1925 was greeted with relief in Bath, and once again groups of German students were welcomed to the city. Yet the rise of Hitler and the rearmament of Germany triggered a growing feeling of insecurity, which was arguably reinforced rather than lessened by the very necessary air raid precautions that began to take shape from 1935 onwards. When war broke out in September 1939, Bath was seen as a 'safe town', and was lulled into a false sense of security until April 1942 when the Baedeker Blitz found the city ill prepared to deal with the fire bombs that caused so much damage and death.

NOTES

A Preliminary note on Bath's newspapers, 1919-39
In 1919 the Wessex Associated News (Ltd) were the proprietors of the *Bath and Wilts Chronicle* and the *Bath Weekly Chronicle*. Messrs William Lewis and Son (LTD) were the proprietors of the *Bath Herald* and the *Bath Weekly Herald*. Both the *Bath and Wilts Chronicle* and the *Bath Herald* were evening papers and the *Weekly Chronicle* and *Weekly Herald* appeared on Saturday. In April 1925 the two evening papers were amalgamated and the new *Bath and Wilts Chronicle and Herald* was published in their place as an evening paper. The *Weekly Chronicle* and the *Weekly Herald* were also amalgamated and appeared each Saturday as *The Bath Chronicle and* Herald. In May 1935 it changed its name to the *Bath Weekly Herald and Chronicle.* In the text below I refer to all editions of both the weekly *Chronicle* and the daily *Bath and Wilts Chronicle and Herald* as simply the *Chronicle*. In the footnotes I give the date and indicate which paper I am quoting from- *The Bath and Wilts Chronicle and Herald* is referred to as the *B&WC&H* and the weekly *Chronicle* simply as the *BC (Bath Chronicle)*. In the inter-war years the *Bath Chronicle* often transcribed speeches into the third person instead of reporting them *verbatim* as is standard practice today.

Chapter 1
1 Duncan Harper, *Bath at Work*, Bath, 1989, p.5.
2 *BC*, 9 November 1918. (Unless otherwise stated *BC* denotes the weekend edition of the *Bath Weekly Chronicle*.)
3 Diary of SH Silvester, 11 November & 7 December 1918, BRO 1052.
4 *Annual Report of the Schools Medical Officer of Health*, 1918, p. 8, BRO.
5 Ibid.
6 East Walcot Girls' School log book,19 September 1918, BRO 0699/2/3.
7 *Annual Report* of the SMO, 1918, p.9, BRO.
8 *Annual Report* of the MOH, 1919, p. 36, ibid.
9 *BC*,16 November 1918.
10 Ibid., 1 & 22 February 1919 (See ibid., 30 November 1918 for the October statistics).
11 K Ainsworth, 10 November 1918, to Mamma and Wyn, BRO 0369/1/26.
12 *BC*, 16 November 1918.
13 Summery of Tape no.64, Oral History Project (OHP), MOBAW.
14 East Walcot Girls' School log book, 11 November 1918, BRO 0699/2/3.

15 CT Foxcroft, *The Night Sister,* London, 1918, p. 20. See also Bath Conservative Association, Press cuttings, 1910-47, BRO 0012/2.
16 *BC*, 14 December 1918.
17 Bath Cooperative Society Minute Book (hereafter BCS), 10 December 1918, BRO 0591/1/1/15.
18 *BC*, 7 December 1918.
19 KA to 'Dearest Mamma', 1 December 1918, BRO 0369/1/28.
20 *BC*, 21 December 1918.
21 KA to 'Dearest Mamma', 22 January 1919, BRO 0369/1/29.
22 *BC*, 29 March 1919.
23 Ibid., 1 February 1919.
24. Tarrant-Bailey to Countess Temple, 11 December 1918, Temple papers, BRO 0442 (uncatalogued). Richard Bailey was better known as Tarrant-Bailey (sometimes with a hyphen, sometimes without) as he advertised his banjo band under that name. Throughout the book I refer to him at Tarrant-Bailey.
25 See Owen Keevil's correspondence, January-April 1919, with G Staddon, FR Withers, G Hull, Mrs. Miles and RD Nicholds , Archives of the FEU, MOBAW H4/12.
26 Ibid., Keevil to Stadden, 30 January 1919.
27 Ibid., Withers to Keevil, 23 January 1919.
28 Ibid., 6 February 1919.
29 N Macmillan with M Chapman, *A History of the Fuller's Earth Mining Around Bath*, 2009, p. 46. For the ceremony at Newton Park see GD Davis, *The Langtons at Newton Park*, Bath, 1980, p. 27.
30 *BC*, 20 June 1919.
31 Ibid., 5 July 1919.
32 Ibid., 22 November 1919.
33 Orlando Figes, *A People's Tragedy*, London, 1997, p. 563.
34 *BC*, 14 June1919.
35 Ibid., 9 August 1919.
36 Charles F Masterman, *England After War*, London, 1922, p.4.
37 Ernest Carter to Chief Constable, 24 October 1919, Bath City Police, BRO 0661/2/3 and correspondence in the scrapbook of the Organist Benjamin C.Maslen, 1916-27, BRO 0414/1.
38 OHP 56, MOBAW.
39 Author's interview with Patricia Connett, 20 January 2020.
40 *BC*, 1 November 1919.
41 Mins. of Bath NUT branch, 29 August 1919, BRO 0394/6
42 See correspondence with Miss Rebecca Rusk, Partis College papers, BRO 0423/16 and 0423/4/2/51.
43 BCS, 9 December 1919 and 17 March 1920, BRO 0591/1/1/16.
44 See BTLC Report and balance Sheet for 1919, pp.4-5, BRO 0591/11/10. See also *BC,* 15 November 1919. Stothert and Pitt's correspondence during the inter-war years 1930s was unfortunately either destroyed by the bombing of the offices of the company in 1942, disposed of as paper salvage during WW2 or destroyed when the firm was wound up in 1989. MOBAW has a complete set

of catalogues, technical information, and promotional literature from Stothert & Pitt as well as a collection of 40,000 images. Consequently for labour relations and policy questions the historian is inevitably dependent on the local press.
45 *BC,* 11 October 1919.
46 Ibid., 21 November 1918.
47 Ibid., 28 June 1919.
48 See *BC,* 30, August 1919.
49 See reference in *BC,* 20 September 1919 to an article by Clifford Essex in the *BMG* , 'a monthly journal devoted to affairs concerning the banjo, mandolin and guitar'.
50 Tarrant-Bailey to Welsh , 28 February 1919, BRO 0442/1/2.
51 see references in BCS mins. for January 1919, BRO 0591/1/1/15.
52 Andrew Swift, *All Roads lead to France*, Bath, 225 p. 30.

Chapter 2

1 *BC,* 2 October 1920.
2 BTLC Report for 1920, BRO 0591/11/10.
3 *BC,*16 October 1920.
4 Ibid., 12 March 1921.
5 Ibid., 22 December 1923.
6 See Ibid., 16 February 1924 for description of the whole incident and Heath's letter.
7 Ibid., 20 December 1924.
8 Foxcroft Papers (undated), BRO 0060/2/1.
9 *BC,*17 September 1921.
10 Foxcroft Papers, July 1922 and July 1923, BRO 0060/1/4 & 0060/1/2.
11 *BC,* 20 August 1921.
12 Ibid., 12 February 1921.
13. Ibid, 18 March 1922 (for text of the play see BRO 0060/1/2). C and R Lanyon (?) to the Misses Foxcroft, 21 February 1929, BRO 0060/2/6.
14 *BC,* 17 July 1920.
15 Letter from Jackman with Tabb's pencil notes in the margin, 13 September 1920, MOBAW, BPM 38. For statistics on free school meals see *BC*, 6 November 1920.
16 *BC*, 6 March 1920.
17 NUT mins., 15 October 1920, Bath Branch, BRO 0394/7.
18 United Alkali Co to BPM,19 October 1920, MOBAW, BPM 38.
19 Tarrant-Bailey to Countess Temple, 8 September 1920, BRO 0442/1/3.
20 Lister to Sidney A Hortsmann, 19 March 1921, Catalogue of Personal and Business papers compiled by Mrs J. Merry, MOBAW. 6/44 (hereafter catalogue). Merry spells Sidney's surname as Horstmann throughout the catalogue.
21 July 1921, ibid., 6/47.
22 22 January, 8 &10 February 1922, ibid., 6/57/1-4, 6/59 & 6/53.
23 Hortsmann to ?, 14 January 1922, ibid 6/56.

24 Ibid., Lister to Horstmann, 19 June 1922.
25 Bethell, Gwyn and Co to BPM, 5 March 1921 and Shell-Mex Ltd to BPM, 11 February 1921, MOBAW BPM 40.
26 BTLC Report for 1921, BRO 0591/11/1-4; BCS, 9 August 1921 & 14 March 1922 BRO 0591/11/10 . For unemployment statistics see *BC*, 12 February &12 November 1921.
27 J Fish and Sons to BPM, 10 June 1921 ; BP to BPM, 27 June 1921, MOBAW BPM 41.
28 Ibid., Piston Collieries to BPM, 4 July 1921.
29 *BC*, 7 May 1921.
30 TCS Mins.,14 & 28 June 1921,BRO 0591/2/1/2.
31 'Report for 1921' BTLC, BRO 0591/11/10.
32 Diary of William Chun, October-December 1923, BRO 0802/1; Ted Ashman, *The Early Years: A Personal Account*,1912-1973, (handwritten account) Bath WEA Records, BRO 0630/13. The unemployment statistics on page 63 are quoted in the *Bath BC*, 7 January & 25 February 1922.
33 Foxcroft papers, BRO 0060/1/4.
34 Ibid., Bagshaw to Foxcroft, 20 October 1922.
35 The Election is covered in: Conservative Association Press Cuttings 1910- 1923, BRO 0012/2/2.
36 *Bath Herald*,14 November 1922.
37 S Horstmann to Manager of City and Midland Bank, 17 September 1923 & W Gough to 'Uncle Sidney' (undated), MOBAW Catalogue 6/81 & 6/83. See *BC*, 24 March & 6 October 1923 for unemployment statistics.
38 *BC*, 8 December 1923. For Foxcroft on referenda see General Committee of Bath Conservative Association, 21 November 1923, BRO 0012/1/3.
39 *BC*, 24 May 1924.
40 Ibid.
41 Ibid. (20 September1924).
42 15 October 1924, BTLC, BRO 0591/11/1.
43 *BC*, 25 October 1924.

Chapter 3
1 *BC*, 22 January 1921.
2 John Hatton, *The hot springs of Bath: medical handbook*, Bath, 1921 (reprinted, 2012).
3 *BC*, 19 November 1921.
4 Ibid., 9 November 1922.
5 Ibid., 29 December 1923.
6 Ibid., 10 June 1922.
7 Ibid., 3 June 1922.
8 Ibid., 3 February 1923 .
9 Undated letter (1920), 'To the Editor', BRO 0442 (uncatalogued).
10 *BC*, 29 October 1921. For a history of Bath's cinemas see Aaron Evans, 'Collective Dreams: A History of Bath's Cinemas' in *Bath History*, vol XII pp. 157-165, 2011.

11 East Walcot Girls' School Log Book, 1911-1969, 22 &25 January 1920, BRO 0699/2/5.
12 Quoted in *BC*, 5 May 1923.
13 Ibid., 19 January 1924.
14 Order to M. Brown (newsagents), 24 December 1918; See letters of 4 December 1919, 29 November & 18 December 1920, Harrington Club papers, BRO 0574/17/1.
15 Mins. of Widcombe's Workingmen's Club, 14 April 1924, BRO 0102F/29.
16 Minute Books of Dickens' Fellowship, 1921-28, 16 March 1921, BRO. 0163/1.
17 *B&WC&H*, 6 & 8 February 1924 . (See press cuttings in ibid.)
18 *Ibid.*, 1 October 1924: 'If Dickens returned to Bath'.
19 *Ibid.,* 29 &30 December 1924.
20 *BC,* 5 November 1921.
21 M Turner, *75 Years, 1912-87, WEA Bath Branch*, Bradford -on-Avon, 1987, p.27 BRO. 0630/1. See also 0630/1/6 for statistics.
22 Turner, *75 Years*, p.29 ; and *Bath WEA: Ted Ashman, The Early Years.*
23 *BC,* 17 February 1923.
24 Ibid., 23 September 1922.
25 Ibid., 14 October 1922.
26 Ibid.
27 Ibid., 13 May 1922
28 Ibid., 24 July 1920
29 Ibid., 12 March 1921

Chapter 4

1 See Robin Pakes, *Tradition and Modernity in Bath Between the Wars*, M.Phil. thesis, Bath University, 2016, p.43.
2 *BC* ,25 October 1924.
3 Ibid., 22 November 1924. This issue also includes a detailed list of proposals.
4 Ibid., 24 January 1925.
5 Ibid., 11 April 1925.
6 Robin Lambert, 'The Bath Corporation Act of 1925', *Transactions of the Ancient Monuments Society*, vol. 44, 2000 p.53.
7 *Bath Chronicle and Herald*, 13 June 1925. (Hereafter still referred to as *BC*).
8 Ibid, 20 June 1925.
9 Ibid, 22 January 1927.
10 City Improvements Committee, 22 November 1927, City of Bath Council and Committee Minutes, 1927, pp.1059-1062 BRO. See also *BC,* 21 April 1928.
11 Ibid., 15 September 1928.
12 Parkhouse interview, MOBAW, OHP 12
13 *BC,* 9 June 1929.
14 Ibid., 12 February 1927. For list of these properties see ibid, 1 January 1927.
15 Special Council Meeting, 24 July 1928, City of Bath and Council Minutes, 1928, pp.578-584 and & City Improvement Committee, 15 March 1929, ibid, 1929, pp.224-25. See also Brochure of the Kingsmead Housing Development, BRO 0128/6/1 and *BC,* 7 & 28 July 1928.

16 See the full report in *BC* 15 June 1929 and the Bath Preservation Trust (BPT) Archives 'A Special Revival Meeting of the Old Bath Preservation Society', 10 June 1929, BPT1/10/1/1. For the quotation from Villiers-Bayley see BC, 20 June 1925.
17 *BC*, 31 March 1928.

Chapter 5
1 FEU Monthly Summaries 1915-67 (internal-external Correspondence), 1925, MOBAW.
2 Ibid.
3 Horstmann to Ernest J White and Co, 14 May 1925; and 'Agreement', Catalogue, MOBAW 6/90 & 6/91.
4 *BC*, 24 January 1925.
5 Ibid., 1 August 1925.
6. 27 & 31 July & 12 August 1925, BTLC, BRO 0591/11/1. See also BC, 15 August 1925.
7 *BC*, 15 August 1925.
8 R. Benewick, *Political Violence and Public Order*, London, 1969, p. 27.
9 *BC*, 19 September 1925.
10 Ibid., 3 October 1925.
11 Ibid., 31 October 1925.
12 Ibid., 13 February 1926.
13 BTCS (Bath Society Minute Book), 23 April 1926, BRO 0591/2/1/13.
14 *BC*, 1 May 1926.
15 FEU, External Correspondence for Combe Hay Works, January-May 1926, MOBAW H3/5.
16 *BC*, 8 May 1926.
17 Ibid
18 Tarrant- Bailey to Countess Temple, 11 March 1926, BRO 0442 /1/3.
19 BTCS, 4 May 1926, BRO 0591/2/1/13.
20 Roy Hattersley, *Borrowed Time*, London, 2009, p.133.
21 *BC*, 8 May 1926.
22 Ibid.
23 Ibid.
24 Chun, Diary, 7 & 8 May 1926, BRO, 0802/1.
25 *BC*, 8 May 1926.
26 Ibid., 15 May 1926.
27 Keevil to J Lambern, 15 May 1926, FEU External correspondence, MOBAW H3/5.
28 BTLC, 27 October 1926, BRO 0591/11/1.
29 See Henderson, Craig and Co. Ltd to BPM, 13 & 27 May1926, MOBAW BPM 60; and Sir John Francis, Ltd to BPM, 29 May 1926, Ibid. BPM 61.
30 BTLC, 27 October 1926, BRO 0591/11/1.
31 *BC*, 30 October 1926.
32 Keevil to Coal Controller, Bath Rural District Council, 26 & 28 May 1926 & his reply of the 27th. MOBAW H3/5.

33 Keevil to J. Wesley Whimster, 29 May 1926 & to Whittington 16 June 1926, ibid.
34 Keevil to Whittington, 1 June and Whittington to Keevil, 2 June 1926, ibid.
35 Keevil to Whittingdon, 3 June 1926; (pp.) Whittington to Keevil 4 June 1926, Ibid.
36 Keevil to Whittington, 14 June 1926, Whittington to Keevil, 15 June 1926 & Keevil to Whittington, 16 June 1926, ibid.
37 Whittington to Keevil, 17 &19 June 26, ibid.
38 See Keevil to Messrs Lowell Baldwin, ltd, 23 September 1926 and further correspondence, September-December 1926, ibid.
39 Circular from Chief Goods Manager, December 1926, ibid.

Chapter 6

1 *BC*, 15 December 1928 . For the development of the council's education programme see ibid., 19 October, 23 November 1929 & 19 March 1932.
2 47 OHP MOBAW.
3 *BC*, 19 September 1925.
4 37, 121 & 39, OHP MOBAW.
5 *BC*, 23 October 1920.
6. Log book, Walcot Senior Boys' School and Bath Diocesan Girls' School, 27 April 1937 BRO 0827/2/2.
7 interviews with Doreen Williams, 18 November.2019 and Patricia Connett, 20 January 2020.
8 113 OHP MOBAW.
9 Ibid. 37.
10 Register of Admission, Progress and Withdrawal, 1917-1941, West Central School BRO 0305/2.
11 42 OHP MOBAW.
12 Interview with Patricia Connett and 152/153 OHP.
13 Ibid.113.
14 Ibid. 42.
15 *BC*, 3 September 1927.
16 122 OHP.
17 For both Blackett's warning and statistics see Annual Report of the MOH, 1930, p.46, BRO
18 *BC,* 26 September 1925.
19 Ibid., 3 September 1927.
20 39 OHP.
21 ibid 152/3.
22 Mary Dale, *Florence Mary Keyes* (memoirs written in 2013 and sent to author, 28 January 2020). For infant mortality see G Davis and P Bonsal, *A history of Bath*, Keele, 1996, pp. 261-2.
23 Interview with Doreen Williams and 39 OHP.
24 *BC*, 5 February 1927. For the statistics re deaths and births see *BC*, 21 January 1928.
25 Ibid., 28 April 1928.

26 See Robert Millard's excellent, *An Unfortunate Incident Has Occurred': The Typhoid Outbreak in Bathwick, 1928* in Ed. Graham Davis, *Bath Exposed*, Bath, 2007, pp.149-182, on which much of this section is based.
27 Typhoid Epidemic, 26 May1928, BRO BC/7/1/15/97/1.
28 For press References and quotations see BRO BC/7/1/15/97/31.
29 Ibid., 'Note of Interview' (signed Basil Ogden) 6 June 1928.
30 Millard *An Unfortunate Incident*, pp. 160-1.
31 See undated min. signed by Croom Johnson: 'Bathwick Water Supply'; draft letter 'Without Prejudice', 28 July1928; letter to 'Dear Sirs', 30 July1928; and Bingham and Sharp to Ogden, 12 July 1928 & 22 November 1928; as well as other correspondence BRO BC/7/1/15/97/1.
32 See min. of 11 November 1928 and other correspondence BRO BC/7/1/15/ 97/2.
33 See Patterson to Blackett, 18 May1928; Blackett to Ogden, 4 June 1928 & to Patterson, 24 May 1928; S.Rouse, Vulliamy and sons to Ogden, 2 October 1928 and see also other correspondence, BRO BC/7/1/15/97/7.
34 Shum to Ogden, 20 June & Thatcher to Ogden, 12 July 1928, BRO BC/7/1/15/97/8.
35 Hoyle to S.Leighton Heard,10 August; Ogden to Ellis, 21 August; & Alice Ellis to Ogden, 27 August1928, BRO BC/7/1/15/97/10; Memorandum on 'Miss Lawson, decd', 25 September 1928 BRO BC/7/1/15/97/9; and Millard, pp.160-61.
36 Blackett to Medical Practitioners in Bath, 26 May 1939 BRO 0219/6/8; Annual Report of the MOH, 1939, p.22 BRO; also *Chronicle*, 26 February and 2 April 1938.
37 *BC*, 5.1.24
38 Ibid., 13 April1929.
39 MOH to 'Doctors practising in Bath', 12 April1938, BRO 01219/6/8.

Chapter 7
1 168 OHP, MOBAW
2 Juliet Gardiner, *The Thirties*, London, 2011, p. 530.
3 Chun, Diary, 14 April 1928, BRO 0802/1.
4 *BC*, 11July 1931.
5 12 &11 OHP MOBAW.
6 Ibid.121.
7 Pauline Forrest, *Childhood Memoirs,* Bath, 2008, p.30.
8 Applications and correspondence, Partis College. BRO 0423/4/1. See also Elizabeth White, 'Your Blessed Asylum: Mrs Partis, and her College for Distressed Gentlewomen', Bath, 1826 in Ed. Graham Davis *Bath Exposed, Bath,* 2007, pp, 39-60.
9 Forrest, p.11.
10 Mary Dale, *Florence Mary Keyes*, interview with author, 15 January 2020 & email 24 November 2022.
11. 26 OHP, MOBAW.
12 See *BC*, 24 November1934 & extracts from the MOH's report for 1934 in ibid., 3August1935.

13 36 OHP, MOBAW.
14 Tarrant-Bailey to Countess Temple, 21 January 1926, BRO 0442/4/1.
15 37 OHP, MOBAW (Mr Perry is recorded erroneously as having said King Feisal of Persia.) See also Sally Festing, 'Charles Richter and the Bath Cabinet Makers. The Early Years', *Bath History vol vii,* 1998, p. 162.
16 123 OHP, MOBAW. For the development of the Slow Motion Suspension system see Catalogue of the Horstman papers: Slow Motion Suspension, MOBAW, 15/1-49.
17 115 OHP.
18 Ibid.63.
19 Ibid. 72 and 65.
20 Ibid. 40.
21 Ibid. 56.
22 Ibid. 34. The original summery erroneously reads 'Spear, Butler and Clarke'.
23 Ibid. 103.
24 Interview with Patricia Connett, 20 January 2020 and 122 OHP.
25 Ibid 61(Gertie Smith), 62 and 28.
26 Newman to Chivers, 14 May 1928. BRO 0490/1/2.
27 103, 11 & 38 OHP, MOBAW.
28 Forrest, *Childhood Memoirs,* p. *38.*
29 56 OHP & Mary Dale, *Florence Mary Keyes* .
30 ibid 2 & 56 ; Mary Dale ibid.
31 Ibid 63.
32 Ibid; and *Florence Mary Keyes.*
33 39 and 41 OHP MOBAW.
34 Forrest, *Childhood memoirs,* pp.36-7.
35 39 OHP, MOBAW.

Chapter 8

1. Foxcroft to Exec. Cttee. of Conservative Association, 27 March 1919, BRO 0012/1/3; Tarrant to H. Foxcroft, 23 February 1929 ibid., 0060/2/6. For Baillie-Hamilton's acceptance speech see *B&WC&H,* 26 February 1929.
2 *BC,* 9 November 1929; R Boyce and EM Robertson (eds.), *Paths to War,* Basingstoke and London, 1989, p. 55.
3 *BC* 2 May 1931. See also for full account of the Annual Meeting and Baillie-Hamilton's relations with the Conservative Party, Conservative Association Press Cuttings, 1929-47, BRO 0012/2/3 and the relevant minutes of the Association's cttees.in ibid./1/4.
4 *BC,* 23 May 1931.
5 Nicholds to OE Keevil, 14 October 1931, Internal correspondence, 1931-32, FEU G2/12, MOBAW.
6 Lloyds Packing Warehouse Ltd, (?)30 September 1931 to BPM, MOBAW, BPM 79.
7 37 OHP, MOBAW.
8 J. Reynolds to Managing Director, 18 August 1931, ibid., BPM 79 .
9 Monthly Summaries, May 1932; and Keevil to Nicholds, 5.& 6 August 1931,

ibid., FEU G2/12.
10 See Cedric Chivers, ltd., 'Report of the Board of Directors for the year, 1931 and 1932'.Meetings of Directors and AGM Shareholder, BRO 0490/2/1/2.
11 Both letters in BC, 30 July 1932.
12 General Order Book, no. 24 , Chief Constable's Office, 28 November 1931. BRO 0661/3/1.
13 NUT mins, 7 October 1932, BRO 0394/8.
14 24 and 113 OHP, MOBAW.
15 BTLC, 12 March 1930, BRO 0591/11/2.
16 Mins of PAC, 21 May 1930, City of Bath Council and Committee mins,1930, p.426.
17 PAC mins, 19 October 1932, ibid. 1932, p. 719; See also *BC*, 22 October 1932.
18 BTLC, 11 January 1933, BRO 0591/11/3.
19 *BC*, 17 February 1934.
20 Leading article in Ibid, 21 January 1933.
21 'Proposed New Central Premises' , BCS,10 March1931, BRO 059/2/1/16.
22 *BC*, 30 May 1931.
23 BTLC ,13.4.32, BRO 0591/11/3.
24 Earl Temple to Farrer and Co, 1 July 1932, BRO 0525/11/3/1. See also G D Davis, *The Langtons at Newton Park*, Bath 1980, p.26.
25 Bath City police, General Order Book, No. 111, 28 November 1932, BRO 0661/3/1.
26 *BC,* 17 December 1932.

Chapter 9
1 *BC*, 21 August 1937.
2 *B&WC&H* 11July 1934 . For the Conservative Party's internal debate on India see Bath Conservative Association, Press Cuttings July-December 1934, BRO 0012/2/3 and the minutes of the Association's cttes, 1932-34 BRO 0012/1/4.
3 Bagshaw to the Chairman, 8 December 1934 BRO 0012/1/4.
4 P. Forrest, *Childhood Memories* , pp. 24-5 & 63.
5 *BC*, 19 June 1939.
6 Ibid., 29 November 1930.
7 BTLC, 11 October 1933, BRO 0591/11/3.
8 *BC,* 6 February 1937.
9 General Order 402, Public Order Act, 1936 BRO 0661/3/1.
10 See *BC*, 27 October 1934.
11 Ibid., 17 November1934.
12 Ibid., 8 December 1934.
13 *B&WC&H*, 17 July 1935.
14 *BC*, 28 September 1935.
15 Interview with Philip Morris, 22 November 2019.
16 41 OHP MOBAW.
17 *BC*, 24 October 1936.
18 Interview with Alan Gait, 6 February 2020.
19 K. Bowers, *Imperial Exile, Emperor Haile Selassie in Britain, 1936-40*, Bath, 2016,

p.99.
20 41 OHP MOBAW and Lutz Haber, 'Emperor Haile Selassie I in Bath, 1936-1940', *Bath History*, p. 168.
21 *BC*, 9 October 1937 , See also Haber, *Emperor*, p. 170.
22 Bowers, *Imperial Exile*, p. 98 Haber, *Emperor*, pp.170-176.
23 *BC*, 29 August 1936.
24 Ibid., 26.Sptember 1936.
25 Leaflet headed 'Air Raid Precautions' from the Home Office, 9 July 1935 And copy of Watch Committee mins.,19 July1935, in ARP Cttee. General Correspondence, Part (hereafter P) 1 (July 1935- 28 September 1936) BRO; 'Appendix to Council Summons, 1 December.1936, City of Bath Council and Committee Mins, 1936, pp. 923-925 (BRO have not yet catalogued these P files).
26 For Hodsell's lecture and report headed 'Air Raid Precautions. Report of Meeting Held in Bristol,15 October 1935 see ibid P.1.
27 For further details see relevant correspondence and Langford Hill's letter to Town Clerk, received 30 September 1935, ibid P.1.
28 Home Office to town clerks, 16 October 1936, ARP Cttee, General Correspondence, P2 (29 September 1936-16 December 1936), BRO.
29 Copy of mins of ARP Sub-cttee, 23 July 1936 in BRO P.1
30. 'Description of an Air Raid showing the services at work', 25 April 1936 ibid., P1
31 'Air Raid Precautions', Blackett to Ogden 30 January 1936, ibid.
32 Memorandum dated 10 June 1936: 'Air Raid Precautions', ibid.
33 'Air Raid Precautions', Chief Constable's Office,15 October 1936, ibid. P.2.
34 'Air Raid Precautions', Appendix to Council Summons Council, 1 December 1936, City of Bath Council and Committee Minutes, 1936, p.925.
35 East Walcot Girls' School log book, 1911-69, 5 June.1935, BRO 0699/2/5.
36 *BC*, 9 November1935.
37 Walcot Senior School and Bath Diocesan Girls School, log book, 20-21 January 1936 &14 December 1936, BRO 0827/2/1 &2.
38 *BC*, 5 December 1936.

Chapter 10
1 '*Bath*, John Betjeman, Mowbray A Green, A W Wills. Broadcast on 17 April 1939 in the Regional Programme and the Western Programme.' See also Robin Lambert, 'Patrick Abercrombie in Bath'. *Bath History*, vol viii, 2000, pp 172-96.
2 *BC*, 24 June 1939.
3 Robin Pakes, *Tradition and Modernity*, p.53. See *BC*, 26 October, 1935 for a summary of the proposals.
4 Robin Pakes, *Tradition and Modernity*, pp 51-3. H A Vachell, *The Golden House*, London, 1937; leaflet in 'Bath Corporation 1935-37', BPT 1/10/2/1.
5 Lambert, *Abercrombie*, p. 180.The report is published in full in *BC*, 2 December 1935.
6 Ibid., 4 January 1936.
7 See ibid., 22 January 1938 for draft schedule of buildings to be preserved. For the text of the Act and the preliminary proceedings in Parliament see *Bath Corporation Bill, Proceedings*, 1936-37, pp.1-68. For a summary of its contents see *BC* 24 October 1936.

8 Annual Reports of the BPT, June 1938 and June 1939, BPT 1/9/1/ 4-5. 'Report on Bath School of Art Supplied by the Head Master on the Occasion of the General Inspection, March 1939 for H.M. Inspectors', Records of Clifford, Rosemary and Penelope Ellis and Bath Academy of Art BRO 1177/3/4.
9 Library and Art Gallery Committee, 21 June 1934, Council and Cttee Mins., 1934, p.487 and ibid., 'Special', 19 February 1936, City of Bath Council and Committee Minutes, 1936, pp.225-226.
10 School log book 19 October 1938. BRO 0699/2/5 (In 1937 East Walcott Girls' School became an infants only school.) ; Author's Interview with Doreen Williams, 18 November 2019 and letter to Doreen's mother from Marjorie Whimster, 24 October 1938; BTLC Report for 1938, BRO 0591/11/10.
11 Report on Bath School of Art ...', BRO 1177/3/ 4
12 Bath WEA: Ted Ashman, 'The Early Years. BRO 0630/13. See also John Kite, 'The Struggle for a Public Library', *Bath History*, Vol IV, 1992, pp.136-154
13 Report of Library and Art Gallery Committee, 21 June 1934, Council and Committee Minutes, 3 July 1934.
14 *BC*, 23 May 36.
15 Ibid. 2, April 1938.
16 *Evening World*, 26 March 1930; *Western Daily Press,*19 March 1930; Cammaerts is quoted in the *Daily Telegraph*, 25 April 1935, newspaper cuttings in BRO 'Festival of Contemporary Arts, 1930, Pump Room, Bath, 20 March to 5 April, 1930' and 'Second Festival of Contemporary Arts, Pump Room, Bath , 24 April to 8 May, 1935' (uncatalogued).
17 'Report on Bath School of Art ...'
18 'To Whom it May Concern' ,13 January 1948; and Bridget Aster to Mrs.Ellis, January 12 (no year given) BRO 1177/3/4.
19 Private and Confidential For HM Inspectors', ibid. See also *BC*, 4 &18 September1937.
20 Sickert to Clifford Ellis, 23 March1939 and Ellis' Broadcast Script: 'Aspects of Walter Sickert (III)'. Recorded 10 August 1960; transmission, 19.11.1966, BRO 1177/3/28.
21 Kate Fryer is quoted in Philippa Bishop, 'Walter Sichert (1860-1942). Painter of the Bath Scene', *Bath History*, Vol IX, 2002, p.161.
22 Report of the Bath Pump Room sub-Committee (Appendix to Spa Committee) 15.12.1938, Council and Committee Mins 1939, pp.91-99. See also *BC* 7 January 1939.
23 Ibid., 12 November 1938.
24 BPT Minute Book, 1934-64, 2 March 1939, BPT 1/2/1.
25 *BC*, 21.1.39.
26 Summary of Statistics, *Annual Report of the MOH and of the Chief Sanitary Inspector* , p.6, 1939, BRO 158.
27 *BC*, 8.May 1937.
28 Ibid., 23 July 1938.
29 Ibid., 30 July 1938.
30 Ibid., 24 June 1939.
31 Ibid., 10 September1938.

32 Ibid., 22 January1938.
33 Free Church Council, Meetings, 12 September, 14 November 1938 & 16.January 1939 BRO 0042/1.
34 *BC*, 12 November 1938.
35 Ibid., 17 December 1938.
36 Ibid., 23 December 1938.
37 *B&WC&H* , 17 March 1939. The situation is covered comprehensively in Bath Conservative Association, Press Cuttings, BRO 0012/2/3.
38 Statistics quoted by J.H. Walker, Managing Director of the *Weekly Bath Chronicle and Herald*, 27 February 1937. See also Robin Lambert, *Patrick Abercrombie*, p.180. The cine film coverage of the Widcombe Children's Cinema Club outing to Weymouth in 1937 contains several street scenes in which only the odd horse drawn vehicle appears. BRO 2588/8.
39 *BC*, 28 May 1938; Appendix to Watch Committee, 13 July 1938, City of Bath Council and Committee minutes, 1938, pp.753-758.
40 BPT to Min of Transport, 1 February 1938, BPT 2/3/11/1.
41 Patrick Abercrombie and Betrand Brueton, *Bristol and Bath Regional Planning Scheme*, London, 1930, p.110.
42 Bath Corporation file (Communication by Air) ibid., BPT 1/10/2/1.
43 See Robin Pakes, *Tradition and Modernity*, pp. 40-101 and Malcolm Hitchcock, 'Public Housing in Bath', *Bath History* Vol XI, p.133.
44 Pakes, *Tradition and Modernity*, p. 73.
45 See Gardiner, *The Thirties*, p.487, *BC*, 31 August 1935 and report in *New Chronicle* [sic] 30 March1939, Bath Sunday School Union, BRO 0466/1/3.
46 *BC*, 29 September1934.
47 Bath Free Church Council, Executive Minutes, 4 October1937, BRO 0042/1.
48 Town Clerk to BVRA , (?) 21.January 1928 BRO 0028D/1/1.
49 East Walcot Girls School, log book, 28 February 1936, BRO 0699/2/5.
50 NUT Special Meeting, 6 November 1938, BRO 0394/9.
51 Mary Dale, *Florence Mary Keyes*, 2013.
52 Bathampton WI Record Book, May 1936-September 1940, BRO 0801/3/1.
53 Interview with Doreen Williams 18 November 2019.
54 Quoted in *BC*, 2.4.38.
55 *Annual Report of the Medical Officer of Health and of the Chief Sanitary Inspector*, 1937, p. 29, BRO
56 BVRA, Executive Committee January 30 1931; and Sir HG Hatt to BVRA, 24 September 1928, BRO 0028D/1/1
57 Gardner, *The Thirties,* London, 201, p.573.
58 *Bath Chronicle* 15.7.1939.
59 Ibid 26 February1938
60 Heffer, ed. *Chips Channon, The Diaries, 1919-38,* London*, 2021,* pp. 729-30
61 *Annual Report of the MOH and of the Chief Sanitary Inspector*, 1937, p. 50 and ibid 1938, p.7 BRO; Gardiner, *The Thirties*, p.565.
62 See Robert Howes, *Gay West: Civil Society and LGBT History in Bristol and Bath, 1970-2010* and his on-line LGBT blog ' the historic sites in Bath'.(http// visitbath.co.uk/blog/read/2022/02.lgbt-historic sites in Bath -b156)

Chapter 11

1 BCS, 30 November 1937, BRO 0591/2/1/18.
2 *BC*, 6 February 1937.
3 Ibid., 13 March 1937.
4 Ibid., 23 December 1938.
5 *BC*, 30 October 1937.
6. Lilly Haprec (?) to Helen Foxcroft, 22 October 1931, BRO 0060/2/6.
7 James Van Sommer, 'Records Personal and National for Five Years' 1933-38', p. 84, BRO VAN/1/1; *B&WC&H*, 6 September 1938.
8 Interview with Phillip Morris, 22 November 2019.
9 NHRD General Cttee mins., 29 September 1938, BRO Hos1/1/1/34.
10 *B&WC&H*, 20 December 1938.
11 BCS, 27 September 1938, BRO 0501/2/1/18.
12 'Your affectionate grandson, Jim' to Grandfather, 1 October 1938 J Van Sommer, Records, BRO VAN/ 1/1
13 Ian Kershaw, *Hitler, vol 2, 1936-1945, Nemesis*, London, 2000, p.119.
14 Van Sommer, Records, BRO VAN/1/1 p. 91.
15 *B&WC&H*, 13 October 1938.
16 *BC*, 27 May.1939, Malcolm Brown and Judith Samuel, 'The Jews of Bath'. *Bath History, Vol.1*, 1986, pp.150-170.
17 Mary Dale, *Florence Mary Keys*, 2013.
18 *BC*, 29 April 1939.
19 *Times* booklet headed 'ARP' (Reprinted from earlier articles in the paper), dated 10,11 and 12 January 1938; Quotation from 12 January 1938 -copy in ARP 'General Correspondence' P3 (17 December 1936 – 18 March 1938) BRO ARP P3.
20 See 'Air Raid Precautions Committee', copy in P3, 31 March 1937, ibid.
21 See Memorandum and subsequent letter from the Home Office 13 October & 5 November 1937, ibid.
22 D Morrison to Town Clerk, 4 March 1937; *Times*, 12.January 1938; and 'Report on Air Raid Precautions ... in the Portsmouth Naval Area, 15-16 July 1937', ibid.
23 letters to Town Clerk, 21 January 1937 & 15 October 1937, Ibid.
24 Poynton to Town Clerk, 17 December 1936; and Chief Constable to Town Clerk, 12 June 1937, ibid.
25 BC, 19 June 1937.
26 'Air Raid Precautions Act, 1937, BRO ARP P3.
27 Hodges to Air Raid Organiser, 4 February 1938 and Ogden's reply 5 February 1938, ibid.
28 Home Office tel., 15 March 1938, ibid.
29 Ogden to Hoyle, 30 March 1938 and Hoyle to Pickard, 8 April 1938, ARP 'General Correspondence' (18 March-19 June 1938), BRO ARP P4.
30 *BC*, 23 April 1938.
31 Ibid., 2.July 1938.
32 Film House to Ogden, 4 May 1938 (in the end the council decided not to hire

it.) (BRO ARP P4; Special Air- Raid Precautions Committee, 26 May 1938, Council and Committee Minutes, 1938, p.547, BRO. See also (undated) 'List of Premises ...' ; and City Engineer 's letter of 20 May 1938 ibid BRO Part 4.
33 'AIR Raid Precautions Progress Report', July 1938, ARP 'General Correspondence' BRO ARP P1 P5. (8 July 1938-26 February 1939).
34 Ibid. and *BC*, 30 July 1938.
35 See Bath Fire and Ambulance Log Books, 6 September 1938, BRO 0282/1/13.
36 *BC*, 9 July 1938.
37 RNHRD General Committee, 8 September1938, BRO HOS1/1/134.
38 Ibid., 24 November 1938.
39 Pickard to Ogden, 9.August 1938, BRO ARP P5.
40 Information and list of 'safety trenches' in Bath *Chronicle,* 1 October 1938.
41 Ibid., 24 September 1938.
42. Special (Air Raid Precautions) Committee, 3 and 30 January 1939, Council and Committee Minutes, 1939, pp.202-206, BRO; *BC,* 4 February 1939.
43 Pickard to Town Clerk, 19 February 1939, BRO ARP P5.
44 RNHRD Building S/ctte., 23 February, 2 March &17 May 1939, BRO HOS1/1/1/35 .
45 Haysman to Ogden, 1 May 1939, ARP 'General Correspondence' (28 February 1939- 16 June 1939), BRO ARP P6. See also *B&WC&H*, 20 July 1939.
46 'Civilian deaths through war, 24 March 1938 '. Ibid (P6).
47 ARP Department Circular no. 86/1939: 'Acceleration of Civil Defence Measures', 18 April 1939 Ibid.
48 NUT Quarterly meeting, 29 September1938, BRO 0394/8 & Clifford Ellis' report headed 'Private and Confidential', BRO 1177/3/4.
49 Hoyle to Pickard, 2.3.39, BRO ARP P6.
50 *BC* 1 April 1939. Also see G Scott, 'Firebomb Fiasco: Civil Defence in World War II' in Ed. Graham Davis, *Bath Exposed ,* 2007, p. 218.
51 *BC* , 21 January 1939.
52 Ibid., 25 February 1939.
53 Meeting 11 April 1939, Bathampton WI Record Books, May 1936 -September 1940, BRO 0801/3/1.
54 Dixon (Deputy town clerk) to Ogden and reply, 6.8.39, (General Correspondence , 17 June 1939-31.6.'40). BRO ARP1 P7.
55 RNHRD Reception Sub Cttee, 21 July 1939, 1939-42. BRO HOS1/1/1/35.
56 *B&WC&H,* 28 July 1939.
57 BCS, 5 May 1939 BRO 0591/2/1/19.
58 121 OHP, MOBAW.
59 113, ibid.
60 *B&WC&H*, 10 August 1939.
61 BCS 'Special Meeting' 25.8.1939, BRO 0591/2/1/19.
62 Bath Gas Company Repair Squads, 28 August 1939, BRO ARP P7.
63 RNHRD General Committee, 31 August 1939, BRO HOSI/1/1/35.
64 East Walcot Infants' School Log Book, 28 August 1939, BRO 0699/2/5.
65 Tel. from Health Ministry to Town Clerk, 31 August 1939, BRO ARP P7.
66 Handwritten note : 'Emergency Committee', 1 September 1939 & also note from

South Western Regional Office, ibid.
67 Walcot Senior School and Bath Diocesan Girls' School Log book, 31 August-12 September 1939, BRO 0827/2/2. (In January 1938 the two schools were amalgamated to form Walcot Mixed School).
68 East Walcot Infants' School log book, 12 September 1939, BRO 0699/2/5.
69 RNHRD General Cttee., 2.September 1938, BRO HOS1/1/1/35. For information about the child evacuees see B&WC&H, 29 & 30 August 1939.

SELECT BIBLIOGRAPHY

Archival Sources

Newspapers
British Newspaper Archive and Bath Record Office
Bath Weekly Chronicle; after 1925 *Bath Chronicle and Herald* and from 1936 onwards *Bath Weekly Chronicle and Herald*.
Bath and Wilts Chronicle (after 1925 Bath and Wilts Chronicle and Herald - the daily edition of the *Bath Weekly Chronicle and Herald*).
The Bath Herald

Published Documents
Abercrombie, Patrick and Brueton, Bertrand, *Bristol and Bath Regional Planning Scheme*, London and Liverpool, 1930
Bath Corporation Bill, *Proceedings, 1936-37*
AW Wills, *The Kingsmead Flats*, Bath Corporation, 1932

BBC Archive
John Betjeman, Mowbray A Green, AW Wills, *Built to Last 1, Bath,* Broadcast on 17 April 1939 in the Regional Programme and the Western Programme (typescript)
Richard Dimbleby, *About Britain: Bath -Queen of the West* shown on BBC TV 21.11.1952. Adrian Hopkins and some other figures who were active in the inter-war period are featured here.(https://bbcrewind.co.uk)

On-line blogs
Howes, Robert, LGBT and History of Bath – a virtual tour, http//visitbath.co.uk/blog/read/2022/02.lgbt-historic sites in Bath -b156

British Pathé archive, 1920-'39
www: British Pathé.com/search/city of Bath
'Marquis of Bath performs ceremony removing tolls from Cleveland Bridge in Bath' (1929)
'Lord Baden Powell visits a large Scout Camp near Bath' (1932)
'Haile Selassie … auctions treasures at London auction house' (1936)

Bath Record Office
Administrative history, 1189-present
Ainsworth, Katherine, correspondence
Bath City Police
Bath Council and Committee Minutes, 1919-39
Bath Council papers dealing with the 1928 typhoid outbreak
Bath Council papers dealing with the general correspondence of the ARP Committee (unsorted files P1-7)
Bath Free Church Council minutes of meetings
Bath Sunday School Union
Bath and Twerton Cooperative Societies, (after 1931 Bath Cooperative) minute books
Bath Trade and Labour Council minute books
Bath Vigilance Society
Bath WEA Records
Chivers, Cedric bookbinders, directors and shareholders meetings
Chivers, Cedric; scrap books on his mayoralty
City of Bath, Annual Reports of Medical Officer of Health, & School Medical Officer's Reports, 1918-39
Conservative Association Press cuttings and minutes of committee meetings
Diary of Williams Chun
Diary of SH Silvester, 1918-19
Dickens' Fellowship, minutes/papers
East Walcot Girls' School, logbook
Foxcroft, Charles, papers
Harrington Club papers/minute books
Maslen, Benjamin, scrapbook
National Union of Teachers, minutes of meetings
Partis College collection
Records of Clifford, Rosemary, Penelope Ellis and Bath Academy of Art
Royal National Hospital for Rheumatic Diseases, minutes of meetings
Stothert and Pitt Scrap book : Tour of George V and Queen Mary, 1917
Earl and Countess Temple's and Newton Park Estate's papers, 1792-1954
J. Van Sommer, Records, 1933-38
Walcot Senior School logbook
West Central School, Register of Admission, Progress and Withdrawals
Widcombe Children's Cinema Club outing to Weymouth, 1937 (film)
Widcombe Workingmen's Club papers/minute books
Women's Institute, Bathampton, 1936-40

Bath Preservation Trust Archives
Old Bath Preservation Society History 10.6.1929
Bath Corporation File
Preserve Bath Movement

Museum of Bath at Work

Bathford Paper Mill
Fuller's Earth Union
Horstman Cars Ltd
Oral History Project, written summaries of tapes
Stothert and Pitt catalogues, technical information and promotional literature as well
 a collection of 40,000 images.

Private Collections
Akeman Press archives
 Collection of illustrations and booklets relevant to Bath
Mrs Mary Dale
 Ms of *Florence Mary Keyes*
Mrs Doreen Williams
 Mainly material concerning her mother's work for the local Conservative Party
  Association

Interviews
Mrs Doreen Williams 18 & 25.11.2019
Mrs Patricia Connett, 20.1.2020
Mrs Mary Dale, 15.1.2020 (with follow-up emails 28.1.2020 & 24.11.2022)
Mr. Philip Morris, 22.11.2019
Mr. Alan Gait, 6.2.2020

Books and Articles

Bone, Mike, 'The Rise and Fall of Bath's Breweries' *Bath History* vol viii, pp. 106-133
Bowers, Keith, *Imperial Exile*, Bath, 2016
Boyce, Robert and Robertson, Esmonde, *Paths to War,* Basingstoke and London, 1989.
Brown, Malcolm and Samuel, Judith 'The Jews of Bath'. *Bath History Vol.1*, 1986, pp.150-170
Brown, W. Henry, *The Jubilee History of the Bath Cooperative Society*, Bath 1939
Buchanan, Angus, 'The Floods of Bath', *Bath History*, vol vii, 1998, pp. 167-188
Davis, Graham, The Langtons at Newton Park, Bath 1980
Davis, Graham and Bonsall, Penny, *Bath. A New History*, Keele, 1996
Elliott, Kirsten, *The Year of the Pageant*, Bath, 2009
Evans, Aaron, 'Collective Dreams: A History of Bath's Cinemas' in *Bath History*, vol XII pp. 157-165, 2011.
Eyles, William, *Electricity in Bath, 1890-1974*, Bath 1974
Fawcett, Trevor, 'Black People in Georgian Bath' , *Avon Past,* vol 16, 1993 pp.2-9
Festing, Sally, 'Charles Richter and the Bath Cabinet Makers. The Early Years', *Bath History*, vol vii, 1998, pp. 146-166.
Figes, Orlando, *A People's Tragedy*, London, 1997
Forest, Pauline, *Childhood Memoirs,* Bath 2008
Forsyth, Michael (with contribution from Stephen Bird), *Bath* , Pevsner Architectural

Guides, Yale University Press, New Haven and London, 2007
Foxcroft, Charles, *The Night Sister*, London, 1918
Gardner, Juliet, *The Thirties*, London 2011
Haber, Lutz , 'Emperor Haile Selassie I in Bath, 1936-1940', *Bath History*, vol 3, pp. 159-180
Haddon, John, *Bath*, London, 1973
Harper, Duncan, *Bath at Work*, Bath 1989
Hattersley, Roy, *Borrowed Time*, London,2009
Hatton, John, *The Hot Springs of Bath: medical handbook*, Bath 1921 (reprinted Ulan Press)
Heffer, Simon., ed., *Chips Channon, The Diaries, 1919-38*, London, 2021
— *Sing As We Go: Britain Between the Wars*, London 2023.
Hill, Andrew, *Biscuits, Banquet and Bollinger, the History of Cater, Stoffell and Fortt., ltd.*, Bradford-on-Avon, 2013
Hill, Dennis, Bath *Fire Brigade and Ambulance, 1891-1974*, Bath 2003
Howes,Robert, *Gay West: Civil Society and LGBT History in Bristol and Bath, 1970-2010*, Bristol, 2011
Hyman, Robert &Nicola, *The Pump Room Orchestra Bath*, Salisbury, 2011
Kershaw, Ian, *Hitler, 1936-'45, Nemesis*, London,2000
Lambert, Robin, 'The Bath Corporation Act of 1925', *Transactions of the Ancient Monuments Society*, vol. 44, 2000 pp. 51-62
— 'Patrick Abercrombie and Planning in Bath', *Bath History*, vol. viii, 2000, pp172-196
Lloyd, Jack, *The Royal United Hospital, Bath*, Bristol, 1982
McCauley, Nick, *Secret Underground Corsham*, Bradford on Avon, 2021
Macmillan, Neil with Chapman, Mike, *A History of Fuller's Earth Mining Around Bath*, Lydney, 2009
Masterman, Charles, *England After War*, London, 1922
Mclaughlin, David 'Mowbray Green and the Old Bath Preservation Society' *Bath History*, vol iv, 1992, pp.155-172
Millard, Robert, '"An Unfortunate Incident Has Occurred": The Typhoid Outbreak In Bathwick, 1928' in Ed. Graham Davis, *Bath Exposed* , Sulis Press, 2007, pp.149-182
Osborne, Honor and Manisty, Peggy, *A History of the Royal School for Daughters of Officers in the Army, 1864-1965*, London 1966
Paikes, Robin, *Tradition and Modernity in Bath between the War*, M.Phil Thesis, University of Bath 2016
Payne, John, *Stothert and Pitt, Rise and Fall of a Bath Company*, Bath, 2007
Rolls, Roger, *Hospital of the Nation; the Story of Spa Medicine and National Mineral Water Hospital at Bath*, Bath 1988
Scott, George, 'Firebomb Fiasco: Civil Defence in World War II' in Ed. Graham Davis *Bath Exposed* , Bath, 2007, pp.217-238
Sealy, Elsie, B., *My Memoirs*, Bath,1970
Skidelsky, Robert, *Britain since 1900: A Success Story?* London, 2014
Smellie, KB, *History of Local Government,.*London, 1946
Swift, Andrew, *All Roads lead to France*, Bath, 2005

Taylor, AJP *The Origins of the Second World War*, London, 1961
Torrens, Hugh, *The Evolution of a Family Firm*, Stothert and Pitt of Bath, Bath 1984
Turner, M. *75 Years, 1912-87, WEA, Bath Branch*, Bradford-on-Avon, 1987
Vachell, Horace, *The Golden House*, London, 1937
White, E., ' "Your Blessed Asylum": Mrs Partis, and her College for Distressed Gentlewomen, Bath, 1826' in Ed. Graham Davis *Bath Exposed*, Bath, 2007, pp.39-60.

INDEX

Abbey, Bath, 9, 29–30, 107, 138, 237, 316
Abdication, 239–40
Abercrombie, Professor Patrick, 241–3, 244, 269, 268
Aberstone, Max, optician, 48
abortion, 274–5
Abyssinia, 225–9; Italian invasion of, 212, 225–7; medical assistance for, 226; reaction to, in Bath, 225–9; Association, 228; *see also* Haile Selassie, Emperor
Addison, Dr C, 38, 39
'aerial' travel, 40–1, 43, 195, 231, 267
Afghanistan, 22, 25
Africa 53, 56, 213, 216, 217, 218–19
air raid precautions (ARP); ARP Act (1937), 291–3; ARP Committee established, 232; appointment of Major H. Pickard, 293; work of, 294–300 *passim*; blackout plans and problems, 233, 235; Bristol regional conference, October 1936, 332–3; decontamination, 291, 295, 296, 300; Emergency Committee, 302; exercises and demonstrations, 296, 302–3; gas masks, 283, 297, 303, 313; gas school at Falfield, 234; last minute preparations in August 1939 and mobilisation, 311, 313; priority to be given to ARP, 301; provision for mortuaries, 300–1; shelters, 233, 235, 284, 293–300 *passim*, 313; and Sudeten crisis, 283, 297–9; wardens, 235, 291, 303–4; and recruitment of; and of other volunteers, 291, 294, 295–6, 301; *see* National Service and Civil Defence Controller
Aitken, General Arthur, 101
Albion Cabinet Works, 27
Ali, Amin, 218
Aliens, German, 27–8
Allen, Dr FJ, 195
Allin, HJ Captain, 46
Altman, Florence Mrs, 85
Amalgamated Engineers Union (AEU), 67–8
Amalgamated Union of Distributive and Allied Workers, 133
Amblin, Councillor SJ, 291

Amritsar, 25
Andrews, Lillian Mrs, 85
Anglo-Persian Oil Company, 130
Ante-natal clinic, 162
Antiquarian Booksellers' Association, 88
Anti-Semitism, 155, 220, 221, 286, 309–10
Anti-War Council, 231; *see also* pacifism
Archdeacon of Bath, 120, 285, 316
Argyle Congregational Church, 93, 95, 98, 212, 223, 230, 241, 262
Armistice, 7–10, 12
art; *see* Bath, cultural life in
Ascension Church, 109, 270
Ashman, Ted, 69, 249
Ashton, Nelson, Chief Constable, 235
Ashwell, Lena, 89
Ashworth, Superintendent Tom, 222–3
Assembly Rooms, 56, 246–7, 249; renovation of, 247; re-opened by Duchess of Kent, 247
Atkins, Joan, 155–6
Austen, Jane, 175
Australia, 30, 53–4, 64
Austria (*Anschluss*), 282–3
Avon, River, 244; Street, 33, 107, 112, 176, 185, 237

Bagshaw, Edmund, 70, 196, 203, 216
Baillie-Hamilton, Hon Charles, 192–3, 195–7, 202; *see also* Conservative Association
Baker, WJ Councillor, 37
Baldwin, Stanley, 73–4, 192, 230
Barker, Sir Herbert, 83
Barrett, Walter, Councillor, 75, 302
Bateman, Councillor Aubrey, 158, 179
Bath, Lord, Thomas Henry Thynne. 5th Marquis of Bath, 4, 63, 117, 196; Lady, 166
Bath and District Employment Exchange, 200–1, 261, 307; Joint Planning Committee, 265
Bath and Portland Stone Firms (Ltd), 137, 200, 258
Bath and West of England Motor Club, 46
Bath Art School, 248, 253–4

INDEX

Bath Attractions Week, 84–5, 87
Bath bills (1925 and 1935); *see* Bath Corporation Acts, 1925 and 1937
Bath Cabinet Makers Ltd., 35, 180–1, 199, 317
Bath City Associated (football) club, 102–3, 278, 317; Supporters Club, 103
Bath, City of: Advertising and publicity, 40–1, 82, 84–8, 210; architecture of, 87–88, 241–8, 268–9 *passim*; births and deaths, 163–5; challenge to, of modernity, 265–70, 273; class system in, 188–90, 203; cultural life in, 41–3, 244, 248–9: art, 251–4; drama, 42–3, 89–91; education in, 151–8; *see also* schools; essence of, 317–19; ethnic diversity in, 56, 216–19; health in, 99–100, 161–6, 172–4; industry in, 1, 3–4, 35–6, 62–4, 67–8, 122–49 *passim* 178-84, 317; music, 41–2, 89, 249–51; nature of, 88–9, 118-20, 256-7, as a spa, 38–40, 82–3, 138, 178, 185, 254–5, 257, 317; threats to, 265; politics in, 125, 197; *see also* elections; population of, 175–6, 178–9, 257; poverty in, 33, 61, 150, 188; *see also* slums and unemployment; as a tourist and conference centre, 38–43, 84, 88, 168, 175, 178, 186–7, 210–11, 306
Bath Council, 9, 106–21 *passim*, 125, 159, 242–8 *passim*; Health Department, 164–8 and the unemployed, 68–9, 207; Council's c'ttees and sub-c'ttees: Air Raid Precautions, 232, 299, 303; Assembly Rooms, 246; Bath Spa Attractions Week, 85; Advertising, 84; Baths, 38, 83, 241, 250, 254, City Improvements, 113, 117, 118, 242–3; Civis, 82; Education, 14, 34, 37, 151–5, 297–8; Electricity, 113; Emergency, 302, 313 (ARP); Finance, 68, 106, 119; Food Control, 12–13, 36; Health, 99–100; 164–8, 166; Housing, 38; Library and Arts, 40, 249; Parliamentary, 106, 242–5 *passim*; Public Assistance, 203–4, 261; Sanitary Committee, 7; Spa, 39, 250, 251, 270; Special (typhoid), 168; Surveying, 106; Watch, 65, 166, 223, 265, 266; Water Works, 115
Bath Coal Office, 65, 129, 143–9 *passim*
Bath Corporation Act (1925) 107–13, 151; clauses, 107–8; Opposition to, 108–9; poll on, 109; Corporation Act, (1937) 242–6; intense opposition to, 243–4; revised bill, 244–5
Bath Corporation Electricity department showrooms, 207
Bath Cricket Week, 101

Bath Dickens' Fellowship, 94–5, 149–50
Bath Electric Tramways Company, 131–3, 141–3, 265
Bath Free Church Council, 52, 262, 270
Bath Gas Light and Coke Co., 207, 246, 312
Bath Horse Show, 43, 227, 230
Bath (health) Insurance Committee, 160–1
Bath Ladies Football Club, 103–5
Bath Literary and Philosophical Association, 94, 96, 119-20
Bath Medical Advisory Committee, 82–3
Bath Municipal Technical College, 157, 253
Bath Pageant (1909), 248
Bath Peace Council, 277
Bath Playgoers Society, 89
Bath police, 132–3, 144, 223, 266, 288; *see also* Constable, Chief
Bath Preservation Trust, 240, 241, 244, 246, 252; *see also* Old Bath Preservation Trust
Bath Public Library, 249
Bath, Rotary Club, 206
Bath Royal Literary and Scientific Institution, 96, 107, 207
Bath Rugby Club, 102
Bath Rural District Council, 91
Bath Schools Rugby Union, 102
Bath Spa Orchestra, 249–51; Save the Bath Spa Orchestra Movement, 250, 254; *see also* Pump Room,
Bath Sunday School Union, 270
Bath Tenement Venture Trust, 271
Bath Trades and Labour Council, 27–8, 30, 34, 48–9, 60, 76–7, 231, 271; and coal strike (1920), 66–7; distrust of NUWM and communism, 60, 141, 203–4, 231; and General Strike and aftermath, 124, 129, 141, 142, 143, and German aliens, 27–8; and Nazi Germany, 219, 237; and Orchestra, 89, 250; Sets up Council of Action, 48–9, 124–5; support for; and Bath Corporation Act (1925), 109; and Royalty, 237; and unemployment, 73, 202, 208
Bath Unemployed Association, 233, 237
Bath Vigilance and Rescue Association, 271–2
Bath War Hospital, 8, 13, 44; *see also* Pension Hospital (after Nov 1919) and hospitals
Bathampton; *see* Women's Institute
Bathavon District Council, 242; and ARP, 292–3
Batheaston, 156
Bathford Paper Mills Ltd., 64, 66, 141–2; and devaluation, 188–9; impact of coal strikes on, 62

Baths, 40, 81-2; Roman, 106; Royal, 39; publicity about, 40-1; *see also* spa
Bathwick Bridge Co., 110; Hill, 167-72 *passim*; Rectory, 173
Baynton, Henry, 90
BBC, 253, 280, 285, 287
Beauchamp, Sir Frank, 144
Beaufort, Duchess of, 165
Beck-Cluckie, Alexander, 51; *see also* 'Bulldogs'
Becker, Rev CM, 122
Beecham, Sir Thomas, 186
Beechen Cliff, 33, 151-2, 207, 393
Bell, Arthur, Bugler, 8
Bell, WW and Co., 282
Bellman (WS Read), 8, 52, 87, 90, 98, 100, 140, 150, 237, 277
Bence, Councillor, 294
Benton Fletcher, Major George, 256-7
Berchtesgaden, 283
Bernstein, Sydney, 256
Besant, Annie, 26
Bethell, Alfred James, 10-11
billeting, 304-5, 314-15; officer, 207; *see also* evacuees
birth control, 273-5
Blackett, J. Dr (MOH), 37, 99, 161-6 *passim*, 167-74 *passim*; role in ARP, 232, 234, 316
Blackmore, Ruth, 228, 229
Blackshirts, 222-3
Blair, Joe, 279
Blakeney, RBD. Brigadier General, 125
Blass, AP, 27
Blathwayt, William, 165
Board of Guardians, 75-7; *see also* Workhouse
Bohemia, 301
Bolshevism, 22-4, 27, 33; *see also* Communist party *and* communists
Bond, Cyril, 185
Borland Advertising Agency, 85
Bowler, JB and Sons Ltd., 183-4, 186; Ernest, 188; and family, 184
Box, 125-8, 128
Boyd, SA, Prebendary, 29
Boyle, Rev J, 34
Bradford-on-Avon, 137, 304
Bragg, AE, 30
Braimbridge, George, 161-2
Brand, John, 41
Brassknocker Hill, 266
Brewer, P, 50
Bristol, 136, 138, 188, 222; and attitudes towards Bath, 53-6, 88-9; Radium Centre in, 161; University, 154; and Zoo, 306

British Broadcasting Company/Corporation, 253, 280, 285, 287
British Empire, 212-16 *passim*; developments in, 53-7, 212-13; Empire Day, 25, 157, 213; Wembley Exhibition, 56-7, 87; and Bath Pavilion, 57, 87; trade, 212
British Empire Shakespeare Society, 218
British Legion, 56, 235, 286
British Union of Fascists, 222-3
Broad, Sapper, 22-3
Brosnan, Alma, 75
Bull, Corporal, 19
'bulldogs' 78
Burdon-Cooper, J. Dr 154
Burraston, William, 184-5
Burgess, J, 75
Bush, Alderman SW, 37, 151-3 *passim*
Butcher, CF, Sergt., 55
Butcher, Richard, 189, 228
Butlin, CJ, 202
Bypasses, 267; *see also* cars

cadets; *see* OTC)
Cammaerts, Prof. Emile Leon, 252
Canada, 53
cancer, 161, 99-100, 164-5
Cannings' College, 154
Carpenter, Councillor Dr, 302
Cars, increase in number of, 265; parks, 265-7; and threat to Bath of, 265; *see also* Horstman
Carter, Ernest 2; Pilot, 31
Carter, Stoffell and Fortt, grocers and restaurant, 66, 95, 157, 178, 217, 228
Carthew, Sergt, W, 7
Case, MV, 14
Cecil, Lord Robert, 323
Cedric Chivers Ltd., Bookbinders, 69, 200, 227
Census (1931), 178-9
Central Ammunition Depot, Corsham, 257-8, 262, 279; *see* 'Corsham workers'
Chamber of Commerce, 39, 43, 81-2, 84-5, 88, 178, 242, 247, 256, 263, 292; supports publicity campaign for Bath, 39, 84-5
Chamberlain, Neville, 282, 283, 285-7, 297
Chamberlain, Tom, Councillor, 32
Chandos House, 120
Chapel, Ernest, Lt, 125
Charlcombe, 176
Charles, W, 84
Charles and Charles, 84
Chesterton, GK, 91
Chilwell, Percy, 91
China, 212, 280-2; Chinese community in

INDEX

Bath, 56, 216–17, laundries, 56
Chivers, Cedric, Alderman, 142, 191; and General Strike, 138–9, 142; supports research into rheumatism, 82–3
Chun, William, 69, 137–8, 175
churches, 97–9 *passim*, 138, 269–70 *passim*; assistance to Somerset miners, 142–3; attendance in decline, 97, 269; Missionary Union, 218; *see also* Smith, Pat, Gypsy, and names of individual churches.
Churchill, Randolph, 195; Winston, 23, 213
Cinemas: Assembly Rooms Cinema, 91–3; Beau Nash Picture House, 91, 226; Forum, 207, 269; Oldfield Park Picture House, 91; Vaudeville, 91; *see also* films
Citizen House, 90–1, 210, 249, 272
Civil Defence Controller, 302
Clarke, WW, 129
Claverton, 267; Down, 159
Cleveland Bridge, 107, 113, 114–17 *passim*
Cleverly, Charles, 7
Clifton, 83, 306; College, 293
clubs, Bath and County, 73; City, 81; for German refugee girls, 288; Left book, 249, 281; Harrington, 93–4; New Empire, 93–4; Widcombe Working Mens', 94
Coal: Controller, 137, 141–7; rationing and shortages, 137, 144–9; *see also* strikes
Cobb, Herbert, 175
Cochran, Charles, 263, 255
Cole, Herbert, 311
Coles, Tom, 127
Collings, EP, 134
Collins, HH, headmaster, 155
Collins, Dr, 6, 7
Colmer, JH, Alderman, 91
Colmer, James, Ltd, 44
Combe Down, 13, 28, 184, 189, 288, 296; Water Company, 167
Combe Hay, 122, 148
Combe Park, 158
Commissioner, Civil, 128, 139; Regional, 313
Committee of the Bath Unemployed (CBU), 75–8; *see also* Bath Unemployed Association
Commons, Private Bills Committee, 111–13 *passim*
Communist Party, 75–8
Communists, 221, 307
Comrades of the Great War, 4, 27
Connaught, Duke of, 250
Coningham, Captain Gerald, 27
Connett, Patricia, 33, 156, 157, 185
conscientious objectors, 308–9
conscription, 307–8
Conservative Association, 229, 272, 286, 290; and Bailly Hamilton, 195–7; India, 213–16; Junior Association (IMPS), 213, 290; Party:; *see* elections, and Foxcroft, and Guinness, Thomas Loel
Constable, Chief, 36, 235, 265–6, 302
Constantine, Learie, 56
Cook, Councillor AE, 99–100, 129, 154, 161, 166
Cook, Ernest, 246
Cooper, George, 161
Cooperative Society, 67, 133, 156, 282; and wage cuts (1921 and 1922), 65; and fund raising for Spanish civilians, 277; and horse Bob, 43–4; and pacificism, 231; and sales, 199; and staff relations, 35; and strikes, 67, 133; new central stores, 207; urges boycott of Japanese goods, 281; on war footing, August 1939, 311–12.
Corps of Honorary Guides, 254
Corsham, 87, 257–65 *passim*
Corsham Bath Stone Company, 43
'Corsham workers', 172, 257–65; debate about in Bath, 257–9; efforts to assist, 266; impact on Bath, 257, 258, 259; *see also* Hopkins, Adrian and Central Ammunition Depot
cost of living, 33–4, 197–9, 201–2
Councils of Action 48, 139; in Bath, 48–9, 139–46
Cowan, Margaret, 154
Craik, Charles, 85
Crawford, Ernest, 120–1
cricket, 101–2
Croome-Johnson, Reginald, KC, Recorder, 170–1
Cuming, LJ, 222
Curd, C. Dr, 158
Czechoslovakia, 283–5 *passim*, 290; *see also* Bohemia *and* Sudeten crisis

Dale, Mary, 163, 177, 188, 189, 272, 288–9
Daniell, John, 101
Daniels, Sidney Reginald, 191, 215, 225
Danzig, 305, 306
Davey, Councillor Colonel HS, 128
Dawes Plan, 52
Day, Councillor Sam, 129, 223
De Reyes, Consuelo, 90, 97, 249, 272
demobilisation, 13, 16–22, 31–2, 44, 55
depressed regions of UK, 199, 204, 208, 257, 258, 261; *see also* hunger marches and unemployment
depressions, economic (1921), 63–70; Great

(1931–33), 193–4, 199–211
Derby, Lord, 186
Derrick, Ada, 185, 187
Desmond, George, 218, 237, 290, 310
Destructor Bridge, 116
devaluation (1931) and impact on Bath, 197–9
Devonshire Arms, 161
Dick Kerr Ladies Football Club, Preston, 103, 104
district nurses, 161
dividends, 122, 129, 209–10
Dobson, Dina, 283
doctors, 160–4, 179, 183
Dog Lane, 118, 119, 129, 145
'dole', the, 201–3
Dolmeads, 38, 118, 119
Domestic Science College, 152; service, 179, 187
Domville, Admiral Sir Barry, 309
Douglas, Brother, 204
Duddridge, Charles, 165–6
Dudley, G., 256
Dyer, Reginald General, 25, 54

Edgar Buildings, 242
Edwards, FP, Air Mechanic, 26
Education, 151–8, 249, 253; Act (1918), 151; Programme (1929), 152–5; *see also* Bath Council, Education Committee and schools
Edward VIII, 239–40; *see also* Prince of Wales
Egypt, 55
elections, by- (1929), 192–3; General, 1918, 9–11; 1922, 70–3; 1923, 74; 1924 78–80; 1929, 192–3 1931, 193–4; 1935, 237–8
electricity showrooms, 207
Ellis, Clifford, 246, 248, 252–4, 272, 298; Rosemary, 253, 272
Elvin, Herbert, 59, 71–3 *passim*
Emmanuel Church, Lower Weston, 270
Employment Exchange, 32, 61, 199–201, 209
Englishcombe Lane, 32, 37, 62, 69; Park, 268
Epstein, Sir Jacob, 251
ethnic minorities in Bath, 53–4, 216–18
eugenics, 173
euthanasia, 99–100
evacuees: plans for their reception, 304–5, 313; attitude towards, 305, arrival in Bath, 314–16; *see also*, billeting and refugees
Evans, DA, 39
Evans, John, 260–1
Evans and Owen, 44, 184–5

Everyman Theatre, 89, 210
Evry, Mrs, 14
Exhibition of Children's Art (1937), 253
Eyres and Sons Milliners, 69

Fairfield House, 227–8
Fanshawe, Captain Guy, 311
Farr, Councillor CB, 247
Fascism, in Bath (1925), 126–7, 226; *see also* British Union of Fascists; Blackshirts and the Link
Fawkes, Guy, 9, 226
Festivals: Contemporary Arts, 1930, 1935 & 1936, 251–2; of the Arts, scheduled for 1939, 254–6; cancelled, 257; Music (1919), 41; (1938), 251
Fielding, Roy, 156
Films 28, 91–3 *passim*, 226; Industry, 43.; *see also* cinema
Floods, 119
Flu', 165–7; 'Spanish', 5–7, 165
Flying squads, 78, 79
Ford, Raymond, 284
Forrest, Pauline, 176–7, 188, 189
Fortt, Bertram, 89
Forum, Southgate; *see* cinemas
Fossberry, Dr, 161
Foxcroft, Charles T, 10–11, 70–3 *passim*, 123, 125, 191; and Bolshevism, 24, 47; and India, 54 and Palestine, 56; and Ireland, 59–60; poet and playwright, 60, 149
Foxcroft, Helen, 192, 214, 225, 272, 280, 285
France, and approach to war, 229, 230; Bathonians serving in, 4–5, 13–14, 19; Ladies Football Team and, 103–4; and Occupation of the Ruhr, 49–50
Franchise extensions (1918), 9, (1929), 192, 193
Franco, General Francisco, 229, 277–80 *passim*
Fraser Forbes, surgeon, 14, 98–9; Mrs, 297
Fred, 'Uncle', 126, 285
Freemantle, Albert, 33
Friends Meeting House, 59, 224, 231; *see also* Quakers
Frome Rd Infirmary, 177, 217
Frome Road House; *see* Workhouse
Fuller's Earth Union: and coal shortages, 130, 146–8; and demobilisation, 19–21; and devaluation, 198–200; sales of, 123, 130, 200; and General Strike, 140; and Great Depression, 200
Fuller's Garage, 183

INDEX 347

Gandhi, Mahatma, 214, 215
Gandy, Miss Violet, 94
Gardner, Juliet, 175
Garforth, Col., 282
Garrick's Head, 276
General Strike; *see* Strikes
George V, 56, 236–39 *passim*
George VI, 239, 240–1
Georges' Brewery, 110
Germany: attitudes towards, 26–9, 47–9, 50–2, 212; and defeat of, 4–5. 15; commercial rivalry with, 28; and poverty in, 50, 51; Nazi, 229, 282–9 *passim*, 290 and Bathonians, 219–22 *passim*, 309–11; its anti–semitism and Bath, 220, 296–9; outbreak of war (1939), 311–16; *see also* Austria, Czechoslovakia, Poland and the Link
Gielgud, John, 256
Gillie, Rev Dr RC, 224
Gilmore, H, 60–1
Gingell, Wilf, 184
Godwin, Jessica, 178
Gold Standard, 124
Gollancz, Victor, 249
Golledge, William, 76; Mrs, 206
Good Neighbours' Club, 206; *see also* unemployment
Gould, Stanley, 76, 143, 204, 310
Grand, Sarah, Mayoress, 51, 212
Great Depression, 193–4, 199–211; *see also* hunger marches and unemployment
Great Western Railway (GWR), 59, 84, 87, 91, 107, 130, 136, 138, 142, 186, 254; and Bath advertisements on, 87; and strikes, 36–7, 136–7, 141, 142, 149
Green, Mowbray, A, 167, 246
Gregory, Mr and Mrs, 177
Grenfell, Major T, 57, 220–1, 230
Gresham Gray, Mr., 170
Grindrod, GH, 97
Grosvenor Bridge, 113, 115, 116
Guildhall, 51–2, 75, 108, 136, 223, 224, 245
guest houses, 178; *see also* hotels
Guinness, Thomas Loel, MP, 237–8; and India 214–16; and Spain, 280; and potential of aircraft, 164; decision not to fight election, 264; the Hon Mrs Joan, 275–6
Gurney, L, Ted and Molly, 226

Haber, Lutz, 229
Hacker, CH, Councillor. 169
Hadow Report, 152
Haig, Field Marshall, Lord, 62
Hailie Selassie, Emperor, 217, 225–9, 239–40; and Bath, 227–9
Hall, Henry, 251
Hambro, Olaf, 256
Hancock, Ellen, 201
Hankow, 180
Hannington, Wal, 70, 75, 203
Harbutt, Owen, 28, 56; and Plasticine Works, 13, 56
Hardy, WE, 141; Mrs, 262
Hardyman, Malcolm, Lt., 23, 139
Harris, Rev, JC, 95
Harrison, Frederic, 16, 85, 87
Harthan, Wendy, 282
Hartnell, Norman, 256
Haslewood, Mrs H.L.
Hatt, Sir Harry, 25, 31, 32, 68, 107, 113
Hatton, John, 40, 81–3, 85, 169, 210, 247
Hawkesyard Priory, Prior of, 49
Hay Hill Baptist Church, 180
Hayward, Thomas, Rev, 97
Heath, Carl, 51–2
Hemmings, Leonard, 69
Hewit, CH, 310
Hepher, Charles, 55
Hill, Lt. J, 14
Hinton Charterhouse, 191
Hitler, Adolf, 219–22 *passim*, 229, 230, 261, 282–6 *passim*, 306; Bath's Reaction to, 220–2; *see* Germany, Nazi
Hoare, Sir Samuel, 23
Hodsell, Wing Commander, 232–3
Holidays, 188–9, 305–6
Holmes, J.T. and Co Ltd, 198
Home Office, 232, 234, 235, 290, 292, 299
Hope, Helena, 97
Hope, RJ, 49, 109, 126
Hopkins, Adrian Alderman, 204, 236, 238, 242, 250, 262–5, 275, 289, 307; Chairman of Bath Conservative Association, 214, 216, 238; decision to stand as National Conservative candidate for Bath, 264; mayor, 270; and Festival of the Arts, 1938–39, 256; and India, 214; and optimism of, 289, 307; and Sunday games, 270; trenchant supporter of 'Corsham' workers, 262–5
Hopkins, Phillip, 212, 283
Hore-Belisha, Leslie, 23, 263–4
Horstmann, Miss P, 221; Sidney, 63–4, 123, 181–3
Horstmann Car Company, 181–3; saved from liquidation, 1922, 63–4, 123; and exports, 73; and the Slow Motion

Suspension Co. 181–3;
Horstmann Gear Company, 3
Horten-Starkie, Le-Gendre George, Prebendary, 50
Hospitals, Bath and Wessex Children's Orthopaedic, 154, 158; Ear, Nose and Throat, 159, 164; Forbes Fraser, 158. Isolation Hospital, 158; Pensions, 46, 158; Royal Mineral Water Hospital (after 1936 Royal National Hospital for Rheumatic Diseases) 83, 164, 283, 284, 297, 306, 312, 316; Royal United Hospital, 83, 98–9, 151, 159, 160–1, 207–8, 312; Bath War Hospital, 8
hotels, 38, 175, 275; Empire, 186; Francis, 41; Grand Pump Room, 38, 89, 186, private, 178; Pulteney, 38; Spa, 38, 42, 187
housing, 32–8, 39, 268, 303; council, 118–19, 268; estates, 246, 268; *see also* slums and Kingsmead Flats
Hoyle, AW, Director of Education, 159, 227, 297
Hughes, Councillor George, 119, 260
Hulance, Pte, 24
hunger marches, 60, 204–5, 262
Hunt, Councillor AA, 202; A.E (head master), 197
Hunter, Sir Charles, 9
Hurd, Percy MP, 23

Imps; *see* Conservative Association
Independent Labour Party, 75, 123, 197
India, 25–26, 31; Bath's links with, 26, 54, 218; Defence League, 213; future of, 213–16; unrest in, 25
industry; *see* Bath, industry in; and individual firms
inflation, 62
influenza; *see* flu
Institution Gardens, 117
Ireland and Bath, 57–60; *see also* Foxcroft.
Isaac Carr and Co, 184
Italy, 225-7, *passim*, 229, 290; *see also* Abyssinia *and* Mussolini

Jackman, Alderman Percy, 58, 84
Jacob Long and Sons Ltd, 87
Japan, 212, 280–2 *passim*
jazz, 42
Jersey, 89; *see also* unemployment
Jews, 55–6, 155, 286–89; *see also* refugees and anti–Semitism
Jolly's department store, 177
Joyce, William, 222

Kaiser, 9, 226
Kapp Putsch, 48
Keevil, Owen, 19–21, 122–3, 130, 140, 145–7, 200
Keir, Lilly J., 215, 251
Kellogg-Briand Pact, 212
Kendal, Father, 52
Kent, Duchess of, 247
Kettle, George W, 85
Khan, Aly, Prince, 275
Kiel Canal, 15
King, Bob, 156, 157–8, 203, 308
Kings; *see* under individual name
Kingsmead, 118, 151; Flats, 119, 207, 208; Square, 33, 181; Terrace, 118
Kingwell Hall, 149
Kipling, R, 213, 241
Kitley, Councillor FW, 115
Knox, Councillor, E, 120, 168
Koo, Miss, 281

labour exchange; *see* Employment
Labour Party, 37, 48, 61, 72–4, 213, 218, 225; *see also* elections
Lacy, Sarah, 176
Lambern, J, 140
Lammond, Frederic, 29
Langford Hall, 34
Lansdown Road, 101
Larkhall, 283
Law, Janet, 286
Lawrence of Arabia, 276
Lawson, SA, 171
League of Nations, 49, 223–5, 318; Union (LNU), 49, 52, 223–5; and peace ballot, 223-5
League of Voluntary Social Service, 206; *see also* unemployment
Leakey, 'big Bill', 179–80
Lee, JJ and sons, 198
Lee, Sergt Maj EA, 30
Lestock, Reid, Major, 215
Lewis, Col. 170
Lewis, J, 93
Liberal Party, 73–4, 215, 225
library, public, 32, 246, 249
Liebmann, R, 282
Link, the, 309–11
Lipscombe, Godfrey, JP, 170
Lister, Charles, 63–4
Lister, Edgar, 256
Literary and Scientific Institution, 96, 245
Littlewood, SR, 39–40, 42
Lloyd, Lord, 214
Lloyd-George, David, 32–3, 37, 70

INDEX

349

LMS, 107, 136, 149, 160
Locarno Agreements, 52
Lock, GD, Major Geoffrey, 295, 302
Lock, W and T, (Cabinet Makers), 35
Locksbrook Rubber Mill, 43; Wharf Timber Company, 198
Logie, Madge, 157, 158
London, Midland and Scottish Railway, 107, 136, 149, 160
Long, Alderman George, 57, 152, 201
Long, Sapper, W, 4
Long, Walter .F. Councillor, 102, 228, 244
Longrove-Hermann, Rev C., 197
Lotz and Kier, 116
Love, Winifrid, 155–6
Lowe, James, 75, 77–8
Lucas, Ella, 184

Macassey, Sir Lynden, 111–13 *passim*
McColl, James, KC, 287
MacDermott, Norman, 89
MacDonald, Ramsay, 52,
Maclaren, Andrew MP, 111–12
Macmillan, Harold, 192
Makonen, Prince, 228
Mallet and Son, 84
Mallet, WE, 84
Mallory, P. and Sons, 84, 197
Manvers Street Baptist Church, 97, 258, 289
Marshall-Selwyn, W Archdeacon, 287
Marxism; *see* communism
Mase, Owen, 256
Maslen, Benjamin, 32; Rosie, 203
Masterman, Charles, 31
Maternity homes, 162–3
Mathews, Private Harry, 18
May Day rally (1935), 237
Mayor's Christmas Fund, 150
Meade, Major, 28
Mealand, Anthony, 265, 267, 268
Means Test, 202–3
Medical Officer of Health (acting), 6–7; (Dr Blackett) 99, 160–74, 179, 234
mental health, 92, 172–4, 284
Mesopotamia, 26, 55
Messel, Oliver, 255, 256
Methuen, Field Marshal Lord, Paul Sanford, 3rd earl, 46; Paul Ayshford (artist) 4th Earl, 253–4
Mettur Dam, 180
Middle Class Union (MCU), 14; *see also* National Citizens' Union
Middle Common, 236
Middle Pitt Colliery, 143–4
midwives, 162–3

Miles, Maurice, 250
Miles, Nurse, 163
Military Training Act, 1939, 307; *see also* conscription
Milk Street, 114; Baby League, 301; Mission, 95
Miller, Rev WR, 289
Milsom Street, 175, 265, 306; proposed extension of, 242–5
miners 123–5, 142–4; *see* Coal, Somerset, and strikes
Mining Federation of Great Britain, 65
Ministry of Health, 68, 100, 106, 115; of Labour, 43; of Pensions, 158; of Transport, 115
Minnis, Major A, 258, 263
missing soldiers, 14, 46–7
'modernity', 241, 265–76, 318
Molton, SS, 278
Monks Wood reservoir, 115, 125, 167; water mains, 115
Monkton Combe, 189, 226
Monmouth Street Society, 35
Moore, Dora, 163
morality, 274–6
Morgan, CH, 14
Morris, Philip, 227, 283
mortality, 164–5; infant, 163
motor traffic, 265–7; *see* road building and parking
Munich crisis; settlement, 285–6, 290; *see also* Sudeten crisis
Munro, Valentine, Mrs, 43
Murray, Brigadier General Edward, 286
Murray, Gilbert, 223
Murschel, Jacob M, 27
Music; *see* Bath, music in
Musicians' Union, 89, 250
Mussolini, Benito, 126, 212, 225–9 *passim*; *see also* Italy

National Citizens' Union,, 68–9, 108–10; *see also* Middle Class Union
National Council of Women, 272
National Dickens' Fellowship, 94–5
National Federation of Furniture Employers, 35
National Government, 193–4, 262
National Insurance Scheme (1913), 160
National Service Scheme, 301–2
National Unemployed Workers. Movement (NUWM), 75–7, 202–3
National Union of Clerks, 62
National Union of Distributive and Allied Workers, 35

National Union of ex-Servicemen, 60
National Union of Railwaymen, 62, 128, 138
National Union of Teachers, 34, 62, 233, 272, 301,
Nazi-Soviet Pact, 309, 311
Nazis; see Germany and Hitler
Neathey, Albert, 7
Nelson, Dr., 160
New, John, 33, 185, 188
New Bond Street, 84, 282
Newton Park, 17, 22, 27, 180
Newton St Loe, 66, 68, 136
Nicholds, RW, 21, 200
North Parade, 107; Bridge, 113, 115–17
North Somerset Coalfields, 66–7, 128, 137, 140–4 *passim*; impact of coal strikes on, 142–4, 149; see also Somerset miners
Norton Hill Colliery, 141
Norwood, Rev F.W, 49
Nuffield, Lord, 186

O'Connell, Harry, 217, 225
O'Connor, TP, 88
Ogden, Basil, Town Clerk, 81–2, 106, 170, 232
Old Bath Preservation Society, 119–20, 241–6 *passim*, 247, 248, 260; see also Bath Preservation Trust, 241
Old Bond Street, 242–5 *passim*
Old Bridge, 9, 107, 118, 132
'Old Contemptibles', 316
Oldfield Park, 32, 33, 97, 165; Baptist Church, 98
Oldham, Dr Hilda, 273, 308; Mr, 310
Orange Grove, 107
Orchestra; see Bath Spa; and Pump Room
Organisation for the Maintenance of Supplies (OMS), 128, 134
Osborne, Margaret, 6–7, 37–8
OTC, 155
Over Thirties Association, 271

pacifism, 231–3, 307
Palace Theatre, 44, 90, 138, 193
Palestine, 288
pantomimes 13, 240, 289
Parkhouse family, 176
parks, 270, 283, 297; Victoria, 118, 120, 230, 236
Parliament, 287; and Bath Bill (1925), 111–13; and 1937 Corporation Act, 245
Parry, William, 44
Partis College, 34–5, 176–7
Patterson, Dr, 171
Pavilion, 144, 245, 187

pawn shop, 209
Payton, George, 237
peace celebrations 29–31; peace Treaty; see Versailles, treaty of; ballot; see League of Nations
Peirse, Sir Richard, Admiral, and Lady Peirse, 50, 257
Penel, Marius, 250
Pennyquick Cemetery, 207
Penrose, Dorothy, 99
Perkins, Mrs AC, 284
Perry George, 155, 181, 199
Perry, Ron, 155, 308
Peto, Mrs Pauline, 125
Pickard, Major H, 293–303 *passim*
Pitman, Alfred and Ernest, 79; CE, 134
Pitman, Isaac and Sons, 317
Playgoers Society, 89, 90, 94
Pointer, G, 75, 203
Poland, 48–9, 290, 312, 313
Pollitt, Harry, 249
Poor Law Board, 75–6
Post Office, 12, 22, 31, 150, 200, 227
Pow, Dorothy, 163–4
Powney, Margaret
Preston Jones, Mr, 160, 185
Preston King, Alderman Dr, 92, 100, 173; see also eugenics
Prince of Wales, 88, 142, 158, 205
prisoners of war (POW), 15; Bathonians, in Germany, 13–14; Germans, 29, 44
Public Order Act (1936), 223
Pulteney Bridge, 112
Pump Room 15, 41, 44, 66, 85, 150, 248, 280, 294; Orchestra, 44, 89, 150, 249–51, 270
Purcell, Albert, 47

Quakers, 51–2, 59, 169, 233, 277, 287
Queen Mary, 306, 316
Queen Square, 76, 297

race meetings, 58, 101, 317
radium, 161
Radstock, 141, 143, 209
Raffety, Frank, 74
Ragtime Banjo Band, 42
Railway Clerks Association, 238
Railways; see GWR & LMS, and rail, strikes
ratepayers, 108, 109, 244
rates, 14, 108
Raven, Canon, 230
Raward, G, 31
Recreation Ground, 69, 236
Red Cross, 232, 234, 292

INDEX   351

Red House, 74, 101, 149
refugees; Belgian, 44; Spanish, 279–80;
  Jewish, 287–9; Refugee fund; 277
Ridley, Arnold, 180
Risdon, William, 222
Rivers Street, 177
road building, 267; *see also* by-passes
Roberts, Brigadier General, H, 214, 215;
  Mrs, 309
Robinson, GB (Music Director) 112
Robson, Paul, 186, 217
Roe, Col. CD, 310
Ronaldshay, Earl of, 264
Rotarians, 124, 172, 215, 221
Royal Air Force, 303
Royal Crescent, 30, 60, 87, 178, 185, 241, 245
Royal Institute of British Architects (RIBA),
  111, 112, 186
Royal Literary and Scientific Institute, 96,
  107, 207, 286
Royal Mineral Water Hospital, 242, 245;
  (after 1936 Royal National Hospital for
  Rheumatic Diseases; *see* hospitals}
Royal United Hospital (RUH); *see* hospitals
Royal Victoria Park, 118, 230; *see also* parks
rugby; *see* Bath
Ruhr crisis, 1923–4, 50; partial occupation
  of, 1921, 49, 50
Russia, 21–2, 47, 48, 290, 311, 318;
  revolution, 22–4

St James Church, 97
St John, Hospital of, 282
St John's Church Lower Weston, 98, 170
St John's RC church, 45
St Luke's, 7
St Mary's, Bathwick, 8, 32, 218
St Stephen's, 17
Salisbury Plain, 19
Salonika, 17,
Salvation Army, 16, 33, 95, 113
Samuel, Lord, 124, 287; Report, 124
Sawclose, meetings and demonstrations in 9,
  23, 50, 66, 75–6, 138–9, 193, 225, 317
schools, Impact of Spanish flu on, 6–7; and
  evacuees, 313–16; Medical Service, 164;
  preparations for war, 297–9, 307, 316;
  and rugby, 102; schools in Bath: Bath
  High School for Girls, 154, 157; Central
  Schools, 155; City Secondary (after 1932
  City of Bath Boys' School), 153, 157,
  236; Combe Down Senior, 155; East
  Walcot, 6, 9, 93, 236, 242, 272, 312,
  315–16; Harley Street, 156; King Edward's

Grammar, 152, 154–5; Kingsmead Infants,
  154–6, 245; Kingswood, 221; Magdalen
  Hospital School, 173; Monkton Combe,
  154; Oldfield Council Boys and Girls,
  73, 151, 152; Royal School, 154, 243,
  272; St John's RC Mixed, 151; St Lukes,
  158, 248; St Michael's, 174 St Paul's, 243,
  245; St Stephen's, 301; Twerton Higher
  Elementary, 151; South, Elementary, 154;
  West, Senior, 152, 197; Walcot Central,
  131, 155, 156; Senior School and Bath
  Diocesan Girls, 156, 238, 315 (Senior
  Mixed School after 1938), West Central,
  102, 156–7; Weymouth House Boys and
  Girls, 151
Scobell, Capt, 78–9, 143, 149; nightingales,
  79
Selfridge, Gordon, 82
sex, 273–6; homosexual, 276
Shakespeare, William, 90, 220
Sham Castle, 30, 129, 167
Sharp, Pritchard and Co, 106
Sheppard, Rev. Dick, 231; Florence, 177
Shopping Week, 84–5
Short, George, 143
Shum, FE, 96
Silcox, Sergt, 25
Silvester, SH, Sergt, 5
Simpson, Wallace, 239
Sims, Gladys, 247
Sims, Leonard, 4
Sing Gour, Sir Hari, 215, 218
single mothers.161–2
Sisson, Frank, 106, 111, 294
'slave bill', 205; *see also* 'means test'
slave trade, 218–19
slums, 107, 109, 114, 119, 175, 176;
  Clearance, 118, 120, 316
Smith, Eric, 157, 162; Gypsy Pat, 98
Smith, Mrs Florence, 247, 273
Snow Hill, 95
Snowden, Phillip, MP, 194
Soccer; *see* Bath City Associated Club
Societies, 94–97, 249; *see also by name*
Society of Friends; *see* Quakers
Somerset, 204; Cricket Club, 101; Boys
  Home, 153; Light Infantry (SLI), 18, 19,
  23, 25, 26, 55, 307; miners, 23, 30, 124,
  128, 140, 142–4
Southgate Street, 33, 102
Spa; *see* Bath as a Spa
Spanish civil war, 229–30, 277–80;
  Bathonians involved in, 278–9;
  humanitarian actions in Bath for, 278,
  279; *see also* refugees, Spanish

Spear, Alderman Frederick, 68, 197
Spender, Harold, 73; Stephen, 73
Stafford, Mrs, 47
Stanhope, 7th Earl of, 139
Statutory Meeting (1925), 108–9
Staynor, Councillor Major, 161
Stead Hostel, 271
Stone, King and Wardle, 185
Stones Opticians, 48
Storr, Captain FH, 286
Stothert, Sir Percy, 68, 79, 101
Stothert and Pitt, 3, 43, 47, 68, 116, 126, 180, 183, 307; and dividends, 122, 209; export of cranes, 43, 122, 180; lays off employees, 199–200; and national engineering dispute, 35–6, 67; and Relief for the unemployed, 68; and Workman's Hospital Fund, 160; and ARP, 294
Strawson, Mr, 191
strikes, 35–6, 62, 65–7; General, 130–9; impact on Bath, 131–9, 144–9; attitude of Churches to, 138, 142; preparations to ensure supplies, 128–30; violence in, 131–3, 140; volunteers in, 134–6; ends, 139–40; in furniture trade, 35–6; Miners, (1921), 65– 7; (1926), 123–49; musicians', 41–2; rail (1919), 36–7; in Stothert and Pitt, 35–6, 67–8
Strutt, Geoffrey, 282, 292
Sturge-Cotterell, T. Councillor, 40, 94, 244, 289
Sudeten Crisis (1938), 283–6; criticism of Chamberlain, 286; impact of, on Bath, 283–5; and relief at outcome, 285–6; see also ARP
Sudetenland, 283–6 passim
Sullivan, BM, 24
Sunday games, 97–8, 269–70; – music, 270
Swain, Walter. 102
Swallow, Eric, 262
Sweetlands Organ factory, 18
Swift, Andrew, 44; Fred, 128
Sydney Gardens, 30

Tabb, Henry S, 66, 141–2
Tarrant, Jas, 138
Tarrant-Bailey, Richard, 17, 22, 42, 89
Tanner, Pte, FW, 30
Tanner, Miss, teacher, 156
Tate, Mrs (Mavis) MP, 273–5
Taylor, AJ, 87, 159; AJPT, 282
Technical College, 157, 253
television, 269
Temperance Association, 150
Temple Earl, 17, 22, 65, 69.133.188, 209, 257; Countess, 22, 27, 63, 133, 180, 257
Terrace Walk, 111, 207
Territorial Army, 307
Theatre Royal, 42, 44, 90, 210, 289; see also Citizen House; and state of contemporary theatre, 89–91, 249
Thompson, Edith, 29
Thompson, Gordon, 282
Three Ways Cottage, 157
Thurstan, Violetta, 178–9
Thynne, Lord Alexander, 4; see also Bath, Lord
Tiley, EJ, Councillor, 245
Toc H, 262
Tollemache, Grace, 205
tolls, abolition of, 107–8; bridges: see individual bridges.
Tomkins, Edward, 153
Tourism; see Bath as a conference and tourist centre
Trade Union Congress, 130, 139, 140, 143
tramps, 203–4
Trowbridge, 135; Carnival, 316
TUC, 130, 139, 140, 143
Tweedy, Rosamond, 271
Twerton, 1, 9, 11, 33, 87, 95, 226; Cooperative Society, 16, 109, 129
Tylee, Florence, 150, 241
typhoid, 167–72; outbreak on Bathwick Hill (1928), 167; council's reaction, 168, 170–1; and deaths, 167; and local residents and Press, 168–9; outbreaks, 1932 and 1939, 172

unemployment, nationally, 32–3, 199–200; in Bath, 32, 60, 63, 67, 73, 75, 122, 200–11; Grant Cttee, 68–9; see also hunger marches and work creation
Usher, WH, 181

Vachell, Horace Annesley, 243, 256, 257
Van Sommer, James, 283, 284, 286
Versailles, Treaty of, 48
Vezey, Alderman Thomas, 174
Victoria Bridge, 113, 116, 118; Park, 230
Vilven and Sons, florist and 'fruiterers', 95

Waldegrave, Lord, 253
Walcot, 33 97, 134; ARP plans for, 300; Methodist Church, 285; Mission Rooms, 95; Street, 132, 134 and widening of, 242, 245
Wales, Prince of, 88, 142, 158, 205; see also Abdication
Wales, South, 205, 258; workers from, 208–

9, 258 and their impact on Bath, 258–9
Wall Street crash, 193–4
Waller, Constance M, 104
Walsh, Shelford, 43
Walton, Sidney, 226
War, World War II, 302; atmosphere in Bath on eve of, 312; move by government departments to, 312–13; outbreak of, 316; *see* ARP and evacuees
war memorials, 31, 46
War Office, 46, 47, 181–2, 263
wardens, air raid; *see* ARP
Wards. Bathwick, 167–72 *passim*; Lansdown, 216, 286; Walcot North, 263; South, 37; St Michaels, 302; Twerton East, 37; Westmoreland, 37; Weston, 129, 145; Widcombe, 37
Warran, Mrs, 31
Warrington, Rev. PE, 189
Wells, City of, 28, 31, 34
Wells, HG, 88
Wells Road, 134, 235
Wellsway, 161
Welton Rovers, 102
Westgate Buildings, 107, 282
Weston, 9, 176; Bridge, 113; Lodge, 174
Wherrett, E. Pte, 25
Whimster, Marjorie, 247; Wesley,146
White, Alderman Ernest J, 223
Whitmore, Henry, 9
Whittingdon, RH 145
Whittle, Sergt., SC, 292
Wicks, Gwendoline, 155, 162, 164, 187, 189
Widcombe, 33; Bridge, 113, 117; Hill; Labour branch, 219

Wilberforce, William, 219
Williams, Doreen, 156, 164
Wills, Alfred, Alderman, 12, 32, 37, 98, 107–13 *passim*, 230, 254; and parliamentary bills of 1925, 109–13; and 1935, 242–4; Thomas, 36, 42
Wireless, 56, 133, 139, 180, 269, 316; and Munich crisis, 285; *see also* BBC
Witham, Miss, 292
Withers, FR Driver, 19–21
Withy, Arthur E. Councillor, 32, 36, 161, 236
Wolfe, General James, 246; WG, 14–15
Women 271–5; and ARP, 294; and birth control, 274–5; Hostels for, 273; impoverished gentlewomen, 34–5, 271; influence of war on status of, 16, married, 272; police, 272; single, 246; working, 32, 272–3
Womens' Institute, 272, 305
Wood, John, the Elder, 120
Woodroffe, Sir John and Lady, 54
Work creation projects, 68–9, 208–209; *see also* unemployment
Work House (Frome Rd), 33, 34, 65, 69, 75, 77, 140, 150, 157, 174, 204, 234, 303; *see also* Board of Guardians
Workers Education Association (WEA) 69, 96–7, 109
Wornham, Joan, 171
Wrayford, JW, 7

Young Man's Christian Association (YMCA), 94, 170, 221, 236, 286

www.ingramcontent.com/pod-product-compliance
Lightning Source LLC
Chambersburg PA
CBHW071734150426
43191CB00010B/1569